DIFFERENT

DIFFERENT
Crimes
Criminals

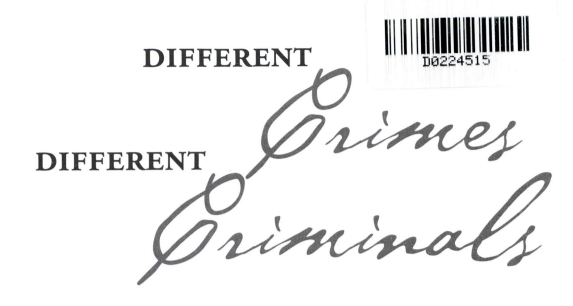

UNDERSTANDING, TREATING AND
PREVENTING CRIMINAL BEHAVIOR

DORIS LAYTON MACKENZIE, PH.D.
LAUREN O'NEILL
WENDY POVITSKY
SUMMER ACEVEDO

UNIVERSITY OF MARYLAND

 LexisNexis®

 **anderson publishing**
A member of the LexisNexis Group

Different Crimes, Different Criminals: Understanding, Treating and Preventing Criminal Behavior

Copyright © 2006

Matthew Bender & Company, Inc., a member of the LexisNexis Group

Phone 877-374-2919
Web Site www.lexisnexis.com/anderson/criminaljustice

MacKenzie, Doris Layton
    Different crimes, different criminals: understanding, treating and preventing criminal behavior -- 1st Ed.
  Doris Layton MacKenzie, Lauren O'Neill, Wendy Povitsky, Summer Acevedo
    Includes bibliographical references and index.
    ISBN 1-59345-334-5 (paperback)

Cover design by Tin Box Studio, Inc./Cincinnati, Ohio

Editor Janice Eccleston
Acquisitions Editor Michael C. Braswell

Acknowledgments

The authors would like to thank the following professionals for their assistance in reviewing the following chapters for content and accuracy:

Bernard Auchter, Ph.D., Senior Social Science Analyst with the Violence and Victimization Research Division of the National Institute of Justice, Office of Justice Programs, U.S. Department of Justice.

James C. Howell, Adjunct Researcher at the National Youth Gang Center.

The Honorable Marvin S. Kaminetz, Circuit Court for St. Mary's County, Maryland.

David J. Kolko, Ph.D., Professor of Psychiatry, Psychology & Pediatrics, University of Pittsburgh School of Medicine and Director of Special Services Unit at the Western Psychiatric Institute and Clinic.

Dr. Martin Lalumiere, research psychologist at the Centre for Addiction and Mental Health, Associate Professor of Psychiatry and Criminology at the University of Toronto, and Associate Head of Research for the Law and Mental Health Program in the Department of Psychiatry at the University of Toronto.

Dr. D. Kim Rossmo, Texas State University Department of Criminal Justice and Dr. Eric W. Hickey, California State University, Fresno Department of Criminology.

Sally Simpson, Ph.D., Department Chair, Department of Criminology and Criminal Justice, University of Maryland, College Park, MD.

Franklin Zimring, J.D., William G. Simon Professor of Law at the University of California, Berkeley.

Table of Contents

Chapter 1

Understanding Criminals and Crime: Theory and Research

Doris Layton MacKenzie

Why do people commit crimes? Why does one person commit a certain type of crime and another person commit another? In this book we examine different types of crimes and criminals. As is evident, no one classification system or theoretical perspective adequately describes all types of crimes and criminals. Our task in this book is to examine these different types of crimes and criminals. For each, we discuss the characteristics of the offenders, theories dominating the current research on the offender or offense, and provide a critical analysis of the research. Effective methods for identifying, classifying, managing, preventing, and treating the diverse types of offenders differ dramatically. The contributing authors examine the effectiveness of various prevention strategies and treatment options for the different types of crimes and criminals. Theories, research, and classification schemes differ widely for the different offenses and offenders. That is the reason for the title of this book; it is in recognition of the many differences that exist among offenders and their crimes.

A Multidisciplinary Perspective: Sociology, Psychology, and Biology

This book demonstrates the changes that have occurred in the theoretical perspectives in criminology and criminal justice. For years, the academic discipline of criminology looked towards the social and physical environment to try to understand criminal behavior. This was, in part, a result of the domination of criminology by sociologists. Sociologists studying crime attempted to propose one theory that would explain all types of crimes. Currently, criminologists have begun to realize that these explanations for crime are not adequate to understand all of the different types of crimes and criminals. The person who commits infanticide differs greatly from the serial murderer and the arsonist who, in turn, differ from each other. Criminologists recognize that individual differences in cognitions and biology are important in understanding criminal behavior.

This book grew out of a graduate course on the topic of "Psychology and Crime." The students were asked to select one type of crime or criminal, and examine the literature. They were asked specifically to: (1) discuss the characteristics of the offender who commits this type of crime; (2) report on the theoretical perspective that is most helpful in understanding this type of offender; (3) review the research on prevention and/or treatment of this type of offender, and (4) evaluate research on effectiveness of treatment and prevention programs. The papers submitted by the students were so outstanding that we decided to combine them in this book. Each chapter discusses the above topics in regard to a different type of crime or criminal. Chapters were reviewed by experts in the field, to ensure pertinent information was included.

A review of the different theoretical perspectives presented in the chapters clearly demonstrates that no one overall theory is adequate to describe all these offenders. Traditionally, criminologists have been trained in the field of sociology and most criminology theories have been based of this perspective. However, sociological theories do not appear adequate to explain all of these crimes. Many sociological theorists search for a general theory of crime. Indeed, one general theory of criminal behavior does not seem sufficient to understand these criminals.

Many of the chapters discuss the importance of biological perspectives in promoting our understanding of the crimes. For example, in her chapter, Jaclyn Smith presents some of the biological explanations that could, in part, explain infanticide. Jennifer Gibbs presents biological theories as one possible explanation for domestic violence. Yet, there is little scientific evidence for how biology directly affects the person who commits infanticide or domestic violence. We are still at a point where these theoretical perspectives appear to present viable possibilities for increasing our understanding of why these offenders commit their crimes, but as yet there is little hard evidence of exactly how this might occur.

Many of the contributing authors to this book refer to psychological theories to help us understand the behavior of these offenders. For example, Summer Acevedo believes stalkers can best be understood using the American Psychiatric Association DSM IV categories of personality disorders, including those who have antisocial, narcissistic, borderline, and histrionic personality disorders (American Psychiatric Association, 1994). Danielle Harris, in the chapter on child molestation, reviews behavioral and cognitive behavior theories that view child abuse as a learned behavior.

The importance of multidisciplinary theoretical perspectives and multiple theories to help us understand the different offenders is demonstrated in many of the chapters. For instance, in Ashlee Parker's (Chapter 6) words: "Because rapists comprise such a heterogeneous sample of offenders, it is difficult to develop theories and paradigms that envelope all types and patterns of rape." Jennifer Gibbs (Chapter 3) makes a similar point in discussing treatment and theory: "Unfortunately, one theory cannot encompass all forms of battering behavior, and batterer intervention programs currently follow a 'one size fits all' approach for those involved in treatment, despite emerging evidence that all batterers are not the same." Another example comes from the chapter by Elizabeth Smith and Wendy Povitsky (Chapter 8), "Individual differences between adolescents may make any blanket explanation of juvenile drug use nearly impossible. There are a variety of sociological, biological, and psychological factors that influence children in different ways and contribute to illegal behavior and drug use." Thus, for many of the criminals examined, multidisciplinary theoretical perspectives or multiple theories are proposed to assist us in understanding their behavior.

Treatment Perspectives

Some crimes are so heinous that no one would expect the offender to be returned to the community; treatment is not considered a viable option. A good example of this type of criminal is the serial murderer. Once such offenders are convicted, they are usually incarcerated for the rest of their lives. They will have no opportunity to return to the community; therefore, little thought is given to what treatment programs would be effective in changing or rehabilitating them. There is some interest in identifying prevention techniques so that children will not grow into the kind of people who commit such crimes. However, although there is interest in preventing serial murderers from committing their crimes, as Raven Korte and Susan Fahey point out in their chapter, we know little about how to this might be done.

Most crimes are not as monstrous as serial murder. And, most convicted criminals do not spend the rest of their lives in prison. Most return to the community. For these offenders, effective treatment that will reduce their later recidivism is critical. Contributing authors to this book were asked to review and report on the treatment and prevention programs available for the types of offender discussed. Furthermore, they were asked to examine research studies of treatment and prevention, and report on the effectiveness of the programs.

Another consistency among chapters is the search for treatment programs guided by specific theoretical perspectives. Some theories do not lend themselves easily to treatment applications. "Psychodynamic approaches have failed to yield empirical support that would help in developing treatment or prevention" (Chapter 5). Perhaps the most consistent perspective for treatment is cognitive behavior or social learning theory. Most of the chapters report on treatment based on some type of cognitive behavior programming.

Evidence-Based Corrections

Contributing authors were asked to evaluate the effectiveness of prevention strategies and treatment programs from an evidence-based perspective. As prison populations continue to grow nationally, and corrections takes up an increasing proportion of state and local budgets, many jurisdictions are seeking to determine if their funds are being spent effectively. They want to know if the money they are putting into prevention strategies and treatment programs is being used most effectively. I argue that these questions can be best answered using scientific knowledge. I refer to this practice as evidence-based corrections or the use of scientific evidence to determine policies and practices. Such evidence-based corrections would implement guidelines and evaluate the performance of agencies and programs. Evidence-based decisionmaking would use research to guide practice. In the words of Larry Sherman (1999), evidence-based practice would "use the best evidence to shape the best practice . . . in a systematic effort to parse out and codify unsystematic 'experience' as the basis for decision-making."

The use of evaluation results is often the missing link in correctional decisionmaking. The basic premise of "evidence-based practice is that we are all entitled to our own opinions but not to our own facts" (Sherman, 1999:4). Without help, practitioners come up with their own "facts," which often turn out to be very wrong. The goal then is to use scientific evidence to hold officials accountable for the outcome of their programs. As is evident throughout this book, we have little scientific evidence to tell whether particular types of interventions are effective in reducing the recidivism of delinquents and offenders, or in preventing youth from becoming involved in certain types of crime. For example, we know little about the effectiveness of different gang intervention strategies, whether sex offender treatment is equally as effective for rapists and pedophiles, or what treatment might be effective in treating violent offenders with schizophrenia.

Determining What Works

All of the chapters in this book review prevention, management, and/or treatment programs for the offenders. The authors discuss the quality of the research and the outcomes in order to determine if the programs are effective. Many authors have based their discussion on the University of Maryland scoring system used in the "What Works Report," while others report on the results of meta-analyses.

What Works Report. University of Maryland researchers developed an innovative technique for answering the question of the effectiveness of various programs. Their work was completed in response to a request by the U.S. Congress for a "comprehensive evaluation of the effectiveness of more than $3 billion annually in Department of Justice (DOJ) grants to assist state and local criminal justice and community efforts to prevent crime" (Sherman et al., 1997). Congress required that the research included in the evaluation be independent, and that it employ rigorous and scientifically recognized standards and methods (MacKenzie, 2000). The culmination of the work was a report to the U.S. Congress, *Preventing Crime: What Works, What Doesn't, What's Promising* (Sherman et al., 1997). In the report, the researchers reported on the results of more than 500 studies of various crime prevention programs. For each study, they assessed the quality of the research methods as well as the direction and significance of the research results. They used this information to draw conclusions about the effectiveness of various crime prevention programs. Later work made use of the technique they developed; it permits scientifically based conclusions about the effectiveness of various treatment programs and management strategies (Sherman et al., 2002; MacKenzie & Hickman, 1998).

One of the goals of this book is to provide a critical analysis of the research examining the effectiveness of prevention strategies and treatment options for the various criminals. Where appropriate, the authors use the University of Maryland scientific methods score to evaluate the quality of the research. If there are sufficient studies in an area, the authors use the decision-making system developed by the University of Maryland researchers.

The University of Maryland decision-making system is a two-stage process to assist in drawing conclusions about what works. The first step involves locating and assessing each individual study for the quality of the research design and methodology and the direction and significance of the outcomes. The second step involves examining each topic area for research quality and the direction and significance of the results. The results of the second step are used to draw conclusions about what works, what doesn't, what is promising, and what we do not know.

The scientific methods scores determined in the first step can vary from 1 to 5, with 5 being the most rigorous experimental designs. Studies with scores of 1 are used to determine some correlation between the program and the outcome but these studies are considered so low in scientific quality that they are not used in decisionmaking. Scores of 2 can be used to determine a temporal sequence between the program and the outcome but are still considered low in scientific quality. University of Maryland researchers reported on studies with scores of 2 but they did not use them for the step two decisionmaking. Studies scoring 3 on the scientific methods score used a comparison group design, those scoring 4 used a comparison group design but also controlled for other factors. Studies scoring 5 were the "gold standard," these experimental designs used random assignment to conditions. This scoring system is helpful because it permits an easy assessment of the quality of the research design in a study. Many of the chapters in this book use this scoring system to determine the quality of the research in the area they are examining.

Step 2 of the decision-making process developed at the University of Maryland involved drawing conclusions about whether the program areas were effective in reducing crime. The researchers developed decision-making rules to classify each program area into one of the following categories: (1) program works, (2) program doesn't work, (3) program is promising, and (4) there are too few studies to determine whether or not the program works.

A very good example of the two-stage process is shown in Lauren O'Neill's chapter on Gangs. She begins by identifying four studies of treatment and prevention of youth gang problems. She identifies four studies that were scored 2 or above on the methods score. Two of the studies scored 3 and one scored 4. She does not draw conclusions about the overall effectiveness of the programs because the programs were extremely varied in the focus and the components so it is not appropriate to group them together to draw a conclusion about effectiveness. Several other contributing authors report on studies that used the scientific methods scoring system. For instance, in the Rape chapter, Ashlee Parker reports on the review Polizzi et al. (1999) completed in which they used the two-stage decision-making system to examine sex offender treatment in prison and in the community.

Campbell Collaboration. Subsequent to the University of Maryland report, a second development occurred in the field of evidence-based public policy: the Campbell Collaboration (http://www.campbellcollaboration.org/). The collaboration is designed to facilitate the preparation, maintenance, and accessibility of systematic reviews and meta-analyses of research on the effects of social science interventions. One section of the Collaboration, the Justice Group, focuses on crime and justice topics. Evidence-based correctional studies will fall under the purview of this group.

There is a growing consensus that systematic reviews and meta-analysis can be important in evidence-based decisionmaking. Researchers have long grappled with the problem of understanding how to interpret the results of separate but similar studies. The University of Maryland's two-step process was one attempt to develop a scientifically based method to assess the research in an area. Another method is the process of systematic review and meta-analysis. Meta-analysis provides a more precise way of determining the "success" of interventions. Systematic review is a term used to describe scientific syntheses using explicit methods for the review. Meta-analysis is a method of summarizing, integrating, and interpreting selected sets of empirical studies that produce quantitative findings. It is a method of encoding and analyzing the statistics that summarize research findings from research reports. The method requires a clear definition of which studies will be eligible for inclusion in the analysis. Once inclusion criteria are clearly identified, an intensive search is made for all studies that fit the criteria. Independent samples from the eligible studies are identified and the data are coded. An effect size statistic, a standardized measure of the difference between the treatment and comparison group, is calculated and analyzed for each study.

Some of the chapters in this book report on meta-analyses that have examined the effectiveness of treatment programs or management strategies. For example, in the chapter on Rape, Ashlee Parker reports on meta-analyses completed by my colleagues and myself (Gallagher et al., 1999), where we identified 25 independent studies evaluating the impact of various treatment programs for sex offenders. Parker reports also on another meta-analysis by Hansen et al. (2002), examining the effectiveness of treatment for sex offenders. Both studies found treatment reduces the recidivism of sex offenders. However, these meta-analyses combined all sex offenders in the analyses so we do not know if the effects of treatment are similar for different types of sex offenders. Thus, we do not know if treatment is effective for rapists. However, in the future, Hansen et al. (2002) plan to examine the effectiveness of treatment programs for different types of sex offenders.

Conclusion

The subjects of the chapters in this book were selected because they are varied and of current interest to criminologists. Furthermore, they represent crimes that are frequently of interest to the public and to policymakers. In each chapter, the authors examine the types of crimes—classification systems used to understand the criminal, theoretical perspectives, prevention, and treatment strategies. They evaluate the research in each area using an evidence-based perspective. There are some consistencies among the different crimes and criminals in these aspects but there are also many differences. Theories of crime and criminal behavior, as well as prevention and treatment strategies, must be designed with an awareness of the wide variety of different crimes and different criminals.

References

American Psychiatric Association (1994). *Diagnostic and Statistical Manual of Mental Disorders,* Fourth Edition. Washington, DC: American Psychiatric Press.

Campbell Collaboration (2005). http://www.campbellcollaboration.org/

Gallagher, C.A., D.B. Wilson, P. Hirschfield, M.B. Coggeshall, and D.L. MacKenzie (1999). "The Effects of Sex Offender Treatment on Sexual Reoffending." *Corrections Management Quarterly,* 9(4):19-29.

Hanson, K., A. Gordon, A. Harris, J. Marques, W. Murphy, V. Quinsey, and M. Seto (2002). "First Report of the Collaborative Outcome Data Project on the Effectiveness of Psychological Treatment for Sex Offenders." *Sexual Abuse: A Journal of Research and Treatment,* 14(2):169-194.

MacKenzie, D.L. (2000). "Evidence-Based Corrections: Identifying What Works." *Crime & Delinquency,* 46(4):457-471.

Polizzi, D. M., D.L. MacKenzie, and L. Hickman (1999). "What Works in Adult Sex Offender Treatment?: A Review of Prison- and Non-Prison-Based Treatment Programs." *International Journal of Offender Therapy and Comparative Criminology,* 43(3):357-374.

Sherman, L.W., B.C. Welsh, B., D.P. Farrington, and D.L. MacKenzie (eds.) (2002). *Evidence-Based Crime Prevention,* London, UK: Harwood Academic Publishers.

Sherman, L.W. (1999). *Evidence-Based Policing: Ideas in American Policing.* Washington, DC. The Police Foundation

Sherman, L.W., D. Gottfredson, D. MacKenzie, J. Eck, P. Reuter, and S. Bushway (1997). *Preventing Crime: What Works, What Doesn't, What's Promising.* Washington, DC: A report to the U.S. Congress prepared by National Institute of Justice.

SECTION I

Relational Crime

Chapter 2

Infanticide

Jaclyn Smith

I wonder if it is normal for a mother to adore her baby
so desperately and at the same time to think about
choking him or throwing him down the stairs."[1]

Introduction

Andrea Yates. Immediately the feeling associated with this name is
either sympathy or revulsion. It is a name that instantly reminds everyone
of the five children murdered by their own mother, Andrea Yates, and the
controversial trial covered extensively by the media. On June 20, 2001,
the world learned of Yates' frantic call to 911 after she drowned her five
children, ranging in age from six months to seven years. On March 13,
2002, there was a myriad of emotions as the judge read her sentence: life
in prison without the possibility of parole (Vatz & Weinberg, 2002).
Many—including the prosecutors, who had sought the death penalty—
believed that Yates' sentence was too lenient. Many in the mental health
field, however, thought her sentence was unjust. In their eyes, Andrea
needed treatment in a hospital for a mental illness from which she obviously suffered. They attacked the jury's judgment, citing it as "ludicrous
and ignorant" (Vatz & Weinberg, 2002). In January 2005, the Texas State
Appeals Court overturned the conviction and ordered a new trial based
on erroneous testimony by the prosecutor's forensic psychiatrist. Although
the prosecutors appealed this decision, the Texas Criminal Appeals
Court, in November 2005, upheld the lower court's decision. Prior to the
new trial, Andrea Yates was released on bond and transferred to a mental institution to await the outcome of her new trial (Parker, 2006). In July
2006 it was announced that Andrea Yates was found not guilty by reason
of insanity. She will be committed to a state mental hospital and held until
she is no longer deemed a threat. As a result of the new trial, the com-
plexities of infanticide are once again the focus of media attention.

Filicide is the generic term used to describe the killing of a child by
the parent. There are generally two types of filicide discussed in the lit-

erature: neonaticide and infanticide (Oberman, 1996). The differences in the terms are sometimes determined exclusively by the age of the victim. Filicide is the killing of a child (at any age) by the parent. The child can be as young as a few hours, or as old as 45. If the murdered child is between 48 hours and two years old, then the term most often used to describe that crime is infanticide. If the child is younger than 48 hours, neonaticide is the term most frequently used (Palermo, 2002). Caution must be taken, however, because there is no readily apparent principle to distinguish between infanticide and neonaticide. The above definitions are not meant to be concrete but instead serve as a general guide. It is not uncommon to find cases of murdered six-month-old children defined as neonaticide and to include murdered four- and five-year-old children as cases of infanticide (Oberman, 1996).

Box 2.1

Definitions

Filicide
The murder of a child by the parent

Infanticide
The killing of infants up to one year or older

Neonaticide
The killing of a newborn within 24 hours

Contrary to popular belief, infanticide is not a new or rare phenomenon. It is best described as ubiquitous, across all cultural and economic lines, throughout history. Wilson (1984) has studied the history of infanticide quite extensively. His main premise is that even primitive people practiced infanticide, although not with the stigma that it carries today. Research conducted in countries such as France, England, Russia, and the United States provides support for Wilson's claim that the act of infanticide is not unusual or a recent crime.

In France, during the seventeenth and eighteenth centuries, fathers had absolute power over their families. The authority included the power to choose life or death for his children (Palermo, 2002). In London in the eighteenth century, Thomas Coram opened hospitals because he could not "bear to see the babies dying in the gutters and rotting on the dung-heaps of London" (Palermo, 2002). Russian writers such as Tolstoy, Dostoevsky, and Chekhov mention infanticide in their writings, although Russia reports infanticide to be uncommon during the nineteenth century (Palermo, 2002). Even the United States did not escape such behavior as women (especially domestic servants) often killed their own children, usually to escape social condemnation (Wheeler, 1997).

China and Fiji are more recent examples of countries that practice infanticide. In China, baby girls still are often killed because of the cultural emphasis on the importance of raising male children. In Fiji, it is common practice for young and unmarried women to murder their offspring; some common ways include stabbing, beating with hands, throwing the infant against hard surfaces, strangling or suffocating, drowning, and depositing in pit latrines (Adinkrah, 2001). The parents in some cultures will also often kill premature or breech birth babies, as well as babies born to mothers that died during childbirth (Oberman, 2002).

It is difficult for historians to collect precise numbers or even rough estimates of infanticide because, in addition to the lack of resources, the rates are considered a "dark figure" of crime (Wheeler, 1997). Generally, the historical forces that affect infanticide are poorly understood. What is known, as illustrated by the aforementioned examples, is that infanticide was a thriving social practice well before the nineteenth century (Wheeler, 1997).

This chapter offers a contemporary descriptive discussion on the prevalence, offender characteristics, and treatment of infanticide. For clarity purposes, this chapter focuses solely on infanticide defined as the murder of a child 24 hours to five years old. This age limitation is set for three important reasons. The first reason is because of the definitional inconsistencies discussed previously. Because offender characteristics and motives vary depending on whether one is discussing infanticide or neonaticide, this distinction is imperative. Second, neonaticide frequently involves the debate over abortion and the issue of when life begins. Thus, it is beyond the scope of this chapter. In addition, this chapter limits the cases discussed to those that occurred in the United States. This limitation is necessary because of varying cultural beliefs and the definitional differences across countries.

Offender Characteristics

Prevalence

Almost 500 children in the United States under the age five were murdered in 1999. Approximately 56 percent of these murders were committed by either a parent or primary caregiver (Szegedy-Maszak, 2002). An extraordinary number of cases involving mothers who kill their own children occur within the first 24 hours of the child's birth (Oberman, 2002). Mothers murdered their babies more often than did fathers, although men are generally more prone to violence. According to one psychologist, a mother kills one or more of her children at least once every three days (Szegedy-Maszak, 2002). Gelles and Cornell (1990) find that young children are more likely to be killed in their homes by other family members, than anywhere else, or by anyone else, in the United States.

It is difficult to fathom the reason for such a high prevalence of infanticide in such an affluent society as the United Sates. Since WWII, the contraceptive pill, the intrauterine device, as well as the legalization of abortion, has removed many of the reasons for unwanted pregnancies and infanticide (Oberman, 2002). However, while Andrea Yates sat in court, a pediatrician was held without bail for murdering her two young children, and another mother was charged with stabbing her son to death (Szedgedy-Maszak, 2002).

Box 2.2

Case That Made Headlines . . .

On October 25, 1994, Susan Smith, a 23-year-old mother and wife, strapped her three-year-old and one-year-old children in their car seats and rolled the car into a lake. She told the media and police that her car was stolen with her children inside. After one week of extensive police searches and investigation in search for the suspects, Susan confessed to the crime.

It was a story that devastated a small South Carolina town and horrified a nation. Susan Smith killed her own children. The motive? To win the affection of Tom Findlay, a man with whom she was having an affair. Tom ended the affair shortly before the murders. In a letter he wrote to her, he said ". . . there are some things about you that aren't suited to me, and yes, I am speaking about your children." The defense tried to portray Susan as a depressed and disturbed woman. The prosecution sought the death penalty. However, the jury convicted her on two counts of murder and sentenced her to life in prison.

Source: http://www.cnn.com/EVENTS/year_in_review/us/smith.html

UPDATE: Susan Smith is currently serving her life sentence in Greenwood, South Carolina. She will be eligible for parole after she has served 30 years (2025) in prison. She will then be 53 years old.

Source:http://www.crimelibrary.com/notorious_murders/famous/smith/phase_10.html?sect=7

Although the prevalence is high, infanticide appears to be declining (Szegedy-Maszak, 2002). The reason for the decline is likely to be a combination of many variables: religious factors, the re-moralization of society, a more humanistic view of life, better social conditions, acceptance of abortion, and better social resources such as easier adoption policies and contraceptives (Palermo, 2002).

Effects

Infanticide has an enormous impact on the offender and the offender's family. Feminists argue that the female offenders are portrayed in the media as mad, irresponsible, hormonally disturbed, and irrational (Wilczynski, 1997). By denying the agency of the offender it resolves society's view that motherhood is a constantly fulfilling reward, but in reality many woman do not experience motherhood this way. The implication of the medicalization of their behavior allows the avoidance of the social causes of infanticide and female violence in general (Wilczynski, 1997). Consequently, most women receive psychiatric treatment that involves not only a social stigma, but that is coercive and harsh.

The offender's family experiences enormous psychological and emotional tribulations. Following the arrest, the other siblings are promptly removed from the home and placed in foster care. The behavioral problems that arise from moving between foster homes are well established in the literature (see Kaufman & Jones, 2003; Leathers, 2003; Orme, 2001; Philpot, 2002). The increased financial burden for the other parent to make ends meet creates additional stress on the family life. In addition, both parents undergo severe scrutiny over their parenting practices not only by the criminal justice personnel and psychologists, but by the media as well. The catastrophic effects of infanticide and the statistics of prevalence only underscore the troubling questions: What kind of person would ever kill their own child?

It is pertinent to begin a discussion of the characteristics of this type of offender with an examination of their upbringing. It is tempting to suppose that the offender's childhood was plagued with problems, maybe with emotional, physical, or sexual abuse. This is a finding in some studies; however, it is not a consistent finding among all research studies (Palermo, 2002). Most women who murder their children enjoyed a relatively normal childhood, without abuse. In addition, they usually lived in a two-parent household (Szegedy-Maszak, 2002). Many infanticidal offenders either have completed or started to complete a college education. A sizable minority of females report a family history of mental illness. In comparison to other female offenders, women who commit infanticide are far less likely to have a previous adolescent or adult criminal record, or to be facing other felony charges at the time of the murder (McKee, Shea, Mogy & Holden, 2001).

Age Differences

Kunz and Bahr (1996) utilized Uniform Crime Report data from the period of 1976 to 1985 to review 3,459 cases of infanticide. They find that 36 percent of the offenders were under the age of 25, and 15 percent of the offenders were teenagers. Of parents that reportedly murdered one of their children, 95 percent murdered their child in the first week, post-birth. Of the five percent remaining, 27 percent murdered their child before the age of one, while 73 percent murdered their child before the child's fifth birthday (Kunz & Bahr, 1996).

Racial Differences

Abel (1986) conducted a retrospective study assessing the racial differences of infanticide cases between the years of 1972 and 1984. He finds a striking difference between Caucasian and African-American offenders. His findings show that African-Americans are nearly eight times more likely to commit infanticide than are Caucasians. The findings presented by Kunz and Bahr, however, contradict Abel's finding. Kunz and Bahr found that Caucasians were about 15 times more likely to commit infanticide than African-Americans (Kunz & Bahr, 1996). Therefore, the true extent of racial differences of infanticidal offenders remains unknown.

Marital Status

Most of the women who commit infanticide are either married or in a common-law relationship at the time of the crime (McKee & Shea, 1998). According to most quantitative studies, less than one-half of the marriages are described as physically abusive (McKee & Shea, 1998). However, when qualitative studies are conducted, such as one by Wilczynski (1997), the marriages are not described as strong and fulfilling. Although abuse is not rampant, many women who commit infanticide feel as if their partner is not supportive enough either emotionally, financially, or both.

Mental Health/Intelligence

Geoffrey McKee reviewed adult women charged with infanticide and referred to a forensic psychiatric hospital for pretrial evaluation. He concluded that more than one-half of the mothers were mentally ill (McKee & Shea, 1998). Furthermore, approximately 25 percent attempted suicide at least once prior to the crime. At the time of arrest, 80 percent of the offenders had a diagnosable mental disorder (according to the DSMIII-R or DSM-IV), and nearly 70 percent had a major thought or affective disorder (McKee & Shea, 1998). The overall IQ was only slightly below average (88.43), but 35 percent could be diagnosed with either borderline intellectual functioning or mental retardation (McKee &

Shea, 1988). Although these statistics are high, they are consistent with other research published (see Kunz & Bahr, 1996; McKee, Shea, Mogy & Holden, 2001; Oberman, 2002; Palermo, 2002).

The four categories of mental health vulnerabilities most commonly discussed in infanticide literature include: Postpartum Psychosis, Chronic Mental Disabilities, Affective Disorder with Postpartum Onset, and Addiction-Related Infanticide (Oberman, 1996). Postpartum Psychosis is extremely rare, affecting only approximately one out of every 1,000 women (Oberman, 1996). Due to the lack of a standardized definition, it is more difficult to estimate how many women suffer from mental disabilities. It is roughly estimated that approximately 40 to 70 percent of the offenders have a chronic mental disability, such as schizophrenia. Approximately five percent are thought to suffer from an Affective Disorder with Postpartum Onset (Oberman, 1996). Addicted-related infanticide involves women who are substance abusers and the infanticide is an indirect result of their addiction (Oberman, 1996). It is more likely that this reason is in combination with an aforementioned explanation and not as a sole factor (McKee & Shea, 1998).

The offenders can further be described and differentiated according to the reason for the infanticide. According to researchers,[2] there are generally six categories of women who commit infanticide. The categories include: neonaticide,[3] battering mothers, retaliating women, unwanted children, mercy killings, and mentally ill mothers (D'Orban, 1979; McKee & Shea, 1998, Palermo, 2002; Oberman, 1996; Oberman, 2002). Each one is discussed in further detail below, and illustrated with an example.

Box 2.3

Classifications of Infanticide Offenders (D'Orban, 1979)	
Type	**Source of Impulse**
Battering Mothers	Sudden impulsive act triggered by victims behavior
Retaliating Women	Mother is usually angry at spouse. Anger Displacement
Unwanted Children	The offenders typically are younger, single, and/or poor
Mercy Killings	Reflection of mothers beliefs. Many times the child has some handicap, either physical or mental
Mentally Ill	Short-term: Postpartum Psychosis Chronic: Schizophrenia

Battering Mothers

D'Orban studied 89 cases of women convicted of infanticide. She finds that the battering mothers accounted for 40 percent of her sample (D'Orban, 1979). The killing is typically a sudden impulsive act, usually triggered by the victims' behavior. This type of infanticide is not intentional but a consequence of harsh punishment and abuse by the parent (Oberman, 1996). Often the mother just wants the baby "to be quiet" or to lie down to take a nap, as illustrated by the following case. The mother laid her two-year-old baby down for a nap, but the child would not stop crying. She became irritated by the child's relentless crying and after several attempts to quiet the baby, grabbed her by her feet and began to whirl her around, hitting her head against the bedroom wall several times (Palermo, 2002).

Retaliating Mothers

Retaliating women are thought to commit infanticide because of anger displacement (McKee & Shea, 1998). In D'Orban's study, 10 percent of the women fit this category (D'Orban, 1979). Usually, the mother is angry and takes it out on the child to retaliate against the husband, father figure, or boyfriend. For example, a 35-year-old woman with a Bachelor's degree and steady job began to feel increasingly frustrated with her relationship with her husband and her inability to relate to him. While he was away on business, she killed their two boys with a baseball bat to get her husband's attention (Palermo, 2002).

Unwanted Babies

Infants that are unwanted are typically murdered by young, single, and poor mothers (Palermo, 2002). A 20-year-old mother was squatting in a nearby alley when pedestrians heard a baby cry. Asking if the mother needed help, she politely said no, but the pedestrians called the police anyway. Near the alley in a dumpster they found the body of a newborn. The father of the baby was married and did not want to assume responsibility. The mother did not want the burden of another child (Palermo, 2002). In D'Orban's sample, she found the unwanted-babies-type to account for only nine percent of her cases. A potential reason for such a low percent is that usually if babies are unwanted they are murdered within the first 24 hours. Thus the "unwanted" reason more adequately explains neonaticide cases (D'Orban, 1979).

Box 2.4

Case That Made Headlines . . .

Marie Noe gave birth to 10 children between the years of 1949-1967, but only one lived to celebrate her first birthday. Her first child was born in 1949 and died within the same year. The cause of death was listed as congenital heart failure. Baby number two was born in 1950 and died within the year. This time the cause of death was listed as bronchopneumonia. Baby number three was also born in 1950 but died suddenly by choking on vomit. Her fourth child, born in 1955 also died of bronchopneumonia. In 1958, she delivered her fifth child, who died of an undetermined cause. Her sixth child was born stillborn at birth. Her seventh child lived six months before she mysteriously died. At the time of this child's death, Noe was already three months pregnant with her eighth child. Her eighth child died of blood abnormalities shortly after birth. Her ninth child lived the longest (one year, three months) before she died. In 1967, her last child was born but he remained in the hospital for five months. Less than three months after he was released from the hospital, he too died. Marie Noe was given a hysterectomy and could no longer have children.

There were no police investigations into the suspicious nature of any of the children's deaths until 33 years after her tenth child died, and 50 years from the death of her first child. In 1997, the *Philadelphia* magazine published an article on the Noes, and this story captured the attention of the media as well as police. In 1999, Marie (age 70) confessed in court to killing eight of her 10 children. The plea agreement was 20 years of probation, with the first five years spent in home confinement and psychiatric analysis.

UPDATE: As of 2006, Marie Noe had yet to be interviewed by any of the experts who were initially contacted. The court-appointed psychiatrist has yet to interview Marie, claiming he was still working on the preliminary evaluation.

Source: http://www.justicejunction.com/judicial_injustice_marie_noe.htm

---

Mercy Killings

Mercy infanticide is sometimes a reflection of the mother's belief that she is incapable of raising a child appropriately (D'Orban, 1979). A child might also be killed if they suffer from a mental or physical handicap. The mother might believe it is better to kill the child than to have them suffer (D'Orban, 1979). This is the least likely reason for a mother to kill her infant, representing at most only one percent of D'Orban's sample (D'Orban, 1979).

Mentally-Ill Mothers

Mental disorders are the most common reason for infanticide, although D'Orban finds this to be the second leading cause of infanticide, accounting for 27 percent of her sample (D'Orban, 1979). Recent research suggests that the percentage is much higher, closer to 80 percent (McKee & Shea, 1998). Mental illness can further be broken down into two types; short-term, such as Postpartum Psychosis or Affective Disorder with Postpartum Onset, and chronic, such as mood disorders and schizophrenia.

The validity of Postpartum Psychosis as a mental disorder is hotly debated. It represents the further end of a spectrum of psychiatric disorders that may be triggered by childbirth (Oberman, 1996). Experts are divided on the etiology, but there is agreement on the symptoms. Symptoms usually appear within the first three months after delivery and are most commonly experienced by women with a prior history of mental illness. There is a break with reality accompanied by a "grossly impaired ability to function, usually because of hallucinations or delusions" (Oberman, 1996). Some of these hallucinations are auditory and all relate to the newborn. Women also suffer from other behavioral tendencies including talking to themselves, sleep-deprivation, and emotional instability. During the event in which they kill their child, the women manifest these characteristics at an extreme level. For example, at Sheryl Massip's murder trial, evidence showed that she pushed her son into oncoming traffic, carried him to her garage, and hit him over the head with a blunt object. She finally killed him by running over him with her car in the driveway (Oberman, 1996). This disorder is only temporary and symptoms virtually disappear (even without treatment) within several months of onset. A mother who suffers from Postpartum Psychosis is at a higher risk to suffer it with future children as well (Oberman, 1996).

Women who suffer from Affective Disorder with Postpartum Onset kill their children in seemingly unprovoked displays of violence. The murders tend to be impulsive and disproportional reactions to an emotionally stressful event in the mother's life (Oberman, 1996). Histories of physical, emotional, and sexual abuse are common for these women (McKee & Shea, 1998). They are likely to live alone at the time they commit infanticide, and have little or no outside financial or emotional support (Oberman, 1996). They have low self-esteem, poor impulse control, and they might also suffer from depression, anxiety, and antisocial behavior. Because parenting requires patience, maturity, endurance, and energy, it is not surprising that some mothers suffering from this illness kill their children under strenuous conditions.

Chronic mental illnesses, however, are long-term. Included in this category are schizophrenia, mental retardation, and mood disorders. Schizophrenic and other psychotic mothers are the most violent compared with mothers with non-psychotic mental disabilities (Palermo,

2002). However, there are fewer cases in the literature of infanticidal schizophrenic parents for several reasons. First, many times, a schizophrenic mother's children are removed from the home shortly after birth if she is determined to be unfit (Oberman, 1996). Second, mothers with schizophrenia have higher rates of spontaneous miscarriages, stillbirths, and induced abortions (Coverdale et al., 1997). And finally, most research indicates that parents with mental illness are quite vulnerable to losing custody of their children, with custody loss rates in some studies as high as 70 to 80 percent (Joseph et al., 1999).

Box 2.5
% of Different Types of Infanticide Offenders (D'Orban, 1979)

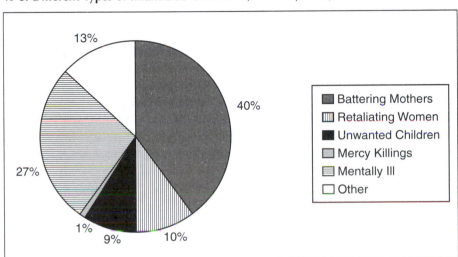

Forensic Characteristics

The methods utilized by a mother to kill her child varied greatly in a study conducted by McKee and Shea (1998). However, all the most common methods entailed close, active, physical contact between the mother and the victim. Almost 70 percent used a manual method, including manual battery (25%), suffocation (25%), or beating with a blunt object (20%). For the remaining 30 percent, the mother used more indirect methods, including arson (20%) and drowning (10%). Curiously, none of the children in this sample were murdered with a weapon. Lewis, Baranoski, Buchanan, and Benedek (1998) recently conducted a study to address the types of weapons used by 60 psychotic and non-psychotic mothers who killed their children. They found that 13 percent utilized a gun and 12 percent utilized a knife. One explanation for such low statistics of weapon use is because the use of a weapon is most likely to be restricted to older children (Lewis et al., 1998). Additionally, psychotic mothers are more apt to use a weapon than are non-psychotic mothers.

Theoretical Perspectives

The myriad of reasons for infanticide make the theoretical conceptualization of infanticide difficult. It is unlikely that one theory can account for all, or even most, infanticide cases. Nevertheless, a discussion on infanticide, albeit brief, is incomplete without a discussion of some relevant theories that provide a partial explanation of infanticide. The two theories discussed are Biological theories and Strain theories.

Biological Theories

Biological theorists argue that biological characteristics increase the probability that individuals will engage in behaviors likely to be labeled deviant (Vold, Bernard & Snipes, 2002). Empirical evidence suggests that various neurotransmitters, some hormones, and the central nervous system effect behavior (see Vold et al., 2002; Fishbein, 2001; Cullen & Agnew, 2003). Neurotransmitters are chemicals that allow for the transmission of electrical impulses within the brain and are the basis for the processing of information (Vold et al., 2002). Three neurotransmitters in particular—serotonin, dopamine, and norepinephrine—are associated with deviant behavior. Individuals with lower levels of these neurotransmitters are thought to be more prone to misconduct than individuals with normal levels.

Although neurotransmitter levels are initially determined by genetics, the levels are also influenced by the environment. For example, changes in the diet can significantly increase the levels of neurotransmitters while disadvantageous environmental conditions can lower serotonin levels (Vold et al., 2002). From the viewpoint of a biological perspective, mothers in stressful conditions (be it financial, emotional, or physical) might not be able to resist the impulse to murder their child. Research is currently devoid of discussions of neurotransmitter levels on mothers at the time they commit the infanticidal act.

It has been established in the literature that testosterone is the hormone most associated with aggression (Fishbein, 2001). Some women are susceptible to cyclical hormone changes that result in an increase in hostility. A small percentage of these women are especially sensitive to the rise in testosterone (Vold et al., 2002). There is validity to this claim, but again, there are no empirical studies on testosterone levels in women who commit infanticide (Haskett, 1987; Fishbein, 1992; Trunell & Turner, 1988).

The central nervous system contains neurons that exist within the brain and spinal cord. Of particular interest in research on aggression and violence is the cerebral cortex, which is the outer portion of the brain. The cerebral cortex is divided into two hemispheres and four lobes

(Vold et al., 2002). The two lobes that are involved with goal-directed behavior, impulses, and emotions are the frontal and temporal lobes (Vold et al., 2002). Irregularities within the frontal lobe influence neuropsychological performance, while the disturbances in the temporal lobe directly affect emotional expression. There are various brain imaging procedures that detect structural and functional abnormalities in both the frontal and temporal lobes including: (1) the electroencephalograph (EEG), (2) computerized tomography (CT), (3) magnetic resonance imaging (MRI), (4) positron emission tomography (PET), (5) and the single photon emission tomography (SPECT) (Vold et al., 2002). Researchers agree that repeat violent offenders have abnormal readings from the aforementioned procedures, but it is unclear what one would expect from mothers who kill their children. With a few exceptions, most infanticidal mothers are not chronic or repeat offenders.

Strain Theories

In contrast with biological theorists, strain theorists believe that the characteristics of society are what lead to criminality. Robert Merton argues that there are certain stable social conditions associated with higher overall crime rates as well as with higher crime rates in the lower class (Vold et al., 2002). Individuals' goals are not natural, but instead are dictated to them by the "American Dream." Because not all individuals are able to obtain societal goals such as wealth, they turn to nonconformity.

Cullen's interpretation of Merton's strain theory is more relevant for explaining infanticide. Cullen considers strain to be feelings and emotions that an individual experiences, i.e., feelings of stress, frustration, anxiety, depression, and anger (Vold et al., 2002). These feelings are what lead to criminality. The behavior acts as an outlet for them to vent their frustrations. Although there is debate whether Merton's original strain theory includes Cullen's version of strain theory, it does offer a testable explanation for reasons why mothers in financial crisis and without support commit infanticide.

At a macro analysis, the economic stress hypothesis is the most useful in explaining cross national variation in child homicide rates (Gauthier, Chaudoir & Forsyth, 2003). The hypothesis suggests that higher levels of economic stress are related to higher levels of child homicide. Homicide rates are not necessarily dependent upon unemployment, but on the range of social programs that provide aid to women and children. Therefore, governments that provide only minimum living standards and places where income inequality is great, homicide rates will be greater for children (Gauthier et al., 2003).

The theoretical conceptualization of infanticide is scarce. As with the biological theories, strain theories have not to date been rigorously tested as an explanation for infanticide. Until empirical tests are published, little can be said theoretically regarding infanticide. The high prevalence of mentally-ill infanticidal women suggests that biological theories have much to offer as both a framework for explaining infanticide as well as for prevention. The importance of the environment, as illustrated in qualitative research, in pushing the women over the edge implies the importance of strain theories.

Treatment/Prevention

Anne Wilczynski argues that not all women are treated sympathetically by the public and the courts (Wilczynksi, 1997). Women who conform to the gender stereotype benefit from the "blameless victimization" and are considered "mad." They "might cause the death of their children, but at that time the balance of their mind was disturbed by not having fully recovered from the effects of giving birth."[4] Women that do not conform to the stereotype (i.e., "bad" mothers) are treated more severely. The "bad" mothers are "ruthless, selfish, cold, callous, and neglectful of their children, or of their domestic responsibilities, as violent and promiscuous."[5] Wilczynski supports her argument by examining a sample of 48 women and the sentences they received. According to her results, the 12 offenders who received prison terms previously physically or emotionally abused the child or drank heavily (Wilczynksi, 1997). The mentally-ill or depressed women sent to prison are unlikely to get proper treatment. It is well established in the literature that prisons lack the funding to have properly implemented programs, if there are programs at all (Pollock, 2002). This is especially the case for women's prisons.

It is important to emphasize that infanticide research has not, and is not, currently focused on treatment of infanticidal women. Although there are exceptions, most infanticidal women are not repeat or chronic offenders. In fact, because most infanticidal mothers kill only once, research on treatment is irrelevant. Instead, what is of utmost importance is prevention. Physicians' and psychiatrists' research suggests that certain medications and drugs can reduce or eliminate deviant or antisocial behavior. This information, while useful for criminologists, has not gained much popularity. Sociological theorists primarily target family risk factors such as poor child-rearing and supervision, or inconsistent and harsh discipline (Farrrington & Welsh, 1999). The latter is abundant in criminological literature, whereas the former is scarce. As a result, sociological preventative programs are emphasized in this chapter. Whether or not the preventative measures are a success is based on the Maryland Scientific Methods Scale (SMS).

Box 2.6

Case That Made Headlines . . .

Melissa Drexler, on June 6, 1997, gave birth to a baby boy at her senior high school prom. For nine months she concealed her pregnancy from her parents, friends, and long-time boyfriend (also the father). She gave birth in a bathroom stall while her unsuspecting friends waited for her outside. She threw the baby in the trash before returning to the dance. The baby was discovered by a janitor who had been called to clean up the blood.

Drexler later confessed to the killing, and was charged with murder. She pled guilty to aggravated manslaughter. On October 29, 1998, she was sentenced to 15 years in prison.

UPDATE: Melissa was paroled on November 26, 2001—after serving only three years of her 15-year sentence.

Source: http://www.answers.com/topic/melissa-drexler

Biological-Based Prevention Techniques

Prevention programs that stem from biological theories are extremely controversial. Lilly, Cullen, & Ball argue there is an ethical danger to focusing on individual differences and such focus is destructive (Lilly et al., 2001). For example, some fear that a focus on biological causes of crime will lead to a eugenics movement. These fears are not unfounded, as exemplified by the laws passed during the years of 1911-1930. During this time, more than 30 states established laws that required sterilization for behavioral traits such as criminality, alcoholism, sodomy, bestiality, feeblemindedness, and the tendency to commit rape (Lilly et al., 2001). Many states also passed laws permitting psychosurgeries, such as a frontal lobotomy. Sterilizations and psychosurgeries were practiced well into the 1970s and it is estimated that more than 64,000 people were sterilized (Lilly et al., 2001). While recognizing these dangerous consequences, biological research and treatment can still be one tool utilized by professionals to decrease the prevalence of infanticide, especially for those mothers who are mentally ill. Unfortunately, biological preventative programs have yet to be embraced by researchers and practitioners in the criminology field. Consequently, the majority of the treatments discussed emphasis sociological-based techniques.

Sociological-Based Techniques

The focus of sociological-based treatment is on the role of the environment in increasing or decreasing the likelihood of a mother committing infanticide. These types of treatments are generally criticized because they do not take into account biological influences and indirectly imply that individuals do not have control over their lives. However, because many mothers who kill their children feel as if they have little support, are under extreme stress, and are lacking parental skills, sociological-based treatments have merit. Sociological-based preventative techniques target two different, but similar high-risk factors; parental support and parental training. The following is a discussion of both high-risk factors and the research that supports preventative programs. Caution must be taken, however, because the research does not directly target infanticidal mothers. Instead, the research and findings target women who are at high risk for abuse. It is plausible to assume that the abuse will have a correlative effect on infanticide cases.

Parental Support

Although the majority of women who commit infanticide are married, many report they lack support from their significant other. They perceive themselves to be the primary caregiver with little outside help (Palermo, 2002). The emotional and physical exhaustion of motherhood is usually viewed as a personal failure. As a result, it is imperative to have parental support programs to help counter this damaging misconception.

There are two private, not-for-profit, and non-punitive parental support organizations: Parents Anonymous and Child-Abuse Prevention Services (CAP). Parents Anonymous consist of eight support groups dispersed throughout the city. Each group has approximately 10 parents that meet weekly to share stories about motherhood and to seek advice (Oberman, 1996). This group has a difficult time recruiting parents because by law they must use their name and report behavior considered to be suspected child abuse. Because of this requirement, parents are afraid to discuss their frustrations and what happens in their household.

The CAP hotline, however, is completely anonymous. It operates 24 hours a day and received an estimated 1.8 million calls in 2002 alone from parents seeking advice, as well as those reporting cases of child abuse. In addition to the hotline, there are also support groups that meet weekly. CAP groups differ from Parents Anonymous because CAP is facilitated by a professional counselor instead of a volunteer parent. CAP is also mandated by law to report suspicious behavior to the proper authorities. Clearly these two programs are a partial solution to alleviate the stresses of motherhood. Although considered successful, the programs are unable to completely fulfill the emotional, social, and financial support the parent needs.

Unfortunately, the two programs discussed above are not common throughout the United States. Most agencies available for mothers to call are child protection agencies that intervene to remove the children from dangerous environments instead of offering parental advice (Oberman, 1996). Parents who utilize these services are at risk for being punished, rather than assisted, and therefore often do not call or seek help. The programs are not scientifically tested to test if the programs can effectively reduce or eliminate abusive behavior. The high numbers of parents who call hotlines each year suggest a definite need for more non-punitive agencies. Scientific research assessing the efficiency and effectiveness will improve the agencies efforts to reach parents.

Parental Training

Motherhood requires tremendous feats of patience, energy, endurance, maturity, and knowledge. The American culture presupposes that all women have a "maternal instinct" and automatically know the tasks of caring for a child. This belief makes it difficult for mothers to seek out help and advice. It is especially difficult when the women are married because it is assumed her husband is supportive. When women seek advice, there can be severe consequences. For example, a mother was breast feeding her first child and found herself to be sexually aroused. She called a child-protective agency to ask if this was normal and what she should do about it. The next day, her child was removed from her home and placed in foster care. She was arrested on the grounds of sexual abuse. It took one year and several thousand dollars for her to reclaim custody of her child. In order to overcome the stereotype that women who seek help are unfit mothers, parenting classes and education should be moved to the forefront of social welfare programs.

Mothers' attitudes and interactions with their children are influenced by a combination of economic stress, environmental forces, and other critical events (Webster-Stratton & Hammond, 1990). Longitudinal studies suggest that children in families under stress have higher rates of child abuse (Elder, Nguyen & Caspi, 1985). Family-based programs that show promising results of decreasing child delinquency or the reduction of parental abusive behavior or neglect can be classified into one of six categories. These categories include; (1) multi-systemic therapy programs, (2) school-based child training plus parent training programs, (3) clinic-based parent training plus child training programs, (4) home visitation, (5) parent education plus day care/preschool, and (6) home/community parent training (Farrington & Welsh, 2002).

Almost all of the above categories help improve the parenting skills but the findings report only on the child's future delinquency and anti-social behaviors. Therefore, they do not warrant further discussion. However, home visitation programs do report on the mother's behavior, and therefore the following paragraphs discuss research studies on home visitations and the assessment of such programs utilizing the University of Maryland Scientific Methods Score (SMS). There are four noteworthy studies carried out in the United States that fall within the home visitation category. All four research studies were based on selective samples of at-risk parents and children. The direct targets of intervention are the parents (most often the mother), the child, or both (Farrington & Welsh, 2002).

The Elmira PEIP Project was established in 1980 by Olds and colleagues to improve the outcomes of pregnancy, to improve the quality of parental care, and to improve the women's own life-course development (Farrington & Welsh, 2002). The sample consisted of 400 at-risk women randomly assigned to one of four treatment or control conditions. In order to be considered at-risk, the expecting mother needed to meet at least one socio-demographic risk factor. The risk factors included: the female was under the age of 19 at the time of pregnancy, she was unmarried, or from a low SES. One criterion that all women had to meet before enrolling in this program is that they had no previous births. The context of the intervention took place in the home, and the risk factors manipulated were parenting skills and family planning. The treatment group received home visits[6] during pregnancy as well as postnatal visits (Farrington & Welsh, 2002).

The results after two years of intervention and a one-year follow-up show a significant reduction of child-abuse and neglect. In addition, the mothers had lower levels of arrests and convictions. According to the SMS this study has a rating of five because they randomly assigned women to both the treatment and control groups.

In 1997, a replication of the Elmira Project was carried out by Kitzman and his colleagues (Kitzman, Olds, Henderson, Hanks, Cole, Tatelbaum, McConnochie, Sidora, Luckey, Shaver, Engelhardt, James & Bernard, 1997). The sample consisted of 1,139 mothers who had at least two of the predetermined socio-risk factors discussed previously. The context of the intervention is in the home and the risk factor manipulated remained the same (parenting and family planning). Both the treatment and the control group received the same parental supplements as in the first study (Kitzman et al., 1997).

The immediate outcome after two years of intervention is a reduction in child injuries. The researchers randomly assigned women to both the treatment and control group, thereby qualifying for a rating of 5 by the standards of SMS.

Another study by Barth, Hacking, and Ash in 1988 focuses on interventions for women who were at high-risk for abusing their unborn child. The sample consisted of 65 women randomly assigned to a treatment and control group. The context of the intervention took place in the home and the risk factor manipulated is the social support system (Farrington & Welsh, 2002). Those women who were assigned to the treatment group received parent education and parental support from family, friends, and community resources. The control group did not receive parental education and parental support.

The results after six months of intervention showed a significant and positive drop in both child temperament as well as episodes of child abuse (Farrington & Welsh, 2002). According to the SMS this study has a rating of five because they randomly assigned women to both the treatment and control groups.

The third home visitation program differs from the first two discussed because the average age of the child was approximately four years old, instead of prenatal. In 1991, Strayhorn and Weidman selectively chose 98 parents who were from the lower SES and who described at least one emotional or behavioral problem in their child (Farrington & Welsh, 2002). The context of intervention, again, took place in the home and the risk factor manipulated was the parenting style. Those parents who were assigned to the treatment group were given group parental training and the control group only received the parental information in the form of brochures and reading packets.

The results after six months of intervention and a one-year follow up showed a significantly positive drop in hyperactivity of the children. Since there was random assignment to both the control and treatment groups, the SMS score is a five. According to the SMS, home visitations can be said to be beneficial because of the consistent rating of a five for the four previously discussed programs.

The Common Sense Parenting Program is another program aimed at increasing parenting skills (Thompson, Grow, Ruma, Daly & Burke, 1993). The program is based on a well-researched approach to providing family-style residential treatment for children with behavior and emotional problems. The program is grounded in social learning principles and designed to teach parental child management skills to the parent. The three main components of the program are (1) family assessment, (2) eight-week skills training, (3) support and follow-up.

The family assessment involves a 60-minute interview with the parents in their home. Some information gathered in this interview includes the general social histories of the parents, family demographics, parent and child strengths and problems, and goals for the training program (Thompson et al., 1993).

The eight-week training program centered around weekly two-hour training sessions to teach a parent concept, for example, discipline, and specific skills to enhance the concept. A variety of teaching methods were employed such as presentations, discussions, role-play, modeling, home assignments, as well as videotapes (Thompson et al., 1993). This meeting provided social support to parents and assisted them with skill acquisition, skill generalization, and intervention strategies for child problem behaviors (Thompson et al., 1993). In between the weekly visits, the counselors maintained contact with the parents via the telephone.

The support and follow-up phase of the program included telephone consultation between weekly meetings and additional meetings after the eight week program, if needed. A support group also met once a month to offer further support for the parents, thereby helping to ensure continued success.

The eight outcome measures were based on three different tests (Thompson et al., 1993). The Eyberg Child Behavior Inventory (ECBI) measured the child's behavior problems. Three scales from the Parent Attitude Test (PAT) measured the change in parent attitudes and perceptions. The first scale was the Home Attitude Scale to reflect the parent's attitude toward the home. The second scale used from the PAT was the Behavior Rating Scale. This scale addressed the behavior problems. The Adjective Checklist Scale consisted of 34 adjectives to describe child attributes or personality characteristics. The third test was the Problem Solving Inventory (PSI). This questionnaire assesses three dimensions of problem-solving ability: problem-solving confidence, approach-avoidance style, and personal control (Thompson et al., 1993).

The results, although preliminary and based on a small sample, were positive. There were significant main effects for all but one of the outcome measures. According to the SMS, however, many alternative explanations for the results are possible. The participants volunteered for the program, so it is unclear whether the findings are generalizable to the general population. Those who volunteered for the program are likely quite different from those who would not. In addition, there was no control group. Each parent acted as there own control (pretest-posttest design), so there are many threats to internal validity that the authors are unable to control. However, this research coupled with the previous research discussed yields strong support for additional programs to help teach parental skills.

The programs that are successful vary on the context of intervention and the duration of treatment. A commonality is a focus on practical skills that can immediately be implemented in the home (Thompson et al., 1993). The attempt to change the familial environment by offering parental advice and guidance appears to be a successful preventative tool. However, one major problem with the programs discussed is that they are multimodal. It is very difficult to disentangle the aspects of the programs that are beneficial to the parent and child from those which are not beneficial.

In the majority of infanticide cases, the women exhibit "warning signs" that indicate that she might hurt herself or her children. If family members, physicians, social workers, neighbors, and friends could detect and recognized warning signs early, then as many as seventy percent of infanticide cases could be eliminated (Rhode, Raic, Varchmin-Schultheib & Marneros, 1998). Some warning signs include: psychotic or depressive symptoms, suicidal ideas or attempted suicide, feelings of hopelessness, inability to sleep, nightmares, or hallucinations (Rhode et al., 1998). Similar warning signals are reported by other authors,[7] showing a need for family members, medical staff, social workers, and legal authorities to act on abnormal behavior exhibited by a mother shortly after birth.

The mentally ill would greatly benefit from individual treatment. Mothers who are stressed and feel hopeless, however, would benefit from social programs and support. Therefore, future treatment programs should contain both biological and sociological components. By building safety nets for mothers who need help, providing resources for those without opportunities (i.e., quality employment, parental training), increasing availability of alternative modes of behavior, revitalizing neighborhoods, assembling multidisciplinary teams to intervene when warning signals are present, and enhancing community involvement could decrease the amount of infanticide cases in the United Sates. Only such integrated preventative programs can ensure that mother's needs are addressed and taken seriously.

Conclusion

"There's just no point trying to comprehend the incomprehensible."[8] This quote summarizes the view of many regarding infanticide. The slaying of innocent children by their mothers is formidable and cannot be integrated easily into our understanding of the world. Indeed, the contributing factors to infanticide are quite complex. It is about a lack of economic resources and a lack of communication and community coupled with biological predispositions. It is also a reflection of a society that places little value on the mental and physical well-being of children and mothers.

The literature reviewed in this chapter, however, suggests that the crime is comprehensible and most importantly, preventable. In order to move beyond our current understanding, future research must be of a multi-disciplinary approach. Much can be learned through criminologist and sociological theories, through physicians/psychiatrists and biological theories, and through psychologists and psychological theories. We must begin to identify the innumerable ways in which our society tolerates and perpetuates infanticidal situations. Finally, we must also acknowledge the role that all of us play in driving these women to the edge of despair.

Notes

[1]   Quote is from source Oberman (1996).

[2]   Resneck, in 1969, developed the first classification system. D'Orban, in 1979 developed a similar classification system but included a category of neonaticide. Resneck's classification system is flawed because it is based on the motive of the offender and so the probability of misclassification is highly dependent upon what the clinician believes to be the primary motive. D'Orban minimizes this risk by basing her reasons on the source of impulse. In 1990, Bourget & Bradford updated the classification categories to include paternal infanticide; however, their system is based on a very small sample and is not cited much in the research.

[3]   As mentioned earlier in the chapter, neonaticide is beyond the scope of this chapter and so is only mentioned as a category, and not further discussed.

[4]   Taken from Wilczynksi, 1991, page 74.

[5]   Taken from Wilczynksi, 1991, page 78.

[6]   Three major activities were carried out during the home visits; parent education about influences on fetal and infant development, involvement of family and friends during the pregnancy and after, and the linkage of family members with other health and human services.

[7]   See Myers, 1970 and D'Orban, 1979.

[8]   A quote by Richard Stengel, an author for Time.com. Source is from Vatz and Weinberg, 2002.

References

Abel, E.L. (1986). "Childhood Homicide in Erie County, New York." *Pediatrics*, 77:709-717.

Adinkrah, M. (2001). "When Parents Kill: A Descriptive Analysis of Filicide in Fiji." *International Journal of Offender Therapy and Comparative Criminology*, 45:144-158.

Barth, R.P., S. Hacking, and J.R. Ash (1988). "Preventing Child-abuse: An Experimental Evaluation of the Child Parent Enrichment Project." *Journal of Primary Prevention*, 8:201-217.

Coverdale, J.M., L.B. McCullogh, F.A. Chervenak, T. Bayer, and S. Weeks (1997). "Clinical Implications of Respect for Autonomy in the Psychiatric Treatment of Pregnant Patients with Depression." *Pyschiatric Services*, 48(2):209-212.

Cullen, F.T. and R. Agnew (2003). *Criminological Theory: Past to Present*, Second Edition. California: Roxbury.

D'Orban, P.T. (1979). "Women Who Kill Their Children." *British Journal of Psychiatry*, 134:560-571.

Elder, G.H., T.V. Nguyen, and A. Caspi (1985). "Linking Family Hardship to Children's Lives." *Child Development*, 56:361-375.

Farrington, D.P. (1999). "Delinquency Prevention Using Family-Based Interventions." *Children and Society*, 13:387-403.

Farrington, D.P., D.C. Gottfredson, L.W. Sherman, and B.C. Welsh (2002). "The Maryland Scientific Methods Scale." In L.W. Sherman, D.P. Farrington, B.C. Welsh, and D. MacKenzie (eds.) *Evidence Based Corrections*. New York: Routelage.

Farrington, D.P. and B.C. Welsh (2002). "Family-Based Prevention." In L.W. Sherman, D.P. Farrington, B.C. Welsh, and D. MacKenzie (eds.) *Evidence Based Corrections*. New York: Routelage.

Fishbein, D. (2001). *Biological Perspectives in Criminology*. California: Wadsworth.

Fishbein, D. (1992). "The Psychobiology of Female Aggression." *Criminal Justice and Behavior*, 19:92-126.

Gauthier, D.K, N.K. Chaudoir, and C.J. Forsyth (2003). "A Sociological Analysis of Maternal Infanticide in the United States, 1984-1996." *Deviant Behavior: An Interdisciplinary Journal*, 24:393-404.

Gelles, R.J. and C.P. Cornell (1990). *Intimate Violence in Families*, Second Edition. Newbury Park, CA: Sage.

Haskett, R.F. (1987). "Premenstrual Dysphoric Disorder: Evaluation, Pathophysiology and Treatment." *Progress in Neuro-Psychopharmacology and Biological Psychiatry*, 11:129-135.

Joseph, J.G., S. Joshi, A.B. Lewin, and M. Abrams (1999). "Characteristics and Perceived Needs of Mothers with Serious Mental Illness." *Psychiatric Services*, 50(10):1357-1359.

Kaufman, L. and R. Jones (2003). "Trenton Finds Abuse High in Foster Care." *New York Times*, 152:D1-5.

Kitzman, H., D.L. Olds, C.R. Henderson, C. Hanks, R. Cole, R. Tatelbaum, K.M. McConnochie, K. Sidora, D.W Luckey, D. Shaver, K. Engelhardts, D. James, and K. Barnard (1997). "Effect of Prenatal and Infancy Home Visitation by Nurses on Pregnancy Outcomes, Childhood Injuries and Repeated Childbearing: A Randomized Controlled Trial." *Journal of the American Medical Association*, 287:644-652.

Kunz, J. and S.J. Bahr (1996). "A Profile of Parental Homicide against Children." *Journal of Family Violence*, 11:347-353.

Leathers, S. (2003). "Parental Visiting, Conflict Allegiances, and Emotional and Behavioral Problems among Foster Children." *Family Relations*, 52:53-60.

Lewis, C.F., M.V. Baranoski, J.A. Buchanan, and E.P. Benedek (1998). "Factor Associated with Weapon Use in Maternal Filicide." *Journal of Forensic Sciences*, 43:613-618.

Lilly, J.R., F.T. Cullen, and R.A. Ball (2001). *Criminological Theory: Context and Consequences*. California: Sage.

McKee, G.R., S.J. Shea, R. Mogy, and C. Holden (2001). "MMPI-2 Profiles of Filicidal, Mariticidal, and Homicidal Women." *Journal of Clinical Psychology*, 57:367-374.

McKee, G.R. and S.J. Shea (1998). "Maternal Filicide: A Cross-National Comparison. *Journal of Clinical Psychology*, 54:697-687.

Myers, S.A. (1970). "Maternal Filicide." *American Journal of Sociology*, 76:213-261.

Oberman, M. (2002). "Understanding Infanticide in Context: Mothers Who Kill, 1870-1930 and Today." *Journal of Criminal Law and Criminology*, 92:707-711.

Oberman, M. (1996). "Mothers Who Kill: Coming to Terms with Modern American Infanticide." *American Criminal Law Review*, 34:1-90.

Orme, J. (2001). "Foster Family Characteristics and Behavioral and Emotional Problems of Foster Children: A Narrative Review." *Family Relations*, 50:13-36.

Palermo, G. (2002). "Murderous Parents." *International Journal of Offender Therapy and Comparative Criminology*, 46:123-143.

Parker, L. (2006). "Judge: Yates Retrial to Move Ahead." *USA Today*, 3/2/2006.

Philpot, T. (2002). "In Need of Attention." *Community Affairs*, 1427:34-46.

Pollock, J.M. (2002). *Women, Prison, and Crime,* Second Edition. California: Wadsworth.

Strayhorn, J.M. and C.S. Weidman (1991). "Follow-up One Year after Parent-Child Interaction Training: Effects on Behavior of Preschool Children." *Journal of the American Academy of Child and Adolescent Psychiatry*, 30:138-143.

Szegedy-Maszak, M. (2002). "Mothers and Murder." *U.S. News & World Report*, 132:23-24.

Thompson, R.W., C.R. Grow, P.R. Ruma, D.L. Daly, and R.V. Burke (1993). "Evaluation of a Practical Parenting Program with Middle- and Lower-Income Families." *Family Relations*, 42:21-26.

Trunell, E.P. and C.W. Turner (1988). "A Comparison of the Psychological and Hormonal Factors in Women with and Without Premenstrual Syndrome." *Journal of Abnormal Psychology*, 97:429-436.

Vatz, R.E. and L.S. Weinberg (2002). "Murderous Mothers: A Challenge for the Insanity Defense." *USA Today*, 131:48-50.

Vold, G.B., T.J. Bernard, and J.B. Snipes (2002). *Theoretical Criminology*. New York: Oxford.

Webster-Stratton, C. and M. Hammond (1990). "Predictors of Treatment Outcome in Parent Training for Families with Conduct Problem Children." *Behavior Therapy*, 21:319-337.

Wheeler, K.H. (1997). "Infanticide in Nineteenth-Century Ohio." *Journal of Social History*, 31:407-419.

Wilczynski, A. (1997). "Mad or Bad?" *The British Journal of Criminology*, 37:419-437.

Wilson, J. (1984). "The Historical Context of Infanticide." *Journal of the History of Science in Society*, 81:769-782.

Chapter 3

Domestic Battery

Jennifer Gibbs

Introduction

Domestic violence, although traditionally considered a private family issue, has received much attention in the past few decades as a societal problem. As with all types of criminal behavior, many theories have attempted to account for spousal abuse. This chapter will focus on defining domestic violence, several theories explaining battering, addressing criminal justice system programs and policies directed at domestic violence in the United States, and the current and potentially future implications of the theories described.

What Is Domestic Abuse?

Domestic abuse—also referred to as domestic violence and intimate partner violence—is a *pattern of behaviors* used by one person to maintain *power and control* over another person in certain types of relationships. Relationships can be current or previous, familial or non-familial, including parent/child, spousal, intimate partner (dating), and having child(ren) in common—but not acquaintances or friendships. The theoretical explanations and treatment options vary greatly depending upon the type of domestic abuse. Therefore, this chapter will focus on a critical examination of intimate partner (spousal, ex-spousal, dating, and formerly dating) relationships.

Abuse may or may not be physical (Johnson, 1995). Domestic violence consists of controlling behavior, usually taking the form of emotional and psychological abuse, social isolation, forced financial dependence and physical violence. However, because it is the most violent and recognized criminally, only physical violence will be discussed in this chapter.

Domestic violence is typified by a *cycle of violence*, which has three repeating stages: tension building, violent outburst/acute battering incident, and the calm, loving stage (also known as the "honeymoon phase") where the abuser is apologetic. As the relationship progresses, the honeymoon phase often decreases and the tension building and violent outburst phases become longer and more severe.

Box 3.1

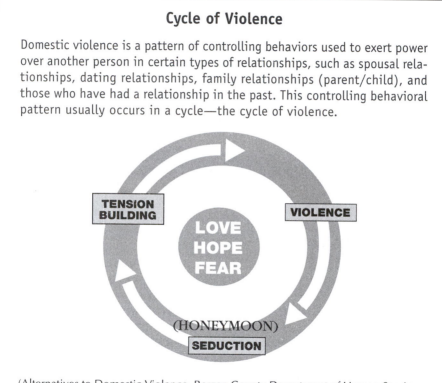

Cycle of Violence

Domestic violence is a pattern of controlling behaviors used to exert power over another person in certain types of relationships, such as spousal relationships, dating relationships, family relationships (parent/child), and those who have had a relationship in the past. This controlling behavioral pattern usually occurs in a cycle—the cycle of violence.

(Alternatives to Domestic Violence, Bergen County Department of Human Services, Hackensack, New Jersey: http://www.co.bergen.nj.us/ADV/WhatIsDomesticViolence.htm)

Physical abuse usually is not constant; rather, it happens in phases. In the calm, "honeymoon phase," the abuser is loving and kind. He may express remorse and make many promises that the violence will not happen again. But a short time later, tension begins to build and the batterer becomes violent again. Over time, the violent phases become longer and more severe, while the nonviolent phases became shorter and even non-existent.

Who Is Victimized by Domestic Abuse?

Domestic violence is a social problem. Domestic violence affects approximately 10 percent of all relationships each year in the United States (Bancroft & Silverman, 2002). The National Institute of Justice calculated that domestic violence costs $67 billion per year (Miller et al., 1996), and the costs related to the criminal justice system could be far greater, as only one-half of all domestic violence incidents are reported to the police (Bureau of Justice Statistics, 2000). Many assaults are witnessed by children, who can be impacted either directly or indirectly in many ways, including being injured while trying to protect the abused parent or calling 911, being in unsafe conditions, being held hostage by the offender to control the behavior of the abused parent, learning negative attitudes toward women, and learning to use physical violence without many consequences (Bancroft & Silverman, 2002; Bartol, 2002; Kitzmann, Gaylord, Holt & Kenny, 2003). In addition, domestic violence increases the likelihood of child abuse, as 30 to 60 percent of children whose mother is a victim of intimate partner violence also are abused (Graham-Bermann & Edleson, 2001).

Both women and men can be victims and perpetrators; however, women are far more likely than men to be victims of domestic violence. According to the 1998 National Crime Victimization Survey (NCVS) published by the Bureau of Justice Statistics (2000), 85 percent the victims of intimate partner violence were female. Tjaden and Thoennes (2000) reported that women are significantly more likely to be injured in a domestic assault than men. Although domestic violence does not discriminate against age, race, or socioeconomic status, African-American women, women who live in urban areas, women between the ages of 16 and 24 years, and women with annual family incomes below $7,000 are most likely to be victimized (Healey & Smith, 1998).

Box 3.2

Victims and Survivors

Domestic violence does not discriminate against age, race, or class. However, victims are more likely to have the certain characteristics. Who is more likely to be a victim?

- Women (and children)
- African-American women
- Women who live in urban areas
- Women between the ages of 16 and 24
- Women who live in poverty

Domestic violence often escalates and, in some cases, can lead to murder. For about one in five women, however, homicide is the first *physically violent* episode committed by an intimate partner (Block, 2003). As reflected in Box 3.3, the Federal Bureau of Investigation's Uniform Crime Reports (UCR) details that, in 2002, more than 1,000 women were murdered by their partners (and approximately 287 men were killed by their partners) (Federal Bureau of Investigation). These numbers remain relatively constant from the previous years.

Box 3.3

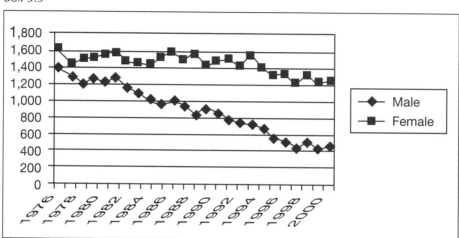

Source: Bureau of Justice Statistics (Rennison & Welchans, 2000).

Offender Characteristics

Who Is a Batterer?

Bancroft and Silverman (2002:3) define a domestic violence batterer as:

. . . a person who exercises a pattern of coercive control in a partner relationship, punctuated by one or more acts of intimidating physical violence, sexual assault, or credible threat of physical violence. This pattern of control and intimidation may be predominantly psychological, economic, or sexual in nature or may rely primarily on the use of physical violence.

Batterers are characterized by their beliefs and need for control; feelings of entitlement; self-centeredness; possessiveness; confusion of love and abuse; manipulativeness; contradictory statements and behaviors; externalization of responsibility; poor social skills; violent backgrounds; denial, minimization of abuse, and victim blaming; and serial battering

(Bancroft & Silverman, 2002; Dixon & Browne, 2003). Typical battering is not characterized by substance abuse, mental health problems, generalized violence and criminality, or race, cultural, and class stereotypes, although these traits may play a role in the type of abusive behavior (Bancroft & Silverman, 2002). Often, batterers may hide their abusive side from society. Batterer public portrayal as kind and gentle people often convinces victims that others will not believe their story, further isolating the victim and continuing the abuse.

Typology of Batterers

Like most criminal activity, there is no commonly accepted description of the "typical batterer." For example, Johnson (1995) found two forms of battering: *common couple violence*, in which both males and females use violence on rare occasions to resolve everyday conflicts, and *patriarchal terrorism*, in which the male systematically uses violence against his partner and family as a control mechanism. In an effort to create more effective batterer treatment, better predict the level of dangerousness, and better predict the likelihood of reoffending, researchers have been developing typologies of battering (Healey & Smith, 1998). However, there is no clear consensus on these typologies.

Based on a comprehensive review of research of batterer typologies, the Holtzworth-Monroe and Stuart (1994) Typology identifies three groups of batterers: family-only violence/non-pathological, generally violent/antisocial, and dysphoric/borderline. *Family-only batterers* limit the violence to the family, present the lowest risk of injury, generally exhibit low frequency and severity of violence, and experienced little childhood trauma. The *generally violent/antisocial batterer* is a psychopath, uses moderate to severe violence to control others (violence is not limited to the family), has an extensive criminal history, and is most likely to have substance abuse problems and have experienced severe childhood physical abuse. The *dysphoric/borderline batterer* is the moderate offender, falling between these two groups: the batterer uses moderate to severe violence primarily in—but not limited to—the family, clearly exhibits the three stages of the cycle of violence, and experienced severe parental rejection and moderate interparental violence during childhood (Dixon & Browne, 2003; Holtzworth-Monroe & Meehan, 2002; Lawson et al., 2003).

Further studies offer strong support for this typology (Lawson et al., 2003). For instance, in a spousal abuse research study by Dixon and Browne (2003), family-only batterers constituted approximately 50 percent of offenders, while the generally violent/antisocial offender represented 30 percent of batterers and the dysphoric/borderline personality offender represented 20 percent of batterers. Dixon and

Browne (2003) suggest that this threefold typology will be of assistance in profiling batterers to better assign treatment protocols.

Although these typologies have been supported in research both before and after the typology was established and the typology may be useful for directing batterers into treatment, Holtzworth-Monroe and Meehan (2002) suggest that more research should be conducted before relying on the typologies, as cut-offs need more clarification. Matching offenders with treatment programs seems to be a promising practice in the future (Saunders & Hamill, 2003), although presently it is not commonly utilized.

Box 3.4

Female Offenders

Domestic violence is commonly described as directed toward women, largely because women are more likely to be to be victims, the frequency and duration of intimate partner violence is far greater for female than for male victims (Tjaden & Thoennes, 2000), and the injuries sustained by females are far more severe than those sustained by males. The differences of the physical domestic assaults by men and women as reported to the police are presented in the table below (Melton Belknap, 2003):

Male offenders	**Female offenders**
Shove or push victim	Hit victim with an object
Grab or drag victim	Throw object at victim
Pull victim's hair	Strike victim with vehicle
Physically restrain victim	Bite victim
Strangle victim	
Prevent victim from calling 911	

The Uniform Crime Reports published annually by the Federal Bureau of Investigation (2002) show that women are murdered far more often by a husband or a boyfriend than men are murdered by a wife or a girlfriend—domestic violence can affect women far more severely than men. (See Box 3.3.)

Although domestic violence is typically directed at women, men can be the recipients of such violence as well. Husband-beating has been present throughout history. The practice of a husband-beating was known as "Riding Skimmington" or "Skimmington" in sixteenth-century England, where an abusive woman was depicted as hitting her husband with a cheese skimming ladle (George, 2003). Battered husbands were made to ride facing backwards on a donkey through town in an attempt to shame the husband into resuming "appropriate" gender roles.

Box 3.4, *continued*

Some studies claim that women are equally as violent as men. In fact, since passage of the mandatory arrest laws, more and more women are being arrested, constituting about 20 percent of defendants entering the criminal justice system (McMahon & Pence, 2003). Female offenders, however, are qualitatively different than male offenders, as mentioned above. For example, women are more likely to tell the police details of their offending, and are more likely to plead guilty instead of going to trial. On the other hand, men prosecuted for domestic offending are less likely to plead guilty; instead, they demand that their defense attorneys attempt to have them acquitted by arguing their innocence (McMahon & Pence, 2003).

Little is known about female offenders with respect to domestic violence against male partners. However, the National Institute of Justice held a Gender Symmetry Workshop in 2000, bringing together researchers, scholars, and experts to address this issue (Swan & Snow, 2003). Although there is a lack of research on female domestic violence offenders, this section will provide a framework for existing research in theorizing causes of female offending.

Masculine Personality Traits

Similar to feminist theory which bases domestic violence in the patriarchal structure of society, some researchers argue that female-perpetrated partner violence is the result of females adopting masculine personality traits. Dietz and Jasinski (2003) studied intimate partner violence in relation to male and female personality traits using a sample of college students and found that women who reported perpetrating psychological, but not physical, abuse toward their partners scored higher on a femininity scale than women who reported mutual psychological abuse. This was expected, as women are socialized to use psychological instead of physical aggression in conflicts. However, they did not find statistically significant support for masculine personality traits and physical aggression by females. Rather, females who endorsed masculine traits were neither victims nor perpetrators of physical aggression, suggesting that these traits or a confounding variable—such as self-esteem—encourage women to leave potentially violent relationships.

Psychopathology

Lesbian batterers report higher levels of psychopathology, including higher levels of antisocial, aggressive, borderline, and paranoid personality traits and higher levels of delusional clinical characteristics, again similar to studies of heterosexual male batterers (Fortunata & Kohn, 2003). Women who report being victims of domestic violence and women who are abused and are aggressors (commit more severe violence against her partner than he commits against her) have significantly higher symptoms of depression, anxiety, and post-traumatic stress disorder than women who report being in a mutually coercive relationship (Swan & Snow, 2003).

Box 3.4, *continued*

Battered Woman Syndrome as a Cause of Female Violence

The Battered Woman Syndrome emerged in the late 1970s and early 1980s as a legal defense in criminal cases (Walker, 1993). Battered Woman Syndrome asserts that an abused woman may react violently toward her abuser in self-defense, most often much later than the violent incident by the abuser, to prevent future harm. Alternatively, a battered woman may initiate the violence, knowing from past experience that she is in danger. Schwartz and DeKeseredy (1993) point out that psychological abuse (for example, name-calling) usually occurs prior to a domestic violence incident, and this preceding abusive behavior may serve as a warning sign that violence is an imminent threat. They suggest that battered women may preemptively strike an abuser to deter his violent behavior—and hitting first may actually be an act of self-defense.

The American Psychological Association recognizes Battered Woman Syndrome as a subcategory of post-traumatic stress disorder. As Lenore Walker (1993:202) explains:

> Battered woman syndrome is the name given to the psychological changes that may occur after the exposure to abuse. The use of trauma theory together with the psychological understanding of feminist psychology, oppression, powerlessness, and intermittent reinforcement theories such as learned helplessness all help us to understand the psychological impact of physical, sexual, and serious psychological abuse on the battered woman.

Feminist scholars argue that women use violence against intimate partners in self-defense, which is supported by a recent study examining police reports, finding male victims of domestic violence more likely than female victims involved in cross-complaints (Melton & Belknap, 2003). Another recent study found that 75 percent of women who used violence in their sample reported using violence in self-defense—to stop violence being inflicted upon them (Swan & Snow, 2003). This research provides support for the Battered Woman Syndrome as a cause of female-perpetrated violence used in self-defense.

While the Battered Woman Syndrome is recognized by courts, the "Battered Husband Syndrome" is not typically permitted in cases of male-perpetrated domestic violence.

Treatment

Unfortunately, there are few services available for female perpetrators of domestic violence (Nicholls & Dutton, 2001). Referring to studies showing that many women who abuse their partners are doing so in self-defense, many women convicted of domestic violence are treated by counselors at a battered women's shelter. While this may assist battered women who use violence to protect themselves, there is a lack of adequate treatment for women who are the sole perpetrators of violence in an intimate partner relationship.

Theoretical Perspectives

What Theories Can Be Used to Understand Battering Behavior?

Studies have shown that many factors can increase the risk of intimate partner violence, including gender (the batterer is overwhelmingly male and the victim female), high unemployment, low academic achievement, alcohol and drug abuse, history of child abuse, witnessing domestic abuse between parents as a child, lack of a support network, and low marriage rates (e.g., Andrews & Bonta, 2003; Healey & Smith, 1998; Moffitt, 1997).

As with all types of crimes, many theories exist regarding the cause of domestic violence. Domestic violence is primarily considered learned behavior, but research indicates the influence of factors outside of the individual also may contribute to domestic violence (e.g., Benson & Fox, 2001). Additionally, biological factors may predispose an individual to violent behavior (e.g., Fishbein, 2001). The following is a summary of support for each of the prominent battering theories.

Learned Behavior

Battering most often is considered a learned behavior. This approach posits that, in homes where intimate partner violence is present, partner violence is modeled for children, who observe that violence is a normal part of adult power dynamics within the family (Perilla et al., 2003). In addition, when the use of violence is effective in changing the victim's behavior with little or no negative consequences for the offender, it is a strong reinforcement for use of violence.

The link between observing interparental violence as a child and adult domestic violence offending is clear. Longitudinal studies show that childhood exposure to parental domestic violence is a significant predictor of future domestic violence offending (Ehrensaft et al., 2003). A longitudinal study conducted by the National Institute of Justice found that children who were abused or maltreated were 29 percent more likely to engage in delinquency and adult criminality than children who were not abused or maltreated; this relationship holds true when controlling for gender, age, race, family structure, and socioeconomic status with a similar matched control group (Widom & Maxfield, 2001). There is a significant correlation between simply witnessing paternal violence against one's mother during childhood and adult domestic abuse offending behavior (Ehrensaft et al., 2003). In comparison with youth who are not exposed to violence, children and adolescents exposed to family violence are more likely to externalize behavior problems such as aggressiveness and delinquency (Osofsky, 1999). This provides evidence that domestic violence, like many other behaviors, can be learned through modeling parental roles. This does not mean that all or even most children exposed to domestic violence grow up to be violent offenders. Rather, of those children that do become violent, a large proportion of them were exposed to domestic violence in their past. Protective factors such as a close relationship with a competent adult, usually a parent, can show youth alternatives to violence (Osofsky, 1999).

Social Disorganization and Strain Theories

Social Disorganization Theory focuses on the structure of the community as a cause of criminal behavior. Social Disorganization Theory posits that delinquency occurs primarily in transition areas, characterized by older, urban areas with ethnic heterogeneity and high residential mobility inhabited by recent migrants and residents that are generally poor (Shoemaker, 1996). Through Social Disorganization Theory, we would expect to find higher rates of batterers living in low-income, urban areas of "transition," which can be measured, in part, by the number of people who rent residences instead of owning houses.[1] The Bureau of Justice Statistics reported that the rates of non-lethal domestic violence victimization are four times more likely for women renting their residence as opposed to those owning their residence, offering support for social disorganization (See Box 3.5).

Similar to Social Disorganization Theory, Strain Theory also examines the impact of economic disadvantage on deviant behavior, but at the individual level. Strain Theory suggests that while everyone has common goals (usually economic) they utilize different means, both legitimate and illegitimate, to achieve those goals (Shoemaker, 1996). Many males aspire to be "real men," and to these men, masculinity[2] is the goal perceived to be widely accepted. Masculinity is thought to be expressed through acting tough, participating in sports, and taking care of one's family. A person who accepts this goal, but who lacks opportunity to achieve it (for example, a man who has a low-paying job that does not adequately support his family), experiences anomie, or strain. The reaction may be to conform (conformity), choose alternative goals (rebellion), or choose alternative means (innovation) to achieve the culturally accepted goal. The alternative, an illegitimate mean for achieving the goal of masculinity, can be domestic violence. Applying Strain Theory, higher rates of domestic violence would be expected among those with lower incomes. Renting one's residence may indicate a lack of funds to purchase a house—one possible barrier to culturally accepted means to exhibiting masculinity. Box 3.5 also provides support for strain theory, showing much lower rates of intimate partner violence among homeowners than those who rent their residences.

Box 3.5

	Rate of Non-Lethal Intimate Partner Violence (per 1,000 males and females)	
	Female	Male
Home ownership	4.8	1.0
Home rented	16.2	2.2
Area in which victim lives:		
Urban	9.5	1.6
Suburban	7.8	1.4
Rural	8.1	1.1

Source: Bureau of Justice Statistics (2000). "Intimate Partner Violence, by Urbanization and Housing," 1993-1998.

In further support of strain theory, studies have shown that male job instability and financial strain are significantly related to intimate partner violence (Benson & Fox, 2002). Also, although intimate partner violence is more prevalent among African-Americans than whites, Benson and Fox (2002) found that the relationship lost significance when controlling for individual economic distress and community disadvantage, suggesting that these factors play a large role in intimate partner violence. As illustrated in Box 3.6, the rates of victim-reported non-lethal domestic violence decrease as household income increases.

Box 3.6

	Rate of Non-Lethal Intimate Partner Violence (per 1,000 males and females)	
Household income of victim	Female	Male
Less than $7,500	20.3	2.6
$7,500 to $14,999	12.3	1.3
$15,000 to $24,999	10.1	2.0
$25,000 to $34,999	7.8	1.7
$35,000 to $49,999	6.3	1.0
$50,000 to $74,999	4.5	1.2
$75,000 or more	3.3	0.9

Source: Bureau of Justice Statistics (2000). "Intimate Partner Violence, by Household Income, 1993-1998."

To examine the effect of strain on domestic violence, Benson and Fox (2002) examined the relationship between economic disadvantage and domestic violence. They found that the risk for battering increases with economic distress, and when economic distress at both the individual level and economic disadvantage at the community level are taken together, the probability of battering increases dramatically both in prevalence and severity, suggesting strain may play a role in domestic violence.

Feminist Theory

The most common theory underlying treatment programs today is feminist theory (Jackson, 2003). The feminist ideology focuses on the patriarchal structure of society as the root cause of violence against women because patriarchy encourages men to dominate and control their partners (Jackson, 2003). According to feminist theory, patriarchal culture upholds the domination of women through economic inequalities between men and women and male attitudes of superiority over women, attitudes that are reinforced by non-egalitarian portrayals of women (Hampton et al., 1999). This theory has been supported by studies finding significant relationships between jealousy and controlling behavior and domestic violence (Andrews & Bonta, 2003). Johnson (1995) adds that male batterers beat their partners an average of more than once per week, and the severity of the beatings increase over time, even though most women do not attempt to defend themselves. Despite the lack of self-defense, battering increases, suggesting the batterer is exercising his desire to control his partner.

Similar to strain theory, the theory of the patriarchal society suggests that men are socialized to define masculinity, in part, as the subordination of women, and there are legitimate means (for example, employment or sports) and illegitimate means (for example, violence) to accomplishing the goal of masculinity (Messerschmidt, 1993). According to the work of James Messerschmidt (1993), battering is a way for some men to affirm patriarchal masculinity. A recent study found that a man's fear of emotions (anxiety, sadness, and positive emotions—all perceived to be feminine emotions) predicted intimate partner violence, suggesting that men react violently not only to threatened masculinity, but also "as a strategy to avoid expressing their feelings of emotional vulnerability" (Jakupcak, 2003:539).

However, feminist theory fails to account for battering committed by upper class males who have access to legitimate means for achieving masculinity, as well as for female batterers. As shown by Box 3.6, domestic violence was reported in households with higher incomes as well as in households with lower incomes.

Box 3.7

In the News . . .

In 1998, former Mötley Crüe drummer Tommy Lee pled no contest to charges of repeatedly kicking his then-wife Pamela Anderson Lee while she was holding their 7-week-old son. Tommy Lee was sentenced to six months in jail, three years of probation, random drug tests, anger management classes, and 200 hours of community service. In addition, he was ordered to donate $5,000 to a domestic violence shelter. Commenting on the case, Pamela said, "I'm very proud of Tommy. I'm happy that he took responsibility for this. I think it's the first step toward healing."

Source: *The Times Union*, April 8, 1998, September 10, 1998.

Biological Theories

Recent research has focused on the impact of biology and genetics on violent behavior (Fishbein, 2001; George et al., 2000; George et al., 2001). Cohen and colleagues (1999) found that neuropsychological performance is significantly related to domestic battery, and batterers differ from both happily and discordantly married men in other cognitive domains, including verbal functioning and memory. Fishbein (2001) suggests that violent offenders (including domestic violence offenders) may be "genetically loaded" for violent behavior, and the environment can either increase or decrease the risk of expressing the violent behavior. This theory is supported through heritability studies and the relationships between neurotransmitters and hormones and violent behavior.

Heritability studies show a higher rate of concordance between monozygotic (identical) twins than between dizygotic (fraternal) twins with respect to repetitive aggressive behavior (including impulsivity and cognitive deficits) and conduct disorder (Fishbein, 2001). Heritability studies also show a higher rate of concordance between children and their biological parents than their adoptive parents with respect to repetitive aggressive behavior (including impulsivity and cognitive deficits) and conduct disorder (Fishbein, 2001).

Fishbein (2001) has suggested that neurotransmitters are correlated with violent behavior. Dopamine, associated with responding to environmental cues, increases with aggression, and drugs that decrease dopamine levels (such as antipsychotic drugs) decrease fighting behaviors. Low serotonin levels (serotonin is related to feelings of pleasure) are correlated with violence and aggression as well (Fishbein, 2001; McKenry, Julian & Gavazzi, 1995). Increases in Norepinephrine, which releases stress hormones as a part of the "fight or flight" response, also are correlated with aggression and violent behavior. Meanwhile, low Monoamine Oxidase (MAO—which metabolizes many neurotransmitters including dopamine, serotonin, and norepinephrine) activity increases dopamine and norepinephrine levels, and irregular MAO levels are associated with antisocial behavior and aggression.

High testosterone levels are related to increased aggressive behaviors (Fishbein, 2001; McKenry et al., 1995) and stress hormones, such as cortisol, also have been related to violence and aggression (Fishbein, 2001). Fishbein (2001) suggests that the risk of violent behavior for a person who is genetically or biologically predisposed to aggression can be exacerbated by child abuse, trauma, poor parenting, and the impact of violence on television.

Box 3.8

In the News . . .

Lorena Bobbitt was a 24-year-old manicurist married to John Wayne Bobbitt, a 26-year-old former swimming instructor. After her husband sexually assaulted and choked her, Lorena severed John's penis with a kitchen knife. Lorena tearfully testified that, while in the kitchen for water, "The refrigerator door was open, and that was the only light. And I turned and saw the knife. I took it. I went to the bedroom. I pulled the sheets off, and I cut him." Both parties were charged: Lorena, with malicious wounding and John, with marital sexual assault (because they were living together and there was no serious physical injury, rape did not apply under Virginia law). John was acquitted; Lorena was found not guilty by reason of temporary insanity and sentenced to 45 days in a mental institution. John has since made a full recovery.

Source: *The New York Times*, November 9, 1993; S. Labaton, November 11, 1993.

Treatment/Prevention

How Can these Theories Be Combined for Effective Treatment?

Unfortunately, one theory can not encompass all forms of battering behavior, and batterer intervention programs currently follow a "one size fits all" approach for those involved in treatment, despite emerging evidence that all batterers are not the same (Maiuro et al., 2001). In addition, researchers have cautioned that the cause of domestic violence (either individual psychopathology or social-cultural foundation) and the source of motivation (either anger or power and control) must first be established before program standards can be effectively formulated (Maiuro et al., 2001). With the growing number of jurisdictions incorporating batterer intervention programs into domestic violence response, understanding effectiveness of these programs is crucial (Healey & Smith, 1998), and understanding the nature of the programs is important, as well.

Batterer intervention programs are different today from when they were first created in the 1970s. Instead of following one ideology, programs today have integrated various models to better address the complexity of domestic violence (Healey & Smith, 1998). The two primary types of batterer intervention programs are the Duluth Model, based on feminist theory, and cognitive-behavioral treatment, based on social learning theory; other programs are combinations of the two, including couples therapy and individual therapy, and psychodynamic treatments (National Institute of Justice, 2002). Although these programs have been empirically examined, research is incomplete and does not provide an accurate picture of the effect of these programs on recidivism, due to limited outcome measures, attrition (or "drop out" of participants), inappropriate comparison groups (Saunders & Hamill, 2003), definitional issues of nonviolent behavior (e.g., push instead of punch), definitional issue of program "success" and program "failures" (Gondolf, 1997a). Geffner and Rosenbaum (2001:4) highlight that "it is as difficult to identify the 'typical batterer treatment' program as it is to identify the 'typical batterer.'"

Feminist-Based Interventions

The first batterer intervention programs emerged in the 1970s and were based on feminist-theory, and many today still operate according to this philosophy (Geffner & Rosenbaum, 2001; Healey & Smith, 1998; Saunders & Hamill, 2003).

MacKenzie (1997) reported that problems with studies of batterer intervention programs include attrition, small sample sizes, and methodological flaws. However, research still may provide useful information. An analysis of six studies of feminist-based interventions by MacKenzie (1997) found that these batterer intervention programs do reduce recidivism of intimate partner physical violence, although only one study reviewed showed significant results. Similarly, another analysis by Saunders and Hamill (2003), using less rigorous standards, found that although feminist-based interventions reduced recidivism, the effect size of such programs was small.

Duluth Model

Most batterer intervention programs today are based on the Duluth Model. The Duluth Model of batterer intervention programs teaches batterers alternatives to violence in resolving disputes, attempts to change traditional views about women and roles of women, and emphasizes awareness of control tactics (Saunders & Hamill, 2003).

The Broward County Experiment (Feder & Forde, 2003) tested the effectiveness of court-mandated counseling based on the Duluth Model and tested "stake-in-conformity" variables (e.g., steady job, stable residence). Although there were problems with random assignment and low response rates, the study found that the batterer intervention programs did not alter battering beliefs, battering responsibility, or views of the proper roles of women. In addition, the program had no significant impact on recidivism. However, the stake-in-conformity variables, including residential stability and months employed, were able to significantly predict violations of probation.

The Brooklyn Experiment (Davis et al., 2003) also examined the effectiveness of court-mandated counseling, Alternatives to Violence (ATV), based on the Duluth Model. Participants in the 39-hour, 26-week ATV program were compared with participants in the 39-hour, 8-week ATV program, as well as a control group of batterers sentenced to the same number of hours in community service—renovating housing units, painting senior-citizen centers and cleaning up playgrounds. Controlling for demographic variables and using multiple sources of data, the 26-week batterer treatment had significantly lower recidivism rates than both the 8-week ATV program and the control group. However, this experiment also had low response rates and high attrition.

Medical Treatment

When considering the role of biology and genetics, medication should be a component of treatment to control the levels of hormones and neurotransmitters. For example, George and colleagues (2000) suggested that antidepressant medications can be used to reduce rage in some domestic violence offenders.

In addition, prevention programs could focus on targeting the environmental conditions that exacerbate aggression. Fishbein (2001) suggests education programs for teachers and parents, programs to reduce bullying in schools, conflict resolution programs for children, the reduction of media violence, and more treatment programs targeting drug and alcohol abuse.

Cognitive-Behavioral Therapy

Cognitive-behavioral therapy is based on social learning theory and uses such activities as skills training (such as communication), behavioral modeling, restructuring faulty patterns of thinking, relaxation, and stress reduction (Rosenbaum & Gearan, 1999; Saunders & Hamill,

2003). Specifically, these programs teach the offender how to identify cues that indicate when they are becoming angry and how to replace the anger-provoking cognitions (Rosenbaum & Gearan, 1999). Many of the treatment programs used today utilize cognitive-behavioral therapy.

An analysis by MacKenzie (1997) reviewing six studies of cognitive-behavioral therapy found that these batterer intervention programs reduce recidivism of intimate partner physical violence, although there were no significant differences in overall recidivism.

Comprehensive Therapy

McKenry, Julian and Gavazzi (1995) attempted to combine the biological, psychological, and sociological theories into a biopsychosocial model of domestic violence. In their sample of over 100 married men, they found both biological and social domains, such as alcohol, family income, marital relationship quality, and testosterone levels, impacted domestic violence.

Bancroft and Silverman (2002:180-183) found 12 successful non-chronological steps a batterer must achieve before having completed a true change in behavior:

1. The batterer must disclose fully the history of physical and psychological abuse toward partner and children.

2. The batterer must recognize that the behavior is unacceptable.

3. The batterer must recognize that the behavior was chosen.

4. The batterer must recognize and show empathy for the effects of his actions on his partner and children

5. The batterer must identify his pattern of controlling behaviors and entitled attitudes.

6. The batterer must develop respectful behaviors and attitudes.

7. The batterer must reevaluate his distorted image of his partner.

8. The batterer must make amends both in the short and in the long term.

9. The batterer must accept the consequences of his actions for him.

10. The batterer must commit to not repeating abusive behavior.

11. The batterer must accept change as a long-term (probably lifelong) process.

12. The batterer must be willing to be accountable.

Criminal Justice Programs

Although wife beating was prohibited in America first by the Puritans in Massachusetts Bay Colony in 1641, domestic violence traditionally has been viewed as a private, family problem not under the jurisdiction of the criminal justice system and the laws banning wife abuse were rarely enforced (Hampton, Vandergriff-Avery & Kim, 1999). In fact, the Supreme Court of North Carolina upheld the ruling of a trial court judge in *State v. Rhodes* (1868) that a defendant was not guilty for beating his wife with a "switch"—as long as it was no thicker than the width of his thumb:

> The laws of this State do not recognize *the right of a husband to whip his wife*, but our courts will not interfere to punish him for moderate correction of her, even if there had been no provocation for it. (emphasis in original)

Discouraging domestic violence was not a priority on the legislative agenda, and changes in the law—permitting battered women to sue saloon owners for injuries sustained by husbands intoxicated at such saloons, for example—were few and far between. In addition, the criminal justice system only intervened in domestic abuse if someone was murdered (Hampton, Vandergriff-Avery & Kim, 1999).

Throughout the first half of the twentieth century, if any action was taken by the police, it was the usual practice to "separate and mediate" disputing spouses. In response to pressure from feminist groups, legislation was changed in the 1970s to bring domestic violence into the public arena and to prohibit violence against women (Hampton et al., 1999; Lilly et al., 2002). However, officers remained hesitant to bring offenders into the criminal justice system.

The 1984 Minneapolis Domestic Violence Experiment, the first controlled, randomized test of the effect of arrest, found that arrest, as opposed to separation and mediation, was a strong deterrent of domestic violence—arrest lowered recidivism rates in a six-month follow-up period (Sherman & Berk, 1984). The same year, a court awarded a battered woman, Tracey Thurman, $2.5 million because police refused to arrest her abusive husband (Hampton et al., 1999). Out of concern for liability suits and the publicity of the Minneapolis Domestic Violence Experiment, pro- and mandatory arrest policies were implemented by police departments across the country. In 15 states, legislation mandated arrest in response to domestic violence incidents, and many police departments adopted such policies in areas where legislation had not been changed (Andrews & Bonta, 2003).

However, replication studies of Sherman and Berk's 1984 experiment conducted in six jurisdictions through the National Institute of Justice (the Spouse Assault Replication Program, or "SARP") found that while arrest deters battering by certain offenders, it can make others more hostile. Schmidt and Sherman (1996:43) observed that "arrest may help some victims at the expense of others and that arrest may assist the victim in the short term but facilitate further violence in the long term." In addition, SARP also found that regardless of the intervention type (arrest versus non-arrest), over half of the offenders did not recidivate during the follow-up period, while some offenders continued to offend (Maxwell et al., 2001), suggesting arrest is not a "one size fits all" solution to domestic violence.

The Violence against Women Act, Title IV of the Omnibus Crime Control Act (Pub. L. 103-322, signed September 13, 1994 by President Clinton) was signed into law in 1994, in part providing funding for research and programs to combat domestic violence. Since that time, many changes have been made within the criminal justice system to respond to domestic violence, such as coordinated community responses, domestic violence units, mandatory and pro-arrest policies, evidence-based prosecution, and domestic violence courts.

Police

As mentioned above, domestic violence historically has been considered a private, family matter that should not involve the police. In the past few decades, much has been done to combat the social problem of domestic violence, especially within the criminal justice system. These changes have been based on lobbying and victim advocacy as well as research.

SARP (the replication studies of Sherman and Berk's 1984 Minneapolis Domestic Violence Experiment) had mixed results, some confirming Sherman and Berk's results and others finding the opposite (Andrews and Bonta, 2003; Schmidt and Sherman, 1996). Since this controversy, some argue that the most effective law enforcement policy should target the arrest of repeat offenders (see Maxwell et al., 2002). Others have suggested that domestic violence offenders having a "stake in conformity," such as those who are employed, married, are college educated, and have stable residences, are more likely to be deterred from future domestic violence offending simply by arrest (Andrews & Bonta, 2003; Lilly et al., 2002; MacKenzie, 1997; Schmidt & Sherman, 1996). However, those offenders who have weak bonds to conventional society are more likely to increase future domestic violence offending following arrest (Andrews & Bonta, 2003; Lilly et al., 2002). Programs such as intensive supervision (as opposed to regular supervision) have been found to reduce the risk of rearrest over a period of three years in employed domestic violence offenders, supporting the importance of community ties in deterring reoffense (Lasley, 2003).

Community/Social Programs

Following a social disorganization or strain theory, any type of batterer treatment should include job training and employment assistance (Moffitt, 1997), as battering is not solely based on personal factors (Benson & Fox, 2002). Again, more intimate partner violence is committed by low (or no) income offenders (Bureau of Justice Statistics, 2000). Becoming involved in the criminal justice system, especially being sentenced to probation, offers batterers access to services with employment that they may not otherwise seek.

Coordinated Community Response

The programs previously discussed included a single type of intervention. However, the most promising results may come from a coordinated community effort, targeting various interventions to reduce recidivism. There is evidence that combining arrest with prosecution and or counseling, drug and alcohol treatment, and mental health programs is more effective than any single intervention (Gondolf, 1997a; Saunders & Hamill, 2003).

Corrections/Treatment

Although the criminal justice system has focused on arresting batterers, incarceration may be detrimental. Rosenbaum and Gearan (1993:363) point out:

> In practice, batterers are rarely given sentences exceeding a few months, and it is hard to imagine how spending time in so misogynist an environment as jail would lead to a reduction in either anger or aggression toward women. Legal remedies, arrest, and incarceration may play a role but are apparently inadequate unless combined with additional intervention.

Domestic Violence Courts, such as the courts in Brooklyn and Broward County discussed above, have been established in many jurisdictions. Domestic Violence Courts are specialized courts in which the batterer is diverted to a batterer treatment program in lieu of probation or incarceration. The batterer must successfully finish the program and complete other conditions set by the court, and the charges are usually dropped. In this way, the batterer receives some sort of treatment and can return to the family without the stigmatization of having a legal record. The few Domestic Violence Courts that have been evaluated have been found to reduce rearrest (e.g., Gover et al., 2003).

However, the terms of domestic violence courts vary, as well as the length and type of treatment. Groups usually meet for about two hours once or twice per week from 6 to 32 weeks (Hampton et al., 1999). The length of treatment, as well as the topics addressed, may determine whether a program is effective for a particular batterer (Gondolf, 1997a). Furthermore, the length of time a batterer participates in a program may determine risk for recidivism, as program completers and those who complete at least three months of a program are less likely than program drop-outs to reoffend (Gondolf, 2000, 1997b).

While examining treatment, it is important to understand the dynamics of domestic abuse: power and control. For this reason, anger management is ineffective in reducing domestic abuse—batterers already manage their anger (Bancroft & Silverman, 2002). Most batterers are very able to control themselves inside and outside the home. Most batterers do not "lose their temper" with their superiors at work, yet this is often an excuse used to explain why their partners are bruised, broken and bloodied. Batterers are manipulative and very capable of controlling themselves when necessary—for example, when trying to convince a judge or a batterer intervention counselor of changed behavior. For this reason, according to Bancroft and Silverman (2002), self-report that a batterer has changed should be taken skeptically and caution should be used when reviewing research using self-reports of changed battering behavior. In addition, because there are long periods of time between battering incidents (batterers attack their partners on average of three times per year), studies reviewing battering recidivism in short periods of time also should be examined with caution (Bancroft & Silverman, 2002). Programs that simply attempt to reduce physical violence also may prove to be problematic, as offenders may use other forms of abuse, such as using verbal and psychological, instead of physical violence (Gondolf, 1997a).

In addition, many researchers and domestic violence victim advocates have found that, although changing battering behavior and attitudes is possible, it is difficult and rare (for example, Bancroft & Silverman, 2002). Bancroft and Silverman (2002:184) cite the most important indicator of batterer change (effective treatment) is consistency in "respectful and responsible behavior." Andrews and Bonta (2003) reviewed studies and found recidivism was related to the length and comprehensiveness of the treatment program. A type of treatment program showing promising reduction of domestic violence recidivism rates is the cognitive-behavioral treatment (Andrews & Bonta, 2003), in which treatment attempts to alter the offender's way of thinking, as well as his beliefs and attitudes (Bartol, 2002). Of course, the ideal treatment would target each offender's specific needs, as well as enlisting the assistance of the surrounding community. One type of multi-systemic treatment program is group practice, which combines the psycho educational curriculum utilized in feminist theory treatment programs with cognitive-behavioral techniques and individual needs assessments (Jackson, 2003). Group practice is commonly used as the preferred treatment ordered by domestic violence courts. However, as the Broward County Experiment (Feder & Forde, 2003) and the Brooklyn Experiment (Davis et al., 2003) show, much research—with improved methodology—is necessary before we can determine whether these programs—and which of these programs—are effective.

Box 3.9

In the News . . .

More than one decade ago, O.J. Simpson was acquitted in the criminal murder trials of his ex-wife, Nicole Brown Simpson, and her friend, Ronald Goldman. Simpson was held liable by a civil jury for damages amounting to $33.5 million, paid to the victims' families. During the trials, it was revealed that Simpson had a history of abusing his wife. On October 25, 1993, while they were separated, Simpson kicked down his wife's door, raged through her home, screaming and cursing. On the 911 tapes, Nicole Brown Simpson told the operator, "he's ranting and raving . . . I think you know his record." On New Year's Eve, 1988, Simpson assaulted Nicole Brown Simpson. He plead no contest to charges that he beat and kicked his wife in 1989, and was sentenced to a $200 fine and 120 hours of community service, but was not placed in a batterers' program because he was already involved in counseling.

Source: Adapted from *The San Francisco Examiner,* June 23, 1994.

Criticisms of Batterer Intervention Programs

Some have argued that batterer intervention programs need to be tailored to cultural differences. For example, programs may be more effective if they incorporate cultural values, such as spirituality, and if programs are racially homogenous (Gondolf, 2002; Healey & Smith, 1998). In addition, language barriers should be taken into consideration, as they may make intervention programs more difficult and less effective (Healey & Smith, 1998).

The emergence of batterer typologies should be incorporated into determining which batterers should attend which treatment programs (Gondolf, 2002). It also has been suggested that the label of "batterers" elicits a negative perception and may shape approaches to research on domestic violence (Corvo & Johnson, 2003). All of these need to be taken into consideration when creating protocols for and evaluating batterer intervention programs.

Conclusions

Each theory discussed holds a strong argument for cause of battering behavior, as well as detailed instructions for treating behavior. Choosing a theory as a base for policy and treatment programs is somewhat difficult; choosing a theory for treatment programs is more difficult when presented with research that not all batterers are the same (e.g., Dixon & Browne, 2003; Johnson, 1995).

Taking the multiple theories together, the best approach seems to be an individual approach. When offenders are brought into the system, either formally through arrest or informally through police referrals (where lack of sufficient evidence prohibits arrest), each should be screened for mental health issues, substance abuse issues, and social needs (e.g., employment, housing). A combination of the above-mentioned theories can provide a multi-systemic approach to reducing violent behavior, which is emerging in many domestic violence courts and treatment programs today (Jackson, 2003). In fact, by incorporating ideas from a variety of fields (health care, social work, psychology, etc.), a very effective comprehensive treatment may emerge (Maiuro et al., 2001). A court monitored program introducing medications or change in diet can reduce the biological factors contributing to violence; employment, education and housing assistance can target the social disorganization/strain of the batterer; individual and group counseling will focus on changing patriarchal perceptions and ideologies and present nonviolent alternatives; and family counseling can help teach successful, nonviolent conflict resolution. The criminal justice system can impose punishments for offenders who do not comply and insure that sanctions are carried out and offenders are held accountable.

Although domestic violence cannot be explained by one all-inclusive theory, we have enough information to provide successful reductions in battering behavior. Future research on batterer typologies is a promising step to more effective interventions so that offenders with differing characteristics and needs can then be addressed through appropriate differential treatment.

Notes

[1]   Renting is usually considered an indicator of temporary residence ("transition"), while owning a home is an indicator of commitment to spend many years in one location.

[2]   See West and Zimmerman (1987) for a detailed explanation of "doing gender."

References

Andrews, D.A. and J. Bonta (2003). *The Psychology of Criminal Conduct,* Third Edition. Cincinnati, OH: Anderson Publishing Co.

Bancroft, L. and J. Silverman (2002). *The Batterer as Parent: Addressing the Impact of Domestic Violence on Family Dynamics.* Thousand Oaks, CA: Sage Publications.

Bartol, C.R. (2002). *Criminal Behavior: A Psychosocial Approach.* Sixth Edition. NJ: Prentice Hall.

Benson, M.L. and G.L. Fox (2002). "Economic Distress, Community Context and Intimate Violence: An Application and Extension of Social Disorganization Theory; Executive Summary." Unpublished manuscript, U.S. Department of Justice. (Available from the NCJRS, No. NCJ 193433)

Block, C.R. (2003). "How Can Practitioners Help an Abused Woman Lower Her Risk of Death?" In *Intimate Partner Homicide.* Washington, DC: National Institute of Justice, Office of Justice Programs, U.S. Department of Justice.

Bureau of Justice Statistics. (2000). *Intimate Partner Violence.* Washington, DC: U.S. Department of Justice, Office of Justice Programs, Bureau of Justice Statistics [Producer and Distributor]. [Online] Available: http://www.ojp.usdoj.gov/bjs/abstract/ipv.htm. Accessed 25 October 2003.

Cohen, R.A., A. Rosenbaum, R.L. Lane, W.J. Warnken, and S. Benjamin (1999). "Neuropsychological Correlates of Domestic Violence." *Violence and Victims,* 14(4):397-411.

Corvo, K. and P.J. Johnson (2003). "Vilification of the 'Batterer:' How Blame Shapes Domestic Violence Policy and Intervention." *Aggression and Violent Behavior,* 8(3):259-281.

Davis, R.C., C.D. Maxwell, and B.G. Taylor (2003). "The Brooklyn Experiment." *Batterer Intervention Programs: Where Do We Go from Here? (NIJ Special Report).* Washington, DC: National Institute of Justice, Office of Justice Programs, U.S. Department of Justice.

Dietz, T.L. and J.L. Jasinski (2003). "Female-Perpetrated Partner Violence and Aggression: Their Relationship to Gender Identity." *Women & Criminal Justice,* 15(1):81-99.

Dixon, L. and K. Browne (2003). "The Heterogeneity of Spouse Abuse: A Review." *Aggression and Violent Behavior,* 8:107-130.

Ehrensaft, M.K., P. Cohen, J.Brown, E. Smailes, H. Chen, and J.G. Johnson (2003). "Intergenerational Transmission of Partner Violence: A 20-year Prospective Study." *Journal of Consulting & Clinical Psychology,* 71(4):741-754.

Feder, L. and D.R. Forde (2003). "The Broward Experiment." *Batterer Intervention Programs: Where Do We Go from Here? (NIJ Special Report).* Washington, DC: National Institute of Justice, Office of Justice Programs, U.S. Department of Justice.

Federal Bureau of Investigation (2002). *Uniform Crime Reports.* Washington, DC: U.S. Department of Justice. [Online] Available: http://www.fbi.gov/ucr. Accessed 09 November 2003.

Fishbein, D.H. (2001). *Biological Perspectives in Criminology.* Belmont, CA: Wadsworth.

Fortunata, B. and C.S. Kohn (2003). "Demographic, Psychosocial, and Personality Characteristics of Lesbian Batterers." *Violence and Victims,* 18(5):557-568.

Geffner, R.A. and A. Rosenbaum (2001). "Domestic Violence Offenders: Treatment and Intervention Standards." In R.A. Geffner and A. Rosenbaum (eds.) *Domestic Violence Offenders: Current Interventions, Research, and Implications for Policies and Standards*, pp. 1-9. New York: The Haworth Maltreatment & Trauma Press.

George, D.T., J.R. Hibbeln, P.W. Ragan, J.C. Umhau, M.J. Phillips, L. Doty, D. Hommer, and R.R. Rawlings (2000). "Lactate-Induced Rage and Panic in a Select Group of Subjects Who Perpetrate Acts of Domestic Violence." *Biological Psychiatry,* 47:804-812.

George, D.T., J.C. Umhau, M.J. Phillips, D. Emmela, P.W. Ragan, S.E. Shoaf, and R.R. Rawlings (2001). "Serotonin, Testosterone and Alcohol in the Etiology of Domestic Violence." *Psychiatry Research,* 104:27-37.

George, M.J. (2003). "Invisible Touch." *Aggression and Violent Behavior,* 8:23-60.

Gondolf, E.W. (2002). *Batterer Intervention Systems: Issues, Outcomes, and Recommendations*. Thousand Oaks, CA: Sage Publications, Inc.

Gondolf, E.W. (2000). "Reassault at 30-months after Batterer Program Intake." *International Journal of Offender Therapy and Comparative Criminology,* 44:111-128.

Gondolf, E.W. (1997a). "Expanding Batterer Program Evaluation." In G.K. Kaufman and J. Jasinski (eds.) *Out of Darkness: Contemporary Research Perspectives on Family Violence,* pp. 208-218. Thousand Oaks, CA: Sage.

Gondolf, E.W. (1997b). "Patterns of Reassault in Batterer Programs." *Violence and Victims,* 12:373-387.

Gover, A.R., J.M. MacDonald, and G.P. Alpert (2003). "Combating Domestic Violence: Findings from an Evaluation of a Local Domestic Violence Court." *Criminology & Public Policy*, 3(1):109-132.

Graham-Bermann, S.A. and J.L. Edleson (eds.) (2001). *Domestic Violence in the Lives of Children: The Future of Research, Intervention, and Social Policy.* Washington, DC: American Psychological Association.

Hampton, R.L., M. Vandergriff-Avery, and J. Kim (1999). "Understanding the Origins and Incidence of Spousal Violence in North America." In T.P. Gullotta and S.J. McElhaney (eds.) *Violence in Homes and Communities: Prevention, Intervention, and Treatment,* pp. 39-70. Thousand Oaks: Sage Publications.

Healey, K.M. and C. Smith (1998). *Research in Action—Batterer Programs: What Criminal Justice Agencies Need to Know.* Washington, DC: National Institute of Justice, Office of Justice Programs, U.S. Department of Justice. (NCJRS No. 171683).

Holtzworth-Monroe, A. and J.C. Meehan (2002). "Typologies of Maritally Violent Men: A Summary of Current Knowledge and Suggestions for Future Research." Paper presented at National Research Council Workshop. Washington, DC: Committee on Law and Justice, National Institute of Justice, Office of Justice Programs, U.S. Department of Justice.

Jackson, S. (2003). "Batterer Intervention Programs." *Batterer Intervention Programs: Where Do We Go from Here? (NIJ Special Report).* Washington, DC: National Institute of Justice, Office of Justice Programs, U.S. Department of Justice.

Jakupcak, M. (2003). "Masculine Gender Role Stress and Men's Fear of Emotions as Predictors of Self-Reported Aggression and Violence." *Violence and Victims,* 18(5):533-541.

Johnson, M.P. (1995). "Patriarchal Terrorism and Common Couple Violence: Two Forms of Violence against Women." *Journal of Marriage and the Family,* 57(2):283-294.

Kitzmann, K.M., N.K. Gaylord, A.R. Holt, and E.D. Kenny (2003). "Child Witnesses to Domestic Violence: A Meta-Analytic Review." *Journal of Consulting & Clinical Psychology,* 71(2):339-354.

Labaton, S. (1993). "Husband Acquitted of Assault in Mutilation Case." *The New York Times,* p. A18.

Lawson, D.M., D. Weber, H.M. Beckner, L. Robinson, N. Marsh, and A. Cool (2003). "Men Who Use Violence: Intimate Violence versus Non-Intimate Violence Profiles." *Violence and Victims,* 18(3):259-277.

Lasley, J. (2003). "The Effect of Intensive Bail Supervision on Repeat Domestic Violence Offenders." *Policy Studies Journal,* 31(2):187-208.

Lilly, J.R., F.T. Cullen, and R.A. Ball (2002). *Criminological Theory: Context and Consequences,* Third Edition. Thousand Oaks, CA: Sage Publications.

MacKenzie, D. (1997). "What Works in Corrections? Domestic Violence Offenders." In Sherman, L.W., D. Gottfredson, D. MacKenzie, J. Eck, P. Reuter, and S. Bushway, *Preventing Crime: What Works, What Doesn't, What's Promising.* Report to the United States Congress. Washington, DC: National Institute of Justice, Office of Justice Programs, U.S. Department of Justice. (NCJRS No. NCJ 165366)

Maiuro, R.D., T.S. Hagar, H. Lin, and N. Olson (2001). "Are Current Standards for Domestic Violence Perpetrator Treatment Adequately Informed by Research? A Question of Questions." In R.A. Geffner and A. Rosenbaum (eds.) *Domestic Violence Offenders: Current Interventions, Research, and Implications for Policies and Standards,* pp. 21-44. New York: The Haworth Maltreatment & Trauma Press.

Maxwell, C.D., J.H. Garner, and J.A. Fagan (2002). "Preventive Effects on Arrest on Intimate Partner Violence: Research, Policy and Theory." *Criminology & Public Policy,* 2(1):51-80.

Maxwell, C.D., J.H. Garner, and J.A. Fagan (2001). "Effects of Arrest on Intimate Partner Violence: New Evidence from the Spouse Assault Replication Program." National Institute of Justice, Office of Justice Programs, U.S. Department of Justice. (NCJRS No. NCJ 188199)

McKenry, P.C., T.W. Julian, and S.M. Gavazzi (1995). "Toward a Biopsychosocial Model of Domestic Violence." *Journal of Marriage and the Family,* 57(2):307-320.

McMahon, M. and E. Pence (2003). "Making Social Change: Reflections on Individual and Institutional Advocacy with Women Arrested for Domestic Violence." *Violence against Women,* 9(1):47-74.

Melton, H.C. and J. Belknap (2003). "He Hits, She Hits: Assessing Gender Differences and Similarities in Officially Reported Intimate Partner Violence." *Criminal Justice and Behavior,* 30(3):328-348.

Messerschmidt, J.W. (1993). *Masculinities and Crime: Critique and Reconceptualization of Theory.* Totowa, NJ: Rowman & Littlefield.

Miller, T.R., M.A. Cohen, and B. Wiersema (1996). *The Extent and Costs of Crime Victimization: A New Look.* Washington, DC: National Institute of Justice, Office of Justice Programs, U.S. Department of Justice. (NCJRS No. NCJ 184372)

Moffitt, T.E. (1997). *Partner Violence among Young Adults.* Washington, DC: National Institute of Justice, Office of Justice Programs, U.S. Department of Justice. (NCJRS No. 154277)

National Institute of Justice (2002). *Batterer Intervention: Where Do We Go from Here?* Violence against Women and Family Violence Workshop Notes. [Online] Available: http://www.ojp.usdoj.gov/nij/vawprog/batterer_intervention.html. Accessed 20 November 2003.

The New York Times (1993). "Tearful Woman Tells Jury Why She Cut Off Her Husband's Penis." *The New York Times,* (November 9):B8.

Nicholls, T.L. and D.G. Dutton (2001). "Abuse Committed by Women against Male Intimates." In B.J. Brothers (ed.) *The Abuse of Men: Trauma Begets Trauma,* pp. 41-57. New York: The Haworth Press, Inc.

Osofsky, J.D. (1999). "The Impact of Violence on Children." *Future of Children,* 9(3):33-49.

Perilla, J.L., K. Frndak, D. Lillard, and C. East (2003). "A Working Analysis of Women's Use of Violence in the Context of Learning, Opportunity, and Choice." *Violence against Women,* 9(1):10-46.

Rennison, C.M. and S. Welchans (2000). "Bureau of Justice Statistics Special Report: Intimate Partner Violence." Washington, DC: Bureau of Justice Statistics, Office of Justice Programs, U.S. Department of Justice. (NCJRS No. NCJ 178247) Available online at: http://www.ojp.usdoj.gov/bjs/pub/pdf/ipv.pdf.

Rosenbaum, A. and P.J. Gearan (1999). "Relationship Aggression between Partners." In V.B. Van Hasselt and M. Hersen (eds.) *Handbook of Psychological Approaches with Violent Offenders: Contemporary Strategies and Issues,* pp. 357-372. New York: Kluwer Academic/Plenum Publishers.

The San Francisco Examiner (1994). "911 Record of O.J. Raging Visit to Nicole; 'He's O.J. Simpson, I Think You Know His Record,' Terrified Ex-Wife Told Operator in October." *The San Francisco Examiner.* San Francisco: The Hearst Corporation. (June 23):A-1.

Saunders, D.G. and R.M. Hamill (2003). "Violence against Women: A Synthesis of Research on Offender Interventions." Washington, DC: National Institute of Justice, Office of Justice Programs, U.S. Department of Justice. (NCJRS No. NCJ 201222)

Schmidt, J.D. and L.W. Sherman (1996). "Does Arrest Deter Violence?" In E.S. Buzawa and C.G. Buzawa (eds.) *Do Arrests and Restraining Orders Work?,* pp. 43-53. Thousand Oaks, CA: Sage Publications, Inc.

Schwartz, M.D. and W.S. DeKeseredy (1993). "The Return of the "Battered Husband Syndrome" through the Typification of Women as Violent." *Crime, Law and Social Change,* 20:249-265.

Sherman, L.W. and R.A. Berk (1984). "Minneapolis Domestic Violence Experiment." Police Foundation Reports, no. 1. Washington, DC: Police Foundation.

Shoemaker, D.J. (1996). *Theories of Delinquency: An Examination of Explanations of Delinquent Behavior,* Third Edition. New York: Oxford University Press.

Swan, D.L. and S.C. Snow (2003). "Behavioral and Psychological Differences among Abused Women Who Use Violence in Intimate Relationships." *Violence against Women,* 9(1):75-109.

The Times Union (Albany, NY). (1998) "No-Contest Plea Will Net Tommy Lee 6 Months in Jail." *The Times Union (Albany, NY) Three Star Edition,* (April 8):A2. The Hearst Corporation.

The Times Union (Albany, NY). (1998). "Jailed for Abuse, Drummer Freed Early." *The Times Union (Albany, NY), Three Star Edition*, (September 10):A2. The Hearst Corporation.

Tjaden, P. and N. Thoennes (2000). "Prevalence and Consequence of Male-to-Female and Female-to-Male Intimate Partner Violence as Measured by the National Violence against Women Survey." *Violence against Women,* 6(2):142-161.

Walker, L.A. (1993). "Legal Self-Defense for Battered Women." In M. Hansen and M. Harway (eds.) *Battering and Family Therapy,* pp. 200-216. Newbury Park, CA: Sage Publications.

West, C. and D.H. Zimmerman (1987). "Doing Gender." *Gender & Society,* 1(2):125-151.

Widom, C.S. and M.G. Maxfield (2001). *An Update on the "Cycle of Violence".* Washington, DC: National Institute of Justice, Office of Justice Programs, U.S. Department of Justice. (NCJRS No. NCJ 184894)

Cases Cited

State v. A.B. Rhodes, 61 N.C. 453, 1868 N.C. LEXIS 38.

Chapter 4

Understanding the Crime of Stalking

Summer Acevedo

Introduction

When one imagines the typical "stalker," it is common to conceive a middle-aged man with few friends, underemployed, and dangerously obsessed with a female celebrity. The reality is that while the majority of stalking incidents do involve men stalking women, they usually are between parties that know one another, and may be reconciliation attempts rather than constant threats to a victim's life (Tjaden & Thoennes, 1998). There is an increasing amount of research on the topic, but despite the emerging presence of stalking in our society, it has not achieved the status of being considered highly important when compared with the many other issues in criminology.

The topic has often been left to psychologists to theorize on the causes of stalking behavior, while the role criminologists play involves interviewing prisoners or examining laws. Stalking is a difficult crime to study because it has wide variability; offenses range from unwanted phone calls, to following a person, to actual physical attacks on the victim. Furthermore, it is difficult to determine exactly when and how an incident can escalate from its fledgling stages. While these problems make studying the phenomenon of stalking difficult, they should not take away from the importance of researching, understanding, and ultimately preventing the crime.

Defining the Term

In the past, the word "stalking" described the act of following prey. Animals, not people, were stalked. Its adaptation to the current meaning can be credited in part to the media and its efforts to sensationalize incidents such as the murder of Rebecca Shaffer by an obsessed fan in 1989. Prior to1994, there were no officials laws against stalking; harassment, trespassing, and other laws attempted to cover all circumstances of an offense (Mullen et al., 2000).

Depending on the state, in legal terminology, the crime of stalking is determined by the presence of an act, a threat, or intent to cause harm or fear. Some states require one, two, or all three elements for the crime of stalking to take place (Morewitz, 2003). A comprehensive definition is difficult because in many cases a specific number of incidents cannot be arbitrarily chosen. This allows for the commission of one additional act to make the difference between criminal stalking and a non-criminal event in the eyes of the law.

Victims of stalking react in various ways, making the criterion of invoking fear difficult to determine as well. If two people are in a dating relationship and one party ends communication, should the other be legally considered a stalker for calling a former partner more than three times, causing alarm? What if the partner is at first fearful, but then decides to reconsider the relationship? Was the person a stalker at point a, but not point b? These are difficult questions to answer and legal definitions attempt to define the offense as well as possible. For example, the state of Maryland defines stalking as "a malicious course of conduct" (a persistent pattern of conduct composed of a series of acts over a period of time that evidences a continuity of purpose) "that includes approaching or pursuing another person with intent to place that person in reasonable fear of serious bodily injury or death or that a third person likely will suffer serious bodily injury or death" (Maryland Art. 27, § 121B). The Federal Statute for stalking makes it illegal to cross state lines to stalk, either physically or by mail or internet, and carries the requirement of intent to kill or injure or place the victim in fear of serious bodily injury or death (18 U.S.C. § 2261A, 1996). Mullen et al. (2000) make the argument that defining stalking is rooted in cultural beliefs. Fifty years ago, behavior defined as stalking today was commonly seen as "courting" or other efforts by potential suitors. Today, Americans have higher expectations of privacy, and therefore have adopted more stringent legal definitions of stalking to protect it.

There are some benefits and criticisms to current anti-stalking laws. Morewitz (2003) states that the benefits include heightened awareness of the crime, improved protection of victims' rights, and the real possibility of sanctions or imprisonment for persistent offenders. The criticisms include duplication of laws already on the books, vagueness, ineffectiveness, and the criminalization of behaviors that may normally occur between parties in intimate relationships. Kinkade et al. (2005) add that discretion is a serious problem in enforcing such laws. Due to the difficulty in interpreting human behavior and intentions, stalking acts may be considered so by one officer, but another may feel all the necessary components of a legal definition were not satisfied.

Bartol (2002) raises the issue of cyberstalking, stating that there is little known about this phenomenon, and that this vulnerability leaves open a large legal loophole for stalkers to victimize others. He points out that little research has been done on incidence and prevalence of cyberstalking, as well as possible deterrents and the psychological impact the occurrence has on victims. Several states currently include email and message board postings as forms of contact in defining stalking behavior, yet local law enforcement agencies may not be properly trained on how to handle the technical aspects of this new crime (United States Department of Justice, 2001).

Box 4.1

What to Do if You Are Being Cyberstalked

- If you are receiving unwanted contact, make clear to that person that you would like him or her not to contact you again.

- Save all communications for evidence. Do not edit or alter them in any way. Also, keep a record of your contacts with Internet system administrators or law enforcement officials.

- You may want to consider blocking or filtering messages from the harasser. Many e-mail programs such as Eudora and Microsoft Outlook have a filter feature, and software can be easily obtained that will automatically delete e-mails from a particular e-mail address or that contain offensive words. Chat room contact can be blocked as well. Although formats differ, a common chat room command to block someone would be to type: /ignore <person's screen name> (without the brackets). However, in some circumstances (such as threats of violence), it may be more appropriate to save the information and contact law enforcement authorities.

- If harassment continues after you have asked the person to stop, contact the harasser's Internet Service Provider (ISP). Most ISPs have clear policies prohibiting the use of their services to abuse another person. Often, an ISP can try to stop the conduct by direct contact with the stalker or by closing their account. If you receive abusive e-mails, identify the domain (after the "@" sign) and contact that ISP. Most ISPs have an e-mail address such as abuse@(domain name) or postmaster@(domain name) that can be used for complaints. If the ISP has a website, visit it for information on how to file a complaint.

- Contact your local police department and inform them of the situation in as much detail as possible. In appropriate cases, they may refer the matter to state or federal authorities. If you are afraid of taking action, there are resources available to help you, Contact either:
  –The National Domestic Violence Hotline, 800-799-SAFE (phone); 800-787-3224 (TDD)
  –A local women's shelter for advice and support.

(United States Department of Justice, 1999).

Box 4.1, *continued*

Cyberstalking Prevention Tips

- Do not share personal information in public spaces anywhere online, nor give it to strangers, including in e-mail or chat rooms. Do not use your real name or nickname as your screen name or user ID. Pick a name that is gender- and age-neutral. Do not post personal information as part of any user profiles.

- Be extremely cautious about meeting online acquaintances in person. If you choose to meet, do so in a public place and take along a friend.

- Make sure that your ISP and Internet Relay Chat (IRC) network have an acceptable use policy that prohibits cyberstalking. And if your network fails to respond to your complaints, consider switching to a provider that is more responsive to user complaints.

- If a situation online becomes hostile, log off or surf elsewhere. If a situation places you in fear, contact a local law enforcement agency.

(United States Department of Justice, 1999).

Prevalence

When estimating the prevalence of stalking in our country, we return to the same problems found in forming a comprehensive definition of the crime. An important consideration when measuring prevalence are the words used to describe stalking behavior. Researchers cannot simply ask subjects if they have been "stalked" due to the highly subjective nature of the term. Instead, questions may or may not be asked based upon the legal definition of the crime, but this may not solve problems with the arbitrariness and operationalization of terms involved.

An important concern raised by Mullen et al. (2000) in estimating prevalence is that many studies will have some sort of sampling bias. This is due to various reasons such as attempting to generalize findings from a convenience sample (often college students), or voluntary responsiveness skewing data. In these instances, women with experience in the matter may be more eager to respond to researchers, or they may be less likely because they see it as intrusive or don't want a reminder of a negative experience. Standard of fear is another aspect that is plagued by uncertainty of definition when measuring prevalence. The exact same act may produce very different levels of fear in a victim. Should we determine if an event is stalking solely based on victim perception when it is known to be so variable? Or should a "reasonable person" standard be used? Many times men have a different perspective on the issue than women; therefore the beliefs of a reasonable man may differ from those of a reasonable woman.

There are several estimates of lifetime prevalence. The most frequently cited estimate is by Tjaden and Thoennes (1998) from the National Violence Against Women Survey (NVAWS). They calculate that women have a 1:12 risk of being stalked in their lifetime, while the lifetime risk for men is 1:45. The prevalence varies with the level of fear included in the definition provided by the researchers. A higher level of fear requirement produces lower lifetime rates, while a lower level of fear provided in the definition may elevate rates (Tjaden & Thoennes, 1998). Another interesting finding of the NVAW study is that there is no difference in the prevalence of the crime between white women and non-white women, though when the non-white category is broken down, there are some differences between Asian/Pacific Islander and other minority women. Unfortunately, the sample size was too small to test for statistical significance (Tjaden & Thoennes, 1998).

The NVAWS, sponsored by the National Institute of Justice and Centers for Disease Control, is the most comprehensive study on stalking victims to date and for that reason is often cited to describe general stalking characteristics. With a telephone random-digit-dialed sample of 8,000 women and 8,000 men, the researchers were able to gather a large amount of information on victims and their reactions to the crime (Tjaden & Thoennes, 1998). The survey may also be considered the most generalizable in stalking research, due to the large, randomized sample.

One factor not strongly considered in prevalence estimates is the cost to society due to the effects of stalking on victims. These costs cannot be easily measured, nor can a specific dollar figure be applied to each incident. Examples of such costs are healthcare needs such as therapy, administrative costs of following the crime through the criminal justice system, and civil actions brought against employers by victims in the workplace (Schell & Lanteigne, 2000). In the NVAWS, Tjaden and Thoennes (1998) found that 30 percent of female victims and 20 percent of males seek psychological counseling in response to being stalked, while 26 percent missed time from work, and 7 percent leave and never return to work because of the events. These findings show that there is a significant societal cost to stalking that prevalence rates may fail to capture.

Victim and Offender Characteristics

For stalking in particular, the behavior of the victim can have an influence on the outcome and/or duration of the crime. The profile of the average victim is a female, under the age of 40, who has had a prior relationship with the offender (Tjaden & Thoennes, 1998). Dependent upon the researcher, victims can be categorized by relationship to the offender, using various divisions that include intimates, acquaintances, and strangers. Many victims are single and live alone, thus making them more accessible to their stalker, who does not have to worry about a roommate or boyfriend taking his phone calls or shielding the victim from contact (Mullen et al., 2000). The data presented in Box 4.2 are taken from the NVAWS, and illustrate that 86 percent of all male and female victims were below the age of 40 when their first reported stalking incident took place (Tjaden & Thoennes, 1998).

Box 4.2

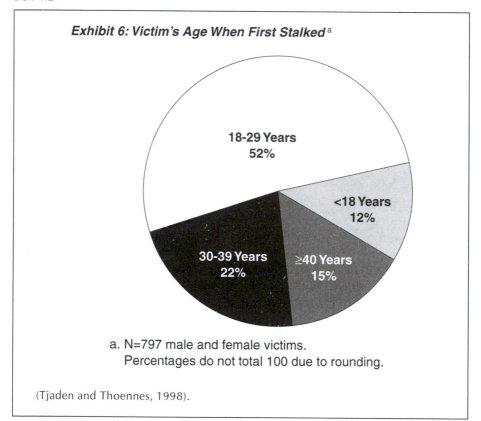

Exhibit 6: Victim's Age When First Stalked [a]

18-29 Years
52%

<18 Years
12%

30-39 Years
22%

≥40 Years
15%

a. N=797 male and female victims.
   Percentages do not total 100 due to rounding.

(Tjaden and Thoennes, 1998).

Box 4.3 summarizes the reported relationships between victims and stalkers in the NVAWS data (Tjaden & Thoennes, 1998). As previously mentioned, the most common relationships are those of former intimate partners. Another important finding of the study was that over 80 percent of women in the sample who were stalked by a current or former intimate partner were also physically assaulted by that person, and 31 percent were raped by that partner (Tjaden & Thoennes, 1998). It seems that stalking behavior may be an extension of the physical violence or psychological abuse suffered by the victim while in the relationship.

Box 4.3

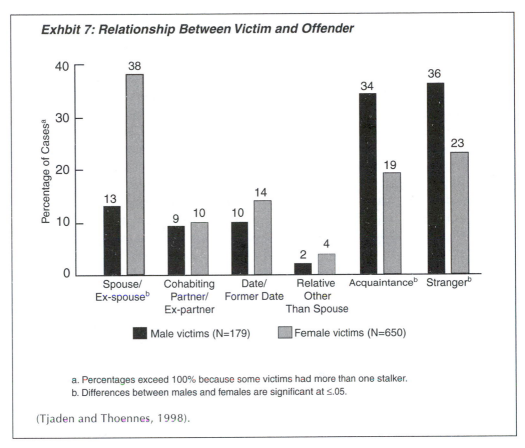

Exhbit 7: Relationship Between Victim and Offender

a. Percentages exceed 100% because some victims had more than one stalker.
b. Differences between males and females are significant at ≤.05.

(Tjaden and Thoennes, 1998).

In studying those incarcerated for stalking offenses, a typical offender tends to be male, middle age, single, intelligent and resourceful, and may have some sort of personality disturbance (Mullen et al., 1999). The problem in studying incarcerated stalkers is that they may not be representative of the general population of stalkers. Specifically, they may represent only the most serious offenders, and not the typical perpetrator that most victims will encounter. Additionally, many may be charged with other crimes such as trespassing or harassment, therefore making it difficult to determine if an offender is a stalker unless the jurisdiction is particularly consistent with charging offenders with the crime of stalking.

Stalking Typologies

There are many classification systems that attempt to distinguish different types of stalkers. These categories are based primarily on the motive of the stalker, as well as the nature of his or her relationship to the victim and possible psychoses of the offender. While most stalkers can be placed in one of the following categories, caution must be used in misunderstanding or misinterpreting their behavior. If a stalker is categorized as a less harmless variety and the victim therefore makes decisions about her reactions based upon this, there is a chance that she may be unpleasantly surprised by his behavior, possibly at a most inopportune time.

Mullen et al. (2000) began with outlining their categories of stalkers based primarily on motivation for the crime. They are listed as the Rejected, the Intimacy Seekers, the Resentful, the Predatory, and the Incompetent. According to Zona et al. (1998), the categories of stalkers can simply be described as Simple Obsessional, Love Obsessional, and Erotomaniac. There are other breakdowns and categorizations of types of stalkers or stalking behaviors, each dependent upon the opinions and focus of the researchers. For example, some groupings may be more psychologically based because they are formulated by mental health professionals as opposed to criminologists. Regardless of labels, there appears to be a central theme that separates those having previous relationships, those that are strangers, and/or those that have violent or delusional motivations.

The Rejected stalker's motives range from attempting reconciliation to exacting revenge on an ex-partner. Whatever the case, a previous relationship is required for this type of stalking to take place. These types of stalkers are commonly the most persistent, possibly due to the feelings that previous contact has given them, as well as knowing personal information about the victim, such as an address or telephone number. A very high percentage of these offenders are males stalking their previous intimate partners (Mullen et al., 2000).

Intimacy seekers share the ultimate goal of a loving relationship with their victims. Delusional offenders are commonly found in this category, along with schizophrenics and those with narcissistic personalities. Celebrities or figures of authority frequently fall victim to this type of stalker. Mullen et al. (2000) classified one third of their sample of 145 stalkers as intimacy seekers. Their communications with the victim are often impersonal, such as email, letters, phone calls, or mailed gifts. The ignorance of rejection is a serious flaw that this type of stalker possesses. Even after being told numerous times by the victim, friends or colleagues of the victim, and even the courts via restraining orders, this group remains persistent. Though not usually violent, intimacy seekers may become so if triggered by perceived unfavorable events. This aggression can be towards the target, but also towards a third party believed to be in the way.

The Resentful category is comprised of stalkers motivated by the fear and distress they cause their victims. They may believe that *they* are the victims caused harm, and their actions are a justified means of fighting back. The sense of power or control felt during the stalking behaviors is very satisfying, and possibly coupled with a desire for retribution. This group may not be as long term as the other groups; in many cases there is a short period of backlash that may include harassing phone calls or letters, but may desist after a few days or weeks (Mullen et al., 2000).

Box 4.4

Mullen et al. (2000) Classification of Stalkers
The Rejected   – Prior relationship between victim and offender   – Motive can be revenge or reconciliation   – Not easily discouraged
Intimacy Seekers   – Little or no prior relationship between victim and offender   – Ultimate goal is a loving relationship with the victim   – Ignorance of rejection tactics by the victim
The Resentful   – Almost always a prior acquaintanceship or relationship between victim and offender   – Motivated by fear created in the victim   – Stalking may be short in duration, dependent upon stalker's attention span
The Predatory   – May or may not have a prior relationship with the victim   – Ultimate goal is attack on the victim; Most potential danger   – Commonly dramatized in the media as the "typical" stalker
The Incompetent   – Has either no or an insignificant prior relationship to the victim   – Goal is to have a relationship, regardless of the victim's wishes   – May be found on college campuses

The Predatory stalker is perhaps the most dangerous because his or her ultimate goal is an attack on the victim; either violent, sexual, or both. Stalking is a means to an end, or a way to best set up the attack situation. Predatory stalkers do not derive pleasure from inflicting fear in their targets; they prefer to watch from afar until it is time to make their move. Victims may not even be aware they are being stalked until the attacker makes his presence known. While predatory stalkers are the rarest group, they are also the most dramatized and represented in the media and entertainment industry. This is probably due to the shock value attached to being assaulted by a mysterious and unknown stalker. Most predatory stalkers are men, but their victims can be either sex, and may even include children. Sexual offenders sometimes fall into this category because their ultimate motive may be a sexual attack (Mullen et al., 2000).

The final category is that of Incompetent stalkers who possess a sense of entitlement to have a relationship, while disregarding the preference of their target. They continually "initiate persistent inept attempts" to start a relationship with their victim (Mullen et al., 2000). This type of stalker may be found on college campuses due to the unsophisticated nature of their behavior.

The previous categories may be considered extensively detailed. Therefore, Zona et al. (1993) attempted to parsimoniously categorize stalkers into three categories. The first category is that of Simple Obsessional stalkers. This typology includes those that have had a previous relationship with the victim, be it intimate, a brief period of dating, or a work relationship. Similar to the rejected stalker, the primary motive is to re-establish a relationship or get revenge for a perceived wrong by the victim.

Love Obsessional stalkers lack a previous or existing relationship with their victim and include celebrity stalkers as well as ordinary citizens. The stalker believes that if he or she could make contact with the victim, then the feelings of love or adoration would certainly be returned. There are frequently phone calls made or letters mailed, but often the victim may not ever know the identity of his or her stalker. This type is categorized as less dangerous than the simple obsessionals, due to the often impersonal nature of their crime (Zona et al., 1993).

The final distinction of stalker according to Zona et al. (1993) is the Erotomaniac. Pure erotomaniacs can be delusional and easily misinterpret words and actions of others. Once a fixation has been established, the erotomaniac lives his or her life around the single object of affection. The offender can honestly believe that the slightest gesture, such as a person sneezing, is a secret sign between the two that the target is showing his or her love. While not listed as a separate category of stalker, the erotomaniac is also given attention by Mullen et al. (2000). The term is defined as, "an exaggerated and irrational sentimental attachment, usually to someone who in reality has little or no relationship to the sufferer." Both definitions of erotomaniacs attempt to explain why an offender would continue stalking behavior after receiving no encouragement from a victim.

Box 4.5

Zona et al. (1993) Classification of Stalkers

Simple Obsessional
    – Previous relationship between victim and offender
    – Goal is to re-establish a relationship or get revenge

Love Obsessional
    – May not have a previous relationship (victim may be a celebrity)
    – Believes the victim will return feelings of love upon repeated contact

Erotomaniac
    – May or may not have a prior relationship with the offender
    – Possibly delusional and may interpret everyday circumstances as "signs of love" from the victim

Female Offenders

As with many other crimes, females are more likely to be victims than perpetrators of stalking. The NVAWS found that the lifetime risk of men being stalked is 1:45, though some of these cases involve males stalking other males (Tjaden & Thoennes, 1998). Therefore, female offenders are rare, but not non-existent. Many well-known celebrity stalkers have been female. In 1988 David Letterman was stalked by a schizophrenic woman who broke into his home, stole his car, was convinced she was his wife, and, years later, committed suicide (New York Daily News, March 18, 2005). Psychiatrist Doreen Orion was victim to a female stalker who suffered from a multitude of psychological disorders, the most prevalent being depression and Erotomania (Orion, 1998). Because female stalkers are so rare, little attention is given in the literature to their motives and conduct. Mullen et al. (2000) only discuss female stalkers when exploring same-gender stalking cases. The authors state that female stalkers who stalk other females may be more likely to do so within the workplace with primary motives of revenge.

While female stalkers may be the minority when compared to their counterparts, this does not suggest that future research should limit samples to only male offenders. A research limitation that may be biasing samples is the possible differential reporting and processing of female offenders by the criminal justice system. If male stalking victims, or even female staking victims embarrassed to be stalked by another female, do not report the crime to the police or the police are not aggressive in charging the female offenders, this group may be excluded from samples taken from official records. This possibility strengthens the argument for the need of self-report or victimization data when studying the crime.

Theoretical Perspectives

While stalker typologies attempt to characterize groups of offenders and sift through their motivations, there are several psychological theories that attempt to explain the origins or reasons for their behavior. Popular theories used to explain the behavior of stalkers consist of what the DSM IV would call personality disorders, specifically those in the sub-categorization of Cluster B (American Psychiatric Association, 1994). These include antisocial, narcissistic, borderline, and histrionic personality disorders. It is not very common for stalkers to suffer from depression, because their stalking behaviors require effort and motivation, while depression is characterized by a lack of those factors (Rosenfeld & Harmon, 2002). It should be noted that all stalkers do not necessarily have a diagnosable disorder; therefore researchers should refrain from attempting to place them neatly into such categories.

Antisocial personality disorder is characterized by impulsivity, aggressiveness, and manipulativeness. These characteristics are often found in stalkers, particularly those that eventually resort to violence. A less volatile diagnosis is that of narcissistic personality disorder, which is characterized by the beliefs the offender has about possession of the subject, or victim, coupled with an inflated ego or superiority complex (American Psychiatric Association, 1994).

Borderline personality disorder is characterized by impulsivity, self destructiveness, and instability (American Psychiatric Association, 1994). A unique trait to this type of disorder is difficulty with therapeutic relationships, specifically maintaining boundaries (Mohan, 2002). This is explored in a book written by psychiatrist Doreen Orion (1998) in which her patient becomes her stalker. Because the relationship in therapy was difficult for her patient "Fran" to deal with, she resorted to stalking Orion by leaving notes in her office and coming to her home. This behavior continued for a number of years and eventually led to Orion moving out of the state. This represents an extreme case of how a mental disorder can manifest itself in stalking, and in turn have a significant impact on a victim's life.

Another possible diagnosis of stalkers is histrionic personality disorder. These offenders tend to be highly emotional, dramatic, and theatrical (American Psychiatric Association, 1994). It is important to note that one individual may suffer from multiple problems and therefore have a combination of many of the above traits. All of these disorders list possible characteristics that stalkers may possess, but should not be used to formulate diagnoses based upon incomplete information about a case.

Two additional diagnoses for stalkers are that of obsessive compulsive disorder (OCD) and schizophrenia. OCD is characterized by obsessions about things in the environment, as well as compulsions to complete certain tasks to remedy perceived problems or to satisfy superstitions, while schizophrenics may experience delusions or severe misperceptions about reality (American Psychiatric Association, 1994). These symptoms are manifested in stalking behavior when the offender becomes obsessed with his or her victim and the victim's life, and acts on compulsions to make contact, or even injure the parties involved. Although the presence of a psychological disorder may seem disturbing in stalking cases, some research has shown that it is negatively associated with violence during the crime; in other words, stalkers with mental disorders may be *less* likely to commit violence against their victims (Rosenfeld & Harmon, 2002).

All of the theoretical perspectives mentioned above come from the field of psychology. This is not to say that the roots of all offender behavior in stalking cases have an entirely psychological component. However, due to their sociological nature, it may be more difficult to apply criminological theories to stalking behavior. First, the intent or motivation of the stalker may be highly variable, as well as difficult to determine; is it hate, revenge, love, or manifestation of some other characteristic? Different theories may be applied dependent upon the answer. Also, most stalking behaviors would be difficult to evaluate as "rational" choices, therefore following the thought process of calculating costs and benefits in the mind of the offender would be a difficult task. One solid possibility is power-control dynamics, which may play a role in motivation to offend. Brewster (2003) studied a sample of 187 stalking victims of former intimate partners. She found that 98.9 percent reportedly felt they were being psychologically controlled, and 68.4 percent felt social control from their stalker. She also concludes that stalking may be an extension of power and control dynamics that exist throughout a relationship.

Due to the lack of official records, data on stalkers is difficult to find. Moreover, it is possible that very different results may be obtained dependent upon which source of information is used in a sample. It is more common to get information from stalkers themselves rather than victims when asking questions about violence. Rosenfeld's meta-analysis (2004) looked at 11 different samples, 9 of which used mental-health obtained samples instead of victim self-report data.

Treatment/Prevention

Treatment

Because there is no single diagnosis that can be applied to all stalkers, they must be assessed individually and treated according to their specific characteristics. Unfortunately, treatments for convicted stalkers have been non-existent. They have instead been dealt with through threat assessment, separation, or incapacitation. There has not been a research focus on therapy or treatment of these offenders beyond what the mental health community offers any other criminal offender.

Those that are diagnosed with personality disorders may best be treated as any other inpatient or outpatient with similar disorders, yet therapy should be undertaken in the context of their crimes. Medication such as lithium and methods such as cognitive behavioral therapy are currently the most beneficial options for this particular group (Mohan, 2002). Those offenders that are incarcerated for stalking but do not have a diagnosable disorder may still require some form of therapy in order to address their misconceptions about relationships, and the fact that their actions were a crime and must not continue while incarcerated or upon release.

An important finding in situational treatment comes from Jasinski and Mustaine (2001). This study reanalyzed the NVAWS data gathered by Tjaden and Thoennes to determine if stalking is treated similar, with respect to police response, to domestic violence. Results show that the factors that prompt formal police actions are different between stalking and domestic violence. Specifically, the study found that a formal police response, such as arrest, was more likely for domestic victims of physical assault than for stalking victims. Possible explanations for this include the elusive presence of stalkers when police arrive, and officer unfamiliarity with laws and policies surrounding the issue. Recommendations of this research are to treat domestic violence cases and offenders separately and differently than stalking cases and offenders, as well as police response being more educated and thus able to vary in response to the situation (Jasinski & Mustaine, 2001).

Incapacitation has been rare in stalking cases due to the many new state laws. Therefore, there is no solid information about its effects on offending. It is possible that the crime could continue while an offender was incarcerated or on probation, but only one study has been conducted describing stalker recidivism. Rosenfeld (2003) found a recidivism rate of 49 percent over 2.5 to 13 years of follow-up data. Interestingly, 80 percent re-offended within the first year after their court-ordered mental health evaluation. Most of the sample was on probation for stalking-related offenses, not incarceration; therefore, answers on incapacitation effects still remain elusive. Unfortunately, it may take more offenders to be processed through the criminal justice system before we are able to gather better data on circumstances following release.

Prevention

The most progress in stalking research has been made in the area of prevention rather than treatment. The ultimate goal of stalking research is to prevent the crime from occurring, but a more realistic goal is ensuring that a victim can identify when stalking behavior is taking place, and

Box 4.6

Federal Sentences for Stalking Crimes

The following is the penalty for violation of the federal statute against stalking:

(1) Life or any term of years, if death of the victim results;
(2) Not more than 20 years if permanent disfigurement or life threatening bodily injury to the victim results;
(3) Not more than 10 years, if serious bodily injury to the victim results or if the offender uses a dangerous weapon during the offense;
(4) As provided for the applicable conduct under chapter 109A (18 U.S.C. § 2241 et seq.) if the offense would constitute an offense under chapter 109A (without regard to whether the offense was committed in the special maritime and territorial jurisdiction of the United States or in a Federal prison); and
(5) Not more than 5 years, in any other case, or both fined and imprisoned.

Interpretation – Penalties for violating §§2261, 2261A or 2262 are either a fine, imprisonment, or both. There are no minimum sentences, but there are maximums based on the extent of the victim's injuries. The maximum sentences are listed below along with the corresponding injury.

- life imprisonment if victim dies;
- 20 years if victim is permanently disfigured;
- 20 years if victim suffers life threatening bodily injury;
- 10 years if victim suffers serious bodily injury;
- penalties set forth in Chapter 109A (18 U.S.C. § 2241 et seq. – sex offenses) if offender's conduct meets the elements of any of those offenses (conduct does not have to occur in federal prison or within special/maritime jurisdiction of U.S.); or
- 5 years for any other situation.

In addition, the maximum sentence is 10 years if the offender uses a dangerous weapon.

18 U.S.C. §2261(b).

---

he or she has some sort of recourse and steps to take to reduce the possibility of prolonged victimization, as well as physical injury. Rosenfeld and Harmon (2002) examined a sample of stalkers and attempted to determine if there are any key characteristics that make one stalker more likely to be violent or carry out threats than another. The final model the authors used to predict violence was found statistically significant and contained the independent variables of age, race, education level, previous threats given, and a prior intimate relationship. Specifically, those offenders who were young (under 30), non-Caucasian, less than high school educated, previously threatened, and had a prior intimate relationship with their victim (Rosenfeld and Harmon, 2002) were more likely to commit violence.

A "preliminary" meta-analysis completed by Rosenfeld (2004) gathered a total of 11 studies to determine what stalking research has concluded about the possible risk factors of violence. Significant factors included threats, substance abuse, and the absence of a psychotic disorder. Other correlates were a history of stalker violent behavior, and a prior intimate relationship with the victim. The author concluded that there is a need for prospective research designs in studying violence in stalking situations. Possible resources for such samples include mental health sources, as well as domestic violence offenders.

Additionally, there are certain actions by victims that may help discourage or eliminate stalking behavior directed towards them. Recommendations include avoiding any and all contact with the offender, having a close peer or family group to rely upon for support and in drastic cases, moving and protecting their identity from public records (Bates, 2001). While it is true victims have some degree of control over whether they continue to be victims of stalking or not, in some cases the offender is so persistent that legal action must be taken. Even then, a victim can be stalked by a perpetrator for many years, with no reliable opportunities for recourse (Orion, 1998).

Conclusion

What we know about stalkers, their victims, and their offenses is greatly overshadowed by what we do not know. Professionals and researchers in the fields of criminology and psychology remain in the early stages of understanding the crime. While the 1998 study by Tjaden and Thoennes represents the first comprehensive effort to study the crime on a national level across populations, there is still much work to be done in exploring the many aspects of stalking, especially theories underlying offender behavior, and most importantly, treatment and prevention techniques.

The limitations of many studies, such as small sample sizes and little generalizability to the entire population, should not completely discourage researchers from attempting new studies and finding new ways to test their prevention or treatment hypotheses. Victims of stalking, like all other victims of crime, deserve to have the best information possible on preventing victimization, as well as understanding the crime that was committed against them. Criminology and psychology have much more work to do until this obligation is fulfilled.

References

18 US Code. Sec. 2261(b) (1996). Online. Findlaw.com. 11 October 2005.

American Psychiatric Association (1994). *Diagnostic and Statistical Manual of Mental Disorders*, Fourth Edition. Washington, DC: American Psychiatric Press.

Bartol, C.R. (2002). *Criminal Behavior: A Psychosocial Approach*, Sixth Edition. Newark, NJ: Prentice Hall.

Bates, L. (2001). *Safety for Stalking Victims*. New York: Writer's Showcase.

Brewster, M. (2003). "Power and Control Dynamics in Prestalking and Stalking Situations." *Journal of Family Violence*, 18(4):207-217.

Connor, T. (2005). "Dave's No Stranger to Woe." *New York Daily News,* (March 18):2.

Jasinski, J.L. and E.E. Mustaine (2001). "Police Response to Physical Assault and Stalking Victimization: A Comparison of Influential Factors." *American Journal of Criminal Justice*, 26(1):23-41.

Kinkade, P., R. Burns, and A.I. Fuentes (2005). "Criminalizing Attractions: Perceptions of Stalking and the Stalker." *Crime and Delinquency*, 51(1):3-25.

Meloy, J.R. (1998). *The Psychology of Stalking: Clinical and Forensic Perspectives*. San Diego, CA: Academic Press.

Mohan, R. (2002). "Treatments for Borderline Personality Disorder: Integrating Evidence into Practice." *International Review of Psychiatry*, 14:42-51.

Morewitz, S. (2003). *Stalking and Violence: New Patterns of Trauma and Obsession*. New York: Plenum Publishers.

Mullen, P., M. Pathé, and R. Purcell (2000). *Stalkers and Their Victims*. Cambridge, UK: Cambridge University Press.

Mullen, P., M. Pathé, R. Purcell, and G. Stuart (1999). "Study of Stalkers." *American Journal of Psychiatry*, 156(8):1244-1249.

Orion, D.R. (1998). *I Know You Really Love Me: A Psychiatrist's Journal of Erotomania, Stalking, and Obsessive Love*. New York: Doubleday.

Rosenfeld, B. (2004). "Violence Risk Factors in Stalking and Obsessional Harassment: A Review and Preliminary Meta-Analysis." *Criminal Justice and Behavior*, 31(1):9-36.

Rosenfeld, B. (2003). "Recidivism in Stalking and Obsessional Harassment." *Law and Human Behavior*, 27(3):251-265.

Rosenfeld, B. and R. Harmon (2002). "Factors Associated with Violence in Stalking and Obsessional Harassment Cases." *Criminal Justice and Behavior*, 29:671-691.

Schell, B. and N. Lanteigne (2000). *Stalking, Harassment, and Murder in the Workplace*. Westport, CT: Quorum Books.

State of Maryland (1997). Maryland Code Annotated. Art. 27, § 121B.

Tjaden, P. and N. Thoennes (1998). "Stalking in America: Findings from the National Violence against Women Survey." Washington, DC: NIJ.

United States Department of Justice (2001). "Stalking and Domestic Violence. Report to Congress." Washington, DC: Office of Justice Programs.

United States Department of Justice (1999). "Cyberstalking: A New Challenge for Law Enforcement and Industry, A Report from the Attorney General to the Vice President." Washington, DC.

Zona, M.A., K. Sharma, and J. Lane (1993). "A Comparative Study of Erotomaniac and Obsessional Subjects in a Forensic Sample." *Journal of Forensic Sciences*, 38:894-903.

SECTION II

Sex Crimes

Chapter 5

Child Molestation

Danielle A. Harris

Introduction

Sexual abuse of children is a deeply complex phenomenon. It is 'steeped in contradiction, confusion and emotion' (Innes, 1997:63), 'violates the norms of almost every culture' (Ryan, Metzner & Krugman, 1990:260) and has been considered the most hated crime in the criminal justice system (Briggs, 1995). When public interest intersects with correctional philosophy this particularly abhorrent offense becomes a 'highly charged issue guided less by sound information than by emotion-laden attitudes and rhetoric' (Broadhurst & Maller, 1992:54; Samenow, 1984). In the past, these concerns have confounded an academic criminological comprehension of child sexual abuse. Borrowing from psychology however, allows for the useful application of behavioral and cognitive-behavioral theories. This chapter is concerned only with sexual offenders who abuse children (hereafter called child molesters). The major focus is on adult males because this reflects the emphasis of the field. However, recently there has been an increased interest in research and treatment on female and adolescent child molesters. Therefore, these offenders are discussed where appropriate.

The term, 'child molester' is used in this chapter to describe offenders who abuse extra-familial children exclusively. Importantly, this is distinguished from incest offenders who offend within the context of family and abuse their own biological, foster, adoptive, or step children. Incest will not be discussed in this chapter and any mention of child abuse shall refer only to extra-familial children. It is important to note there are substantively significant differences between incest offenders and child molesters and therefore, automatic comparisons between the two should not be drawn.

Child sexual abuse is often used to illustrate the concept of the dark figure of crime because the exact number of offenders, offenses and victims is unknown and underestimated (Grant, 2000; Lee, 1993; Morrison, 1999). Definitional variance across jurisdictions regarding offense type, age of consent, age of adulthood and age of criminal responsibility, for example, obscure these data also. One might measure how many members of the population have been victimized, how many members of the population have offended (prevalence), how many offenses an average offender might commit (incidence) or how many offenses a particular victim might experience.

Using official statistics to gauge the extent of child sexual abuse is perhaps the most unreliable measure of its actual prevalence. While it is necessary to provide some overview of the problem, it is with hesitation that the following statistics are offered. The most commonly cited prevalence data estimate that one in five women and one in 11 men has been sexually victimized (Finkelhor, 1984). Sex offenders (not delineated by offense type) make up approximately 4.7 percent of the total national correctional population with approximately 60 percent of these convicted offenders living in the community (Bureau of Justice Statistics, 1997).

Sexual abuse of children typically occurs secretly, usually within an existing relationship (Lee, 1993) where there is a marked disparity of power (Ryan, Metzner & Krugman, 1990). A victim's subsequent disclosure therefore becomes unlikely, dangerous, or even impossible (Lee, 1993). For these reasons estimates of child molestation are likely to be understated (Lee, 1993; Mathews, 1997; Worling, 1995a). Disclosure is even less likely for victims of incest and/or female offenders.

Offender Characteristics

A broad review of the emerging knowledge from international literature reveals that extra-familial child molesters share common and identifiable characteristics. These include chaotic family environments, (Stenson & Anderson, 1987) inconsistent parenting, and significant marital discord (Friedrich & Luecke, 1988), little or no contact with fathers (Ford & Linney, 1995; Graham, 1996), physical or sexual parental abuse, witnessing domestic violence (Higgs, Canavan & Meyer, 1992), chronic isolation from same age peers (Ford & Linney, 1995) difficulty making friends (Prentky & Knight, 1993), early childhood sexualization and prior victimization (Veneziano, Veneziano & LeGrand, 2000).

Seriousness of Child Sexual Abuse

The inherent social conscience of the average citizen is sufficient to accept unconditionally the gravity of this phenomenon. This however makes it particularly necessary to illustrate the effects of abuse and the likelihood of recidivism from a scholarly and empirical standpoint.

Effects of Abuse: The negative effects of child sexual abuse are well documented and include feelings of betrayal, powerlessness, stigmatization, traumatic sexualization, depression, guilt, substance abuse, suicidal ideations, anxiety, somatic complaints, phobias, and severely impeded emotional development (Friedrich & Luecke, 1988; Grant, 2000; Bartol, 2002; Worling, 1995a). The impact of abuse depends heavily on the child's age at the time, the number of perpetrators, their relationship to the child, the type of abuse, its frequency and duration and whether force was used (Friedrich & Luecke, 1988). Abuse is particularly traumatic where bodily penetration and aggressiveness are combined, as the experience is more likely to be "split off" (or denied) by the child, who is unable to integrate the experience and make sense of it (Friedrich & Luecke, 1988; Prentky & Knight, 1993).

Likelihood of Recidivism: The high probability of sex offender recidivism has been supported by numerous clinical results (Hanson, 2002) and this finding has informed much legislation. Sexual Predator laws, for example, allow for the civil commitment of violent sexual offenders (Andrews & Bonta, 2003) and Megan's Law and other iterations of community notification and registration require that individuals be informed of a child molester residing in their neighborhood (Bartol, 2002).

Sex offender criminal activity differs from the offending of many other offender types. For many other offenders, the age crime curve clearly describes their criminal careers (Gottfredson & Hirschi, 1983). As the offenders get older they age out of crime. The reality of sexual offending against children is dramatically different. While early onset age is evident (Prentky & Knight, 1993), 'unlike other juvenile delinquents who typically grow out of their offending' (Erooga & Masson, 1999:4) many child sexual abusers continue offending and 'get better' or 'grow into it' with time (Grant, 2000; Stenson & Anderson, 1987). The sexual experience has a positively reinforcing physical element and when this occurs at an early age, (sometimes even in the context of victimization) it may lead to repetitive and ingrained deviant patterns of arousal (Elliot & Smiljanich, 1994; Graham, 1996).

Theoretical Perspective

Child molestation as a topic for research and theory has typically not been a focus of traditional criminologists. Most work in this area has been done by the 'helping professions' of psychology, psychiatry and social work (Gelles & Wolfner, 1994). American criminology was born mostly out of schools of sociology. This perspective has lead to a rejection of the psychological ideas of offender typologies and classifications. The very title of this book however, indicates an appreciation for crime specific theory; a new approach for traditional criminology.

Box 5.1

In the News

'Expecting a school district and a police department to be on guard against female teachers in their 30's out to ravish 12-year-old boys is like expecting a weather bureau to be on the watch for showers of frogs'[1]

An exhaustive search for mention of female sexual offenders in international press over the last five years yields extremely little. What *is* reported however, reveals an extreme dearth of insight, research and understanding which generally perpetuates uninformed or worse, ill-informed public perception. This perception evidently influences the way in which these individuals are treated by the media and by all levels of the criminal justice system.

Society's general reluctance to accept that women can commit sex crimes against children[2] is documented in articles that describe the 'prevailing sentiment that it's not a big deal'[3] and the belief that it is 'more of a fluke of nature than a miscue by authorities.'[4] Not surprisingly, various criminal justice personnel are repeatedly quoted with their arms in the air saying 'it's very shocking . . . you just don't see things like that'[5] and 'I never could have imagined it . . . I have never heard of such a thing.'[6]

The well-publicized case of Mary Kay LeTourneau (the 34-year-old Seattle married mother of four who bore two additional children to a 12-year-old male student and was recently released after serving a seven and a half year prison sentence for child rape) is doubtless the most well-known and is referred to by almost all journalists in their discussions of this phenomenon.

In the press coverage of her case, LeTourneau is described as 'America's most infamous female child molester,'[7] a 'randy Miss,'[8] 'a nut, out in the ozone layer,'[9] and 'a troubled person whose list of psychiatric difficulties goes well beyond delusions that she is romantically in love with a 12-year-old boy.'[10] Interestingly, her 12-year-old *victim* is described as 'her grade school lover.'[11] The 'couple' were reported to be 'tangled in an intimate relationship'[12] that was described by one journalist as a 'steamy 18-month affair.'[13] The abuse was defined as a relationship by four additional writers,[14] and was once considered to be 'torture' rather than 'true love.'[15]

---

[1]   Hall, May 24, 2002.
[2]   Stanley, June 9, 2002; Taylor, April 1, 2002.
[3]   Adamson, June 16, 2002.
[4]   Hall, May 24, 2002.
[5]   Stanley, June 9, 2002.
[6]   Hall, May 24, 2002.
[7]   Haskell, March 29, 2002.
[8]   Flynn, April 5, 2002.
[9]   O'Reilly, May 29, 2002.
[10]   Hall, May 24, 2002.
[11]   Radue, May 6, 2002.
[12]   Gold and Dirmann, May 3, 2002.
[13]   Flynn, April 5, 2002.
[14]   Giles, May 19, 2002; Gold and Dirmann, May 3, 2002; Mitchell, May 15, 2002; Young, June 3, 2002.
[15]   Mitchell, May 15, 2002.

Box 5.1, *continued*

Curiously, two separate journalists describe LeTourneau and Tanya Hadden (a 33-year-old teacher who was found with her 15-year old student in a Las Vegas hotel room[16]) as 'blonde'[17]—an interesting choice of adjective given that the hair color of a male sex offender is rarely considered significant enough to report.

This skewed public perception is best displayed by the recent case of Pamela Diehl-Moore, 43, who abused a 13-year-old boy in New Jersey,[18] where Judge Bruce Gaeta made the following statements during her trial: 'It's just something between two people that clicked beyond the teacher-student relationship[19] . . . I really don't see the harm that was done here[20] . . . people mature at different rates[21] . . . certainly society doesn't need to be worried[22] . . . it was simply an opportunity for the boy to satisfy his sexual needs.'[23]

The point is repeatedly made that had the genders been reversed, public reaction, legal responses and media coverage would have been very different.[24] Thus, when compared to their male counterparts these women received incredibly disproportionate sentences. For example, 'in 1993 in Virginia, a male teacher who had sex with three teenage female students was sentenced to 26 years in prison—while the next day [in the same jurisdiction] a female swimming coach who had an "affair" with an 11-year-old boy and sexual encounters with two others got 30 days.'[25] Additionally, when LeTourneau received her initial sentence of six months probation [which she broke upon falling pregnant for a second time to the same boy] at the same time in Seattle, there was another case where a male teacher was caught with a female student and received four years in prison.[26] Further, in reporting LeTourneau's case, Flynn's recent article is titled, 'See me after History Class . . . and I'll Strip!' One gets the feeling that this headline would be considered in extremely poor taste if gender roles were reversed.

While the incidence of female perpetrated abuse is under-reported, the popular explanations given in the media have disastrous reinforcing qualities in terms of public perception. These include: 'some boys may see sexual contact at the hands of an older woman not as molestation but as early initiation,'[27] the boys 'who are usually willing partners, do not consider themselves victims,'[28] a boy is 'going to enjoy this, and it's going to be the fantasy of a lifetime,'[29] young boys dream about 'experienced older women,'[30] 'in some way it is difficult to blame frisky teachers.'[31]

[16] Gold and Dirmann, May 3, 2002.
[17] Giles, May 19, 2002; Flynn, April 5, 2002.
[18] Young, June 3, 2002.
[19] Associated Press (AP), May 24, 2002.
[20] Adamson, June 16, 2002; Young, June 3, 2002.
[21] AP, May 24, 2002.
[22] Adamson, June 16, 2002; AP, May 24, 2002; Young, June 3, 2002.
[23] Young, June 3, 2002.
[24] Mitchell, May 15, 2002.
[25] Young, June 3, 2002.
[26] O'Reilly, May 29, 2002.
[27] Kluger, April 1, 2002.
[28] Stanley, June 9, 2002.
[29] O'Reilly, May 29, 2002.
[30] Peters, June 9, 2002.
[31] Adamson, June 16, 2002.

It is difficult to use criminology theories to understand the phenomenon of child molestation. Psychoanalytic perspectives that dominated psychology for many years also seem inadequate. Child molestation may perhaps be best understood as both a criminological and psychological problem and theories must combine both perspectives.

This chapter pays particular attention to behavioral and cognitive-behavioral theories. When behavioral theory is applied to sexual offending, the emphasis is on learning sexual deviations as part of masturbation fantasies. As its title suggests, cognitive-behavioral theory attaches the assumption that thoughts and feelings mitigate one's actions (Schwartz & Cellini, 1996).[1]

Behavioral Theory

Consistent with some features of criminological learning theories, behavioral theory assumes that sexual deviation is 'another form of learned behavior' (Schwartz & Cellini, 1996:2-14). Classical conditioning is a relevant consideration 'in which a repetitious or traumatic pairing of sexuality and some negative experience, produces some type of intensive emotional response that distorts subsequent sexual gratification' (Schwartz & Cellini, 1996:2-14).

Clinicians use the tenets of behavioral theory to explain the unconscious compulsion to re-enact the abuse or gain mastery over the abusive experience (Wyatt & Johnson-Powell, 1988; Worling, 1995a). Also known as the 'vampire effect' (Veneziano, Veneziano & LeGrand, 2000) or the 'abused/abuser hypothesis' (Worling, 1995b) re-victimization (or inappropriate sexual acting out in a normative way) is considered a function of the individual's own sexual abuse victimization (Graham, 1996; Fagan & Wexler, 1988). When re-victimization occurs, one's past abuse is triggered and the compulsion to repeat produces the 'same tragic conditions for pleasure' (Miller, 1999:108). Sometimes, the behaviors in which they engage are often completely reflective of the offender's own victim experiences (Veneziano, Veneziano & LeGrand, 2000). The child molester re-enacts in literal and repetitive ways their own victimization (Elliot & Smiljanich, 1994).

This explanation assumes that all child molesters have histories of child abuse. To clarify, the broader umbrella of victimization encompasses early exposure to pornography, witnessing parental abuse, neglect and early sexualization. Importantly, there is an evident paradox that only a small proportion of the thousands of child sexual abuse victims become perpetrators (Blues, Moffat & Telford, 1999). One consistent interpretation of this data is that while victimization is a strong correlate of subsequent sexual offending, it is certainly not a causal factor.

Cognitive-Behavioral Theory

Cognitive-behavioural theory holds that individuals are affected not by events but by the views they take of them. In this sense, a child molester's thoughts and feelings allow them to become preoccupied with deviant fantasies (Schwartz & Cellini, 1996). The specific appeal of this approach to child molesters is its ability to describe the subtle manner in which an individual denies, minimizes, justifies and rationalizes his behavior. The criminological parallel of this perspective with which readers may be more familiar are the 'Techniques of Neutralization' described by Sykes and Matza (1957). These techniques include 'denial of responsibility,' 'denial of injury,' 'denial of victim,' 'condemnation of the condemners' and 'appeal to a higher loyalty.' They are used to describe the way in which an individual is able to overcome certain internal and external inhibitors and commit an offense.

The cognitive-behavioral approach implies that sexual arousal to abusive or deviant acts can develop over time (Veneziano, Veneziano & LeGrand, 2000) and that severe sexual abuse in childhood might contribute to a 'predilection for sexually aggressive behavior' in later life (Friedrich & Luecke, 1988:159). Operant conditioning offers a similar explanation where reaching orgasm (even in the context of abuse) is a powerful behavioral reinforcement, particularly when paired with relevant thoughts and emotions. So arousal (if any) stems not from sadism or sexual deviance, but is instead a product of the way the offender has 'processed' his own abuse. The victim comes to 'regard these behaviors as appropriate, normal and worthwhile' (Burton, Nesmith & Badten, 1997:160). Sometimes, inappropriate sexual behavior might also be rewarded with a level of intimacy that is otherwise lacking in the child's relationships (Erooga & Masson, 1999).

Treatment/Prevention

Consistent with the discussed theoretical perspective, cognitive-behavioral therapeutic techniques are considered to be the most appropriate for child molesters. Importantly, while surgical, pharmacological and purely behavioral treatments (outlined in Box 5.2) exist, research is conflicting at best. The strongest research with the most rigorous methodologies and most promising conclusions are drawn from cognitive-behavioral programs.

In the following sections, the objectives and difficulties of sex offender treatment are outlined and the characteristics of cognitive-behavioral therapy are illustrated. A short review of past and existing attitudes towards sex offender treatment will follow with a discussion of the effectiveness of treatment programs. Finally, to answer the all important question of determining 'what works,' recent meta-analyses will be reviewed and discussed.

Box 5.2 outlines the important link between theory and practice (treatment). The goal of behavioral theory is summarized and the treatment modalities that have been informed by this perspective are detailed. These include (but are not limited to) aversion therapy, covert sensitization, masturbatory satiation therapy and shame therapy. For more detail on these specific treatment types, readers are referred to the footnoted citations.

The goals of cognitive-behavioral theory are also provided in Box 5.2. In addition, the widely applicable treatment modalities of this perspective are discussed. Contemporary cognitive-behavioral treatment is probably best represented in the form of Relapse Prevention techniques. This is the most common and well regarded treatment option today. Other treatment options with cognitive behavioral components include sexual education, social skills training and reducing cognitive distortions. It should be noted that unlike the behavioral approaches in the table, the cognitive-behavioral approaches are most often provided in concert with each other.

Despite our acknowledgement of the detrimental effects of abuse and the high likelihood of recidivism, there is little public currency and even less political will to promote or fund necessary programs for child molesters. Effective treatment is further hindered by the absence of a solid theoretical basis for this work. And finally, it is especially hard to change entrenched sexual arousal and deviant sexual preferences in an adult who has likely spent years 'refining' and 'hiding' his behavior (Hanson & Bussiere, 1998).

Cognitive Behavioral Therapy

Cognitive-Behavioral Therapy (CBT) is the historically favored approach for adult offender treatment (Orr, 1991). Its consistent application in the field and its evident relationship to cognitive-behavioral theory makes it an appropriate choice for the present discussion. According to CBT, the most effective change is said to come from recognizing the connection between thoughts, emotions and beliefs about offending and actual offending behavior (Lakey, 1994; Whitford & Parr, 1995).

The paramount goal of all sex offender treatment is the prevention of further victimization and the cessation of sexually inappropriate behavior (Orr, 1991; Perkins et al., 1998). CBT achieves this by employing the relapse prevention model to circumvent 'the build up to inappropriate sexual gratification' (Thomas, 1999:6) and to alter negative thoughts and cognitive distortions (Gabor & Ing, 1991:43). CBT focuses

Box 5.2
Treatment Goals, Components, Definitions and Findings from Behavioral and Cognitive-Behavioral Perspectives

Theoretical Influence	Goals	Treatment Type and Components	Treatment Definition and Description	Advantages, Disadvantages and Evaluative Findings
Behavioral Theory	Aims to reduce deviant arousal or remove libido	Aversion Therapy[1]	Pairing a noxious stimuli with images of the target behavior (can include nausea inducing agent, electrical shock, foul odor)	Mixed results. Very little empirical evidence. The most rigorous meta- analyses have found temporary advantages only.
		Covert sensitization[2]	Pairing an imagined aversive consequence with deviant thoughts to eliminate that thought or behavior	
		Masturbatory Satiation Therapy[3]	Continuation of masturbation during the unresponsive period immediately following orgasm while repeatedly evoking deviant fantasies	
		Shame Therapy[4]	Client acts out his molestation on a mannequin in front of staff or family members who do not respond to produce a feeling of extreme anxiety and shame	
Cognitive Behavioral Theory	Aims to increase self control and reduce the cognitive distortions that allow offending to occur	Relapse Prevention[5]	Focuses on deviant arousal, lapses are deviant, controllable and stoppable—addresses cognitive distortions that lead to offending	Is widely applicable. Meta-analyses consistently support the relapse prevention model. Limitations include that it requires high verbal intelligence and admission of the offense.
		Sexual education and social skills training[6]	Teaching appropriate sexual arousal patterns and pro-social attitudes	
		Reducing cognitive distortions[7]	Examining minimizations, denial and justifications of offending	

[1] Righthand and Welch, 2001.
[2] Righthand and Welch, 2001.
[3] Righthand and Welch, 2001.
[4] Schwartz and Cellini, 1996.
[5] Pithers in Schwartz and Cellini, 1996.
[6] Perkins et al., 1998.
[7] Perkins et al., 1998.

primarily on the individual's criminality in a confrontational and non-sympathetic manner, pays direct attention to abusive behaviors (Orr, 1991) and is characterized by logical, straightforward and highly structured techniques (Gabor & Ing, 1991). An additional advantage of CBT is its cost. It is less expensive and more flexible than some of the more invasive behavioral techniques as well as those that might require surgical expertise.

Importantly, because CBT requires 'a high level of cognitive ability on the part of the client,' (Gabor & Ing, 1991:50) its relevance for special populations including adolescents and developmentally delayed offenders has been questioned.

Sex Offender Treatment Program Evaluation

The paramount question of 'what works' and 'how do we know?' should be answered by rigorous research evaluations. Unfortunately, evaluative research of Sex Offender Treatment Programs (SOTPs) is still considered to be extremely problematic (Perkins et al., 1998). This is most often attributed to methodological weaknesses in research design, such as lack of randomization, use of small unmatched samples, variation in treatment approach and absence of control groups (Polizzi, MacKenzie & Hickman, 1999; Rasmussen, 1999; USGAO, 1996). Further, no two studies of SOTPs are directly comparable (Perkins et al., 1998).

Martinson's now legendary 1974 conclusion that 'nothing works' evidently shook the foundations of criminology and has had lasting effects on the level of commitment shown to offender rehabilitation. Despite psychology's dedication to treatment and rehabilitation ideals, the sexual abuse field was similarly devastated over a decade later. In a landmark meta-analysis of existing SOTPs, Furby, Weinrott, and Blackshaw (1989) came to their own damning conclusions that treatment had no effect on sexual recidivism. Researchers have spent the last fifteen years lamenting the effects of Furby et al. (1989) on the field and professional ideas have been contaminated by an echo of 'nothing works.'

Selected Sex Offender Treatment Program Evaluations Meta-Analyses

Treatment can be evaluated on a number of dimensions such as integrity, intermediate impacts, costs and outcome (Perkins et al., 1998). Since outcome measures of recidivism are the most accessible, most telling and most commonly provided, they will be used here. It is important to consider the re-offending rates of untreated offenders as a baseline against which to judge treatment effects (Perkins et al., 1998). Hanson and Bussiere (1998) achieve this in their meta-analysis of recidivism rates in the absence of treatment. The research findings and conclusions cited in this chapter come from a selection of recent meta-analyses and qualitative reviews conducted in the field. The three major evaluations that are outlined in Box 5.3 are described below.

The most noticeable obstacle to comparing different programs is the inconsistent definition and measure of recidivism. Recidivism has been operationalized as reconviction, re-arrest, failure of a polygraph, or violation of probation or parole (Hanson et al., 2002). Some studies delineate by sexual or nonsexual and violent or non-violent re-offense, and others use general re-offending regardless of offense type. Further, the measure of recidivism and data collection techniques that are employed range from police records to self report data, family interviews and community records.

Hall (1995) reviewed all treatment studies published since Furby et al.'s (1989) damning review in 1989. Perhaps in an attempt at neutralization, his conclusions are curiously positive. While treatment providers and professionals in the field of sexual abuse evidently appreciated this perspective, his findings have more recently been interpreted with caution.

Gallagher et al.'s (1999) meta-analysis of 25 sex offender treatment programs has been considered the most comprehensive and technically sophisticated review available (Hanson, 2002). The biggest advantages of this study are its international focus; attention to both published and unpublished treatment initiatives and its ability to delineate by offense type.

Hanson et al. (2002) provide the most recent and most highly anticipated and definitive meta-analytic review of psychological treatment for sex offenders to date. These researchers share all of the advantages that Gallagher and colleagues offer but boast a larger sample size, longer follow-up periods and inclusion of studies that randomly assigned cases to non-treatment control groups.

What Works in Sex Offender Treatment?

The summary provided here is drawn from the conclusions of various meta-analyses and qualitative reviews of sex offender treatment programs over the past 15 years. Clinical findings from various treatment programs are mostly consistent with theoretical predictions. However, because clinical significance does not equate to statistical significance, it is impossible to tell to what degree CBT is effective. Evidence suggests that a combination of group treatment and individual therapy works better than either in isolation; residential community programs are more effective than custodial programs for incarcerated offenders and the most promising results are coming from programs catering specifically to adolescents (Hall, 1995). Given a youth's greater capacity for change and the established advantages of early intervention, this is not surprising.

Box 5.3
Comparison of the Three Most Important Meta-Analyses of Sex Offender Treatment Programs in the Last Decade

	# studies	total n of SOs	Published or not published	# CM # R # all or mixed	Dominant Treatment type	Follow up period	Definition of recidivism	Data source	Average Treatment recidivism	Average control recidivism	Characteristics of programs with strongest treatment effects
Hall 1995	12	1,313	Published since Furby et al. (1989)	R (6) CM (10) mixed (5)	Not specified	Mean 6.85 years (SD 5.95)	Reconviction (2); other (10)	Official records (5); self-report (3); combination (4)	SRO 19%	SRO 27%	CBT over hormonal programs; longer follow ups; adolescent programs; community over institutional;
Gallagher et al. 1999	25	N/A	Both	R (13) CM (22) mixed (12)	CBT	N/A	Reconviction (3); re-arrest (18); other (4) (1)	Official records (18); combination (6); not specified	N/A	N/A	CBT; surgical castration;
Hanson et al. 2002	43	9,454	Both	N/A	CBT	12 months – 16 years (median 46 months)	Reconviction (8); Re-arrest (11); Parole violation, community reports and readmission (20)	CJ records (26); state records (19); self-report (9); not specified (6)	SRO 12.3% NS 27.9%	SRO 16.8% NS 39.2%	unpublished; when compared to alternative treatment than to untreated group; community over institutional;

SOs: sex offenders; # CM: number of programs for child molesters; # R: number of programs for rapists
all: number of programs for both child molesters and rapists, or programs that did not specify their clientele
CBT: Cognitive-Behavioral Therapy; SRO: sexual re-offense; NS: non-sexual re-offense

Other Populations

Discussions of female and adolescent populations are too often considered exclusively by a last minute paragraph before the conclusion. And regretfully, they are also addressed here.

In recent years, attention has turned to the reality of sexual abuse of children that is perpetrated by adolescents. At least one-half of the adult males who are known to have sexually offended against children admit to having started their offending before the age of 16. Findings from retrospective self-report surveys administered to sexually aggressive adults indicate a need to focus on the likelihood of juveniles to continue offending across the life course (Grant, 2000).

The number of adolescents who sexually abuse children as a percentage of all child sexual abusers is unknown (Grant, 2000; Erooga & Masson, 1999). Self-report studies with adult and adolescent offenders and their victims give some indication of the actual figures. Generally, it has been found that adolescent perpetrators are responsible for between one fifth and one third of all child sex offenses (Cavanagh-Johnson, 1988; Ford & Linney, 1995; Morrison, 1999; National Clearinghouse on Family Violence, 1997; Ryan, Metzner & Krugman, 1990; Stenson & Anderson, 1987). Some studies have found the figure to be well over 50 percent (Elliott & Smiljanich, 1994; James & Neil, 1996).

Sexual offending by females is less understood than offending by males. They are generally considered to make up 5 to 10 percent of all sexual offenders (Hislop, 2001). Female child molesters are often described in one of three ways. The *teacher/lover* offender non-violently instructs the child (usually a prepubescent boy) in love-making. The *male coerced* offender is directed into the abusive role by a persuasive male (Higgs, Canavan & Meyer, 1992; Briggs, 1995:138). The third type is the *predisposed* offender who usually has a transgenerational history of sexual abuse and may have had previous psychiatric diagnoses or treatment (Higgs, Canavan & Meyer, 1992). It is unclear whether female child molesters begin offending in adolescence, one study found that a conservative estimate of 75 percent had engaged in age inappropriate sexual behavior by the time they entered adolescence (Saradjian, 1996:66).

The official responses to females who sexually abuse are seldom consistent (Blues, Moffat & Telford, 1999; Elliott, 1993). Women criminals are consistently 'perceived to be either not women or not criminals' (Worrall, 1990:31). They are treated either with forgiving lenience or severe harshness. Exhibitionism by a female for example, might 'more readily be labeled promiscuity than viewed as a legal offense such as indecent exposure' (Fehrenbach & Monastersky, 1988:150). Consistent with the chivalry thesis, Miller et al. (1995) assert that most judges are reluctant to place girls in correctional settings. Prosecution for a sexual offense is a crucial step in acknowledging victim harm and in providing the offender with a chance to take responsibility for her behavior and seek treatment. Despite this, prosecutors have a tendency to decriminalize sexual offenses committed by women (Elliott, 1997:105). 'By discounting the existence of female offenders, researchers have invalidated the experience of hundreds of thousands of victims and denied female offenders the help they might have received in treatment' (Turner & Turner, 1994:11).

While women and girls have very specific treatment needs (Miller et al., 1995) they are considered better candidates for treatment than men and boys. It has been found that offending girls are less likely to deny their offense, blame the victim, or describe it incorrectly as 'love' (Cavanagh-Johnson, 1989). Further, they are far more likely to feel that their behaviour was wrong and to assume total responsibility for the incident (Fromuth & Conn, 1997). Importantly, therapy for female sex offenders is particularly beneficial when there is an opportunity to address their own victim/survivor issues (Blues, Moffat & Telford, 1999; Hirshberg & Riskin, 1996).

Box 5.4

Why Females Are Less Likely to Be Identified as Sex Offenders

Male victims seldom disclose abuse by females. Male conditioning teaches that sexual initiation by an older female is 'the ultimate beneficial educational experience for boys' (Briggs, 1993:36). The victim is generally assumed to be "lucky" because she made the first move (Cavanagh-Johnson, 1989:572). This leads to traumatic sexualization, which is one of the effects of child sexual abuse that Finklehor (in Saradjian, 1996) identified.

Boys are socialized to be the initiators of sexual activity and it is therefore quite difficult for them to admit to 'sexual subjugation'. This situation is 'magnified if the abuser is a woman' (Saradjian, 1996:16).

Briggs (1995:138) describes how the women's movement was at the 'forefront of publicizing the abuse of female children by men' and pioneered the establishment of women's shelters and help lines and survivor groups across the western world. These developments 'gave women the courage to reveal childhood abuse, which they had previously kept secret. In the meantime there was no similar recognition by male society of the existence and needs of abused boys' (Briggs, 1995:138). Regardless of their offender's sex, male victims 'have a long way to go to get past the resistance and backlash' that still exists (Mathews, 1997:58).

Conclusion

There are still a number of questions remaining about treatment. Future research should examine three issues. One relates to whether deniers should be admitted into a treatment program with admitters. Some argue that acceptance is the first step to recovery and having admitters and deniers in the same group can be disruptive. A second important topic for research is whether mandatory attendance should be required. While treatment is often required by court order, some treatment providers argue treatment is useless unless it is voluntary. The third issue concerns the importance, necessity or likelihood of family reunification. This is considered to be particularly relevant for incest offenders.

Traditional criminology fails to provide a theoretical understanding of sexual offending against children. Sources of official statistics, which are mostly accepted by criminologists, are equally inadequate since this crime is so rarely identified, disclosed or discussed. The knowledge we have garnered instead from clinical samples and psychological perspectives is useful in furthering our understanding of child molestation. Whether the offense is considered a modeled behavior, an alternative sexual preference or a rational act of criminality, behavioral and cognitive-behavioral theories hold that there is some level of learning (conscious or unconscious, intended or not) that encourages, disinhibits, and reinforces this behavior. The cognitive-behavioral perspective offers the most consistent explanation of child molestation and cognitive-behavioral therapy specifically, offers the best approach for individual therapy, group treatment and overall management of this troubled and troubling population.

Note

[1]   In regard to sexual offending, Finkelhor's (1984) four factor model integrates both of these perspectives and remains one of the most frequently cited theories in the field.

References

Adamson, R. (2002). "Don't Turn a Blind Eye When Boys Are Sexually Exploited by Women." *Ottawa Citizen*, (June 16):A14.

Andrews, D. and J. Bonta (2003). *The Psychology of Criminal Conduct,* Third Edition. Cincinnati, OH: Anderson Publishing Co.

Associated Press (AP) (2002). "New Jersey Teacher Who Had Sex with 13-Year-Old Student Gets Probation." *AP State and Local Wire* (May 24).

Bartol, C. (2002). *Criminal Behavior: A Psychosocial Approach*. New Jersey: Prentice Hall.

Becker, J. (1988). "The Effects of Child Sexual Abuse on Adolescent Sexual Offenders." In R. Wyatt and G. Johnson-Powell (eds.) *Lasting Effects of Child Sexual Abuse*. London: SAGE Publications.

Blues, A., C. Moffat, and P. Telford (1999). "Work with Adolescent Females Who Sexually Abuse: Similarities and Differences." In M. Erooga and H. Masson (eds.) *Children and Young People Who Sexually Abuse Others: Challenges and Responses,* London: Routledge.

Briggs, F. (1995). *From Victim to Offender*. Sydney: Allen and Unwin.

Broadhurst, R. and R. Maller (1992). "The Recidivism of Sex Offenders in the Western Australian Prison Population." *British Journal of Criminology*, 32(1):54-80.

Bureau of Justice Statistics (1997). http://www.ojp.usdoj.gov/bjs

Burton, D., A. Nesmith, and L. Badten (1997). "Clinician's Views on Sexually Aggressive Children and Their Families: A Theoretical Exploration." *Child Abuse and Neglect,* 21(2):157-170.

Cavanagh-Johnson, T. (1988). "Child Perpetrators: Children Who Molest Other Children – Preliminary Findings." *Child Abuse and Neglect,* 12:219-229.

Elliott, D. and K. Smiljanich (1994). "Sex Offending among Juveniles: Development and Response." *Journal of Pediatric Health Care*, 8(3):101-105.

Erooga, M. and H. Masson (eds.) (1999). *Children and Young People Who Sexually Abuse Others: Challenges and Responses*. London: Routledge.

Fagan, J. and S. Wexler (1988). "Explanations of Sexual Assault among Violent Delinquents." *Journal of Adolescent Research*, 3(3):363-385.

Finkelhor, D. (1984). *Child Sexual Abuse: New Theory and Research*. New York: The Free Press.

Finney, D. (2002). "Breaking the Silence: Sexual Abuse of Kids Causes Untold Misery." *Omaha World-Herald,* (April 7):LIVING, 1.

Flynn, B. (2002). "See Me after History Class . . . and I'll Strip!" *The Sun,* (April 5).

Ford, M. and J. Linney (1995). "Comparative Analysis of Juvenile Sex Offenders, Violent Nonsexual Offenders, and Status Offenders." *Journal of Interpersonal Violence*, 10(1):56-70.

Friedrich, W. and W. Luecke (1988). "Young School-Age Sexually Aggressive Children" *Professional Psychology: Research and Practice*, 19(2):155-164.

Fromuth, M. and V. Conn (1997). "Hidden Perpetrators: Sexual Molestation in a Non-Clinical Sample of College Women." *Journal of Interpersonal Violence,* 12(3):456-465.

Furby, Weinrott and Blackshaw (1989). "Sex Offender Recidivism: A Review." *Psychological Bulletin,* 105:3-30.

Gabor, P. and C. Ing (1991). "Stop and Think: The Application of Cognitive-Behavioral Approaches in Work with Young People." *Journal of Child and Youth Care,* 6(1):43-53.

Gallagher, C., D. Wilson, P. Hirschfield, M. Coggeshall, and D. MacKenzie (1999). "A Quantitative Review of the Effects of Sex Offender Treatment on Sexual Reoffending." *Corrections Management Quarterly,* 3(4):19-29.

Gelles, R. and G. Wolfner (1994). "Sexual Offending and Victimization: A Life Course Perspective." In A. Rossi (ed.) *Sexuality Across the Life Course.* Chicago: University of Chicago Press.

Giles, D. (2002) "Pupil 'Kidnapped.'" *Perth Sunday Times,* (May 19).

Gold, S. and T. Dirmann (2002). "Teacher Held in Kidnapping; Police Discover 33-year-old Woman in a Las Vegas Hotel Room with a 15-year-old Boy from Her Science Class. She Faces Felony Charges." *Los Angeles Times,* (May 3):CALIFORNIA METRO, 1.

Graham, K. (1996). "The Childhood Victimization of Sex Offenders: An Underestimated Issue." *International Journal of Offender Therapy and Comparative Criminology,* 40(3):192-203.

Grant, A. (2000). "The Historical Development of Treatment for Adolescent Sex Offenders." *Trends and Issues in Crime and Criminal Justice,* 145:1-6.

Hall, B. (2002). "Of Course, the Police Didn't Suspect LeTourneau." *Lewiston Morning Tribune,* (May 24):12A.

Hall, G. (1996). *Theory-Based Assessment, Treatment and Prevention of Sexual Aggression.* New York: Oxford University Press.

Hall, G. (1995). "Sex Offender Recidivism Revisited: A Meta-analysis of Recent Treatment Studies." *Journal of Consulting and Clinical Psychology,* 63(5):802-809.

Hanson, K. and M. Bussiere (1998). "Predicting Relapse: A Meta-Analysis of Sex Offender Recidivism Studies." *Journal of Consulting and Clinical Psychology,* 66(2):348-362.

Hanson, K., A. Gordon, A. Harris, J. Marques, W. Murphy, V. Quinsey, and M. Seto (2002). "First Report of the Collaborative Outcome Data Project on the Effectiveness of Psychological Treatment for Sex Offenders." *Sexual Abuse: A Journal of Research and Treatment,* 14(2):169-194.

Haskell, D. (2002). "Analysis: Molesters Lurk Anywhere." *United Press International,* (March 29):GENERAL NEWS.

Higgs, D., M. Canavan, and W. Meyer (1992). "Moving from Defence to Offence: The Development of an Adolescent Female Sex Offender." *The Journal of Sex Research,* 29(1):131-139.

Hirschberg, D. and K. Riskin (1994). "Female Adolescent Sexual Offenders in Residential Treatment: Characteristics and Treatment Implications." Available at http://www.germainelawrence.org/web/fasort.html

Hirschi, T. and M. Gottfredson (1983). "Age and the Explanation of Crime." *American Journal of Sociology,* 89:552-584.

Hislop, J. (2001). *Female Sex Offenders: What Therapists, Law Enforcement and Child Protective Services Need to Know*. Washington: Issues Press.

Innes, M. (1997). "Commentary." *Journal of Child and Youth Care*, 11(1):63-64.

James, A. and P. Neil (1996). "Juvenile Sexual Offending: One Year Period Prevalence Study within Oxfordshire." *Child Abuse and Neglect,* 20(6):477-485.

Kluger, J. (2002). "Why Do They Target Kids?: The Molesters' Mind-Set." *Time,* (April 1):37.

Lakey, J. (1994). "The Profile and Treatment of Male Adolescent Sex Offenders." *Adolescence,* 29(116):755-761.

Lee, R. (1993). *Doing Research on Sensitive Topics*. London: SAGE Publications.

Mathews, F. (1997). "The Adolescent Sex Offender Field in Canada: Old Problems, Current Issues and Emerging Controversies." *Journal of Child and Youth Care,* 11(1):55-62.

Martinson, R. (1974). "What Works? Questions and Answers about Prison Reform." *The Public Interest,* 36:22-54.

Mitchell, M. (2002). "LeTourneau's Relationship with Boy 'Torture Not True Love' Lawyer Says." *AP State and Local Wire,* (May 15).

Morrison, T. (1999). "Is There a Strategy Out There? Policy and Management Perspectives on Young People Who Sexually Abuse Others." In M. Erooga and H. Masson (eds.) *Children and Young People Who Sexually Abuse Others: Challenges and Responses*. London: Routledge.

National Clearinghouse on Family Violence (1997). "Adolescent Sex Offenders." Available at http://www.hc-sc.gc.ca/hppb/familyviolence/html/adosxof.htm.

O'Reilly, (2002). "Back of the Book." *The O'Reilly Factor,* (May 29).

Orr, B. (1991). "Male Adolescent Sex Offenders: A Comparison of Two Treatment Approaches." *Journal of Child and Youth Care*, special issue:87-101.

Perkins, D., S. Hammond, D. Coles, and D. Bishopp (1998). *Review of Sex Offender Treatment Programmes* – prepared for the High Security Psychiatric Services Commissioning Board (HSPSCB) Department of Psychology, Broadmoor Hospital.

Peters, B. (2002) "Sex with an Adult Just as Harmful for Boys." *Lewiston Morning Tribune,* (June 9):1A.

Polizzi, D., D. MacKenzie, and L. Hickman (1999). "What Works in Adult Sexual Offender Treatment? A Review of Prison and Non-Prison Based Treatment Programs." *International Journal of Offender Therapy and Comparative Criminology,* 43(3):357-374.

Prentky, R. and R. Knight (1993). "Age of Onset of Sexual Assault: Criminal and Life History Correlates." In G. Nagayama Hall, R. Hirschman, J. Graham, and M. Zaragoza (eds.) *Sexual Aggression: Issues in Etiology, Assessment and Treatment,* Washington: Taylor & Francis.

Radue, A. (2002). "Students Address Teacher-Student Relationships in Light of Area Cases." *Milwaukee Journal Sentinel*, (May 6):4E.

Rasmussen, L. (1999). "Factors Related to 'Recidivism Among Juvenile Sexual Offenders." *Sexual Abuse: A Journal of Research and Treatment,* 11(1):69-85.

Righthand, S. and C. Welch (2001). *Juveniles Who Have Sexually Offended: A Review of the Professional Literature*. Washington: Office of Juvenile Justice and Delinquency Prevention.

Riley, R. (2002). "Sex with Kids Illegal for the Right Reasons." *Detroit Free Press*, (May 29).

Ryan, G., J. Metzner, and R. Krugman (1990). In K. Oates (ed.) *Understanding and Managing Child Sexual Abuse*. Sydney: Harcourt Brace Jovanovich Publishers.

Samenow, S. (1984). *Inside the Criminal Mind*. New York: Time Books.

Sapp, A. and M. Vaughn (1990). "Juvenile Sex Offender Treatment at State-Operated Correctional Institutions." *International Journal of Offender Therapy and Comparative Criminology,* 34(2):131-145.

Saradjian, J. (1996). *Women Who Sexually Abuse Children: From Research to Clinical Practice*. Chichester, West Sussex, England: John Wiley and Sons.

Schwartz, B. and R. Cellini (eds.) (1996). *The Sex Offender: New Insights, Treatment Innovations and Legal Developments*. New Jersey: Civic Research Institute.

Sefarbi, R. (1990). "Admitters and Deniers among Adolescent Sex Offenders and Their Families: a Preliminary Study." *American Journal of Orthopsychiatry*, 60(3):460-465.

Stanley, S. (2002). "Reports of Sex Abuse by Women Increase: Experts Say Attacks Not as Rare as Thought." *The Times-Picayune*, (June 9):METRO, 1.

Stenson, P. and C. Anderson (1987). "Child Care Commentary: Treating Juvenile sex Offenders and Preventing the Cycle of Abuse." *Journal of Child Care*, 3(2):91-101.

Sykes, G. and D. Matza (1959). "Techniques of Neutralization: A Theory of Delinquency." *American Sociological Review*, 22.

Taylor, P. (2002). "Beyond Myths and Denial: What Church Communities Need to Know about Sexual Abusers." *America*, 11(186):7.

United States General Accounting Office (1996). *Sex Offender Treatment: Research Results Inconclusive About What Works to Reduce Recidivism*. Report to the Chairman, Subcommittee on Crime, Committee on the Judiciary, House of Representatives. (GAO/GGD-96-137)

Veneziano, C., L. Veneziano, and S. LeGrand (2000). "The Relationship between Adolescent Sex Offender Behaviours and Victim Characteristics with Prior Victimization." *Journal of Interpersonal Violence,* 15(4):363-374.

Ward, T. and S. Hudson (1998). "The Construction and Development of Theory in the Sexual Offending Area: A Meta-Theoretical Framework." *Sexual Abuse: A Journal of Research and Treatment,* 10(1):47-63.

Weisburd, D. (2000). "Randomized Experiments in Criminal Justice Policy: Prospects and Problems." *Crime & Delinquency*, 46(2):181-193.

Whitford, R. and V. Parr (1995). "Uses of Rational Emotive Behavior Therapy with Juvenile Sex Offenders." *Journal of Rational-Emotive and Cognitive-Behavior Therapy*, 13(4):273-283.

Worling, J. (1995a). "Adolescent Sex Offenders against Females: Differences Based on the Age of their Victims." *International Journal of Offender Therapy and Comparative Criminology*, 39(3):276-293.

Worling, J. (1995b). "Adolescent Sibling-Incest Offenders: Differences in Family and Individual Functioning When Compared to Adolescent Non-Sibling Sex Offenders." *Child Abuse and Neglect*, 19(5):633-643.

Young, C. (2002). "The Bias against Male Victims." *The Boston Globe*, (June 3):A13.

Chapter 6

Rape

Ashlee Parker

Introduction

Rape is a destructive crime, to both victims and the social structure. Estimates indicate the United States has the highest incidence of rape in the world (Bartol, 2003). Understanding rape is a difficult venture, because sometimes what we think we know is actually a misconception. This chapter will begin by discussing the incidence and prevalence of rape in this country along with the sources and weaknesses of rape data. Perspectives of rape and rape myths will also be presented. The chapter also explores some of the patterns and characteristics that have emerged to describe the victims, offenders, and the contexts in which rape occurs. Attempts to create useful typologies will be summarized followed by theoretical perspectives of rape and discussion of possible treatment for rapists.

Data on Rape

The Uniform Crime Report (UCR) is a set of data collected from law enforcement agencies of crimes reported to police. The definition of rape employed by the UCR limits the scope of acts and victims included in statistics of rape:

> *Forcible rape . . . is the carnal knowledge of a female forcibly and against her will. Assaults or attempts to commit rape by force or threat of force are also included; however, statutory rape (without force) and other sex offenses are excluded* (FBI, 2001:29).

According to the Uniform Crime Report, 90,491 rapes were reported in 2001, at a rate of 31.8 per 100,000 inhabitants. However, because the UCR defines victims of rape as female, the actual rate is 62.2 rapes for every 100,000 females (FBI, 2001). The rates of rape reported vary by region: the Northeast Region reported 13.4 percent of the nation's rapes (44.0 per 100,000 females); the West reported 23.7 percent (65.2 per 100,000 females); the Midwestern States reported 25.1 percent (68.6 per 100,000 females); and the South reported the highest percentage of rapes in the nation with 37.8 percent (65.8 per 100,000 females) (FBI, 2001). The highest incidence rate for rape occurs in metropolitan areas, at 67.7 per 100,000 females (FBI, 2001).

Reported rapes faced a relatively low rate of clearance in 2001, defined by the UCR as arrest and charge of a suspect for the offense or the involvement of conditions that prevented an arrest from occurring. For example, when the victim refuses to cooperate with prosecutors the case would be classified as cleared (FBI, 2001). Overall, rape has a 44.3 percent rate of clearance, with the Northeast clearing 50.1 percent of reported rapes. Other regions clear less than half of all reported rapes (FBI, 2001). For juvenile offenders the UCR considers a case cleared when the case is turned over to juvenile court, which accounts for 12.4 percent of all clearances (FBI, 2001). The number of arrests for rape in 2001 was 23,270 and 45.4 percent of those arrested were under 25 years old, 62.7 percent were white, and 98.8 percent were male (FBI, 2001).

The UCR data on rape gives us some idea about the incidence, prevalence, and dispersion of rape in the United States, even if the definition employed is exclusionary and the cases included in the determination of clearance are overly inclusive. According to the UCR data, of the 90,491 reported rapes, only 40,088 of those rapes were cleared, with 4,971 of those cleared going to juvenile court. Of reported rapes, 50,404 were never cleared (FBI, 2001). Unfortunately, the very nature of rape and the trauma rape victims experience, both during and after the act, make the reported statistics on rape suspect. In fact, the National Crime Victimization Survey (NCVS) estimates that two-thirds of all rapes (and sexual assaults) go unreported (BJS, 2002). This drastic rate of underreporting of rape masks the extent of rape in this country.

The NCVS is a longitudinal self-report of victimization for various crimes in the United States by randomly surveyed households. The NCVS definition of rape is very different from that used by the UCR:

> *Rape is forced sexual intercourse, including* both psychological coercion and physical force. *Forced sexual intercourse means* vaginal, anal, or oral penetration *by the offender(s). . . . This definition includes attempted rapes*, male and female victims, *and* heterosexual and homosexual rape (BJS, 2002:14; emphasis added).

According to the NCVS, there were 146,000 rapes or attempted rapes in 2001, a rate of 60 rapes per 100,000 persons 12 or older (BJS, 2002), nearly twice the rate expected by UCR data (which also includes victims under the age of 12). The NCVR estimates that most victims are female, between the ages of 16-24, and 65 percent knew their rapists (BJS, 2002). For all rape and sexual assault cases revealed to the NCVS researchers, only 38.6 percent were reported to police (BJS, 2002). Similar to UCR data, the NCVS data shows that more rapes occur in urban areas, but the NCVS data gives us more information about the victim. A large portion of rape victims live in poverty, but they can be found at all income levels (BJS, 2002). Finally, except for the Northeast Region, which showed somewhat lower victimization, the regional occurrence of rape is fairly even (BJS, 2002).

Box 6.1
Information on the Occurrence of Rape with Different Data Sources

	UCR		**NCVS**
Incidence	90,491 offenses reported in 2001.		146,000 rapes/attempted rapes in 2001
Prevalence (2001)	31.8 per 100,000		60.0 per 100,000 persons 12 or older
	62.2 per 100,000 females		190 per 100,000 persons 12 or older for females
Reported to Police			38.6% rape/ sexual assault
Arrests	27,270 persons	45.4% under 25 62.7% white 98.8% male	
Clearances (Arrested and Charged, or Beyond Control of Law Enforcement	44.3% rapes cleared		
	12.4% juveniles		
Victim			34% between age 16-19 24% between age 20-24 65% nonstranger rape 35% stranger rape

FBI (2001). Uniform Crime Report; Bureau of Justice Statistics (2002). The National Crime Victimization Survey.

Perception of Rape and "Rape Myths"

How rape is perceived and understood by offenders, victims, and outside observers is often a function of society. As a result, much of the past literature on rape maintained that the main causes of rape were attributed to the uncontrollable impulses and urges of men, the presence of mental illness or disease, a momentary loss of control due to mitigating factors (drugs, alcohol), and instigation by the victim (Bartol, 2002). These rape myths have persisted in the general public's perception of the causes of rape, the victim, and the offender. These themes are also often used to explain rape by offenders themselves.

Box 6.2

Rape Myths

1. Men's sexuality is uncontrollable and impulsive

2. Rapists are inherently pathological

3. Loss of control due to external factors, like alcohol or drugs

4. The victim instigated the attack by wearing provocative clothing or behaving in a sexual way

---

Lea and Auburn (2001) present a case study of a convicted rapist, focusing on the language he used to describe the rape and the patterns that emerged in his discussion of the offense. According to the authors, "rape myths operate as 'practical ideologies'" made up of "the often contradictory and fragmentary complexes of notions, norms and models which guide conduct and allow for its justification and rationalization" (Lea & Auburn, 2001:13). Lea and Auburn (2001) found certain patterns emerging in the talk of the rapist they investigated (through recordings of treatment sessions). Three particular themes emerged that supported the dominant practical ideologies: the ambiguity of the victim's role and motive, the storyteller as passive and empathic, and the co-perpetrator as a brutal rapist. The rapist used rape myths to describe his own behavior and motives and his vocabulary was more descriptive of a consensual act than a rape. The rapist had learned how he was "supposed" to speak about particular people and circumstances, and corrected his mistakes, despite consistent language throughout that limited his culpability. Language, then, should be considered by therapists in the talk of rapists, and practitioners should be trained to recognize such cognitive distortions represented in discourse.

Research has shown that more rape victims are young, with 61 percent of victims below the age of 18 (Cowan & Campbell, 1995). Offenders also tend to be young (UCR, 2001) and to commit their first offense during adolescence (Groth, 1982). Therefore, it is important to understand how adolescents perceive rape. Cowan and Campbell (1995) investigated adolescents' attitudes about what causes rape based on familiar rape myths and theoretical ideologies (psychopathological, physiological, and sociocultural). Accordingly:

People accepting rape myths often tend to blame the female victim, suggesting that she asked to be raped, deserved rape, or wasn't really raped. Other rape myths focus on the perpetrator in two ways—first, that rapists are crazy or pathological men, and second, that men rape because they cannot control their sexuality (Cowan & Campbell, 1995:145).

The authors measured attitudes of high school aged boys and girls (n=453) for five causes of rape: male dominance, female blame, male sex drive/biology, society, and male pathology/anger. The findings show that boys were more likely to believe that female precipitation, male pathology and male sexuality caused rape, whereas girls were more likely to support male pathology as the major cause for rape. Girl's scores for female precipitation decreased as age and grade level increased. Communication with parents about rape increased systemic views (society and male dominance) with girls being more likely to report having discussed rape with parents than boys. Students who discussed rape with their parents scored lower on female precipitation scales. Students who discussed rape in class scored higher on societal and male pathology scales. No effects were found for students who discussed rape with siblings, friends, or in a rape-education program. Ultimately women are less likely to blame women for rape than men are, because of the potential for identification and projection of responsibility. Boys feel less responsibility when they attribute rape to "sick" men while girls use this myth to feel safe from potential rape. These views and the gender difference in variables of rape causal attitudes have important implications for rape educators, perhaps indicating a need for gender-specific rape prevention education and an increased understanding of the specific rape myths each group most strongly believes (Cowen & Campbell, 1995).

Trying to understand variability of support for rape myths, Kleinke and Meyer (1990) investigated perceptions of the rape victim by gender based on the just world hypothesis.

The just-world hypothesis holds that people can restore their belief in a just world by eliminating the suffering of innocent victims or derogating them for their plight. Since it is not possible to reverse a crime of rape, rape victims are subject to derogation. However, when observers identify with a victim by recognizing a common vulnerability, they are likely to respond with empathy rather than derogation (Kleinke & Meyer, 1990:344).

Their findings suggest that men with high just-world thinking were more negative toward the victim, but also viewed the crime as more serious. Women with high just-world thinking were more sympathetic toward the victim and placed more responsibility on the rapist. Participants who saw a video of the rape victim during an interview, versus merely reading a transcript, were more favorable toward the victim. This may indicate minimal familiarity has some effect on observer perception. Overall, participants with low just-world thinking recommended longer prison sentences. These findings could have important implications for jury trials on rape (Kleinke & Meyer, 1990).

Box 6.3

Rape in the News

The reality of rape is lost in many media depictions and impersonal news reels. The rape myths society uses to explain this behavior are often embedded in media accounts of rape. At the 2002 Cannes Film Festival, controversy erupted over the graphic representation of rape in *Irreversible,* a film by French director Gaspar Noe (CNN.com, 2002). The scene lasted a full nine minutes and resulted in 250 audience members walking out, 20 people fainting, and critics barraging the film as 'sick' and 'gratuitous' (BBC News, 2002). The discomfort in discussing rape, especially in entertainment media, was fully realized with this film, but the inability to present rape in the public discourse could be halting the progress we have been making in changing how people think about rape. As a side note, the remaining audience at the Cannes screening of *Irreversible* conferred a five-minute ovation on the film.

The news media seems most willing to report stories that most fully represent rape as it is conceived of in rape myths. While stories involving serial rapists are important, especially as warning to the community, the fact that these stories are seen as newsworthy while the epidemic of acquaintance rape in this country is not is quite telling. The stories involving serial rapists give us a disturbing picture of how this crime rips apart communities and its victims. In May of 2003, police in Columbus, Ohio faced the daunting task of tracking down a serial rapist that had been on the loose since 1991. Twenty-one victims had been linked to the suspect, including a mother and daughter, the fourth and first victims of the rapist. DNA evidence placed the rapist both in the Columbus community and in Los Angeles, California (Narciso & Mayhood, 2003). A similar scene was unfolding around the same time in Charlottesville, Virginia, where police were seeking public assistance in identifying and catching a serial rapist who had attacked six women since 1997 and six more were being investigated as possibly linked to the same suspect. In this case the rapist had attacked within the university community, including five University of Virginia students and one employee (Associated Press, 2003). A string of four rapes in Idaho were linked to one attacker in early 2004. The rapist illegally entered the homes of the victims and hid his identity from victims by wearing a mask, approaching from behind, or flashing a light in victims' eyes (Taylor, 2004).

Rape law reforms have been enacted in most states since the 1970s, in an attempt to increase victims' willingness to come forward and to eliminate practices that re-victimize rape victims in the courtroom. Legislation in many cases has included Rape-Shield Laws to protect the victim from being put on trial for past behaviors or the use of rape myths as detractors from the trial of the defendant.

Box 6.3, *continued*

The Rape-Shield laws have faced their most recent test in the highly charged, media frenzy that surrounds the trial of Kobe Bryant, the basketball player facing trial for rape in Colorado. Since accusations hit the media in 2003, the victims' past sexual and mental health history, among other unseemly details, have emerged outside of the courtroom (Paulson, 2004). The Kobe Bryant case is not a typical rape case. Bryant's celebrity status made the case of national interest. The stories and discussion coming out about the case are riddled with rape myths: Bryant could not have raped the accuser because he has a beautiful wife at home; the victim allegedly had sex with other men and "a slut cannot be raped"; women cry rape to get revenge or attention; Bryant is a "nice guy" and a "role model;" and the list goes on (Vachss, 2003). In reality, rape is not tied to need or opportunity for consensual sex. The idea of a "real" or worthy rape victim is malicious and questioning a victim's behaviors or actions within the lens of traditional sex role stereotypes is both dangerous and prejudicial. According to FBI statistics, false accusations of rape are no more common than for other crimes. Alice Vachss (2003), former New York prosecutor, points to one case in which a rapist pleaded to 80 charges of sexual assault and had been voted local "Man of the Year." These and other rape myths that people use to color their understanding of rape are not only wrong in most cases, but dangerous. Prosecutors of the Bryant case will be lucky if they can find potential jurors without some knowledge of the media's portrayal of the victim and the case (Vachss, 2003). Current and future victims are also seeing the destruction of the victims' credibility and reputation in the media, which could very likely prevent them from coming forward and reporting their victimization. However this case turn out, no one wins. The plight of rape victims being re-victimized by the judicial system is a set-back and if the case turns out to be a false accusation, women reporting rape will be scrutinized.

Offender Characteristics

When studying the data, certain patterns emerge between victim, offender and situational factors of rape. The investigation of these patterns, especially those surrounding the offender, will not only help in our understanding of the crime of rape and those who commit such crimes, but will also pave the way toward improved treatment and management of these offenders, with the ultimate goal of preventing victimization.

The view that offenders are different than non-offenders, or that individual differences can be identified as causes of criminal behavior has historically been restricted to the field of psychology. The issue of specialization among offenders is also controversial, with some researchers positing that sex offenders are no different than non-sex offenders (Andrews & Bonta, 2003), while others tending to focus on perceived differences. It is the opinion of the author that understanding differences between sex offenders and between rapists and other sex offenders in particular, will greatly benefit research on sex offenders and eventually policy. As it stands, the current research available on rapist characteristics group rapists into one group, which could mask potential differences between different types of rapists.

Official data indicate that a near majority of arrested rape offenders are 25 years or younger (UCR, 2001). In a study investigating age and history of sexual convictions, Dickey, Nussbaum, Chevolleau, and Davidson (2002) found that rapists were most represented in young adult (18-25) and adult (26-40) age groups in their sample of sex offenders. Non-sadistic rapists showed the greatest decline in offending after the age of 40, whereas sadistic sex offenders (age of victim not used to classify) offend consistently throughout their life (Dickey et al., 2002). While sadistic sexual offenders were most likely to have previous sexual offenses (66% of young adults), non-sadistic rapists tended to commit more offenses when they were young (39.6% for young adults) (Dickey et al., 2002). Hanson (2002) also found age to be a significant factor for rape and recidivism levels. Rapists tended to be younger than other types of sex offenders, with about half being under age 30. Rapists' risk for recidivism decreased with age, with the average recidivism rate at 17 percent (Hanson, 2002).

Because sexual offending often begins at an early age, research on adolescent offenders is important in understanding rapists. Hagan and his colleagues (Hagan, Gust-Brey, Cho & Dow, 2001) compared juvenile sex offenders, juvenile non-sex offenders, and the general juvenile population (male). Delinquents with any offense have higher risk of sex offending than "normal" juveniles. No difference in risk of sex offending between juveniles who raped peers and juveniles who raped/molested children. Juvenile sex offenders have higher risk of future sex offending than juveniles convicted of a non-sex offense. This study illustrates the point that sex offending and rape behavior in particular likely start in adolescence, and that while all adolescent delinquents are more likely to commit rape than your average adolescent, some seem to have a predilection and present a higher risk at sex offending than adolescents with non-sex related delinquency (Hagan et al., 2001).

The idea that rapists are somehow different from the non-sex offending population has been explored. Dreznick (2003) looked into the presence of heterosocial competence as a characteristic of rapists. Heterosocial competence is the ability to successfully and adequately interact with members of the opposite sex and to correctly interpret romantic cues. In a meta-analysis (n=119 different studies), Dreznick (2003) found that rapists had higher levels of heterosocial competence than child molesters, but lower levels than non-sex offenders; non-incarcerated rapists had lower levels of heterosocial competence than non-incarcerated non-sex offenders; and incarcerated rapists had lower levels of heterosocial competence than non-incarcerated non-sex offenders, but showed no difference with incarcerated non-sex offenders. Dreznick (2003) concludes that rapists do not have a great deficiency in heterosocial competence and disputes the argument that rapists engage in sexual coercion because they cannot form consensual relationships.

This theme of deficiency in the offender has inspired further research into offender characteristics. Porter et al. (2000) investigated the existence of psychopathy in offender populations at a medium-security Canadian prison that housed 10 percent of Canada's adult sex offender population (n=329). Using psychopathy scores from the Psychopathy Checklist-Revised (PCL-R), from a varied sample of sex offenders (including child molesters and mixed rapist-molesters) and non-sex offenders, the authors compared the prevalence of psychopathy as a function of offender type. Findings indicate that mixed rapist/molester types had the highest prevalence of psychopathy (64%), while rapists and non-sex offenders had similarly high scores (about 35%). They also found that while these groups showed similarly high levels of psychopathy, rapists scored higher on Factor 1 measures (glibness/superficial charm, grandiosity, pathological lying, lack of remorse, shallow affect, lack of empathy, and failure to accept responsibility), while non-sex offenders scored higher on Factor 2 measures (need for stimulation/prone to boredom, poor behavioral controls, promiscuity, early behavioral problems, lack of realistic goals, impulsivity, irresponsibility, juvenile delinquency, and revocation of conditional release). Understanding differences between offenders convicted of sexual violence and other offenders is important to issues like security, sentencing, and ultimate release of offenders.

Dangerousness is often measured by potential recidivism. In an effort to understand the low recorded recidivism rates in combination with the general clinical belief that sex offending is not situational, but likely to reoccur, Groth et al. (1982) compared a sample of rapists and child molesters (n=83 and n=54, respectively). Two-thirds of the rapists (65%) had one or more prior convictions, with an average of 2.8 priors. Undetected rapes were reported for 81.4 percent of the first group and 48.5 percent of the second, averaging 5.2 undetected rapes combined. In order to obtain a more conservative average, rapists who reported the highest numbers of undetected rapes were excluded from these calculations. Had they been included, rapists would have averaged 14 undetected offenses, indicating that like non-sex offenders a small number of individuals offend at a much higher rate. The findings suggest an early onset of rape behaviors in adolescence (most between ages 16-18, average of 17.6-19.6) (Groth et al., 1982). Overall, the authors suggest that the offenders studied were serious recidivists and avoided detection twice as often as they are caught for their crimes, displaying a recidivism rate comparable to non-sex offenders. Additionally, this type of offending is chronic and more psychologically than situationally determined. The low recidivism rate of these offenses reflects the low visibility, and thus cannot be used as a measure of a program's effectiveness. Finally, the onset of rape behavior during juvenile years has implications for treatment, and can mislead officials who often do not see juvenile records once they are expunged. Overall, the undetected levels of rape correspond with victimization surveys, and go to show that far more rapes occur than are reported to officials, and of those reported few will result in a conviction, leading to unrepresentative conclusions about the actuality of rape (Groth et al., 1982).

One would expect those rapists that make it into the criminal justice system to be the most serious offenders; however, undetected rapes occur in which the offender is never caught. Lisak and Miller (2002) investigated the occurrence of rape among a sample of male students who had never been arrested for an offense (N=1,882). Of those surveyed, 120 (6.4%) self-reported committing rape, with 63.3 percent of those reporting multiple rapes (average 5.8 each). These undetected rapists were serious offenders (the majority reported committing other violent crimes) showing similarities with incarcerated rapists. However, they tended to choose victims they were acquainted with and did not cause extensive physical injury, making victims less likely to report the offense and prosecutors less likely to charge (Lisak & Miller, 2002). These disturbing findings highlight the fact that many rapists are never detected by the criminal justice system and remain in the community committing violent sexual criminal acts.

Box 6.4

Female Rapists and Sexual Assaulters

Rape and sexual assault are typically considered crimes only committed by men, however, recently attention has turned to the existence of female rapists and sexual assaulters. This topic is still fairly new and the rarity of female sex offenders (of adult victims) makes research difficult. According to the Bureau of Justice Statistics (2000), 1 in 50 violent sexual offenders is a woman, accounting for 2 percent of all violent sexual offenders with about 10,000 reported annually by their victims. Felony convictions for rape/sexual assault for women varies from year to year, reaching 630 in 1994 and dropping to 442 in 1996 (BJS, 2000). Female offenders of rape and sexual assault make up about 1 percent of state prison admissions (BJS, 2000), comprising .4 percent of offenders in state prisons for rape and 1.2 percent of offenders in for sexual assault (BJS, 2002). The accumulation of these statistics by the Bureau of Justice Statistics (2000) stems from various sources that differ on definitions of rape. This could be a problem in determining actual numbers of female sexual assaulters and rapists, because the victims' ages are not reported making it impossible to tell if these offenses are rapes/sexual assault of adult or child victims.

Box 6.4, *continued*

Much of the literature on female sex offenders involves the abuse of children. Until recently, criminal justice officials did not take seriously the fact that women can sexually aggress and that female rapists can victimize other women as well as men (Travin, Cullen & Protter, 1990). Sarrell and Masters (in Travin et al., 1990) attempted to classify female rapists into four groups: (1) the forced sexual assault of adults, (2) abuse by hired caregivers/babysitters, (3) incest, and (4) "dominant woman abuse" of adult victims. This typology, however, is based on a case study of eleven, making the methodology weak, and the typology itself groups all female sex offenders. Stemming from research on clinical treatment of men raped by women, Masters (1986) speculates that female rapists may not be much different from male rapists in their reasons and methods. Based on interviews with male victims, Masters interjects,

As the sexual assaults continued, other distractive elements entered the victim's level of awareness: his attackers' derogatory comments, feelings of humiliation, threats of castration, sadistic manipulation of the genitals, and even threats on his life . . . Although the women who carried out the sexual assaults have not been interviewed, a possible parallel exists in the motivations of male and female "perpetrators" of sexual attack (Masters, 1986:40).

More research is needed to determine if actual differences exist between male and female sex offenders. Until this is done, creating separate typologies for female offenders is fruitless. As sex offenders are typically differentiated on the basis of the age of their victim, grouping female child molesters with rapists of adult victims seems counterintuitive. It is evident by the lack of knowledge on this topic, that research on female rapists and sexual assaulters can and should be undertaken with attention focusing on possible differences from male sex offenders, and from females who abuse children. Additionally, female victims of female sexual assaulters cannot be forgotten, as male victims of rape have been until recently. At this point in time, we know women can and do sexually assault and rape men and women, either alone or with other male or female attackers. This may be a rare occurrence, but we cannot ignore these offenders or their victims in research or in policy.

Victim and Situational Characteristics

Victims of rape and sexual assault tend to display some general characteristics. Young women between the ages of 16-24 are most likely to be victims of rape and sexual assault (BJS, 2002a). Women between the ages of 16-19 have a 34 percent rate of victimization among persons ages 12 and older (BJS, 2002a). Victims of rape and sexual assault tend to be single at the time of their victimization, with women who have never been married having a victimization rate of 21 percent and divorced or separated women being victimized at a rate of

20 percent for persons 12 and older (BJS, 2002a). Women in urban areas are more likely to be victims of rape and sexual assault, having a 19 percent victimization rate for persons 12 and older (BJS, 2002a). Additionally, like men who are at greater risk of committing sexual assault and rape, women who hold more traditional beliefs are at higher risk of being raped (Rosenthal, Heesacker & Neimeyer, 1995). Characteristics of traditionality (sex role stereotyping) include the belief that men should be aggressors in sexual relationships, while women remain passive. A woman's refusal is considered a sign of her femininity and need to retain her reputation and not necessarily a demand to stop sexually aggressive behavior. Women who believe leading a man on is a justification for rape are more likely to experience rape and sexual assault (Rosenthal et al., 1995). The acceptance of such rape myths and attitudes that incorrectly identify causes of rape place women at great risk, just as men with such attitudes are more likely to display sexually aggressive behavior (Rosenthal et al., 1995; O'Donohue, Yeater & Fanetti, 2003).

Alcohol and other substances are commonly involved in most rape cases. A large number of convicted rapists and victims of acquaintance rape report alcohol or substance abuse (Bartol, 2002). Brecklin and Ullman (2001) further investigated offender alcohol use in rape attacks (n=362) by analyzing data from the NCVS. Two thirds of offenders (75.9%) were judged to be under the influence of alcohol. The assaults tended to take place indoors (83.5%), at night (78.1%), and involved physical aggression (97%). Sixty-one percent of rapes were completed and 37.9 percent of victims sustained some injury. Findings suggest that offender use of alcohol is related to more risky situations, including stranger assaults, night assaults, outdoor locations, and greater victim resistance. However, alcohol use by the offender actually leads to less rape completion, and was unrelated to severity of physical injury. In addition to offender alcohol use, victims of rape have also been found to have past histories of alcohol and drug problems (Karp, Silber, Holmstrom & Stock, 1995) and more frequent drinking in bars has been associated with greater risk of sexual victimization (Parks & Zetes-Zanatta, 1999). These results have important implications for rape-prevention education. Women should be informed about the relationships between alcohol use, situational factors and rape outcomes.

The issue of victim resistance can have important implications for victims of sexual assault. Some researchers claim that resistance on the part of the victim may lead to increased injury from certain rapist types, specifically pervasively angry or sadistic types, which will be discussed later (Bartol, 2002; Ullman & Knight, 1995). Ullman and Knight (1995) analyzed police reports and court testimonies of raped and rape avoidant women (n=147), looking specifically at rape avoidance strategies and rapist type. Resistance types included forceful fighting (i.e., punching, kicking, pulling offender's hair, using a weapon or martial arts technique; used by 28 percent of women in the study; fleeing/pushing the offender away (53%); screaming, yelling or threatening the offender (42%); and pleading, crying, or reasoning with the offender (57%). Findings suggested that rapist type had little effect on increased sexual abuse as victims increased resistance strategies. In fact, while increased force in resistance does not increase the amount of violence experienced by victims, it can decrease the probability that the rape will be completed. Thus, Ullman and Knight (1995) suggest that level of violence employed by offender, not rapist type, should be used to determine resistance strategies, with an equal level of resistance for the level of physical violence experienced. This finding is dramatically important for victims, as they are not likely to be able to differentiate rapist type during the offense, and ultimately by resisting, they could avoid the more serious psychological damage associated with rape completion (Ullman & Knight, 1995). Educating women on appropriate resistance strategies, as opposed to telling them to avoid any resistance, could save women from the trauma of rape while allowing them some sense of control.

Box 6.5

Male Victims of Rape and Sexual Assault

The sexual assault and rape of adult males is largely ignored by researchers and misunderstood by the public. Like rape of female victims, male-male sexual assault is misperceived as a function of rape myths. These myths are, that: (1) Men cannot be raped, (2) Rape of males is confined to prisons and other sex-segregated institutions, (3) Offenders who rape men and adolescent boys are homosexual and their victims are heterosexual, and (4) Women do not sexually assault or rape men (Stermac, Sheridan, Davidson & Dunn, 1996). Male victims of rape and sexual assault may be less likely to report rape or seek medical or psychiatric help, because of perceived and actual stigma. Like female victims, males face "victim blame." In a study of counselor-trainees, an average overall acceptance of rape myths was found and male victims were more likely to face blame when they failed to make an active attempt to resist their attacker (Kassing & Prieto, 2003). The limited research that has been conducted on this topic gives us some idea that this problem is largely underestimated and that assumptions about male victims of sexual assault are incorrect.

According to the National Crime Victimization Survey (BJS, 2002a), there were 22,930 rapes or sexual assaults of male victims in 2001. Of these, 6,770 were completed rapes and 16,160 were sexual assaults, at a rate of 0.1 rapes and 0.1 sexual assaults per 1,000 persons age 12 or over (BJS, 2003). This translates into 1 rape/sexual assault of a male victim for every 5,000 male residents age 12 or older (BJS, 2002b). Based on respondent information, 67 percent of these incidents were

Box 6.5, *continued*

committed by a friend or acquaintance and 33 percent were committed by a stranger (BJS, 2002a). These statistics are undoubtedly massive underestimations, due to the stigma attached to rape in general and to male victims in particular. Some estimates indicate that 5 percent to 10 percent of all sexual assault victims are male (Kaufman, Divasto, Jackson, Voorhees & Christy, 1980).

A study conducted by Stermac et al. (1996) found that male victims seeking help at a rape crisis center made up about 7 percent of the total number of victims entering the unit. More than half (55%) of the men were under 25, and the average age was 26.86 (SD = 10.36, range 18-65). The authors (Kaufman et al., 1996) were surprised to find their sample was made up of highly vulnerable victims, with 14 percent having physical disabilities and 21 percent cognitively impaired. Most of the offenders reported were lone males (86%), half were strangers, nearly half (43%) reported two or more assailants and multiple assaults (48%), and many of the cases involved victim use of alcohol (46%) or drugs (18%). Overall, Stermac et al. concluded that many male-victim rapes are similar to heterosexual date rapes, involving young, gay men. This study employed a small sample (N = 29) and occurred at a rape crisis center, and as a result may not provide us with generalizable results.

In a more recent study, Hodge and Canter (1998) collected data from victim self-report surveys (N = 83) and police reports (N = 36). Hodge and Canter (1998) found the sample of offenders to fall into two distinct categories: heterosexual offenders who target unknown males regardless of age or sexuality with control and domination-based motivation; and homosexual offenders with some relationship to the victim, who target young men (aged 16-25 years) through manipulation and coercion. This study found a higher occurrence of sexual assault by heterosexual offenders (55%). Differences emerged in sexuality of victim-offender depending on whether the data was from self-report or police report. More heterosexual victims reported their assault to police (60% vs. 32%), more offenders in the self-report sample were believed heterosexual in comparison with the police sample (45% vs. 22%), and most victims in self-report knew their attacker (51%). This study found, in contrast to Stermac et al. (1996) that most sexual assault involved only one offender. The high number of gang assaults (34%), however, is disturbing, and most (66%) of these involve heterosexual offenders and are likely a function of homophobia and gay bashing. Homosexual victims in this study experienced more serious injuries (45% vs. 36%). Overall, Hodge and Canter (1998) suggest the sample characteristics vary significantly depending on the source of the data. Specifically, offender populations may involve more heterosexual offenders (though sex offenders misrepresent their sexuality) with prior criminal records and violent stranger assaults, official data may miss the homosexual offender who assaults in dating contexts, and rape crisis/medical centers may produce a specific type of victim.

Isely and Gehrenbeck-Shim (1997) found similar results, however results indicated most victims and offenders of male-male sexual assault are white, heterosexual men. Most victims were between the ages of 16-30, faced physical force or threat, and were under the influence of drugs and alcohol. Most assaults involved a single offender (60%). Very few of the institutions tapped for this study

Box 6.5, *continued*

responded, and most that did respond were primarily rape crisis centers. Very few men in this study sought medical help and those who did were not likely to report the sexual aspect of their assault. Additionally, very few men reported their assault to police. Male victims of rape and sexual assault experienced high levels of Post-traumatic Stress Disorder and 46.3 percent of victims (where agencies had such information) experienced suicidal thoughts, 76 percent of which actually tried to kill themselves. This study drives home the seriousness of male-male sexual assaults and the need for medical and psychiatric staff to understand the extent of this crime.

Typology and Classifying Rapists

There has been a concerted effort to categorize rapists into types based on certain characteristics of the offense and the offender. Prentky and Knight, working at the Massachusetts Treatment Center (MTC) developed a classification system which ordered rapists into four types: displaced aggression, compensatory, sexual aggressive, and impulsive rapists (Bartol, 2002). A similar model was developed by Groth, however its usefulness as a taxonomic system for classifying and predicting rapist types has been questioned (Knight et al., 1998).

The MTC model has since been revised to include more types broken down by offender motivation, level of social competence and presence of sexualized aggression (Box 6.6). The MTC:R3 contains nine types, with four primary motivations: opportunity, pervasive anger, sexual gratification, and vindictiveness (Knight et al., 1998). Types 1 and 2 are motivated by opportunistic factors (like the previously mentioned impulsive rapist) with their assaults being largely a function of situational stimuli. These impulsive, predatory rapists are broken down by the level of social competence they exhibit, which is manifested either in adolescence (Type 2) or adulthood (Type 1) (Knight et al., 1998). Type 3 rapists are motivated by a strong and overarching pervasive anger (like displaced aggression rapists) that is not aimed at a specific target but generally at all areas of life. This type has a long history of anti-social aggression and their behavior is marked by expressive anger, which results in serious injury to victims (Knight et al., 1998). Types 4 through 7 are motivated by sexual factors, with types 4 and 5 making up the sadistic breakdown (representing overt or muted sexually aggressive fantasies) and types 6 and 7 making up the non-sadistic rapists, broken down by level of social competence. These types have in common some form of sexual fixation that could be distorted by sexualizing violence (Types 4 and 5) or the need to dominate their victims (Types 6 and 7) (Knight et al., 1998). Finally, the vindictive rapists, types 8 and 9, are motivated by anger and aggression, but unlike the pervasively angry, their aggression is directed at women and as a result the victim usually experiences violent physical attacks. These types are separated by level of social competence also (Knight et al., 1998).

Box 6.6
Categorization of Rapist Types and Subtypes According to the MTC:R3

Primary Motivation			Type
Opportunistic	High Social Competence		1
	Low Social Competence		2
Pervasively Angry			3
Sexual	Sadistic	Overt	4
		Muted	5
	Non-Sadistic	Low Social Competence	6
		High Social Competence	7
Vindictive	Low Social Competence		8
	Moderate Social Competence		9

Source: Knight et al., 1998.

Typology as a Crime-Scene Instrument

While the Groth model has been developed into a crime-scene assessment tool for law enforcement agencies to investigate serial rape, Knight et al. (1998) criticizes the Groth model of rape classification and instead feel the MTC:R3 would be a more useful classification tool for profiling serial rapists. In an effort to prove this typology's usefulness in the field to predict rapist type, Knight et al. (1998) analyzed three samples of serial rapists (n=116, n=25, n=254) that allowed them to compare specific rape types and crime-scene indicators. The results showed predictive ability for adult antisocial and expressive aggression domains (based on the defining dimensions/characteristics of rape types), which are included in types 1-4, 8 and 9 of the MTC:R3 taxonomy (opportunistic, pervasively angry, vindictive, and overtly sadistic sexual types). Possible predictive scales were found for the domains of sadism, offense planning, and relationship with victim during the crime (types 4-7, sexual sadistic and non-sadistic), which showed high internal and cross-crime consistency (Knight et al., 1998). Although this area of research needs to be further studied and replicated, it provides practical application of rapist typology, in this case for criminal investigative analysis (profiling). However, this research sampled populations of serial rapists who had been placed in custody, which is a limited sample of all rapists. It was not stated but could be inferred from this study that the sampled rapists did not know their victims, and as stranger rapes are a small portion of all rapes, may represent very different characteristics from those who rape women they know (acquaintance and intimate partner rape) and those who are not detected by the criminal justice system.

Theoretical Perspectives

Because rapists comprise such a heterogeneous sample of offenders, it is difficult to develop theories and paradigms that envelope all types and patterns of rape. The use of general theories of crime to understand rape, while typical of criminologists, is not generally accepted by psychologists. Sex crimes seem to demand a crime-specific approach, especially when one considers the heterogeneity of sex offenders. A brief discussion of the theoretical paradigms that could be used to support and conduct research on rape and treatment options follows.

Psychodynamic theories view rape as originating early in life and continuing into adulthood as a character disorder. From this perspective, the rapist feels inadequate and sexually aggressive, which leads to failure of the ego to control the individual. However, psychodynamic approaches have failed to yield empirical support that would help in developing treatment or prevention (Polaschek, Ward & Hudson, 1997).

Behavioral theories move away from the unquantifiable arena of the mind and unchangeable past, into addressable behavior. Such theories see sexual arousal resulting from rape cues as a causal mechanism for sexual assault. By retraining individuals' behavioral reinforcers, it is believed the deviant sexual behavior can be stopped. While this perspective allows for the heterogeneity of rape offenders, the focus on behaviors and conditioning leaves aspects of the offense process unexplained (Polaschek et al., 1997).

Sociological theories of crime have gained recent popularity, focusing on cultural attitudes and practices that tolerate and facilitate rape. Rape myths, which were previously discussed, had at one time been the dominant and accepted "reasons" for rape, but research has since looked into the violence of our culture paired with the dominant cultural ideology that degrades and devalues women (Bartol, 2003). Since the second wave of the Women's Movement, greater attention has been paid to patriarchal causes of crime. Feminist theories identify rape as motivated by male violence serving to uphold a system of male supremacy through the control of women (Lilly et al., 2002; Polaschek et al., 1997).

Social-cognitive theories combine aspects of social knowledge and the cognitive processes of the individual to understand rape and its underlying factors. This process allows cultural implications, like rape myths, to be considered within an individualist paradigm, placing importance on both social factors and individual differences. Social-cognitive theories are useful in helping researchers in understanding rape, while also providing a reasonable basis for treatment (Polaschek et al., 1997).

Sociobiological theories identify rape as having some genetic indicator in males. For example, evolutionary theory views rape as an adaptive behavior that helps certain men who would otherwise be unable to reproduce to forcefully pass on their genes (Archer & Vaughan, 2001; Polaschek et al., 1997). However, a purely biological, sexual motivation for rape ignores the heterogeneity of rapists and the support found for other causes and associations with rape. Additionally, placing the cause of rape behavior on a single factor like testosterone oversimplifies an obviously complex human behavior, allows for no prediction of sexual aggression, and wrongfully blames the victim while easing offender culpability (Polaschek et al., 1997).

Comprehensive theories that are rape-specific have become more popular in recent years. For example, Malamuth, Heavey, and Linz (1993, in Polashchek et al., 1997) hypothesize that rape is caused by motivation to commit aggressive acts, reductions in internal and external inhibitions, and opportunity" (1997:129). Detrimental early experiences lead to the development of antisocial attitudes surrounding male-female relationships. These hostile attitudes combined with sexual promiscuity facilitate sexual aggression (Polaschek et al., 1997). Malamuth and associates identified six risk factors for rape: (1) sexual arousal, (2) dominance as a motive, (3) hostility toward women, (4) attitudes facilitating aggression against women, (5) antisocial personality characteristics, and (6) sexual experience (Polaschek et al., 1997). This framework, and others, combines multiple factors and causes in an attempt to create a crime-specific theory of rape that allows for the heterogeneity of offenders.

Many theoretical paradigms have been used in rape research and have found empirical or rational support. In the past few decades, researchers have made great strides in understanding rapists and an increasing effort has been made to address the seriousness of rape, both to its victims and to any society within which it is allowed to exist. Continued research into causes and factors that characterize rape will continue to focus on varied paradigms and theoretical constructs. The ultimate goal is to identify the best methods of rape prevention and the most successful treatments for rapists.

While much research on rapists and rape does not follow a particular theory, criminologists still value theory and the ability understand why crime occurs. The heterogeneity of sex offenders and the nature of violent crimes may suggest the need for crime specific theory, but this does not have to be the case. Currently, the most useful method of treating sex offenders may also provide a theoretical perspective on rape. A cognitive-behavioral paradigm is not only useful as a general approach to understanding crime, but is especially explanatory for rape and other sex crimes.

Cognitive-behavioral theories, also known as social learning theory in sociological criminology, build on behaviorism and their focus on learning mechanisms. In essence behavior is learned through interactions with the environment, both social and non-social influences. Cognitive-behavioral theories allow for individual experience and difference, while still including social/environmental factors. Akers' social learning theory, one example of a cognitive-behavioral approach, is becoming popular as a general theory of crime that can logically be applied to rape (Akers, 1998). According to social learning theory, learning can occur in direct interaction and modeling, and through both social and non-social reinforcement for behaviors. In this way social learning theory provides a general theoretical approach for factors known to be present in sex crimes. For example, some rapists may be more influenced by the actions and attitudes of those around them, while others may be more likely to act based on previous experiences that were gratifying and pleasurable. Social learning theory and cognitive-behavioral paradigms can account for these heterogeneous offending types.

Treatment/Prevention

Treatment and rehabilitation for offenders is considered an important component of corrections these days, however, problematic issues arise when rape treatment and the evaluation of rape treatment programs is discussed. Research on effective sex offender treatment programs is sparse and in most cases employs small samples of rapists and undifferentiated groups of sex offenders (Polaschek et al., 1997). The differences between rapists and other types of sex offenders make undifferentiated sex offender research unreliable. Likewise, even research that differentiates between rapists and child molesters may fall short due to the heterogeneity between types of rapists. Additionally, measures of recidivism used to determine a treatment's effectiveness may not be useful, because so many rapes go undetected (Groth et al., 1992; NCVS, 2001).

Systematic Reviews and Meta-Analyses of Sex Offender Treatment

Polizzi, MacKenzie, and Hickman (1999) conducted a systematic review of 21 studies of sex offender treatment. The studies were classified as prison and non-prison-based programs and all employed some measure of recidivism to evaluate effectiveness. Findings indicate that non-prison-based sex offender programs using a cognitive-behavioral model were somewhat effective in reducing recidivism and prison-based programs show promise. However, the researchers were not able to examine the impact of the programs on specific offender types due to the small samples of rapists and the failure of studies to investigate the impact of treatment on different offender types. Box 6.7 shows the studies used in evaluating non-prison based sex offender programs and their effect sizes.

Box 6.7
Non-Prison-Based Sex Offender Treatment Program Studies

Study	N	Sample	Type of Program	Results Significant?
Marques et al. (1994)	602	Child molesters and adult rapists	Cognitive-Behavioral	NO
Marshall and Barbaree (1988)	126	Child molesters	Cognitive-Behavioral	YES
Marshall, Eccles, and Barbaree (1991)	44	Exhibitionists	Unspecified	NO
	61		Cognitive-Behavioral	YES
Rice et al. (1991)	58	Child molesters	Behavioral	NO

Source: Polizzi et al. (1999).

The deficiency of research specific to rapists calls into question the usefulness of identical treatment programs across sex offender types. Gallagher, Wilson, Hirschfield, Coggeshall, and MacKenzie (1999) found similar results in a meta-analysis of 25 independent studies evaluating various treatment programs by type taking into account similarity between treatment and control groups, follow-up period, type of recidivism measure, and attrition. Overall, findings suggest treatment reduces recidivism for sex offenders; however, cognitive behavioral programs, especially those including relapse prevention, are most effective. Surgical castration showed significant improvement; however, this analysis was based on one study and should be viewed cautiously. Box 6.8 summarizes the effects found for different treatment programs.

Box 6.8
Results of Meta-Analysis for Types of Sex Offender Program Effectiveness

Program Type	# of Studies	Treated Group Significantly Different from Control?
Behavioral	2	NO
Behavioral Plus	2	NO
Cognitive-Behavioral/ Relapse Prevention	10	YES
Cognitive-Behavioral/ Other	3	YES
Surgical Castration	1	YES
Chemical Castration Plus	4	NO
Other Psychosocial	3	NO

Source: Gallagher et al. (1999)

Again, these results may not necessarily be generalizable to rapists, given the sample. Despite the usefulness of meta-analyses in reviewing research findings, the current lack of offender specific research for rapists makes determining appropriate treatment programs a guessing game.

In a more recent meta-analysis, Hanson, Gordon, Harris, Marques, Murphy, Quinsey, and Seto (2002) summarized the findings from 43 studies, resulting in data for 5,078 treated sex offenders and 4,376 untreated sex offenders. Hanson and associates (2002) took great care in coding only methodologically sound studies that used comparison groups, had consistent follow-up periods, and used similar measures of recidivism for comparison. The resulting meta-analysis found a lower average sexual recidivism rate for treatment groups over comparison groups (12.3% and 16.8%, respectively). General recidivism was also reduced for sex offenders treated with psychological programming over those receiving no treatment or treatment deemed useless (27.9% versus 39.2%). Results were strongest when studies compared treated sex offenders to those who had dropped out of treatment; however, studies employing random and incidental assignment also showed statistically significant reductions in recidivism for treatment over comparison groups (9.9% and 17.3% for sexual recidivism and 32% and 51% for general recidivism). This research provides strong evidence that some treatments (cognitive behavioral and systemic) are effective for sex offenders. Future research should examine the effectiveness of treatment programs for different types of sex offenders.

Cognitive-Behavioral Therapy for Rapists

Research results demonstrate cognitive-behavioral treatments are effective for sex offenders, of which rapists make up some portion in the studies, however small. Additionally, studies of rapists generally consider cognitive factors in etiology, such as misperception and mislabeling of cues when interacting with women, lack of inhibitory self-talk, associations of sex with power, rape myth acceptance, attitudes supportive of victim attribution, macho attitudes upholding notions of masculinity, authoritarian attitudes, and an underestimation of the negative effects of rape on the victim (Drieschner & Lange, 1999). Until more thorough and reliable research on appropriate treatment for rapists exists, cognitive-behavioral therapy may be useful in treating rapists; however, evidence-based programming should integrate findings of potential shortfalls and possible improvements.

Cognitive-behavioral therapy is typically composed of several components. One focus is arousal control, as it is thought that deviant sexual stimuli and fantasies lead an offender to rape. Arousal control involves techniques like covert sensitization and masturbatory satiation. Additionally, therapy seeks to discover and modify cognitive distortions that are deviant and rape supportive, thus allowing offenders to understand the offense process and themselves. This often involves empathy training and victim awareness. Another component is skills training, particularly for social and interpersonal development, but may also include life skills, problem-solving, and anger and/or stress management. Particularly high risk offenders may also receive biological treatments like chemical castration, psycho-pharmaceuticals and psychosurgery. Finally, relapse therapy is administered to allow offenders to identify behaviors, emotions, cognitions and situational cues that precede offending and approaches to prevent deviant sexual behavior (Marx, Miranda & Meyerson, 1999).

Maletzky and Steinhauser (2002) used a retrospective review of sex offenders from a community-based sex offender cognitive-behavioral treatment program between 1973 and 1997 differentiating by offender type. This study employed a large sample size (n=7,275) over an extensive follow-up period (25 years) employing multiple measures of failure, including new sexual charges, self-report lapses (covert) and relapses (overt), failure of plethysmographic test (for deviant sexual urges), and failure of polygraph examination. Treatment lasted an average of 1 3/4 years and involved aversive conditioning, plethysmographic biofeedback, aversive behavior rehearsal, masturbatory reconditioning, vicarious sensitization, sexual impulse control training, relapse prevention, cognitive therapy, and empathy training. Problems with this study involve attrition due to inability to maintain contact with subjects over time, lack of a control group, and failure to conduct statistical tests due to insufficient data. However, despite attrition, a large sample was followed through the entire follow-up period (n=2,837, 39%). Additional problems with this study involve changes in treatment protocol, with more focus on cognitive-behavioral and relapse prevention therapy in recent years, making it difficult to target which factors are most successful. Despite its weaknesses, this study provides some indication of failure rates for different types of offenders over a long period of time.

As noted in Box 6.9, rapists had an overall failure rate of 21.2 percent, with most failure (83.7%) resulting from a new sexual charge.

Box 6.9
Self-Reported Failures and Recidivism by Offender Type at Follow-up

Offender Type	N	Overall Failures Rate	% Failure Due to New Sexual Charge
Child Molester, female victim	833	6.4%	24.5%
Child Molester, male victim	279	9.4%	30.8%
Heterosexual pedophiles	302	9.7%	55.2%
Homosexual pedophiles	419	16.3%	75.0%
Exibitionists	570	13.5%	62.3%
Rapists	434	21.2%	83.7%
Totals	2,837	12.2%	61.7%

Source: Maletzky and Steinhauser (2002)

The failure rate for rapists increased rapidly in the first five years after treatment, then leveled off and remained stable. Dropping out of treatment increased the failure rate dramatically for rapists (9.8% vs. 74.5%), however rapists had relatively low rates of leaving treatment (11.4%). Rapists had the highest level of failure among different types of offenders for this treatment program, and failure rates were consistent over cohort groups. Despite limitations due to methodology, these findings suggest that this type of treatment may decrease recidivism among rapists, though less effectively than other sex offender types and most effectively where offenders complete treatment. However, the high rate of failure (recidivism) for rapists suggests further research is needed and perhaps more refined treatment methods uncovered for rapists.

Nicholaichuk, Gordon, Gu, and Wong (2000) compared differentiated sex offenders treated with cognitive-behavioral therapy and relapse prevention to an untreated, matched control group (n=296 and n=283 respectively). The residential treatment community housed high-risk sex offenders, while the control data were drawn from official records. The treatment group had slightly more convictions. The rapist sample was fairly large, giving us a better picture of the rapists in treatment than we might see of other sex offenders in this study. Nicholaichuk and associates (2000) examined initial recidivism and recidivism over time. They found that the treatment significantly impacted initial sexual recidivism with the control group having a 20.5 percent initial recidivism rate, compared to 6.1 percent for treatment groups. Through the follow-up period, the treatment group showed 14.5 percent sexual recidivism, while the control group recidivated sexually at twice the rate of the treatment group (33.2%). Treatment did not reduce nonsexual convictions and the treatment group had more technical violations, however they had lower overall readmission when compared to the control group. Rapists treated had lower recidivism than a control group of rapists (14.3% versus 42.0% for untreated). Treatment for first time rapists was more effective (11.1% versus 32.0% for untreated first-time rapists) than treatment for repeat rapists (20% versus 52% for untreated repeat rapists).

Box 10

Comparison of Sex Offenders Treated with Cognitive-Behavioral Therapy and Matched Controls: Sexual Recidivism

	Treatment Group (N = 296)	Control Group (N = 283)
Initial Recidivism Rate	6.1%	20.5%
Recidivism at Follow-up	14.5%	33.2%
Recidivism for All Rapists	14.3%	42.0%
Recidivism for First Offense Rapists	11.1%	32.0%
Recidivism for Repeat Rapists	20.0%	52.0%
Source: Nicholaichuk, Gordon, Gu, and Wong (2000).		

This study gives us a much better picture of rapists than other studies looking at general sex offender treatment. It additionally shows support for cognitive-behavioral therapy with relapse prevention for rapists, indicating that the high failure rates for rapists may be due in part to the inclusion of repeat offenders, who in this study showed much higher rates of sexual recidivism.

Important Considerations and Suggestions

Differences between rapists and other sex offenders may limit the success of cognitive-behavioral therapy. Concern has been voiced by researchers on several issues. Rapists may learn to exhibit socially desirable responses in treatment that may prevent identification of rape supportive cognitive distortions (Lea & Auburn, 2001). The importance of language should be recognized and the potential benefits of a discursive psychological approach, focusing on distortions within the talk of rapists, should be investigated (Lea & Auburn, 2001; Auburn & Lea, 2003). Some research suggests rapists do not have deficient heterosocial competence and that teaching social and interpersonal skills may give offenders manipulation techniques that facilitate victimization (Dreznick, 2003; Drieschner & Lange, 1999). Also, empathy training and awareness of negative consequences of victimization may not be appropriate for rapists who seek to humiliate their victims (Drieschner & Lange, 1999). Rapists display high levels of psychopathy compared to other sex offenders, which may reduce the success of treatment because they are more resistant to conditioning (Porter et al., 2000). Emotional recognition skills and affect regulation to improve moral and social consciousness may be beneficial for psychopathic rapists (Polaschek et al., 1997; Marx et al., 1999).

Due to the heterogeneity of rapists, successful treatment must address offense related needs that give attention to functional differences among offenders (Polaschek et al., 1997; Marx et al., 1999). Attention to rapist type, motivation, possible developmental factors, and cues associated with the deviant behavior should be considered in individualizing treatment (Drieschner & Lange, 1999; Marx et al., 1999). Additional suggestions for future treatment include creating a functional analysis to assist in customizing treatment and not applying treatment that may have an adverse affect on particular offenders. Also, promoting psychological acceptance of deviant cognitions instead of attempting to suppress them and informing offenders they do not have to act on cognitions has been suggested, though not tested (Marx et al., 1999).

Community Prevention

Research has shown that most rapists will not come into contact with the criminal justice system due to low levels of reporting (BJS, 2002; Groth et al., 1982). Essentially undetected rapists continue to live in the community. Prevention of rape through the targeting of high risk groups, like college students and adolescents, could potentially be useful. Rosenthal, Heesacker, and Neimeyer (1995) found attempts to change rape-supportive attitudes within the community can be successful. In their study, they targeted college students who were particularly at risk of raping or being raped. This group of men and women hold traditional attitudes of gender role stereotypes, especially in the context of sexual relationships. Rosenthal and colleagues (1995) targeted these students with high traditionality measures (n=122 males, and n=123 females), exposing them to a psycho educational intervention, and comparing them to a control group. The treatment group showed significant reductions across 10 measures of rape-relevant attitudes and beliefs compared with the control group, showing support for rape education programs for both low and high traditionality men and women. This study shows that community prevention programs show promise in reducing rape-supportive attitudes that could culminate in the occurrence of rape. O'Donohue, Yeater, and Fanetti (2003) also studied rape prevention via the reduction of rape myth acceptance, increased victim empathy, and changing outcome expectations (rewards and costs). This study found improvement in these variables for college males, and most notably, for males who reported a past history of coercive sexual behavior (O'Donohue et al., 2003). Further research on the efficacy of community prevention programs needs to be conducted, but this type of programming shows potential and should be embraced.

Conclusion

Understanding rape and rape offenders in this country proves a difficult task. The data sources measuring occurrence of rape consistently underreport its incidence and prevalence. Even victimization surveys are relatively conservative estimates and though they tend to catch a greater number of incidences, they also recognize a greater sample of victims. In addition to low rates, our research on rapists themselves may not be capturing the differences of the heterogeneous population of rapists. This research is typically conducted on rapists within institutional settings like prisons, which could potentially introduce bias and threaten the ability to generalize to the population. More recently research is being done in the community, particularly with college students. The lack of representative research on rapists ultimately means we know less about them than we would like. More research on rapists will increase our ability to capture serial rapists (who tend to have high numbers of undetected rapes), increase the adequate prosecution of all types of rapists (not only the most violent), and eventually allow us to treat them more effectively.

At the moment, we have little research that evaluates the effectiveness of different treatment programs. More attention is given to sex offenders in general than to rapists in particular. More reliable research is needed that differentiates by sex offender type, and ultimately by rapist type. Increased understanding of how different types of rapists react to and benefit from treatment is vital if we are to reduce sexual reoffending. Sex offenses are some of the most damaging and disheartening offenses our criminal justice system handles, thus it is in our best interest to know as much as we can and to utilize that knowledge to reduce sex crimes. There seems to be some promise that the appropriate treatment programs could reduce further victimization. Additionally, more research needs to be targeted toward acquaintance and intimate partner rape in this country, because these offenses make up the majority of cases yet are frequently ignored. Prevention is the most appropriate goal, given the effect of rape on victims, and that effort needs to begin in the community. Teaching adolescents about the facts of rape and eliminating rape myths early is important in helping young women protect themselves. Needless to say, society has some hand in how rape is understood and how serious we are going to be in punishing and preventing rape.

References

Akers, R. (1998). *Social Learning and Social Structure: A General Theory of Crime and Deviance.* Boston, MA: Northeastern University Press.

Andrews, D.A. and J. Bonta (2003). *The Psychology of Criminal Conduct.* Cincinnati, OH: Anderson Publishing Co.

Archer, J. and E.A. Vaughan (2001). "Evolutionary Theories of Rape." *Psychology, Evolution & Gender,* 3(1):95-101.

Associated Press (2003). "Police Seeking Serial Rapist in Charlottesville." *The Associated Press State & Local Wire.* Retrieved May 5, 2004, from LexisNexis Academic database.

Auburn, T. and S. Lea (2003). "Doing Cognitive Distortions: A Discursive Psychology Analysis of Sex Offender Treatment Talk." *British Journal of Social Psychology,* 42:281-298.

Bartol, C.R. (2002). *Criminal Behavior: A Psychosocial Approach.* Upper Saddle River, NJ: Prentice Hall.

BBC News (2002). "Cannes Film Sickens Audience." Retrieved May 7, 2004, from http://news.bbc.co.uk/1/hi/enterntainment/film/2008796.stm.

Brecklin, L.R. and S.E. Ullman (2001). "The Role of Offender Alcohol Use in Rape Attacks: An Analysis of National Victimization Survey Data." *Journal of Interpersonal Violence*, 16(1):3-21.

Bureau of Justice Statistics (2003). "Criminal Victimization in the U.S., 2001: Statistical Tables." Retrieved 4/12/04, from www.ojp.usdoj.gov/bjs/pub/pdf/csus01.pdf.

Bureau of Justice Statistics (2002a). "The National Crime Victimization Survey." Retrieved 10/23/03, from http://www.ojp.usdoj.gov/bjs/pub/pdf/cv01.pdf.

Bureau of Justice Statistics (2002b). "Sex Offences and Offenders." Retrieved 4/12/04, from http://www.ojp.usdoj.gov/bjs/pub/pdf/soo.pdf.

Bureau of Justice Statistics (2000). "Women Offenders." Retrieved 4/12/04, from http://www.ojp.usdoj.gov/bjs/pub/pdf/wo.pdf

CNN (2002). "Walkout at Cannes Rape Film." Retrieved May 7, 2004, from http://www.cnn.com/2002/SHOWBIZ/Movies/05/25/cannes.walkout.

Cowan, G. & R.R. Campbell (1995). "Rape Causal Attitudes among Adolescents." *The Journal of Sex Research*, 32(2):145-153.

Dickey, R., D. Nussbaum, K. Chevolleau, and H. Davidson (2002). "Age as a Differential Characteristics of Rapists, Pedophiles, and Sexual Sadists." *Journal of Sex and Marital Therapy*, 28:211-218.

Dreznick, M.T. (2003). "Heterosocial Competence of Rapists and Child Molesters: A Meta-Analysis." *The Journal of Sex Research*, 40(2):170-178.

Drieschner, K. and A. Lange (1999). "A Review of Cognitive Factors in the Etiology of Rape: Theories, Empirical Studies, and Implications." *Clinical Psychology Review*, 19:57-77.

Federal Bureau of Investigation (2001). "Uniform Crime Report." Retrieved 10/23/03, from http://www.fbi.gov/ucr/ucr.htm

Gallagher, C., D. Wilson, P. Hirschfield, M. Coggeshall, and D. MacKenzie (1999). "A Quantitative Review of the Effects of Sex Offender Treatment on Sexual Reoffending." *Corrections Management Quarterly*, 3(4):19-29.

Groth, A., R. Longo, and J. McFadin (1982). "Undetected Recidivism among Rapists and Child Molesters." *Crime & Delinquency*, 28(3):450-458.

Hagan, M., K. Gust-Brey, M. Cho, and E. Dow (2001). "Eight-Year Comparative Analyses of Adolescent Rapists, Adolescent Child Molesters, Other Adolescent Delinquents, and the General Population." *International Journal of Offender Therapy and Comparative Criminology*, 45(3):314-324.

Hanson, K. (2002). "Recidivism and Age: Follow-up Data from 4,673 Sexual Offenders." *Journal of Interpersonal Violence*, 17(10):1046-1062.

Hanson, K., A. Gordon, A. Harris, J. Marques, W. Murphy, V. Quinsey, and M. Seto (2002). "First Report of the Collaborative Outcome Data Project on the Effectiveness of Psychological Treatment for Sex Offenders." *Sexual Abuse: A Journal of Research and Treatment*, 14(2):169-194.

Hodge, S. and D. Canter (1998). "Victims and Perpetrators of Male Sexual Assault." *Journal of Interpersonal Violence*, 13(2):222-239.

Isely, P. and D. Gehrenbeck-Shim (1997). "Sexual Assault of Men in the Community." *Journal of Community Psychology*, 25(2):159-166.

Karp, S., D. Silber, R. Holmstrom, and L. Stock (1995). "Personality of Rape Survivors as a Group by Relation of Survivor to Perpetrator." *Journal of Clinical Psychology*, 51(5):587-593.

Kassing, L.R. and L.R. Prieto (2003). "The Rape Myth and Blame Based Beliefs of Counselors-in-Training Toward Male Victims of Rape." *Journal of Counseling and Development*, 81:455-461.

Kleinke, C. and C. Meyer (1990). "Evaluation of Rape Victim by Men and Women with High and Low Belief in a Just World." *Psychology of Women Quarterly*, 14(3):343-353.

Knight, R., J. Warren, R. Reboussin, and B. Soley (1998). "Predicting Rapist Type from Crime-scene Variables." *Criminal Justice and Behavior*, 25(1):46-80.

Lea, S. and T. Auburn (2001). "The Social Construction of Rape in the Talk of a Convicted Rapist." *Feminism and Psychology*, 11(1):11-33.

Lilly, J., F. Cullen, and R. Ball (2002). *Criminological Theory: Context and Consequences.* Sage Publications: Thousand Oaks, CA.

Lisak, D. and P. Miller (2002). "Repeat Rape and Multiple Offending Among Undetected Rapists." *Violence and Victims*, 17(1):73-84.

Maletzky, B.M. and C. Steinhauser (2002). "A 25-Year Follow-up of Cognitive/Behavioral Therapy with 7,275 Sexual Offenders." *Behavior Modification*, 26(2):123-147.

Marx, B., R. Miranda, and L. Meyerson (1999). "Cognitive-Behavioral Treatment for Rapists: Can We Do Better?" *Clinical Psychology Review*, 19(7):875-894.

Masters, W.H. (1986). "Sexual Dysfunction as an Aftermath of Sexual Assault of Men by Women." *Journal of Sex and Marital Therapy*, 12(1):35-45.

Narciso, D. and K. Mayhood (2003). "Police Seek Assistance in Finding Serial Rapist." *Columbus Dispatch,* Retrieved May 5, 2004, from LexisNexis Academic database.

Nicholaichuk, T., A. Gordon, D. Gu, and S. Wong (2000). "Outcome of an Institutional Sexual Offender Treatment Program: A Comparison between Treated and Matched Untreated Offenders." *Sexual Abuse: A Journal of Research and Treatment*, 12(2):139-153.

O'Donohue, W., E. Yeater, and M. Fanetti (2003). "Rape Prevention with College Males: The Roles of Rape Myth Acceptance, Victim Empathy, and Outcome Expectancies." *Journal of Interpersonal Violence*, 18(5):513-531.

Parks, K. and L. Zetes-Zanatta (1999). "Women's Bar-Related Victimization: Refining and Testing a Conceptual Model." *Aggressive Behavior*, 25:349-364.

Paulson, A. (2004). "Is the Rape-Shield Law Working?" *Christian Science Monitor*. Retrieved May 5, 2004, from LexisNexis Academic database.

Polaschek, D., T. Ward, and S. Hudson (1997). "Rape and Rapists: Theory and Treatment." *Clinical Psychology Review*, 17(2):117-144.

Polizzi, D., D. MacKenzie, and L. Hickman (1999). "What Works in Adult Sex Offender Treatment? A Review of Prison- and Non-Prison-Based Treatment Programs." *International Journal of Offender Therapy and Comparative Criminology*, 43(3):357-374.

Porter, S., D. Fairweather, J. Drugge, H. Hervé, A. Birt, and D. Boer (2000). "Profiles of Psychopathy in Incarcerated Sexual Offenders." *Criminal Justice and Behavior*, 27(2):216-233.

Rosenthal, E., M. Heesacker, and G. Neimeyer (1995). "Changing the Rape-Supportive Attitudes of Traditional and Nontraditional Male and Female College Students." *Journal of Counseling Psychology*, 42(2):171-177.

Stermac, L., P. Sheridan, A. Davidson, and S. Dunn (1996). "Sexual Assault of Adult Males." *Journal of Interpersonal Violence*, 11(1):52-64.

Taylor, K. (2004). "DNA Testing Confirms Serial Rapist; Analysis Shows One Man Committed Four Attacks." *Spokane Spokesman-Review*. Retrieved May 5, 2004, from LexisNexis Academic database.

Travin, S., K. Cullen, and B. Protter (1990). "Female Sex Offenders: Severe Victims and Victimizers." *Journal of Forensic Sciences*, 35(1):140-150.

Ullman, S.E. and R.A. Knight (1995). "Women's Resistance Strategies to Different Rapist Types." *Criminal Justice and Behavior*, 22(3):263-283.

Vachss, A. (2003). "Common Myths Remain a Strong Force in Rape Cases." *Milwaukee Journal Sentinel*. Retrieved May 5, 2004, from LexisNexis Academic database.

SECTION III

Youth Crime

Chapter 7

Violent Juvenile Offenders

Wendy Povitsky

Introduction

Picture a child climbing the steps of the school bus on his first day of school; a seven-year-old at his first Boy Scouts meeting; a teenager on the first day of high school; a young girl after her first kiss. These are the tender images that may make us smile, cringe, or blush. These same innocent experiences and memories are the ones we desire for our children. However, this is not always possible. What happens in a young mind to transform an innocent child into a "monster"? What makes a child run through the halls of his school, a place that should be as familiar and comfortable as home, and shoot his classmates, children he has grown up with since elementary school? What transforms a child from a baby-faced toddler into a violent juvenile offender (VJO)?

Zimring (1998) defines VJOs as those who "make an immediate threat or imposition of injury to another person" (1998:18). Murder, forcible rape, robbery, and aggravated assault are the possible violent juvenile crimes, as identified by the FBI (McCord, Widom & Crowell, 2001; McShane & Williams, 2003; Federal Bureau of Investigation [FBI], 2000; Zimring, 1998). Others categorizing violent crime also include assault in their definitions and, most recently, arson (Zimring, 1998). The above-mentioned offenses vary significantly in seriousness. Homicide and forcible rape are the most harmful of those offenses, and are identified in the high seriousness category. Those youth who commit aggravated assaults and robberies are classified as heterogeneous in seriousness due to the high variability in the amount of physical harm they impose on the victim. Finally, assaults are recognized as the least serious offense and are placed in the lower seriousness category. Assaults falling into this last category are deemed to not be aggravated assaults, and thus are not categorized as violent by the FBI (Zimring, 1998).

Revisiting our original question; who is the violent juvenile offender? Based on television and other forms of media, we might imagine him to be the kid in the trench coat or the inner city African-American teenager. While both of these examples profile violent youth in America, it would be incorrect to stereotype all juvenile offenders into those categories. In reality, VJOs come from all socioeconomic backgrounds, religions, and ethnic groups (McShane & Williams, 2003). It is true that crimes by certain groups are more common (e.g., African-American juveniles were arrested for 42.3% of juvenile violent offenses in 1999) than others, but it would be a grave oversight to stereotype youth based solely upon demographics (McCord et al., 2001). Juvenile crime can be unpredictable; therefore overlooking certain variables creates dangerous assumptions that can lead to severe injustices against specific groups of people.

As stated above, there is much variability in violent juvenile crime. The next section will review juvenile violence trends over the last 30 years. Next, there will be a closer look at the definitions and characteristics of the types of VJOs identified by the FBI's crime index and some background on their prevalence in our society. Additionally, the female violent offender, an offender becoming increasingly familiar in our society (Zimring, 1998), will be examined along with risk factors currently being proposed as causes of violent juvenile crime. Lastly, a review of issues and options in treating VJOs will be presented.

Trends in Violent Juvenile Crime

In 1999, 2.47 million juveniles were arrested for committing illegal acts (McShane & Williams, 2003). While this number may seem high, it reflects a decrease in juvenile crime since 1994 when juvenile crime was at its peak. Between 1995 and 1999 juvenile crime decreased by 25 percent (McCord et al., 2001; McShane & Williams, 2003; Zimring, 1998). No one is absolutely certain what prompted this decrease but correlates are being researched. It is important to note that the above numbers represent all juvenile crime, from violent offenses such as homicide, to status offenses such as truancy.

Violent juvenile offenders (VJOs) in 1998 made up four percent of all juvenile arrests (McCord et al., 2001). In 1999, 18 percent of violent offenders arrested were juveniles (McShane & Williams, 2003). This is a substantial number when we are discussing the crimes of homicide, forcible rape, robbery, and aggravated assault. Perhaps a more settling fact is that the numbers of juveniles being arrested (e.g., those under 18) for each of the four crimes designated as violent are less than the number of 18- to 24-year-olds being arrested for the same crimes. This statistic also stands when comparing juveniles to those ages 25-34 in cases of homicide, forcible rape, and aggravated assault. However, juveniles do commit more robberies than those in the 25-34 age group (McCord et al., 2001).

Despite the differences in arrest rates for juvenile and adult offenders, the continuum of severity that is found in violent offenses applies to both youth and adult offenses. However, Zimring (1998) found some characteristics of committing violent crime that are unique to youth. The majority of adolescents committing crimes are male (although female violence is on the rise). The rate of adolescent male arrests is higher than for any other group of males. A more positive characteristic of violent juvenile crime is a low mortality rate. Fewer deaths result from juvenile violence than adult violence. Essentially, VJOs are less likely to kill their victim during an attack. Finally, VJOs typically act in groups. Most violent juvenile offenses involve one or more co-offenders. These three characteristics (males, co-offenders, and fewer deaths) have been observed consistently across all types of violent juvenile crime (Zimring, 1998).

The bountiful research on juvenile offenses indicates that trends are changing in violent juvenile crime. Just 10 years ago we were facing a serious rise in juvenile crime, while today, we are experiencing a decline. However, this does not mean that the problem does not still exist. Criminologists, sociologists, psychologists, and others are still trying to determine why youth become involved in crime. What are the social and psychological factors that contribute to rises and dips in juvenile crime rates? Already, much has been discovered. By simply knowing that youth are more likely to act together helps us to create theories of causal factors. The following section provides a breakdown of violent juvenile crime. As will become evident, VJOs are still a harsh reality, somewhat unique to America. While it is simple to give statistics, such as juveniles were responsible for 18 percent of violent offenses in 1999, there is variability within each type of violent offense (McShane & Williams, 2003).

Offender Characteristics

The Breakdown of Violent Juvenile Crime

Homicide

The FBI defines criminal homicide as "death caused by the willful killing of one human being by another" (FBI-Homicide; McCord et al., 2001:315; Zimring, 1998:18). Homicide is justifiable only in the case of a law enforcement officer killing a felon in the line of duty or a private citizen killing a felon during the commission of a crime. Homicide is undeniably the most serious of the violent offenses. While there is less likelihood of a juvenile killing a victim during a violent interaction, it does occur. In 1999, 1,400 juveniles were arrested for homicide (McShane & Williams, 2003). Similar to other violent crimes, the early 1990s were characterized by a substantial increase in juvenile homicides (McCord et al., 2001; Williams & McShane, 2003; Zimring, 1998). However, that number dropped in 1995 when 84 percent of counties reported no juvenile homicides, with most occurring in urban areas such as New York City, Los Angeles, Chicago, Houston, and Detroit (McCord et al., 2001). Similar to other violent offenses, over half of the juvenile homicides include more than one offender (Zimring, 1998). In order to explain the causes of homicide as well as the trends in homicide rates, researchers have examined juvenile homicide offenses in terms of a number of different social factors, perhaps most importantly, school violence and gun availability.

Homicides and Other Forms of Violence in Schools. When studying school violence one must be very apprehensive of the media. The media is biased in their reporting and often does not accurately depict the trends in school shootings and other forms of school violence. Since the 1992-1993 school year, 286 violent deaths have occurred on school property, 77 percent with handguns (McShane & Williams, 2003). When a shooting occurs on school property, the media reports the story, analyzes the causes, and predicts the effects. To those who depend on the media alone for facts, school shootings may appear to be very prevalent in our society. Fortunately, this is not the case. School shootings do occur, but most often the school years with higher violent death rates are due to a low number of incidents with multiple fatalities. Since 1992, death tolls in schools have ranged from 21 in the 1994-1995 school year, to 54 in the 1992-1993 school year (McShane & Williams, 2003). The year of Columbine, when school murder became a popular topic of conversation and research, was not the year with the most violent school deaths. When looking at the true facts of school violence, while it is a serious issue, it is not as widespread as other offenses. During the 1996-1997 school year, only 10 percent of schools reported any violent crimes, most being physical assault and fights without a weapon (McShane & Williams, 2003). An interesting qualification to consider when examining school violence is intent. Was the intent of the offender in a physical altercation to commit a homicide or rather to physically harm the other student? As research has shown, despite intent, VJOs are less likely to kill their victim than adult offenders. However, based on the lack of weapons in most school violence, it would be reasonable to assume that the intent is not to kill. In fact, from 1992 to 1995 there was a decline in the reported number of weapons students brought to school. Unfortunately, that number rose in the 1996-1997 school year with 6,000 students being expelled for carrying a firearm (McShane & Williams, 2003). It is important to note that most assaults occurring in school would not be considered violent crime because they do not involve the use of a weapon.

In 1997 the trend in school violence was for such events to involve multiple offenders and multiple victims. Over the past five years, schools have made a concerted effort to increase security and take greater measures to protect their students. Many schools have adopted a zero-tolerance policy where all acts of aggression and violence are immediately punished. This approach seems to have had an effect. During the 1999-2000 school year, the nation had only 15 incidents of serious violent offenses (McShane & Williams, 2003). School crime is a critical issue that demands close examination. The media, while at times misleading, has been helpful in bringing these issues to the attention of the public and researchers. In order to prevent school violence before it occurs, schools must use the available research to identify risk factors, such as previous aggressive acts, and attempt to deal with these problems before they escalate.

Guns. The impact of handguns and automatic weapons on juvenile homicides is undeniable. Between 1980 and 1987, 54 percent of juvenile homicides were committed with handguns. In 1994, the height of juvenile crime, that number rose to 82 percent (McShane & Williams, 2003). Victim studies indicate that the majority of juvenile homicide victims (76%) are acquaintances of the offender and are killed with a gun. Sixty-three percent of those homicide offenders were over the age of 16 (McShane & Williams, 2003; Zimring, 1998). The impact of guns on juvenile homicide is most evident when looking at possible causes for the rise in juvenile homicides in the late 1980s though 1994. The increase and decrease of juvenile homicide has been shown to be directly related to gun availability, especially illegal gun availability (McCord et al., 2001; Stolzenberg & D'Alessio, 2000; Zimring, 1998).

Whether it is by gun or other method, juvenile homicide is a significant issue in our society. While these types of crime may not be as rampant as assaults or robberies, the results are much more serious. This issue, as we have seen, spans from urban areas to suburban schools; from gang violence to desolate children. While it is difficult to create a profile of the typical juvenile homicide offender, we do know that 93 percent of these offenders are male, with more than one-half being African-American (56%). Eighty-eight percent are over the age of 15. From 1980 to 1997, only 10 children under the age of 10 were found to be involved in murders (McShane & Williams, 2003). Of those, about half included the use of a gun. Because of the finality of this offense, even a small number of these offenses is unacceptable. For this reason, criminologists must work with politicians to create gun regulations. Guns are indisputably a major problem. This is evident through statistical evaluations or by simply opening the newspaper. As long as guns are available, our youth will have a powerful method with which to kill.

Box 7.1

Columbine High School
Littleton, Colorado
April 20, 1999

That infamous day in history, when Eric Harris, 17, and Dylan Klebold, 18, decided to enter their high school with the intent to kill as many people as they possible could, embodies the harm caused by youth violence. Twelve students and one teacher were executed in what was supposed to be the safe haven of their high school hallways, classrooms, and library. The two young killers had no previous offenses besides one arrest for breaking into cars in 1998. The intentions of Eric and Dylan were clear—they carried with them into the school an assault-style rifle, two shotguns, and at least one handgun. Additionally, police estimate that the boys brought more than 30 explosive devices with them into the school. While intent was clear, what propelled them toward these heinous crimes that took the life of their peers and themselves?

On April 20, 1999, our country took notice of the potential travesties that can occur at the purposeful hands of youth. Such instances as Columbine are not the typical instances of violence performed by youth, but examples such as these do exist. Efforts to curb such violence must be evaluated and implemented in order to prevent the further use of violence to solve adolescent issues. When children are killing other children, all those involved become victims.

Information extracted from *Littleton Begins Searching for Answers*. April, 22, 1999. www.cnn.com

---

Forcible Rape

Until the 1980s, rape was not considered to be a juvenile issue. Boys who committed such offenses were shrugged off with the statement, "boys will be boys." Most thought such behavior was simply part of growing up (Bischof & Stith, 1992). However, this view has drastically changed over the past 20 years. Today rape is considered one of the most serious offenses a juvenile can commit. The FBI's 1997 report, Crime in the United States, defines forcible rape as "the completed or attempted act of sexual intercourse accomplished by force or the threat of imminent force" (FBI-Forcible Rape; McCord et al., 2001:315; Zimring, 1998:316). This number has been fairly consistent over the past 20 years. In 1980, 100 VJOs were convicted of forcible rape. That number began to increase in 1988, and reached its peak in 1992. During that year, juveniles committed 32 percent more rapes than in 1980. Like other violent crimes, the number of juvenile rapes started to decline in 1995. Nineteen ninety-six had the lowest forcible rape rate since 1977. As is evident from these numbers, there have been some noticeable trends in juvenile rape rates. At this point, the causes of such trends are unknown by researchers (Zimring, 1998). Today, VJOs are responsible for at least 20 percent of the rapes that occur in the US (Bischof & Stith, 1992; McShane & Williams, 2003). This is most likely an underestimate due to the large number of sexual crimes that go unreported or unprosecuted. In 2000, the FBI reported that juveniles were involved in 12.1 percent of the cleared rapes (FBI-Forcible Rape). Thirty-five percent of victims report vaginal or anal penetration by juvenile rapists. More often with juvenile rape offenders than adult rape offenders, victims are acquaintances or siblings. The juvenile offender is typically male and chooses victims of the same age or older. Similar to the juvenile homicide offender, juvenile rapists vary in socioeconomic status, ethnicity, and religious backgrounds. While certain characteristics such as the influence of others and the sexual aggressiveness of the offender have had some correlation to sex crimes, much is still unknown about the causes of these offenses (McShane & Williams, 2003).

Robbery

"Taking or attempting to take anything of value from the care, custody or control of a person by force or by threat of force or violence, or by putting the victim in fear" is the FBI's definition of robbery (FBI-Robbery; McCord et al., 2001:316; Zimring, 1998:19). In 1995, a period of decline in juvenile crime, youth under the age of 18 made up 32 percent of robbery arrests (Zimring, 1998). By the year 2000, this number had been cut in half. At this time, 15.5 percent of cleared robberies were attributed to juveniles. This was a 4.6 percent drop from 1999, a larger decrease than that experienced by adult offenders of the same kind (1.8%); (FBI-Robbery). Despite the changes in the number of youth committing robberies, researchers can not define the reason for these rises and declines.

The seriousness of the robbery influences who gets arrested and who does not. For instance, robberies with a firearm are taken much more seriously than those without. Despite being treated more critically, research shows fewer gun robberies result in injury to the victim than robberies with knives. Other factors taken into consideration when deciding the seriousness of the offense are the amount of property taken, whether the attempted robbery was successful, the nature of the threat issued by the offender, the offender's age, and the characteristics of the victim (e.g., race, employment, etc.; Zimring, 1998). In determining who is committing these acts, researchers find that there is an overrepresentation of males and African-Americans committing these offenses (McCord et al., 2001).

Aggravated Assaults

In 1995, 15 percent of aggravated assault arrests were determined to be juvenile arrests. In that same year, there were 51 times more juvenile arrests for aggravated assault than for homicide (Zimring, 1998). The FBI defines aggravated assault as "an unlawful attack by one person upon another for the purpose of inflicting severe or aggravated bodily injury." These offenses are "often accompanied by use of a weapon or by means likely to produce death or great bodily harm" (FBI-Aggravated Assaults; McCord et al., 2001:316; Zimring, 1998:19).

Trends in juvenile aggravated assaults are similar to those of other violent offenses. Rates were relatively steady in the early 1980s and began to rise by the end of the decade. By 1994, the rate of juvenile aggravated assaults had doubled that of 1980. While in 1995 there was a 20 percent decline in the aggravated assault rate, numbers were still 56 percent above the 1980 rate. Juvenile aggravated assault rates experienced a much slower decline in the mid and late 1990s than did homicide (Zimring, 1998).

Similar to robberies, there is a continuum of seriousness when defining aggravated assaults. Some researchers have proposed that the slower rate of decline for aggravated assaults may not have as much to do with the number of assaults occurring as it does with the changes in definition of simple assaults. The FBI does not classify these more minor assaults as violent crimes. As the definition of simple assaults was modified, the aggravated assault definition became broader. Much discretion is given to police when deciding whether to charge a youth with a violent or aggravated assault versus a simple assault (McCord et al., 2001; Zimring, 1998).

By the year 2000, a noticeable decrease in juvenile aggravated assaults was evident. That year, 11.7 percent of cleared aggravated assaults were attributed to juveniles, a decline of 4.2 percent from 1999 (FBI-Aggravated Assaults). Despite this decrease, juvenile aggravated assaults are still very prevalent in America, especially in examining gang violence. The only information researchers can confidently report pertaining to aggravated assaults is that, similar to robberies, juvenile males and African-Americans are overrepresented in this offender population (McCord et al., 2001).

Juvenile Female Offenders

The final group of VJOs we will examine is not specifically cited in the FBI Crime Reports but is important to understand. The number of female offenders in America is on the rise at a pace faster than male offenders (McShane & Williams, 2003). In 1999, females made up 27 percent of juvenile arrests and 22 percent of aggravated assault arrests. The typical female offender does not currently become involved in many violent offenses, however these numbers are changing. From 1981 to 1994 there was a 64 percent increase in male arrests for violent offenses. During the same time period, female arrests for the same offenses rose 120 percent (McCord et al., 2001). Despite the steep increase in the number of female VJOs, males still offend at a higher rate. In 1998, the FBI reported that male VJOs committed 603 violent crimes per 100,000 people. That same year, female VJOs committed only 127 violent crimes per 100,000 people (McCord et al., 2001).

Researchers have taken great interest in this recent increase in female crime. There is a general consensus that the reason for the increase is not because young females have become more criminal but rather because the justice system is beginning to treat them in a similar manner to males (McCord et al., 2001; McShane & Williams, 2003; Zimring, 1998). Despite this claim, there is evidence that cases involving females are still less likely to be petitioned or adjudicated. If cases involving females do get that far, typically such offenders are less likely to be put on formal probation or in out-of-home placements (McShane & Williams, 2003). Nevertheless, female crime is on the rise and there is evidence that the punishments for males and females are becoming more similar.

Theoretical Perspectives

What Makes a Child Violent?

The above question has been pondered for more than a century. Are the causes biological, social, or psychological? Most researchers have come to the conclusion that all of these factors play some role in predicting the violent behavior of youth. Let us go back to our young children we introduced at the beginning of this paper. The youth, who innocently got on the school bus on his first day of kindergarten 15 years ago, is found standing over a deceased peer, gun in hand. Exactly one century ago, this crime would have been attributed to social factors (MacQueary, 1903). Perhaps the youth lived in poverty or did not attend school. The youth would have entered a residential school with hopes of being rehabilitated and able to reenter society. Just 50 years later, researchers might claim the youthful offender is helpless to the social factors that influence one's personality as he develops. Jones (1941) asserted that youth could not be "morally responsible but rather [acted] in response to the various factors and experiences in his or her social environments over which he had no control. . . . [the youth] adjust[ed] to society based on how he was trained and directed" (1941:439). For this reason, punishment was viewed as useless. Despite the age of these views, much of the same themes can be found in more recent research.

The risk factors that cause juvenile crime are relatively uncertain. While many studies indicate the existence of risk factors, replications often find alternative results. Despite inconclusive research on specific factors, studies indicate definitive results concerning the overall impact of psychological and social factors on violent behavior (Blumstein, Cohen & Farrington, 1988; Cottle, 1998; Gerstein & Briggs, 1993; Haller, 2000; McShane & Williams, 2003; Stouthamer-Loeber & Loeber, 2002). Psychologically speaking, the Pittsburgh Youth Study found VJOs were three times as likely to be diagnosed with Disruptive Behavior Disorder by 13.5 years old than were non-offenders (Stouthamer-Loeber & Loeber, 2002). VJOs were also more likely than non-offenders to be placed in special classrooms due to poor behavior. While such placements were more frequent for VJOs, the authors believed not enough attention was being paid to such offenders. They claimed that 48 percent of VJOs received no help in or outside of school to deal with their behavior problems. Perhaps if parents dealt with the issues when they first surfaced, the 47.1 percent of youth who displayed chronic criminal behavior by age 12 could have been saved from such behavior. Haller (2000) found that as many as 60 percent of youth who entered the juvenile justice system suffered from some sort of mental disorder. VJOs have also been found to be more impulsive, adventurous, emotionally responsive, and carefree (Gerstein & Briggs, 1993). Further research must be done on how mental disorders of youth are diagnosed and treated.

The social factors that are believed to cause increased risk of violent behavior range from poverty to abuse to family structure (Cottle, 1998; Gerstein & Briggs, 1993; McShane & Williams, 2003; Stolzenburg & D'Alessio, 2000; Zhang, Welte & Wieczorek, 2002). VJOs self-report to have been more involved in violent offenses before their current arrest. This finding has been shown to discriminate between violent and non-violent juvenile offenders (who did not have a history of violent offenses) (Gerstein & Briggs, 1993).

Family structure and abuse are believed to have a major influence on violent behavior in youth (Cottle, 1998). Without parent attachment and appropriate socialization, it is unlikely for a youth to comply with the expected behaviors of society. Symptoms of post traumatic stress disorder, caused by parental abuse, are common in juvenile offenders. Such symptoms as well as the abuse itself have been linked with juvenile homicide numbers, especially matricide and patricide (killing of mother and father) (Cottle, 1998; McShane & Williams, 2003).

The prevalence of crack cocaine in the mid-1980s also seemed to have some relationship to the increase in juvenile homicides (McCord et al., 2001; McShane & Williams, 2003). Researchers have predicted that as more youth began to deal crack there was an increase in the number of guns being carried by youth. Both juvenile dealers and non-dealers carried guns as a form of protection. In the mid-1990s, as the homicide rate fell, researchers cited the maturity of the crack market, the improvement of the economy, and the crackdown on drugs as the reasons for this decline (McCord et al., 2001). Youth were getting conventional jobs and the police were making it more difficult to deal drugs.

Alcohol has also been linked with increased violent juvenile crime. A Buffalo study of young men (ages 16 to 19) indicated that alcohol was frequently used to attain violent consequences (Zhang et al., 2002). For those youth who had high expectancies of violence, an interaction was found between the use of alcohol before a violent act and a high level of alcohol use in general. Certainly the effects of alcohol on violence are affected by many variables (e.g., where consumption takes place, etc.) but, there is a general consensus among researchers that alcohol reduces inhibitions and makes a potential offender more likely to take risks and act in an anti-social and/or violent manner (McShane & Williams, 2003; Zhang et al., 2002).

Whether it is family related, chemical dependency, or other factors, predictors of criminal behavior seem to be evident at a young age (Cottle, 1998; Stouthamer-Loeber & Loeber, 2002). Three developmental factors have been cited as being linked to violent juvenile crime. The following behaviors, often found before age 12, indicate the possibility of more serious offenses later on in adolescence: conflicts with authority, covert behaviors such as lying, and overt behaviors such as minor aggression (McShane & Williams, 2003). These early behaviors lead to avoidance of authority, actions that damage property, fighting, and other forms of violence. Most research indicates that risk factors are the same for all four violent offenses, although some have attempted to claim that etiology of sex offenders differ from that of homicides, robberies, and aggravated assaults. However, when examining family variables such as family cohesion, adaptability, and social-environmental factors, no differences have been found between sex offenders and other violent offenders (Bischof & Stith, 1992; Bischof & Stith, 1995).

Violent juvenile offenders are clearly a subject of great concern for criminologists. However, in order to curb this violence, more research must be done to find definitive risk factors that predict these crimes. The community must then use these predictors to prevent and end the criminal careers of our youth. Another benefit of defining the factors that most relate to violent behavior is their relationship with treatment options. Prison administrators, psychologists, program specialists, and any other treatment providers must be able to identify what about the youth needs treatment. For example, if the youthful offender scores high on family cohesiveness, a program designed to improve family functionality may not be appropriate or necessary. A Midwestern juvenile facility collected background psychological information, as well as information about health, education, family life, demographics, and criminal history on 276 inmates (Auffrey, Fritz, Lin & Bistak, 1999). Among other things, this data allowed the facility to examine what treatment had previously been administered as well as what treatment might be beneficial. The collection of such data occurs in many facilities across the country. As researchers continue to investigate risk factors, treatment options will become more defined and tailored to individuals. In gathering any information on offenders, the goal is to find a way to turn them into upstanding community members. Thus, the next step will be to examine what treatment options exist currently and where they are headed in the future.

Box 7.2

Lionel Tate vs. State of Florida: An Example of Other Problems Youth Can Incur When Involved in the Justice System

At age 12, Lionel Tate murdered six-year-old Tiffany Eunick. He was found guilty of first degree murder for the 1999 offense. Mr. Tate is an example of the growing number of youth entering the adult justice system. Tate was charged with felony murder, aggravated child abuse, and premeditated murder. Such severe charges left him without the option of going through the juvenile system. However, despite the heinous nature of the offense (the victim suffered from approximately 35 wounds including internal injuries to her kidneys, pancreas, and liver), could the effect of entering the adult criminal justice system be more detrimental to the youthful offender than satisfying to the community in which the offense took place? The possibility of Tate not being prepared to enter into an adult court proceeding and fully understand the consequences such a setting were brought to light when Tate's attorney entered a motion to appeal Tate's original trial citing Tate as incompetent. According to Tate's attorneys, "Tate did not know or understand the consequences of proceeding to trial and . . . he was unable to assist counsel before and during the trial" (p. 2). An example of support for this notion came when Tate refused a plea that could have saved him from life in prison. Tate's attorneys believed that had Tate fully understood that going to trial and being found guilty meant life in prison without parole, he would have taken the plea which promised a less harsh punishment.

With the verdict in the hands of the Court of Appeals, information came out that Tate was not given a competency hearing prior to the trial beginning despite a written motion that Tate was not competent at pretrial. The judge presiding over the trial claimed that competency was never brought up as an issue. Nevertheless, the Court of Appeals found that Tate was incompetent at time of trial and that the court should have ordered

Box 7.2, *continued*

a pretrial competency hearing or one at post trial due to the defendant's age and lack of experience with the justice system. In essence, the Court said that Tate's due process rights were violated and the results of the trial were overturned.

The Tate case provides us a visual image of young children committing heinous crimes. But, the question is what we do about such children? Say Tate had taken a plea bargain and did not have a life sentence. When he got out, he would have been robbed of his childhood and that time to develop. Would he be safe to himself or others on the street? When we put young offenders through the adult criminal justice system do we take away any chance of them being able to lead a normal life? Do they have a right to lead a normal life? These are all questions that must be thought about and researched. The answers are not easy but are crucial in finding solutions to the issue of juvenile crime in America.

Tate v. State, 864 So.2d 44 (2003).

Treatment/Prevention

Methods

All articles cited in the treatment portion of this paper were taken from online databases. Searches used pertinent key words for each treatment in order to discover what research was available. Date limits were set to find articles published after 1990. All articles were reviewed using the Maryland Methods Scale to determine methodological rigor (Sherman et al., 1997). All research was used as long as the Maryland Methods score did not fall below a two.

The common phrase "what works in corrections" exemplifies the conflict that has been especially strong since Martinson's 1974 article in which he stated that no rehabilitation programs currently being used in correctional facilities were effective in reducing recidivism. Corrections in America has moved back and forth between providing and not providing treatment to offenders. The critics of treatment programs would argue that they are expensive and have not been shown to be effective in reducing recidivism. Despite such beliefs, when dealing with juveniles, there seems to be a stronger push to incorporate treatment into corrections, if for no other reason than to ensure the safety of staff while offenders are in prison. The type of crimes discussed in this paper most often result in the youth entering some out-of-home placement. Research indicates that without treatment programs, the safety of facility staff, other inmates, and the offender himself, is put at risk (Cellini, 1994).

On a broader level, treatment is designed to rehabilitate youth. Unlike in the adult criminal justice system, the premise of juvenile justice is that youth are capable of being rehabilitated. Their limited capacity does not allow them to make sound judgments and for that reason they are not necessarily responsible for their actions (Vogel & Vogel, 2003). Due to the belief that all juveniles can be rehabilitated, a plethora of programs exist in an attempt to reach this goal. However, it would be impractical to review all of the existing treatment programs used in American corrections. Instead, an examination of three current and popular treatment programs will be discussed along with their pertinent research. The reviewed treatments will include boot camps, Moral Reconation Therapy, and Multisystemic Therapy.

Boot Camps

As an alternative to entering a traditional juvenile facility, a growing number of states offer boot camp as a placement option. Boot camps are often described as a military-style environment characterized by strenuous exercise and strict disciplinary measures (Kempinen & Kurlychek, 2003; MacKenzie et al., 1999; McShane & Williams, 2003; Tyler, Darville & Stalnaker, 2001). Typically offenders spend a shorter period of time in a boot camp than a typical detention facility. The purpose of boot camps is to create a stressful environment and in doing so, the youth may become vulnerable to change and susceptible to influence. Thus, when the treatment portion of the program is introduced the youth may be more likely to experience permanent positive changes. Although boot camps differ in day to day function, an example of a typical day in a boot camp is as follows: youth wakes up very early, eats breakfast, attends the mandated hours of school, and spends the rest of the day participating in hard physical labor, physical exercise, or drill and ceremony. The evenings are spent in programs such as life-skills or addiction treatment (McShane & Williams, 2003).

Research on the effectiveness of boot camps is ample and typically not positive. Tyler, Darville, and Stalnaker (2001) conducted a review of boot camps literature to come up with some very critical results. Being that we live in a political world, cost is the first problem cited with such programs. The researchers claimed that boot camps cost $33,480/year for each inmate while detention centers cost only $31,354/year. This difference is fairly significant if boot camps may not be effective. The researchers cite a number of factors other than the boot camp routine as possible contributors to the mediocre results boot camp studies have experienced. Research has revealed abuse of inmates, especially younger ones at the hands of older ones, in boot camp facilities (Tyler, Darville & Stalnaker, 2001). This behavior can seriously harm a child and stand in the way of any positive treatment the child may have received otherwise. Another factor the researchers claim contributed to poor results is the lack of aftercare for boot camps. Youth enter these intense programs and then go back into the community with no transition or help in reentry. The researchers posit that if aftercare treatment was available upon leaving the boot camp facilities perhaps the positive impact of the boot camp would be more fully displayed in behavior.

Despite the pessimistic view points noted above, researchers have found some positive aspects of going to boot camp as opposed to traditional facilities. However, such results are still commingled with proof of ineffective programming. Kempien and Kurlychek (2003) compared adults in a boot camp to a sample of adults in a state penitentiary from 1996 to 1997. The study, receiving a Maryland Methods score of three, looked at an adult sample and sought to discover whether boot camps reduced recidivism when providing a program that "promoted discipline, structure, and characteristics of good citizenship" (2003:586). The boot camps had a strong emphasis on rehabilitative programming as did the prison. Regardless of that similarity, significant differences were found between the two samples. Results indicated that overall the boot camp group was more likely to recidivate than the prison group (44% vs. 39%); however this was only true when looking at both new convictions and violations of probation. Boot camp participants actually had a lower rate of recidivism when only looking at new convictions (12% vs. 15%). Results also indicated that older boot camp participants were less likely to recidivate than younger participants. Offense type, employment, county of origin, and maximum sentence length also contributed to likelihood of recidivism. Despite limitations concerning the comparability of the samples, results indicated that boot camp participants were less likely to have a new conviction. This could be helpful in determining where improvements could be made to boot camp programs in the future.

A stronger study was conducted by MacKenzie et al. (1999), in which 27 boot camp programs for juveniles were identified and matched with comparable institutions youth would have been sent to if not in a boot camp. This study received a Maryland Methods Score of four. The researchers in this study made site visits to each institution and surveyed juveniles and staff. Administrators were interviewed and researchers conducted walkthroughs with cameras. In general, juveniles indicated that boot camp had a more positive environment except when looking at safety from staff. Staff also favored the environment of the boot camp claiming that they had more favorable working conditions. In a survey that was given at two separate times, levels of anxiety and depression were more greatly reduced in boot camp youth. A final positive finding in the MacKenzie et al. study was that boot camp youth reported decreased dysfunctional stress attitudes and increased positive social attitudes while the comparison facilities reported increased dysfunctional stress and a decrease in positive social attitudes. While the study did not discover the impact of boot camp on recidivism, it implied that there could be some positive aspects to such programs.

Moral Reconation Therapy (MRT)

The purpose of MRT is to increase the moral reasoning abilities of youthful offenders. The sixteen step program (see Box 7.3) begins during incarceration and continues into aftercare. While there has not been a lot of research on the treatment program, initial results are mixed. MacKenzie and Hickman (1998) reviewed what research does exist in a report to the Washington State Legislature. Preliminary studies displayed a reduction of hedonistic orientation and an increased level of moral reasoning in MRT participants. Other research has shown that improved reasoning skills in juvenile offenders could be related to a reduction in recidivism. This has proven to be true in five different studies comparing MRT participants to non-participating juvenile offenders.

While MRT appears to be a promising program for correctional facilities, most of this research was conducted by the program's originators. This implies that MRT was most likely implemented in a strict methodological environment. When such implementation took place without the program's creators and in a "real-life" environment, the program did not fare as well. In fact, Armstrong's (2003) study using a randomized sample found no differences in recidivism between treatment and comparison groups. The success of a program under research conditions does not indicate the program's ability to reduce recidivism when implemented by program staff (e.g., prison social workers and counselors). Further research is necessary to determine the benefit of MRT.

Multisystemic Therapy (MST)

The goal of multi-systemic therapy is to "impact anti-social behavior by altering key aspects of youths' social contexts in ways that promote prosocial behavior rather than anti-social behavior" (Huey, Henggeler, Brondino & Pickerel, 2000:452). MST is premised on the belief that the client's behavior is a reflection of the interaction between the individual, peer system, school system, and community. Family also has a large influence. For this reason, repeat offending is related not only to previous offenses but also the relationships between the individual and his surroundings (e.g., family, peers, school, etc.) (Henggeler, Melton & Smith, 1992). MST differs from other treatments in that it is custom designed

Box 7.3

Moral Reconation Therapy Freedom Ladder

MRT provides each participant with a four-hour orientation which explains the steps of the program. Each step involves related activities. Participants must indicate acceptance and understanding of each step before moving on to the next.

Freedom Ladder
1.	Honesty
2.	Trust
3.	Acceptance
4.	Awareness
5.	Healing damaged relationships
6.	Helping others
7.	Long-term goals and identity
8.	Short-term goals and consistency
9.	Commitment to change
10.	Maintain positive change
11.	Keeping moral commitments
12.	Choosing moral goals
Steps 13-16.	Evaluate relationship between inner self and personality

---

to the individual. It addresses a long range of criminogenic needs and incorporates different modes of therapy, including family therapy and cognitive behavior therapy.

Research on MST has been consistently very positive. Aside from one study, which had a Maryland Methods rating of two, the remaining studies reviewed for this paper were very rigorous; all receiving ratings of five (see Appendix B). Research has examined many different aspects of MST to determine its effectiveness.

Huey et al. (2000) looked at therapists' adherence to MST principles and its relationship to the participant's success. While the methods of the study indicated that participants were randomly assigned to an MST group or a usual services group, no further mention of the usual services group was provided throughout the article. Despite this, the authors measured MST adherence on the part of the therapist, family functioning, parent monitoring, delinquent peer affiliation, and delinquent behavior on a pre and post test. Appropriate portions of the test were given to the caregiver, youth, and therapist. Results indicated that therapists varied greatly in their adherence to the MST model. However, when adherence was strong, there was significant improvement in family, peer, and youth functioning. Measures also indicated that improvements to family functioning and parent monitoring decreased delinquent peer affiliation and delinquent behavior over time. Despite the weakness of the research (Maryland Methods Score of two), the study provides a foundation for doing more research on what contributes to successful MST therapy.

While the study by Henggeler, Melton, Brondino, Scherer, and Hanley (1997) was evaluated as a methodologically rigorous study, the findings were not conclusive. One hundred fifty violent and serious offending youth and their families were randomly assigned to participate in MST or traditional juvenile services. Measures included individual emotional adjustment and adolescent behavior problems, criminal activity, family relations, parent monitoring, and peer relations. Surveys relating to the listed measures were given to offenders and parents twice during the treatment. Therapists also completed a survey measuring adherence. Arrest and incarceration information were collected during the 1.7 year follow-up. The emotional and behavioral function of MST youth was found to be significantly improved when compared to the traditional services group. Treatment effects were not observed in peer relations or family functioning. Although recidivism was 26 percent lower for the MST group than for the traditional services group, this number was not significant. However, significance was found in the incarceration rates; MST participants were incarcerated for significantly less days than the traditional services group. Results in this study were encouraging for the future of MST.

Two other studies, both with ratings of five, indicate that MST is influential in reducing recidivism among juvenile offenders. Henggeler, Melton, and Smith (1992) studied the effects of MST on serious, violent juvenile offenders. Using similar procedures to Henggeler et al. (1997), the current study had much more favorable results. Fifty-nine weeks after the treatment was completed, the number of arrests for the MST group was nearly one-half as many as for the usual services group (42% vs. 62%). Additionally, only 20 percent of the MST group who were rearrested was taken into custody while 60 percent of the usual services received incarceration. The MST group showed an increase in family cohesion and a decrease in peer aggression. The usual services group decreased in family cohesion and displayed no change in peer aggression. Many say that the only important measure of a treatment is recidivism rate. This rigorous study succeeded in indicating that MST can have a positive affect on recidivism.

Borduin et al. (1995) found similar results in another methodologically strong study of MST. In a design similar to that of Henggeler et al. (1997), the researchers used a pre and post test measure as well as a four-year follow-up. MST was shown to decrease adjustment problems, decrease behavior problems, increase family cohesion and adaptability, and improve family interactions. Those in the usual services group experienced either no change in measures or negative outcomes. At the

Box 7.4
Maryland Methods Ratings of MST Research

Evaluation Study Review	Methods Score	Evaluation Study Findings
Huey, Jr. et al. (2000)	2	MST participants were more successful when therapists strictly followed the treatment plan and MST principles (e.g., family functioning and parent monitoring) Improvements to family functioning and parent monitoring decrease delinquent peer affiliation and delinquent behavior over time
Henggeler et al. (1997)	5	MST participants experienced a reduction in symptomatology whereas comparison group experienced increases MST participants experienced a 26% reduction in recidivism but *not significant* Incarceration rates were 47% lower for those in MST condition vs. comparison group (33.2 days/year, vs. 70.4 days/year No effect on family relations or peer relations
Borduin et al. (1995)	5	MST sample has increase in behavior problems and symtomatology; no difference in individual therapy (IT) group MST group experienced increase in family cohesion and adaptability; family functioning decreased for comparison group No effect on peer relations 4 years after completion of treatment, MST completers experienced less recidivism (22.1%) than MST dropouts (46.6%), IT completers (71.4%), IT dropouts (71.4%, and treatment refusals (87.5%). MST completers were arrested less often than IT (M=1.71,SD=1.04 vs. M=5.43, SD =3.62), and for less serious crimes (M=5.17, SD=5.01 vs. M=9.40, SD=3.37) MST had significant effect on predicting violent recidivism
Henggeler et al. (1992)	5	MST group experienced increased family cohesion and decreased peer aggression 59 weeks after treatment, MST group had less recidivism than comparison (42% vs. 62%) and fewer days incarcerated (20% vs. 68%)

end of the four-year follow-up MST completers had significantly less recidivism (22.1%) than usual services completers (74.1%), usual services dropouts (71.4%), treatment refusers (87.5%), and MST dropouts (46.6%). MST participants were arrested less often than usual services participants. MST participants were also arrested for less serious crimes than usual service participants.

Of all of the treatments available today, MST has been shown to be one of the most promising. In addition to positive research findings, studies are done with the appropriate amount of rigor. Assuming future research on MST is conducted in a similar manner and findings are replicable, MST will continue to provide positive experiences and promising futures for its participants. Future research will determine whether MRT follows the same path. As for boot camps, despite dismal findings in the research, rigorous studies continue as does funding for such programs.

Conclusion

As the research indicates, promising programs exist to help rehabilitate violent juvenile offenders. However, in order to provide youth with the opportunity to improve themselves, we must allow them that chance. As violent juvenile crime increasingly becomes a topic of public interest, there is a growing movement to move these offenders into the adult system (Feiler & Sheley, 1999; Sprott, 1998; Vogel & Vogel, 2003). The National Center for Juvenile Justice polled citizens and found that the public wants to see youth held more accountable for their actions (Torbet, 1997). No more will people accept that youth aren't capable of making decisions. This evolution of juvenile justice is especially pivotal in the sentencing of violent juvenile offenders. Their crimes are the most devastating and heinous and are thus the ones being waived into adult court. As younger and younger offenders move into the adult system they lose the opportunity to benefit from treatment. Often times, adult facilities are not prepared to handle youth and their specific needs (Feiler & Sheley, 1999).

It is estimated that over the next 25 years, the juvenile population will increase by 31 percent (Haller, 2000). Chances are violent juvenile crime is not going to go away. For this reason, researchers must determine the costs and benefits of juvenile waivers while continuing to study the effectiveness of treatment programs. As seemingly effective treatment is available, policy makers and the general public must dedicate themselves to discovering a solution to the epidemic of juvenile violence.

References

Armstrong, T.A. (2003). "The Effect of Moral Reconation Therapy on the Recidivism of Youthful Offenders." *Criminal Justice and Behavior,* 30:668-687.

Auffrey, C., J.M. Fritz, B. Lin, and P. Bistak (1999). "Exploring Differences between Violent and Nonviolent Juvenile Offenders Using Juvenile Corrections Facility Client Records." *Journal of Educational and Psychological Consultation,* 10:129-143.

Bischof, G.P. and S.M. Stith (1995). "Family Environments of Adolescent Sex Offenders and Other Juvenile Delinquents." *Adolescence,* 20:157-170.

Bischof, G.P. and S.M. Stith (1992). "A Comparison of the Family Systems of Adolescent Sexual Offenders and Nonsexual Offending Delinquents." *Family Relations,* 41:318-323.

Blumstein, A., J. Cohen, and D.P. Farrington (1988). "Longitudinal and Criminal Career Research: Further Clarifications." *Criminology,* 26:57-74.

Borduin, C.M, B.J. Mann, L.T. Cone, S.W. Henggeler, B.R. Fucci, D.M. Blaske, and R.A. Williams (1995). "Multisystemic Treatment of Serious Juvenile Offenders: Long-Term Prevention of Criminality and Violence." *Journal of Consulting and Criminal Psychology,* 63:569-578.

Cellini, H.R. (1994). "Management and Treatment of Institutionalized Violent Juveniles." *Corrections Today,* 56:98-102.

Cottle, T.J. (1998). "The Child at Risk: The Case for the Youthful Offender." *Journal of Education,* 180:95-114.

Federal Bureau of Investigation (n.d.). *Uniform Crime Reports.* Retrieved October 5 2003, from http://www.fbi.gov/ucr/ucr.htm

Federal Bureau of Investigation (2000). *Uniform Crime Reports: Aggravated assault.* Retrieved October 5, 2003, from http://www.fbi.gov/ucr/cius_00/00crime2_6.pdf

Federal Bureau of Investigation (2000). *Uniform Crime Reports: Forcible Rape.* Retrieved October 5, 2003, from http://www.fbi.gov/ucr/cius_00/00crime2_4.pdf

Federal Bureau of Investigation (2000). *Uniform Crime Reports: Homicide.* Retrieved October 5, 2003, from http://www.fbi.gov/ucr/cius_00/00crime2_3.pdf

Federal Bureau of Investigation (2000). *Uniform Crime Reports: Robbery.* Retrieved October 5, 2003, from http://www.fbi.gov/ucr/cius_00/00crime2_5.pdf

Feiler, S.M. and J.F. Sheley (1999). "Legal and Racial Elements of Public Willingness to Transfer Juvenile Offenders to Adult Court." *Journal of Criminal Justice,* 27:55-64.

Gerstein, L.H. and J.R. Briggs (1993). "Psychological and Sociological Discriminants of Violent and Nonviolent Serious Juvenile Offenders." *Journal of Addiction and Offender Counseling,* 14:2-13.

Haller, L.H. (2000). "Forensic Aspects of Juvenile Violence." *Juvenile Violence,* 9:859-881.

Henggeler, S.W., G.B. Melton, M.J. Brondino, D.G. Scherer, and J.H. Hanley (1997). "Multisystemic Therapy with Violent and Chronic Juvenile Offenders and Their Families: The Role of Treatment Fidelity in Successful Dissemination." *Journal of Consulting and Clinical Psychology,* 65:821-833.

Henggeler, S.W., G.B. Melton, and L.A. Smith (1992). "Family Preservation Using Multisystemic Therapy: An Effective Alternative to Incarcerating Serious Juvenile Offenders." *Journal of Consulting and Clinical Psychology,* 60:953-961.

Huey Jr., S.J., S.W. Henggeler, M.J. Brondino, and S.G. Pickrel (2000). "Mechanisms of Change in Multisystemic Therapy: Reducing Delinquent Behavior through Therapist Adherence and Improved Family and Peer Functioning." *Journal of Consulting and Clinical Psychology,* 68:451-467.

Jones Jr., W.B. (1941). "An Educational Problem in Juvenile Delinquency." *Journal of Educational Sociology,* 14:437-441.

Kempinen, C. and M.C. Kurlychek (2003). "An Outcome Evaluation of Pennsylvania's Boot Camp: Does Rehabilitative Programming within a Disciplinary Setting Reduce Recidivism?" *Crime & Delinquency,* 49:581-602.

MacKenzie, D.L, A.R. Gover, G.J. Styve, and O. Mitchell (1999). *A National Study Comparing the Environments of Boot Camps to Traditional Facilities for Juvenile Offenders.* Washington, DC: U.S. Department of Justice.

MacKenzie, D. and L.J. Hickman (1998). *What Works in Corrections: An Examination of the Effectiveness of the Type of Rehabilitation Programs Offered by Washington State Department of Corrections.* College Park, MD: Crime Prevention Effectiveness Program of the University of Maryland.

MacQueary, T.H. (1903). "Schools for Delinquent, and Truant Children in Illinois." *The American Journal of Sociology,* 9:1-23.

McCord, J., C.S. Widom, and N.A. Crowell (eds.) (2001). *Juvenile Crime Juvenile Justice.* Washington, DC: National Academy Press.

McShane, M.D. and F.P. Williams III (eds.) (2003). *Encyclopedia of Juvenile Justice.* London: Sage Publications.

Sherman, L., D. Gottfredson, D. MacKenzie, J. Eck, P. Reuter, and S. Bushway (1997). *Preventing Crime: What Works, What Doesn't, What's Promising.* Washington, DC: National Institute of Justice.

Sprott, J.B. (1998). "Understanding Public Opposition to a Separate Youth Justice System." *Crime & Delinquency,* 44:399-411.

Stolzenberg, L. and S.J. D'Alessio (2000). "Gun Availability and Violent Crime: New Evidence from the National Incident-Based Reporting System." *Social Forces,* 78:1461-1482.

Stouthamer-Loeber, M. and R. Loeber (2002). "Lost Opportunities for Intervention: Undetected Markers for the Development of Serious Juvenile Delinquency." *Criminal Behavior and Mental Health,* 12:69-82.

Torbet, P.M. (1997). "State Response to Serious and Violent Juvenile Crime." *Corrections Today,* 59:121-123.

Tyler, J., R. Darville, and K. Stalnaker (2001). "Juvenile Boot Camps: A Descriptive Analysis of Program Diversity and Effectiveness." *The Social Science Journal,* 38:445-460.

Vogel, B.L. and R.E. Vogel (2003). "The Age of Death: Appraising Public Opinion of Juvenile Capital Punishment." *Journal of Criminal Justice,* 31:169-183.

Zhang, L., J.W. Welte, and W.W. Wieczorek (2002). "The Role of Aggression-Related Alcohol Expectancies in Explaining the Link between Alcohol and Violent Behavior." *Substance Abuse and Misuse, 37*:457-471.

Zimring, F.E. (1998). *American Youth Violence*. New York: Oxford University Press.

Chapter 8

Juvenile Drug Offenders

Elizabeth Smith and Wendy Povitsky

Introduction

Among the multitude of challenges facing today's youth, many would say drugs are the most pervasive and also the most persistent. Every few decades for the past century, American society has experienced a moral panic and widespread fear over a particular drug (Goode, 1999). In the early 1900s, cocaine took the spotlight and became cause for alarm and concern. In the 1930s, marijuana was recognized as the new menace and widespread propaganda emerged warning against the evils of the drug. The film *Reefer Madness* is a cinematic example of the prevalence of substance use in society during this period. The 1960s brought about the hippie subculture as well as the popularity of LSD, which quickly became the nemesis of conservative parents. Marijuana continued to be popular throughout the 1960s as well. During the 1980s, the use of crack cocaine was brought into the living rooms of all Americans with images of crack babies and kids dealing drugs on street corners. Due to the moral panic over crack cocaine, the war on drugs escalated during the 1980s and many in the United States pushed for harsher punishments for drug use. Slogans, such as "Just Say No," and "This is your brain, this is your brain on drugs" bombarded the popular culture (Goode, 1999). In addition to widespread media campaigns, a mirage of treatment and prevention programs was implemented; most proving to be unsuccessful.

Two surveys used to measure the prevalence of drug use among American juveniles over the past twenty-five years are the Monitoring the Future (MTF) and Parents' Resource Institute for Drug Education (PRIDE). These surveys allow us to evaluate the current degree of drug use among youth, and also examine the patterns of drug use among juveniles over time. After discussing these surveys and the findings, this chapter will examine a number of typologies proposed to classify juveniles based on their level of drug use and drug dealing behavior. In addition, the link between drug use and criminality will be examined as well as various sociological, psychological, and biological theories of drug use. The chapter ends with a review of drug treatment, correctional interventions, and management strategies used to reduce the drug use of juveniles. While the choices are numerous, ranging from rehabilitation and incarceration to prevention strategies, many have been shown to be ineffective. Court-mandated treatments such as juvenile assessment centers and juvenile drug courts will be focused upon due to their growing popularity.

Major Tools for Tracking Drug Use

A large variety of surveys are available to estimate juvenile drug use in the United States. Most of these self-report surveys are anonymous and administered through schools. Two representative surveys highlighted here are the Monitoring the Future (MTF) survey and the Parents' Resource Institute for Drug Education (PRIDE) survey. Both have been widely used across the country.

Monitoring the Future Survey

The Monitoring the Future (MTF) survey, conducted by the Institute for Social Research at the University of Michigan, has questioned over 45,000 students in 433 secondary schools. It is one of the most influential and longest running surveys that exist to date. Beginning in 1975, the survey was used to evaluate high school seniors' drug use, attitudes towards drug use, and peers' drug habits. In 1991, the MTF survey broadened its sample to include 8th and 10th graders. Goals of the MTF include tracking drug use among middle and high school students, understanding changing patterns in drug use, and impressing upon people the importance of practical research (Mieczkowski, 1996).

According to the MTF survey, drug use was on the rise during the 1960s and 1970s, and peaked in the late 1970s. Drug use appeared to decline through the 1980s and early 1990s, but then went on the rise, peaking again in 1996 and 1997. Since then, drug use has remained relatively stable with minute increases and decreases (Johnston, O'Malley & Bachman, 2003).

Despite the perceived stability of juvenile drug use, the numbers of youth involved with drugs is alarming. According to the 2003 MTF survey, by the end of 8th grade, 32 percent of students have tried an illicit substance and by 12th grade, 55 percent have done so. Such illicit substances include inhalants (the illicit inhaling of gases in legal household substances). Forty-eight percent of 12th graders report having tried marijuana and 6 percent of 12th graders admit to smoking daily. During the past year, 8 percent of 12th graders admit to cocaine use, 3.8 percent report crack cocaine use, 7.4 percent tried ecstasy and 4 percent admit trying Oxycontin. Heroin use among 12th graders decreased by half between 1975 and 1979; dropping from 1 percent to 0.5 percent. The rates of heroin use then stabilized for the next fifteen years until 1994 and 1995 when it increased by 2-3 times its previous rate. In 2000, heroin rates decreased for 8th graders from 1.4 percent to 1.1 percent but increased for 12th graders from 1.1 percent to 1.5 percent. The increase in heroin use by seniors was mostly due to non-injection heroin use. Both groups showed significant decreases in heroin use in 2001 (Johnston et al., 2003).

The MTF survey also examines drug use among different socio-demographic groups and has found that males show much higher rates of drug use than females. This is to be expected as males have higher overall delinquency rates than females. When examining drug use among different racial/ethnic groups, the MTF indicates that Hispanics have the highest rates of use of marijuana and drugs included in the "dangerous" category, such as heroin with a needle, crack, and crystal methamphetamine. Whites have the highest rates of use of inhalants, hallucinogens, narcotics, and ecstasy. Finally, the MTF indicates that African-Americans have the lowest rates of use for all substances (Johnson et al., 2003).

Regardless of who has the highest or lowest rate of drug use among youth, most demographic groups are experiencing the repercussions of drug use. The MTF indicates that treatment and prevention must become a focus if we want to eliminate this epidemic of drug abuse.

PRIDE Survey

Another survey used to capture information on the prevalence of drug use is the Parents' Resource Institute for Drug Education (PRIDE). This survey, in use since 1982 and also conducted in schools, gathers data on alcohol and drug use, violence, attitudes toward drug use, lifestyle choices, ease of obtaining drugs, age of first use, and parental roles. The PRIDE survey chooses students from grades 6-12 to include in their yearly sample (PRIDE, 2002). Because PRIDE captures information on younger children, it is seen as an improvement over the MTF survey which only looks at 8th, 10th, and 12th graders. A criticism of PRIDE is that it uses broader categories for drug use such as marijuana, cocaine, heroin, uppers, downers, inhalants, hallucinogens, and steroids. It does not ask about "trendier" drugs that have recently been on the rise such as ecstasy and oxycontin. Another downside to this survey is that it only asks about use for the year prior to the administration of the survey, thus precluding information on lifetime use rates (PRIDE, 2002).

Despite such criticism, PRIDE is considered reliable and useful in tracking drug trends among juveniles.

Rates of use according to PRIDE closely mirror findings of the MTF survey, with drug use on the rise through the early 1990s with a peak in 1996 and 1997. Again, similar to MTF, drug use rates have remained relatively stable since 1997 with some small decreases. Surpassing the information MTF can provide, PRIDE found that for 6th-8th graders, drug rates have dropped significantly since 1996-1997 and rates have only remained stable for 9th-12th graders (PRIDE, 2002). This is an encouraging finding as it suggests that younger children are using fewer drugs, which could lead to less drug use as they get older. Despite this reduced rate of use among younger students, similarities for rates of use in MTF and PRIDE are evident as PRIDE indicates that 35.7 percent of 12th graders smoked pot sometime over the past year and 7.5 percent admitted to smoking daily. Within the past year 7.1 percent of 12th graders had tried cocaine, 4.3 percent had tried inhalants, 8.3 percent had tried hallucinogens, 3.7 percent had tried heroin, and 37.4 percent had tried any illicit drug (PRIDE, 2002).

Box 8.1

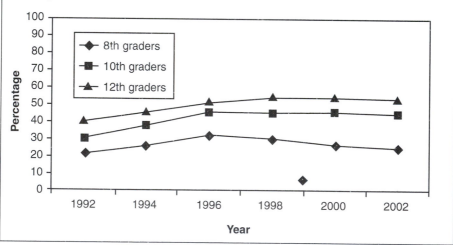

Drug Use declined steadily from the 1970s until the early 1990s. Then the use of drugs among juveniles rose steadily until it peaked in 1996 and 1997. Since then, it has remained relatively stable with slight decreases (MTF, 2003).

Problems with the Use of Surveys

Unfortunately, the results of school surveys may not be completely accurate for many reasons. For example, by conducting these surveys in school many juveniles are precluded from the sample. It is possible that the chronic drug abusers could have dropped out of school, skipped the day the survey was administered, or had already been arrested and placed in detention centers at the time of the survey. Another problem with school surveys is that many students feel that they cannot tell the truth on such surveys because they will somehow get punished for their behavior. Research shows that if students can be convinced of either confidentiality or anonymity, their answers will be more reflective of their actual drug use (Bjarnason & Adalbjarnardottir, 2000). Other problems include inaccurate memories of use and dishonest answers, which can threaten the reliability and validity of the data. Evidence indicates a high probability that the amount of drug use reported in these surveys is slightly underrepresented, however research has found that generally school surveys are reliable and valid estimates of substance abuse (Bjarnason et al., 2000). Despite the challenges associated with school surveys, such problems have not changed. The amount of error is likely consistent through the years; thus not greatly impacting the ability to make conclusions about trends of drug use.

Offender Characteristics

Chaiken and Johnson (1988) categorize youthful drug users in the following typology: recreational users, adolescents who distribute small amounts of drugs, adolescents who frequently sell drugs, teenage dealers who commit other delinquent acts, losers or burnouts, and persistent offenders. These categories share many similar qualities and offenders frequently move between them depending on their amount of use and/or criminal behavior.

The recreational user, who uses drugs only moderately, usually engages in drug use in order to get high or enhance a social setting. These youth rarely distribute drugs and typically do not come to the attention of authorities. It is uncommon for these offenders to commit other crimes aside from drug use. They are very high functioning and often, as they grow older, they develop more stakes in conventional society and desist from drug use. The majority of juvenile drug offenders can be labeled as recreational users (Chaiken & Johnson, 1988).

The small amount distributors are juveniles who distribute small amounts of drugs and do so in order to support their habit. Despite their actions, these youth usually do not consider themselves to be seriously involved in either drug use or trafficking. Similar to recreational users, they are very high functioning and rarely come to the attention of the criminal justice system (Chaiken & Johnson, 1988). They differentiate themselves from those who frequently sell drugs by bridging the gap between the adult dealer and the juvenile user. Many of these youths are daily drug users but still function in normal activities such as school and employment.

Those individuals who frequently sell drugs do so in order to make money or to free themselves of drugs. These youths only sometimes come to the attention of authorities because their drug trafficking is usually in small amounts and informal settings (Chaiken & Johnson, 1988).

Losers and burnouts, another category of juvenile drug users, do not associate with other users and dealers but rather commit individual unplanned crimes. Their heavy drug use decreases their usefulness in an organized drug distribution network and increases their probability of arrest. Although these users occasionally work for dealers to market the product, they are very unreliable and are looked down upon by drug traffickers. They are frequently arrested and if untreated, they often become entrenched in the addiction subculture and continue their drug use and criminality into adulthood (Chaiken & Johnson, 1988).

Box 8.2
Drug Typologies

Recreational
Consists of the majority of drug users
Very moderate drug use and most desist in use as they grow older
Rarely come to the attention of authorities

Distributing Small Amounts
Distribute in order to support own habit but do not consider themselves to be heavily involved in drug use or trafficking
Also rarely come to the attention of authorities

Losers and Burnouts
Juvenile addicts that commit unorganized individual crimes
Heavy drug use decreases usefulness in gangs because of unreliability and increases the probability of arrest
Very likely to continue drug use and criminal behavior into adulthood

Teenage Dealer
Usually commits property crime or violent crime
Comprises 2 percent of juvenile population and commits 40 percent of robberies and assaults and 60 percent of teenage felony thefts and drug sales
May work for adult dealers and then advance in drug trade
This type commonly forms gangs with highly organized drug-networking systems.
Usually only use drugs recreationally
Very likely to become persistent offenders and continue crime into adulthood

Chaiken & Johnson (1988).

Out of the numerous types of juvenile drug offenders, teenage dealers who commit other delinquent acts cause the most societal problems. These offenders not only distribute drugs but also commit property and/or violent crimes. While this group comprises 2 percent of the teenage population, they commit up to 40 percent of juvenile robberies and assaults and 60 percent of teenage felony thefts and drug sales. This group usually works for adult dealers as runners and advance their status in the drug trade industry as they grow older and more experienced. Often, juveniles in this group join together to form gangs and develop organized drug-networking systems. Because their focus is on the business of drug trafficking, the majority of these juveniles are only recreational users and rarely use highly addictive substances (Chaiken & Johnson, 1988). This category frequently leads to persistent offending in adulthood. In fact, about two thirds of all juvenile drug offenders continue using drugs into adulthood and about one-half continue their criminal activities.

The Link between Drug Use and Criminality

Although an association between drug use and criminality has been established in the research literature (Bui, Ellickson & Bell, 2000; Bui et al., 2000; Cantor, 1995; Chaiken & Johnson, 1988; Elliot, Huizinga & Ageton, 1985; Johnston, 1988), the exact link is unclear. Does drug use lead to criminality, delinquent behavior lead to drug use, or do certain outside factors lead to both? All of the above options may be true depending on the circumstances and types of people. Despite disagreements regarding causality, it seems clear that directional certainty would lead to better prevention and treatment solutions. Even if directionality is conditional, researchers could attempt to better understand said conditions and ultimately the link between drug use and criminality.

There are three key associations between drug use and criminality (Johnston, 1998); the first being that crime is an instrument of the drug trade. This is likely due to the fact that drug trafficking is mainly conducted on the black market—an industry already fraught with violence and property crimes. The second link between drug use and crime is the necessity of crime to obtain and use drugs. The final link between drug use and crime is that use of drugs is likely to cause crime by lowering inhibitions. This makes offenders more willing to take risks and thus more likely to commit crimes while under the influence (Johnston, 1998).

Contrary to the evidence that drug use leads to delinquency, as described above, some believe that the opposite is true. The National Institute of Justice's Arrestee Drug Abuse Monitoring System tracks drug use among arrested juveniles. It has found that 40 percent of male and 20 percent of female arrestees tested positive for marijuana. The tracking system also indicated that incarcerated youth are more likely to be involved with drugs than adolescents in the general population (Cantor, 1995). Chaiken and Johnson (1988) found, using data from national self-report surveys, that less than 2 percent of juveniles reported using cocaine or heroin and committed more than two index crimes per year. However, this 2 percent accounted for 40-60 percent of all index crimes reported in the sample. This suggests that there is a small core of substance abusing juveniles that are committing a significant proportion of all crimes. In an effort to pinpoint the exact causation between drug use and criminality, Bui et al. (2000) found that higher levels of delinquency in 10th grade led to higher levels of drug use in 12th grade.

To further complicate matters, Elliot et al. (1985), proposed that certain factors that lead to criminal behavior are also favorable to substance abuse, thus that there may be no causation between drug use and delinquency. He suggests that both drug use and delinquency reflect developmental problems and both are part of a general pattern of deviance. Many youth begin by committing petty crimes and drinking alcohol and gradually move toward more serious crimes and drugs. Both substance abusers and delinquents are often part of an urban underclass that consists of a certain lifestyle that involves limited education, few job skills, unstable families, few social skills, and a pattern of law violating behaviors (Elliott et al., 1985).

Box 8.3
Red Ribbon Week

Red Ribbon Week is a national program sponsored by the National Family Partnership. The weeklong event is designed to promote awareness of drugs and alcohol and to motivate citizens to keep their communities free of the harms of drug trafficking and drug abuse. Throughout the United States, there are rallies, events, and memorials for those who have fallen victim to drug and alcohol abuse. People wear red ribbons to signify their commitment not only to keeping themselves clean but also to protecting their communities. It is estimated that, today, more than 80 million Americans participate in this event.

This well-supported national movement indicates that people are ready to end drug abuse among both adults and youth. In order to do so, we must have a good understanding of why certain people become involved with drugs and what treatments are effective in ending this addiction.

Red Ribbon Week is the most far-reaching and well-known drug prevention event in America. The National Family Partnership, which coordinates Red Ribbon activities nationally, estimates that more than 80 million Americans participate in Red Ribbon events. It's also a chance for Drug Enforcement Administration to show their support for citizens throughout the United States who support their efforts to keep communities free from the ravages of drug trafficking and drug abuse.

http://www.usdoj.gov/dea/ongoing/redribbon02.html

Theoretical Perspectives

Individual differences between adolescents may make any blanket explanation of juvenile drug use nearly impossible. There are a variety of sociological, biological, and psychological factors that influence children in different ways and contribute to illegal behavior and drug use. Examples of explanations for juvenile drug use include a desire to experience new behaviors and sensations, to act in a manner that they feel is more adult and mature, to relieve peer pressure, or to enhance a social setting. Most adolescents will only be recreational drug users and never go on to develop an addiction. They may try drugs experimentally a few times and then cease the behavior to live fully functional lives (Hanson & Venturelli, 2001).

Such behavior might be explained by Moffitt's theory of delinquency. This theory encompasses sociological, biological, and psychological facts. According to Moffit's theory, there are two types of juvenile offenders: adolescent-limited and lifecourse-persistent. Adolescent-limited juvenile offenders commit an array of delinquent acts in adolescence including drug use and eventually age out of their delinquency patterns to lead productive, law-abiding lifestyles in adulthood. However, there are the select few that are lifecourse-persistent offenders that also become juvenile addicts or involve themselves in substance abuse related crime and continue their criminal behavior into adulthood (Moffitt, 1993). These are the juveniles that create concern in society. Additionally, much of the research has focused on trying to understand the causes of their delinquency. With a better understanding of the causes of their behavior, treatment professionals could be more effective in implementing prevention and treatment efforts that work towards eliminating the problem of juvenile drug use.

Sociological Theories

Social Disorganization Theory

Shaw and McKay's Social Disorganization Theory has aided in explaining juvenile substance abuse. The theory states that neighborhoods become socially disorganized when they have high population growth and transience, ethnic heterogeneity, and high rates of poverty. These elements create a disconnection among neighbors and block strong social ties in the community. In turn, delinquent social groups emerge, and cannot be controlled by the neighborhood. Shaw and McKay found empirical support for their research in Chicago. Through their investigation it was discovered that the highest rates of social disorganization were in the center of the city, along with the highest rates of delinquency (Shaw & McKay, 1942).

Researchers have proposed an explanation of juvenile drug use using Social Disorganization theory. From their perspectives, the highest rates of drug use will be found in poverty-stricken urban neighborhoods that have high rates of social disorganization. However, research support for this proposal has been mixed. Jang and Johnson (2001) proposed that neighborhood disorder provided an environmental context that supported juvenile drug use. In a longitudinal study that measured neighborhood disorder and drug use, they found a significant correlation between socially disorganized neighborhoods and juvenile drug use. In contrast, research done by Elliot et al. (1985) indicated that there was almost no association between drug use and class. Middle class, suburban juveniles were as likely to engage in substance abuse as those living in poor, urban areas (Elliot et al., 1985). Because research findings are mixed, it is likely that this theory may explain only a small portion of juvenile substance abuse at best, and further explanations are necessary.

Social Bond Theory

Hirschi's Social Bond Theory has also been used to explain juvenile drug use. The theory suggests that the causes for crime and drug use are not just the neighborhoods but instead the weakened social bonds in the socially disorganized neighborhoods. Through attachment, commitment, involvement, and belief in conventional social bonds, social control can be achieved and crime decreased (Hirschi, 1969). If positive bonds are created between the family and school, individuals will be less likely to turn to drug use (Hirschi & Gottfredson, 1995). Studies have found that the majority of drug abusers have had unhappy childhoods, which included harsh punishments and parental neglect. Substance abusers tend to also have large families with parents that were separated, divorced, or absent (Bucky, 1973). This research indicates that weakened bonds with the family lead to drug use and criminality.

Physical or sexual abuse can also lead to weakened ties within the family and are highly correlated with drug abuse among juveniles. A study by Ireland, Smith, and Thornberry (2002) examined the role of maltreatment on delinquency and drug abuse. They found maltreatment that occurred during childhood did not play a large role in later delinquency and drug use, but maltreatment that occurred in adolescence and persistent maltreatment that occurred throughout both childhood and adolescence, were significantly correlated with juvenile delinquency and drug use (Ireland et al., 2002).

Other social bonds have been shown to reduce drug use include individual religiosity and sports participation. Research by Jang and Johnson (2001) found that although disorganized neighborhoods have a significant effect on juvenile drug use, this effect was tempered by religiosity. Juveniles with higher levels of religiosity were much less likely to be involved in drug use, suggesting that social bonds to religion could influence delinquent behavior. A study conducted by Eitle, Turner, and Eitle (2003) found that for African-Americans, participation in sports throughout high school significantly reduced drug use. Unlike with Social Disorganization Theory, the evidence is convincing that an individual's bond with conventional society has an effect on the amount of delinquency and drug use.

Social Learning Theory

Despite empirical support, social control theory cannot fully explain juvenile drug use because some individuals do maintain conventional social bonds and still experiment with drugs and engage in criminality. Akers's Social Learning Theory attempts to explain this behavior. The key concepts in this theory are differential association, imitation, and differential reinforcement. Differential association suggests that if the surrounding environment, particularly intimate social relationships, has favorable attitudes concerning drug use, then an individual will be more likely to adopt these favorable attitudes and engage in drug use. It is thought that an individual first adopts these favorable definitions towards criminality and then begins to imitate the behavior. Once the individual engages in criminal acts they receive positive or negative reinforcement, which leads to desistance or further criminality (Akers, 1973). Research by Bachman, Johnston, and O'Malley (1998) found that attitudes and perceptions about particular drugs significantly predicted drug abuse.

Social Learning Theory is a particularly important theory when examining the peer groups of an individual. From peer groups where the prevalence of substance abuse is high, youth can learn positive attitudes concerning the use of drugs. In addition to learning favorable attitudes that can lead to drug use, juveniles learn the techniques and language that helps them to become more proficient in their use and immersed in the drug subculture. Research has shown that the amount of drug use by an individual's peers is one of the strongest predictors of drug use (Jang & Johnson, 2001; Johnston, 1998). Families also influence juvenile attitudes toward drugs mainly through observation of other family members' drug use. Youth can learn favorable attitudes about drugs, drug techniques, and drug language from family members as well (Mio et al., 1986).

Box 8.4

Steroid use is becoming a serious problem within high schools across the nation. Experts fear that these youth don't know the serious dangers that are in store for those who abuse steroids, such as heart and liver damage. Despite the dangers, the number of youth using this drug is alarming. "The National Institute for Drug Abuse reports more than half a million eighth- and 10th-grade students are now using steroids. The federal Centers for Disease Control reports steroid use among high school students is up 67 percent since 1991. And there are even younger kids involved, with reported use among seventh-, sixth-, even fifth-graders" (http://www.msnbc.msn.com/id/7223231/).

Strain Theory

Merton's Strain Theory also aids in explaining juvenile substance abuse. Strain theory postulates that in the United States there is a specified "American Dream" involving economic success, which people strive to achieve. When individuals do not have the means to achieve this goal they become frustrated and respond in one of five ways: conformity, innovation, ritualism, retreatism, and rebellion (Merton, 1938). Drug abuse is mostly associated with retreatism. This occurs when individuals become frustrated due to a lack of acceptable means for achieving society's goals, and thus escape society through drug use (Merton, 1938). Although this theory appears to explain juvenile drug use, a study done by the Rand Corporation found that many of the youth who have been arrested for drug trafficking also held legitimate jobs. This shows that some youth do not turn to drugs out of frustration because of unemployment and poor socioeconomic status, but do so for some other reason (Reuter, MacConn & Murphy, 1990).

Biological Causes

At times, sociological factors are not the sole reason for drug use; factors such as genetics may also play a role. Research studies with twins and adopted children have shown that addictive behaviors may be biologically based. Twin studies look at the similarities in behavior between fraternal twins and identical twins. Because identical twins share the same exact DNA, if their behavior is similar it would suggest that behavior is genetically based. If the fraternal twins behave in a similar manner, it would indicate that behavior is environmentally based since they do not share the exact same DNA. This research has found that the concordance rates between identical twins are much higher than for fraternal twins when examining alcoholism (Rowe, 1983).

Juvenile Drug Offenders   **171**

Adoption studies determine how behavior is passed through genetics by looking at the behavior of adopted children and whether it resembles that of the biological parent or the adoptive parent. If the behavior is similar to the biological parent, this is an indication that the behavior is genetically determined. If the behavior more closely resembles the adoptive parent, the behavior can be assumed to be an environmental trait. This research indicates that children whose biological parents are alcoholics but have been raised by adoptive non-alcoholic parents are very likely to develop alcohol problems. Children who are raised by alcoholic adoptive parents but have no history of alcoholism in their biological families also sometimes develop alcohol problems but not to the same extent (Brennan, Mednick & Jacobsen, 1996). Such research suggests that alcoholism may have genetically determined component.

Scientists have attempted to pinpoint the exact cause of genetically determined behavior, but it has proven to be a daunting task. Many neurotransmitters have been identified that could lead to certain behavioral problems such as serotonin, dopamine, and MAOA. Hormones such as testosterone are also thought to play a role in behavioral problems (Fishbein, 2001). Deviant behavior has also been linked to biological factors related to the environment. If a woman smokes, drinks, or engages in substance abuse during pregnancy, it can have serious repercussions on the life of the unborn child. Fetal Alcohol Syndrome is caused by drinking alcohol while pregnant and is closely linked to a baby's future behavioral and developmental problems (Fishbein, 2001). Although these studies indicate that biology plays an important role in juvenile substance abuse and delinquency, much more research needs to be conducted to determine to what extent. In many cases, biological makeup can predispose a person to have certain traits; however, it is the environment and sociological factors that cause the individual to act on those traits.

Psychological Causes

Psychological factors have also been linked to juvenile criminality and substance abuse. It is theorized that adolescents may use drugs in order to change unsatisfactory emotional states caused by emotional disorders (Bui et al., 2000). Youth who internalize their feelings and blame themselves for their failures may then have strong feelings of self-doubt and inadequacy, which lead them to substance abuse. Similarly, youth who externalize their feelings and blame others for their failures are more likely to engage in many antisocial behaviors, including drug use (Steele et al., 1995). Bui et al. (2000) attempted to determine the causal nature between emotional distress and substance abuse they found that although it is clear that juveniles with emotional problems have higher rates of substance abuse, the causal nature between the two cannot be determined. It is possible that confounding variables exist that lead to both emotional problems and drug use. A correlation between the two has been established suggesting that further research needs to be conducted to obtain clear answers (Bui et al., 2000).

According to some research, up to one half of all drug users may also be diagnosed with antisocial personality disorder (Strain, 1995). One of the elements of antisocial personality disorder is that an individual must be at least eighteen years old in order to be diagnosed. Antisocial personality disorder traits can be present before that age, but then the behavior is diagnosed as a conduct disorder. The DSM-IV defines conduct disorders as the repetitive and persistent patterns of behavior that violate the basic rights of others (APA, 1994). Many children that are diagnosed with this disorder are then classified as having antisocial personality disorder when they turn eighteen. Between 6-16 percent of all juvenile males are affected by conduct disorders (Cohen, Cohen & Brook, 1993). Although drug use is not specifically under the realm of conduct disorders, having this psychological problem can lead to a vast range of deviant behaviors that includes drug use.

Attention Deficit Hyperactivity Disorder (ADHD) is also a psychological cause for much deviant behavior and drug use. ADHD is the most common psychological diagnosis for American children even though the cause of ADHD is unknown. Some speculate that ADHD is caused by biological factors while others believe that it is environmentally based. ADHD causes extreme emotional, behavioral, and developmental problems that can have serious negative effects on productive social functioning. Because of these problems, many juveniles become frustrated and may develop deviant characteristics including drug use. A study conducted by the Long Island Jewish Medical Center and the New York State Psychiatric Institute showed that 16 percent of the individuals diagnosed with ADHD were abusing drugs as opposed to 3 percent of the comparison group (Cowley, 1993). This suggests that ADHD is a psychological problem that can lead to many deviant problem behaviors including drug use.

Treatment/Prevention

Many different treatment options have been implemented to try to alleviate the problem of juvenile substance abuse. These options vary in effectiveness. Treatment efforts have been employed at all stages of development, from school based prevention efforts, to treatment efforts during parole to help offenders re-enter the community. The focus here will be on treatment through the criminal justice system once an offender has already been arrested rather than on self-selected rehabilitation or school-based prevention. First, the ideal treatment plan will be identified and the elements of the plan will be discussed. Then treatment programs that are already in place will be compared to the ideal model to gauge whether they meet the requirements for effective treatment.

The Ideal Treatment Plan

Box 8.5

McBride et al.'s (1999) proposal for an ideal treatment program:

1. Early intervention
2. Comprehensive needs assessment
3. Access to full range of treatment options
4. Cooperation between agencies
5. Single agency should provide management throughout treatment process
6. Management information systems
7. Care should be continued after release
8. Treatment programs must undergo continuous evaluation
9. Interventions should relate to school, family, and peer groups
10. Staff must be sensitive to the unique needs and cultures of juveniles

The traditional juvenile criminal justice system has six key phases that juveniles pass through: intake, social investigation, fact-finding hearing, adjudication, disposition, and continuing care. According to McBride and colleagues (1999) the ideal plan for effective treatment involves altering the current system slightly to cater to juvenile substance abusers. First, the intervention must take place early in order to treat the delinquency problems. Second, a comprehensive needs assessment must be completed to create an effective treatment plan for that individual's needs. Third, juveniles must have access to a full range of treatment options to meet their needs. Effective treatment of juveniles requires cooperation between agencies throughout the system. According to McBride et al. (1999), one agency should provide management through the entire process in order to help the family navigate the system. Management information systems need to be created to organize important information pertaining to the juvenile and the family. This information can be shared between agencies. Care of the juvenile needs to be continued following release to the community. Additionally, treatment programs need to be continuously evaluated for their effectiveness and cost. Interventions need to relate to the school, the family, and the peer groups in order to be truly effective. Staff must be sensitive to the unique needs and cultures of juveniles. Also, educational and vocational training is important to give juveniles skills to succeed in conventional society once they return to the community. Finally, less restrictive programs need to be used primarily so that the juvenile does not get isolated from the community (McBride et al., 1999). Several programs now implement many of these elements in their treatment plans. Research needs to be conducted to determine whether the programs that utilize these methods have greater effectiveness in reducing recidivism and drug use.

Juvenile Assessment Centers

One plan that has been put into practice in the last few years is the idea of juvenile assessment centers (JACs). These centers act as a substitute for traditional intake procedures. They serve as a stepping-stone from the time of arrest to entrance into the court system and then provide case management throughout the process of treatment. The needs of the juvenile are assessed within these centers in order for effective treatment plans to be created. The ideal center should be less focused on criminal justice and should be more of a juvenile health service center that can respond efficiently to the multiple needs of high-risk youth. The purpose of the center would be to link juveniles with special needs to the services that provide them with information systems, assisted planning, resources, and case management processes. The goal is to focus on the overall health of the juvenile that includes physical, mental, and social well being, and also includes prevention efforts in the community. The idea of juvenile assessment centers was first put into operation in Florida in 1993 and has slowly begun to spread throughout the country (Rivers & Anwy, 2000). At this point, little research has been conducted on the effectiveness of these centers however they seem to have several important elements that are proposed in McBride and colleagues' ideal treatment model such as early intervention, needs assessment, and the need for one agency to guide the entire process. Studies need to be completed on the effectiveness of these programs in order to determine whether they reduce recidivism and drug use and are worth the additional cost.

Juvenile Drug Courts

Juvenile drug courts also have many of the elements of the ideal treatment model. They have begun to increase in popularity and become the recent focus of much research. They were initially based on adult drug courts but it was quickly realized that they had to diverge from adult drug court treatment plans as juveniles and adults are so different in their drug use and treatment needs. The goal of the juvenile drug court was to focus

on the family, school, and peer groups so that the child could be rehabilitated and rejoin the community. Currently there are more than 140
courts that have been established and more than 125 in the planning
phases (NDCI, 2003). Many of them have different procedures and
treatment options but they share two things in common. All juvenile drug
courts are comprised of intense judicial supervision that consists of sanctions and incentives to help promote positive behavior and the delivery
of support services such as drug treatment, mental and primary health
care, education, and vocational training. Juveniles with substance abuse
problems that have not committed serious violent offenses are diverted
from the traditional court system to the juvenile drug court system where
a treatment plan is created for that individual's needs. The key purpose
of juvenile drug courts is to obtain help for the juvenile and attempt to
rehabilitate rather than just punish them (Cooper, 2001). Although
this process tends to be a little more costly, it has been found that it is
more cost efficient in the long run because of the lower recidivism rates.
Examples of the sanctions used are short-term incarceration, community service hours, and more frequent drug testing. Examples of incentives are promotion to the next treatment level, gift certificates or
tickets to local sporting events, presentation of a certificate acknowledging good behavior, and the praise of the judge. Many of the juvenile
drug courts have adopted Multi-systemic Therapy, which targets many
factors that lead to delinquent behavior and drug use such as peers and
the family. Multi-systemic Therapy has been shown to be effective in
reducing recidivism in research (Cooper, 2001; MacKenzie, 2006).

According to the OJP Drug Court Clearinghouse and Technical
Assistance Project, juvenile drug courts are effective in reducing recidivism and drug use, while increasing school performance and family functioning. They also found that although juvenile drug court programs have
large failure rates they still have higher retention rates than traditional
programs (Cooper, 2001). Other research has similar findings such as
research by Applegate and Santana (2000) and the Delaware Statistical
Analysis Center (1999), which has shown that juvenile drug courts
can be effective in reducing recidivism and drug use for those who complete the program as compared to those who failed and the comparison
group. The key to the success of these programs is completion of the
program and taking advantage of all the treatment that is provided. They
also acknowledge that there is a large failure rate in juvenile drug
courts and the reason for this has yet to be identified. It was shown that
one-third to one-half of all those assigned to juvenile drug courts fail out
of the program (Applegate & Santana, 2000; Delaware Statistical Analysis Center, 1999). Wilson, Mitchell, and MacKenzie's (in press), meta-
analysis of both adult and juvenile drug courts lend further support to

the program. Their findings indicated that drug court was, overall, more effective in reducing drug use and other criminal offenses than alternative methods of dealing with drug crimes such as probation.

Juvenile drug courts adopt many of the elements in the ideal treatment plan, which indicate that it could be a very effective method. Juvenile drug courts attempt to intervene early and provide needs assessments to create individual treatment plans. They also provide a vast array of services to effectively treat the juvenile and the agencies work together in order to achieve that goal. The judge acts as a case manager to guide the juvenile through the rehabilitation process. Interventions include family therapy plus attempting to improve school performance and vocational training. Support is given to the juvenile even upon completing treatment and rejoining the community, which helps to prevent recidivism. Despite the problems with juvenile drug courts such as their cost and failure rate, they are a very promising method of treatment that needs to be researched further.

Box 8.6

Drug Courts in Practice

Saint Mary's County in Maryland has its own juvenile drug court that was established in 2004. The program is offered as an alternative to formal court proceedings for juveniles involved in substance use and the commission of delinquent acts. The features of the program are as follows:

Juveniles must first admit their involvement in a delinquent act, in addition to substance use or abuse.

Insurance is billed for treatment and medical services provided. The program has a policy that states no one will be turned away due to inability to pay for services.

The program lasts 7-9 months. Upon completion, a finding of "not involved" in the delinquent act is rendered and the pending case is dismissed.

Goals include learning to be drug/alcohol free, learning and improving life skills (e.g., coping, employment, and social skills), and accepting responsibility for past decisions.

There are several aspects to treatment, such as random drug testing, substance abuse treatment, social curfew, mandatory school or work, and community service/restitution.

Incentives and sanctions are given as the juvenile progresses through the program. Examples of incentives are sports or event tickets, verbal recognition by the judge, gift certificates, and decreased mandatory reporting. Sanctions include additional community service, increased reporting, curfew adjustment, and electronic monitoring.

Grounds for early termination of the program consist of missing or positive drug tests, repeated violations of the treatment plan, and violence or threats of violence to staff or other participants.

Graduation is a formal ceremony where the individual is recognized for his or her achievement of completing the program and being drug free.

Other Treatment Options

Incarceration-based drug treatment does not follow the ideal treatment model. In fact, it has been found that incarceration for drug offenders actually increases recidivism and reduces the time until the new crime occurs (Spohn & Holleran, 2002). However, incarceration is one of the most widely used punishments in the United States and will likely not be eliminated in the near future. Therefore, effective incarceration-based treatments need to be identified so that it can potentially reduce some of the negative effects of imprisonment. Unfortunately, it has been found that treatment is available in less than 40 percent of the 3,000 public and private juvenile detention, correctional, and shelter facilities (McBride et al., 1999). Cognitive-behavioral therapy has been shown to be effective in reducing recidivism upon re-entry into the community. Also, therapeutic communities have been found to be effective for adults in reducing drug use and recidivism. Recently, juvenile therapeutic communities have been implemented but there has been very little research to examine the effectiveness. For adults, therapeutic communities have been found to be the most effective treatment while incarcerated, followed by group counseling and methadone maintenance (Mitchell, MacKenzie & Wilson, 2005). Overall, it has been found that some treatment regardless of the type while incarcerated is better than no treatment at all. Although incarceration is not the best way to punish juvenile drug offenders for their actions, until American policy is changed effective prison based treatments need to be established.

Conclusion

Much research has been done on the subject of juvenile drug abuse and many theories have been established as to why these youths engage in this behavior. Now that so much is understood about this phenomenon, treatment methods need to be examined and assessed for effectiveness. Over the years, many different treatment programs have been tried. Many have been reactive and are created in order to treat the person that is already addicted while others are preventive and attempt to reach juveniles before they begin using drugs. Some programs have been shown to be effective, others have had disastrous results and potentially caused juveniles to use more drugs and commit more crimes. An ideal treatment plan has been identified and this paper discussed a few programs already in place that incorporated many of the elements of the ideal model. Juvenile assessment centers and juvenile drug courts seem to be effective in reducing recidivism and drug use among juveniles. Further research needs to be conducted in order to determine the true value of these programs so that positive steps can be made in the future for the treatment of juvenile drug offenders.

References

Akers, R. (1973). *Deviant Behavior: A Social Learning Approach.* Belmont, CA: Wadsworth Publications.

American Psychiatric Association (APA) (1994). *Diagnostic and Statistical Manual of Mental Disorders (DSM IV).* Washington DC: Author.

Applegate, B.K. and S. Santana (2000). "Intervening with Youthful Substance Abusers: A Preliminary Analysis of a Juvenile Drug Court." *Justice System Journal,* 21:281-300.

Bachman, J.G., L.D. Johnston, and P.M. O'Malley (1998). "Explaining Recent Increases in Students' Marijuana Use: Impacts of Perceived Risks and Disapproval, 1976 through 1996." *American Journal of Public Health,* 88:887-892.

Barnes, G.M., J.W. Welte, and J.H. Hoffman (2002). "Relationship of Alcohol Use to Delinquency and Illicit Drug Use in Adolescents: Gender, Age, and Racial/Ethnic Differences." *Journal of Drug Issues,* 32:153-178.

Bjarnason, T. and S. Adalbjarnardottir (2000). "Anonymity and Confidentiality in School Surveys on Alcohol, Tobacco, and Cannabis Use." *Journal of Drug Issues,* 30:335-344.

Brennan, P.A., S.A. Mednick, and B. Jacobsen (1996). "Assessing the Role of Genetics in Crime Using Adoption Cohorts." Ciba Foundation Symposium, 194:115-123, discussion, 123-128.

Bucky, S.F. (1973). "The Relationship between Background and Extent of Heroin Use." *American Journal of Psychiatry*, 130:709-710.

Bui, K.V.T., P.L. Ellickson, and R.M. Bell (2000). "Cross-Lagged Relationships among Adolescent Problem Drug Use, Delinquent Behavior, and Emotional Distress." *Journal of Drug Issues,* 30:283-304.

Cantor, D. (1995). "Drug Involvement and Offending of Incarcerated Youth." Paper presented at the annual meeting of the American Society of Criminology, Boston, MA.

Chaiken, M.R. and B.D Johnson (1988). *Characteristics of Different Types of Drug Involved Youth.* Washington DC: U.S. Department of Justice.

Cohen, P., J. Cohen, and J. Brook (1993). "An Epidemiological Study of Disorders in Late Childhood and Adolescence-II. Persistent Disorders." *Journal of Child Psychology and Psychiatry*, 34:869-877.

Cooper, C.S. (2001). *Juvenile Drug Court Programs.* JAIBG Bulletin by the Office of Juvenile Justice and Delinquency Prevention.

Cowley, G. (1993). "The Not-Young and the Restless." *Newsweek,* 48-49.

Delaware Statistical Analysis Center (1999). Evaluation of the Delaware Juvenile Drug Court Diversion Program.

Eitle, D., R.J. Turner, and T.M. Eitle (2003). "The Deterrence Hypothesis Reexamined: Sports Participation and Substance Abuse Among Young Adults." *Journal of Drug Issues,* 33:193-222.

Elliot, D., D. Huizinga, and S. Ageton (1985). *Explaining Delinquency and Drug Abuse.* Beverly Hills, CA: Sage Publishing.

Fishbein, D. (2001). *Biobehavioral Perspectives in Criminology.* Belmont, CA: Wadsworth.

Goode, E. (1999). *Drugs in American Society.* New York: McGraw-Hill College.

Hanson, G. and P. Venturelli (2001). *Drugs and Society.* New York: Jones and Bartlett Publishers, Inc.

Hirschi, T. (1969). *Causes of Delinquency.* New Brunswick, NJ: Transaction Publishers.

Hirschi, T. and M.R Gottfredson (1995). "Control Theory and the Life Course Perspective." *Studies on Crime and Crime Prevention,* 4:131-142.

Ireland, T.O., C.A. Smith, and T.P. Thornberry (2002). "Developmental Issues in the Impact of Child Maltreatment on Later Delinquency and Drug Use." *Criminology,* 40:359-399.

Jang, S.J. and B.R. Johnson (2001). "Neighborhood Disorder, Individual Religiosity, and Adolescent Use of Illicit Drugs: A Test of Multilevel Hypotheses." *Criminology,* 39:109-144.

Johnston, L.D. (1998). *Reasons for Use, Abstention, and Quitting Illicit Drug Use by American Adolescents.* Commissioned by the Drugs-Violence Task Force of the National Sentencing Commission. MTF Occasional Paper 44.

Johnston, L.D., P.M. O'Malley, and J.G. Bachman (2003). *Monitoring the Future National Survey Results on Drug Use, 1975-2002.* National Institute on Drug Abuse. NIH Publication No. 03-5375.

MacKenzie, D. (2006). *What Works in Corrections? Reducing the Criminal Activity of Offenders and Delinquents.* New York, NY: Cambridge University Press.

McBride, D.C., C.J. Vander Waal, Y.M. Terry, and H. VanBuren (1999). *Breaking the Cycle of Drug Use among Juvenile Offenders.* National Institute of Justice. NCJ 179273.

Merton, R.K. (1938). "Social Structure and Anomie." *American Sociological Review,* 3:672-682.

Mieczkowski, T.M. (1996). "The Prevalence of Drug Use in the United States." *Crime and Justice Abstracts,* 20:349-414.

Mio, J.S., G. Nanjundappa, D.E. Verlur, and M.D. DeRios (1986). "Drug Abuse and the Adolescent Sex Offender: A Preliminary Analysis." *Journal of Psychoactive Drugs,* 18:65-72.

Mitchell, O., D. MacKenzie, and D.B. Wilson (2005). "The Effectiveness of Incarceration Based Drug Treatment: An Empirical Synthesis of the Research." In D.P. Farrington and B.C. Welsh (eds.) *Preventing Crime: What Works for Children, Offenders, Victims, and Places.* New York, NY: Springer.

Moffitt, T.E. (1993). "Adolescence-Limited and Life-Course Persistent Anti-Social Behavior: A Developmental Taxonomy." *Psychological Review,* 100:674-701.

National Drug Court Institute (2003). Juvenile Drug Courts: Strategies in Practice. National Drug Court Institute and the National Council of Juvenile and Family Court Judges. Office of Justice Programs. NCJ 197866.

PRIDE Survey (2000). National Summary Grades 6-12. USO 19999.

Reuter, P., R. MacCoun, and P. Murphy (1990). *Money from Crime: A Study of the Economics of Drug Dealing in Washington, DC.* Santa Monica, CA: Rand.

Rivers, J.E. and R.S. Anwyl (1999). "Juvenile Assessment Centers: Strengths, Weaknesses, and Potential." *The Prison Journal,* 80:96-113

Rowe, D.C. (1983). "Biometrical Genetic Models of Self-Reported Delinquent Behavior: A Twin Study." *Behavioral Genetics,* 13(5):473-489.

Shaw, C.R. and H.D. McKay (1942). *Juvenile Delinquency and Urban Areas.* Chicago: University of Chicago Press.

Spohn, C. and D. Holleran (2002). "The Effect of Imprisonment on Recidivism Rates of Felony Offenders: A Focus on Drug Offenders." *Criminology,* 40:329-357.

Steele, R., R. Forehand, L. Armistead, and G. Brody (1995). "Predicting Alcohol and Drug Use in Early Adulthood: The Role of Internalizing and Externalizing Behavior Problems in Early Adolescence." *American Journal of Orthopsychiatry,* 65:380-387.

Strain, E. (1995). "Antisocial Personality Disorder, Misbehavior, and Drug Abuse." *Journal of Nervous and Mental Disease,* 163:162-165.

Wilson, D.B., O. Mitchell, and D.L. MacKenzie (in press). "A Systematic Review of Drug Court Effects on Recidivism." *Journal of Experimental Criminology.*

Chapter 9

Gangs

Lauren O'Neill

Introduction

Defining Youth Gangs

In order to fully understand a group's motives for committing crimes and to have any hope of treating the members of a particular risk group, it is necessary to define that group. There is a plethora of research dealing with youth gangs, and it is the general consensus that youth gangs need to be defined separately than traditional adolescent groups and adult gangs. How to define a youth gang is one of the most serious problems in the study of this issue (Miller, 2001; Esbensen, Winfree, He & Taylor, 2001; Howell, 1998). Some researchers use definitions that do not necessitate delinquent activity, whereas others have a long list of qualifications to meet before being considered a youth gang. Some definitions are so broad that normal adolescent social groups like the Greek fraternities and sororities, and even the Boy and Girl Scouts, could classify as gangs (Esbensen et al., 2001). However, many contemporary gang researchers agree that two criteria must be met in order for a group to be labeled a youth gang. These criteria are: "(1) youth status, defined as an age classification ranging between 10 and the early 20s or even older, and (2) the engagement by group members in law-violating behavior or, at a minimum, 'imprudent' behavior." (Esbensen et al., 2001:108). Another definition that encompasses almost all contemporary gang research is "a self-formed group, united by mutual interests, that controls a particular territory, facility, or enterprise; uses symbols in communications; and is collectively involved in crime" (Miller, 1992:21). For the purposes of this assessment, the previous definitions will be the criteria used to define a youth gang.

The lack of consensus for a definition of youth gang leads to many difficulties such as accurately stating the gang problem with the best definition for the research question, underestimating the problem by using a definition that is too narrow, or overestimating the problems by using an overly broad definition (Esbensen et al., 2001). This definitional issue can potentially affect research dealing with the prevalence of a youth gang problem in certain areas. Luckily, despite the slight variations in definitions of youth gangs, a review of the literature in this area reveals that research on the prevalence and risk factors for understanding gang behavior has generally concurred.

Box 9.1
Interpreting Gang Graffiti

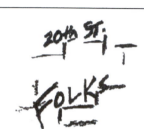

This indicates the name of the gang claiming this territory, usually a neighborhood name.

"Folks" is a reference to the Folk or Hoover Nation gang which is based in Chicago but is popping up all over the South.

These are the individual gang members' street names.

Names are usually given based on a particular trait of the member.

This is the six-pointed star which is the symbol of the Folks. In this example, they have both proudly proclaimed their affiliation and "dissed" (issued disrespect) to the rival Vice Lords by turning the cane handle upside down (Vice Lords use the upright cane in their graffiti). The Folk Nation pitchfork is upright showing respect. The letters at the six points of the star are symbols of the concepts of the Folk Nation: Life, Loyalty, Love, Wisdom, Knowledge, and Understanding.

East Coast represents LA gang orientation. "Cuzz" is a term of endearment used by Crips to address each other. Substituting dollar signs for the S's indicates that this gang is selling narcotics.

BK stands for Blood Killer. Sometimes you will see CK which of course is Crip Killer.

Street names, signature of artists.

(Source: http://www.gangwar.com/dynamics.htm)

Prevalence and Demographics of Youth Gangs in the U.S.

How big a problem is crime related to youth gangs in the U.S.? The majority of youth gang research looks at the increasing prevalence of youth gangs between the 1970s and the present and overwhelmingly shows that crime associated with youth gangs is increasing (Miller, 2001; Howell, 1998). In the 1970s less than one-half of the states in the US reported youth gang problems, but by the late 1990s every state and the District of Columbia reported youth gang activity (Miller, 2001). In addition, "the number of cities with gang problems increased from about 286 jurisdictions with more than 2,000 gangs and nearly 100,000 gang members in 1980 to about 4,800 jurisdictions with more than 31,000 gangs and approximately 846,000 gang members in 1996" (Howell, 1998:1). From 1996 to 2002, all city law enforcement agencies with a service population above 250,000 affirmatively reported gang problems across all seven of the survey years. A large majority of city agencies in the next largest population group (i.e., 100,000-249,999) also reported gang problems during this period. However, in smaller populated areas reports of gang problems declined noticeably from 1996-2001 but increased slightly from 2001 to 2002 (Egley, Howell & Major, 2004). Statistics such as these are seen time and time again in the contemporary research on youth gangs.

In addition to the increasing prevalence of youth gangs in the US, there is also a higher prevalence of violent offenses committed by gang members compared to non-gang members. Howell's (2003) assessment of three longitudinal studies shows that the percentage of the samples that were gang members varied between 14-30 percent. Although the percentage of gang members were smaller than non-gang members, the gang members accounted for between 68-85 percent of the serious violent offenses reported by the samples (Howell, 2003). In some cities gang members committed between three times and seven times the number of serious and violent offenses than non-gang members and in Rochester, two-thirds of chronic violent offenders at a given time were gang members (Howell, 2003).

Offender Characteristics

Despite the definitional differences used in youth gang research, the demographic characteristics of the gang members remain relatively stable across definitions (Esbensen et al., 2001). Demographically, a typical youth gang member is a male between the ages of 12 and 24 (Howell, 1998; Hill, Howell, Hawkins, Pearson, 1999). The demographic that research varies on is ethnicity; depending upon how data were collected.

National law enforcement records estimate a lower percentage of whites involved in gangs (around 5%), whereas student surveys find about 25 percent of gang members to be white. Both means of data collection show the highest percentage among African Americans (between 31-48%), followed by Hispanic (between 25-43%). Asian individuals were the lowest percentage for both means of data collection (Howell, 1998).

Demographic differences between gangs also account for some prevalence variations in different areas. It has been shown that gangs of certain ethnicities commit different delinquent acts. Research finds it apparent that gangs are most likely relatively specialized in the offenses they commit regularly (Sheley, Zhang, Brody & Wright, 1995). "African-American gangs are relatively more involved in drug offenses; Hispanic gangs, in "turf-related" violence; Asian and white gangs, in property crimes" (Howell, 1998:3). Due to the increasing prevalence of youth gangs in the United States it is important to examine the problem more closely in order to work towards understanding these offenders. Demographics are a solid base for beginning to locate gang members, but research has shown that there are many risk factors that affect one's decision to join a life of crime through a gang, and many different gang models and types of gang members that help to understand how much of a danger certain gang members are to society.

Box 9.2
What About Female Gang Members?

There has been very little research done to date specifically focusing on female gang members. Of the existing research, the following conclusions have been made:

- On average, females join gangs at a later age and leave them earlier than their male counterparts (Spergel, 1992).

- According to law enforcement agencies, the percentage of gang members that were female between the 1970s-1998 range from 8-11 percent. However, the proportion of self-identified gang members who were female ranged from 8-38 percent (Moore & Hagedorn, 2001). Other research suggests that the ratio of female to male gang members is 1 to 10 (Spergel, 1992).

- Female gangs are more likely to be founding small cities and rural areas than large cities (Moore & Hagedorn, 2001).

- Most female gangs are African-American or Latina, although there are small but increasing numbers of Asian and white female groups. Ethnicity of female gang members varies by regions with African-American concentrated in the Midwest and Northeast and Latinas in the Southwest (Moore & Hagedorn, 2001).

Box 9.2, *continued*

- One constant in female gang research is that gangs are often a "refuge for young women who have been victimized at home" specifically because high proportions of female gang members have experienced sexual abuse at home (Moore & Hagedorn, 2001). However, Wang (2000) argues that while abuse is a consistent finding, the percentages are not as high as some research suggests. Additionally, a gang provides what a girl needs, protection and acceptance, when other relationships such as family and friends fail her (Wang, 2000).

- Delinquency rates of female gang members are lower than those of male gang members, but higher than those of non-gang females and non-gang males. In general, female gang members commit fewer violent crimes than male gang members (Moore & Hagedorn, 2001; Miller & Decker, 2001; Curry, 1998; Spergel, 1992). Serious offenses that female gang members are committing include carrying a hidden weapon, and selling marijuana and crack cocaine. Serious and violent altercations are usually left to the young men. "Women are likely to be killed in gang homicide events because they are in the wrong place at the wrong time, and with the wrong people, rather than because they are the specific targets of gang retaliation or other violent confrontations." (Miller & Decker, 2001:136).

- The major role of females in gangs is a secondary, auxiliary, or socializing role, specifically acting as sex partners (Wang, 2000; Spergel, 1992).

Risk Factors

Similar to any multidisciplinary view of crime, there are many areas of one's life that can lead someone to joining a gang, including neighborhood factors, family factors, school factors, peer factors, and individual factors (Hill et al., 1999; Howell, 1998). Most gang research incorporates a mixture of a sociological and psychological perspective on crime and evaluates how a juvenile's surroundings and attitudes influence their decision to resist or embrace gang life. The contemporary research is void of a biological perspective on youth gangs. Generally, research supports the idea that adolescents in gangs are more frequently involved in serious delinquent acts than youths who are not in gangs due to a convergence of multiple risk factors that are more prevalent in a gang member's life than a non-gang member adolescent. Therefore, in order to start thinking about prevention of juvenile gangs as a problem in society we need to look at what factors in one's childhood influence a juvenile's decision to get involved in gang life. One of the major studies in this area was the

Seattle Social Development Project by Hill et al. (1999). This longitudinal study followed a sample of 808 juveniles from age 10 to 18 and focused on risk factors in the areas of neighborhood, family, school, peers, and individual students (Hill et al., 1999). Numerous studies concur with the results of this study (Howell, 1998).

In looking at neighborhood level predictors the most significant correlations between predictors and gang involvement were seen in the availability of marijuana to the youths and if other juveniles in the neighborhood were in trouble a lot. In fact, these results showed that children exposed to either of these factors are at least three times more likely to get involved in gangs compared to those with no exposure (Hill et al., 1999). Among family variables, poverty, low parental supervision, and low parental attachment also increased the probability of gang membership (Howell, 1998). The structure of a family has a fairly significant correlation to gang activity. Compared to juveniles living with two parents, either biological or adoptive, youth living with one parent and other adults in the house are most likely to get involved in a gang, followed by those with no parents in the home, and then followed by youth living with one parent. Surprisingly, youth with one biological and one stepparent showed no increase in gang activity. Other family-level factors affecting youth gang membership are the parental attitudes toward violence. Attitudes that favor violence when children are between 10 and 12 led to gang membership later in the child's life, as did antisocial behavior by siblings, and poor family management practices (Hill et al., 1999).

School and peer level predictors were not as heavily looked at in Hill et al.'s study. However, where significance was found, it was highly significant. In looking at school-level predictors significance was found in decreasing level of significance, when the individual was learning disabled, poor academic achievement on standardized tests, low attachment to school, low commitment to school and low educational goals. In addition, other studies concentrated on these factors and found very significant affects on three factors, including low expectations for success in school by the parents and students, low student commitment to school, and low attachment to teachers (Howell, 1998). When analyzing peer-level predictors significance was found when juveniles had friends that got them in trouble in school or had the child try alcohol behind parents' backs (Hill et al., 1999). Also, associating with delinquent peers and unsupervised "hanging around" with these delinquent friends are a "potent combination" (Howell, 1998:8). These results should not be surprising due to the fact that juveniles spend so much time in school and with their peers. Therefore, the exposure to factors in school and peer pressure are much higher than exposure to some of the other areas, dictating more significance in the lives of the youth.

Box 9.3

Gangs in the News . . .

MS-13 Gang Behind Brutal Machete Attack

Three MS-13 gang members were charged in a violent machete attack of a 16-year-old boy in Alexandria, VA. One of the gang members was profiled, while his parents attempted to explain how a happy reunion and the prospects of a new life for their son somehow led to gang involvement and possible death. The victim was allegedly a member of a rival gang, the South-Side Locos (SSL), and doctors were only able to reattach four fingers on his right hand, and only his thumb on the left. The victim denies any gang involvement, and upon admission to the county jail, one of the gang members promptly carved an "MS-13" into his cell window. Public outcry led to an additional $500,000 in funding to combat the Northern Virginia gang problem, as well as promises to fund a new National Gang Intelligence Center.

Source: *The Washington Post,* June 28, 2004

Although the significance levels were not necessarily as high as some of the other factors, there were many more individual level risk factors. This could be because juveniles internalize a lot of what goes on around them and take things personally, which leads to inner conflict, and in some instances aggressive and delinquent behavior may be how a child copes with this inner conflict (Hill et al., 1999). One of the main reasons for delinquency may be to gain attention and a feeling of belonging. This may be important for gang members. Gang membership enhances prestige or status among friends and allows for excitement in an adolescent's life through such activities as selling drugs and making money. Therefore, adolescents see personal advantages to gang membership and rationalize their decision to join a gang (Howell, 1998). After all, this line of reasoning is in tune with some of the oldest theories of crime, such as Beccaria, in which individuals are recognized as rational beings with free will who analyze the cost and benefits of certain behaviors (Beccaria, 1764). Gang activity gives youth a feeling of belonging and a way for internal issues to be masked by acting with a group of others. In decreasing order of significance, the individual-level factors that yielded significant results were: youth having tried marijuana; self-reported violence such as fighting, throwing things, or hitting a teacher; youth whose teachers view them as highly externalizing behavior; rejection of conventional beliefs; youth who have a difficult time turning away from things; hyperactivity; and early initiation of drinking (Hill et al., 1999). Other studies also found that low self-esteem, numerous negative life events, depressive symptoms, and easy access to drugs were significant (Howell, 1998). In fact, "youth who use drugs and are involved in delinquency, particularly violent delinquency, are more likely to become gang members than are youth who are less involved in delinquency and drug use."(Howell, 1998:8).

The research on delinquency shows over and over again that juveniles exposed to these risk factors are rarely exposed to just one of them. Many troubled youth come from areas where exposure to numerous risk factors is a part of everyday life and this research shows that not only does that increase the chance of delinquency, but specifically gang activity. For example, in Hill et al.'s (1999) study, juveniles were asked about 21 risk factors. Exposure to multiple factors had a significant effect on the youth's involvement in a gang. An example of the effect of this multiple exposure was that youth exposed to 7 or more risks during their elementary school years had more than 13 times greater odds of gang involvement than those students with exposure to 0-1 risk (Hill et al., 1999; Howell, 1998). This news should be alarming because it has been corroborated by additional studies, specifically the Rochester study (Thornberry et al., 2003), and shows the likelihood of many of our youth getting involved in gangs. Youths who experience multiple risk factors in numerous domains have been found to be at a much higher risk of gang participation than those who do not face multiple risk factors (Howell, 2003; Thornberry et al., 2003). This lends credence to the idea that instead of focusing on one risk factor, a multidimensional approach to gang prevention needs to be undertaken if we are to have a chance at combating the whole problem.

Theoretical Perspectives

The Effect of Gangs on a Juvenile's Entire Life

The above research shows how adolescents get involved in gangs, but equally as important to treating gang members is understanding the different types of gang members and the likelihood that they will phase out of the activity. Such knowledge will help us know where we should concentrate our resources (e.g., type of gang member). For example, some research suggests that the more hierarchically organized a gang, the greater its involvement in violence (Sheley et al., 1995). Some research has also shown that there are different types of gang members and the type of gang involvement is indicative of how the gang life will affect the overall life of a juvenile. Research by Thornberry and Krohn (1993) and Thornberry et al. (2003) use three different models of explanation of gang involvement: the selection or "kind of person" model; the social facilitation or "kind of group" model; and the enhancement model, to classify gang activity and its effect on ones' life. This research also looks at different types of gang members, such as transient versus stable members. In many studies transient members were only gang members for a year whereas stable members were defined as members for two or more years (Thornberry & Krohn, 1993).

The first model, the selection model, states that gangs recruit their members from adolescents that are already involved in delinquent behavior. This model suggests that gangs look for a certain "kind of person" to join a gang and chances are these individuals would be involved in delinquency regardless of involvement in a gang. The selection model uses the theoretical foundation of control theorists who contend that "birds of a feather flock together" and that delinquent individuals self-select into delinquent peer groups such as gangs due to low social and/or self-control (Gottfredson & Hirschi, 1990; Hirschi, 1969). If this model is accurate results of the research studies would be expected to show that there would be no increase or decrease in one's level of delinquent behaviors before, during, or after gang involvement (Thornberry & Krohn, 1993:57; Thornberry et al. 2003). The social facilitation model has a different approach. This model states that gang members are no different than non-gang members except for their gang involvement, which brings about delinquent behaviors. Therefore, the gang members are a product of a "kind of group" and are only delinquent because they got involved in a gang. This model is based on the idea that normative processes in a gang can create and sustain delinquent activity. At the root of this model are Sutherland's Differential Association Theory (1947) and Akers' Social Learning Theory (1998), which both posit how delinquent activity can be learned and become normative through interactions with delinquent peers. Research concurrent with this view would show that before and after gang involvement gang members would barely differ from non-gang members, however, during gang involvement the delinquency rates of gang members would be much higher than those of the non-gang members (Thornberry & Krohn, 1993:57; Thornberry et al., 2003). The final model, the enhancement model, combines the selection and facilitation models and relies heavily on Thornberry's Interactional Theory (1987). It suggests that gangs attract juveniles that already have a propensity for delinquency, and in some cases are already involved in it, but that the gang encourages delinquency, therefore increasing the gang members' rates of delinquent behavior. Research supporting this view would show a difference in delinquency between gang members and non-gang members at all times, before, during and after gang involvement. However, during gang involvement the delinquency rates of gang members would be much more significant than non-gang members due to the facilitation of delinquent activity through the gang (Thornberry & Krohn, 1993:58; Thornberry et al., 2003).

While Thornberry's study cited researchers that agree with each of these models, the results of the research, say he and his colleagues, did not strongly support any model. There is little convincing evidence that supported the selection model, furthermore the results for transient versus stable gang members differed. For transient members the social facilitation was most widely supported. These gang members did not significantly vary from the non-gang members before or after gang membership, but during gang membership their delinquency rates were much higher than non-gang members. An explanation for this could be that transient gang members spend less time with their delinquent peers and are not as close to the core of the gang. Presumably, being distanced from the core of the gang provides them with less knowledge of the extent to which the gang commits serious, delinquent acts, which makes it easier for them to decrease their involvement in delinquent behaviors once separated from the gang. In addition, being on the perimeter of the gang, as opposed to the core, makes it easier to break away from gang activities (Craig, Vitaro, Gagnon & Tremblay, 2002).

Box 9.4

Gangs in the News . . .

Gang Members Charged with Murder of Federal Witness

According to officials, a gang member in jail awaiting trial for murder arranged for a federal witness to be killed. The 17-year-old victim was pregnant, and a witness in the prosecution of several Mara Salvatrucha (MS-13) gang members. She was stabbed repeatedly and told she was being killed because she had chosen to cooperate with law enforcement. Four gang members were charged with her murder, including the mastermind already in jail. The victim, who grew up as the daughter of a gang member and was formerly involved with the MS-13, was put in witness protection, but had recently come out onto the street voluntarily. Friends claim she returned to the street because she missed the "allure of gang life." The plot went undetected, despite the monitoring of communications from one defendant's jail cell, primarily due to street-gang dialect that was difficult for officials to interpret.

Source: *The Washington Post*, June 25, 2004.

For stable gang members there was more support for the enhancement model more than any other model or group. While these members' delinquency rates were substantially higher during gang involvement, there was also some significant difference between the delinquency rates of them and the non-gang members before and after gang involvement (Thornberry & Krohn, 1993:69). In many situations, stable gang members were found to have behavior problems prior to gang membership and to often have friends who engaged in delinquent behaviors and who supported the values and structure of joining a gang, leading to a facilitation of increased delinquent activity during gang membership (Craig et al., 2002). In this case the enhancement model would be representative of a large facilitation effect and a small selection effect (Thornberry et al., 2003). Therefore, in some aspects, the social facilitation model and enhancement model were both supported by this research but a pure selection model was not. In addition, it is vital to note that multiple longitudinal studies show that gang members who no longer claim gang status exhibit substantially more pro-social attitudes and behavior than those still involved with gangs (Esbensen et al., 2001). This finding lends credence to the above findings by Thornberry and the hope for rehabilitation of gang members of the past.

Why Should We Care: Implications of Gang Research

People may wonder why we should focus so much attention on a problem that has been around for years and why we have not been able to combat it successfully over those years. There are a few reasons, the first being the countless success stories of gang members who are now living healthy lives, with some even giving back to the community by helping to educate youth about the consequences of gang involvement. The second reason is to educate the public on the truth because portrayal of gangs that are readily available to the public are not always accurate, as with the depiction of many crime problems, and too often society's reactions are based on their perceptions of a problem, not the reality of it. For example, a study by Swetnam and Pope (2001) compared the perceptions of gang activity between students, teachers and police officers and found interesting results. Although all three groups were generally on target for the demographics of gang members and the fact that gang members can be found in many different parts of town, in other instances, their perceptions varied. For example, the police officers and teachers were more likely than students to see gangs as being a problem, more involved in the sale of drugs, and more violent than the students viewed them. In addition, the police officers had the most negative perceptions of gang members. It is likely that the varying perceptions are based on the type of exposure each group has to gangs, but who is to say which view is a most accurate depiction of a true gang? (Swetnam & Pope, 2001). After all, police may have the most exposure when a delinquent act has been committed, but students have the majority of daily interactions.

The media portrayal of gangs gives many false impressions to those who do not interact with them. Although gangs existed in the 1970s media, research attention to the issue did not really increase until the early 80s when police began to rebuild their crime units. The link between media and research is directly related. The media began to focus on gangs as "distributors of drugs, especially crack, and as perpetrators of much violence, especially gun shots that have hit innocent bystanders." (Horowitz, 1990:39). The media attention exploded and, unfortunately, was full of incorrect or exaggerated images. In response to the media craze, which was sending the public and police into a frenzy over gang activity, researchers decided to uncover the truth in order to combat the fiction. Some of the research focused on gang locations to disprove that gangs in small suburban areas are not mere extensions of big city gangs, not all gangs deal with drug distribution, and that gang members are not necessarily the most likely victims or perpetrators of homicides in all inner-city neighborhoods (Horowitz, 1990). These were all news stories that were discovered to have been false and research has continually uncovered more and more stories like them. The media portrayal overemphasized some gang problems and led to an increase in fear among the public. People living in fear may not be willing to take part in gang prevention due to the perceived dangerousness of gangs that they witness in the media. Research can help shed light on youth gangs for these individuals and help them understand the problem, as well as give suggestions for getting involved. Important studies include those that emphasize most gang violence is directed at other gangs, not random individuals (Howell, 1998). In fact, the most traditional and common gang offense, fighting, is relatively sporadic and not often a planned goal of a gang. Instead, it is usually a response to threats to gang solidarity (Sheley et al., 1995).

At the other end of the spectrum are the people who are ambivalent to youth gang violence. Research has shown that some communities are ambivalent toward gangs because the community members are often parents of the gang members, the gangs provide some sense of protection for the residents, the residents identify with gangs because of their own or relatives' prior involvement, or they fear too much policing if a gang problem is acknowledged (Howell, 1998). Therefore, research can help open the eyes of these individuals and highlight the harmful effects of gang involvement for their neighborhood's youth and the effective alternatives and success stories to give the neighborhood hope. The fact that success is possible but people are not educated is a huge reason to continue studying this area. In order to expect people's full participation in prevention programs we must first educate them on the realities of the issue, so that they realize the actual severity of the situation and the potential for reform.

Youth gang research has varying implications for different groups of people, but continued research will be valuable for all. For researchers, it is necessary to refine measurement techniques in order to assess the reliability and validity of processes being used. For theorists it is necessary to better understand the risk factors associated with gang members in order to test existing theories' applicability to gangs and to construct new theories (Esbensen et al., 2001:122). For example, some of the research cited here seems to heavily support Sutherland's theory of differential association because they show time and time again that one of the major risk factors for adolescents choosing gang involvement is being surrounded by people who have favorable attitudes towards delinquent behaviors. Therefore, these antisocial attitudes and behaviors become the norm and are easy to validate through gang life. In addition, continued gang research is necessary for policy makers in order to assess the severity of youth gang delinquency in certain areas and create policies to alleviate the problem, evaluate the effectiveness of existing prevention programs and create new programs (Esbensen et al., 2001:122).

Box 9.5

Gangs in the News . . .

RICO Statute Used Against Gang Members

The Racketeer Influenced and Corrupt Organizations (RICO) Act was first used in 1970 to target violent criminal business operations. It is most widely known for its use against Mafia crime families, but prosecutors have recently expanded its use against gangs. It has successfully been used to prosecute street gangs in Los Angeles, New York, Atlanta, and Utah, and is currently being tried in Maryland. A critical element in using this statute against gang members is establishing that the individuals being prosecuted are part of an "established organization with a hierarchy of leaderships and rules" as opposed to a "loose confederation of violent criminals" (The Washington Post, 2005, C6). A Maryland U.S. Attorney attempts to do this by alleging that the MS-13 gang has factions all over the US that meet in person and communicate via cell phones to discuss rules and activities, that dues are paid to support incarcerated members in the US and El Salvador, and that in order to stay in good standing members must commit acts of violence. So why is this statute not used against more gangs? Establishing this tight network is difficult, as viewed by the choice to not use the RICO statute against the Los Angeles Bloods and Crips gangs because a structure, leadership, or business model could not be established. One of the main benefits of the use of the RICO statute is in the targeting of gang leaders. Often times the leaders are the individuals who make the plans and set them in action. They believe that as long as they don't pull the trigger they are protected. The RICO statute says otherwise and allows gang leaders to be prosecuted.

Source: *The Washington Post*, August 28, 2005

Treatment/Prevention

Treatment and Prevention of the Youth Gang Problem

The research in Seattle and Rochester, as well as other studies, demonstrate that there are many different areas of one's life in which risk factors exist. The studies show that exposure to multiple factors highly increases the likelihood of gang involvement. Therefore, we need to implement programs in all areas of a juvenile's life in order to combat each aspect of the correlates to gang activity. It is for this reason that the primary response to the youth gang problem is a comprehensive approach combining many different prevention techniques. The current literature does not address treatment attempts, such as getting people out of gangs, but instead focuses on prevention of gang involvement.

Currently the Office of Juvenile Justice and Delinquency Prevention's Comprehensive Community-Wide Approach to Gang Prevention, Intervention, and Suppression, also known as the Spergel model, is a common approach to curbing the youth gang problem. This program has been developed over time and is comprised of five core strategies (Howell, 2000). The reason this is viewed as the comprehensive approach is because the programs that have been developed and deemed successful can all be classified into one of the core strategies of this model. Therefore, it is believed that incorporating the successes together will be most effective. These five components are community mobilization; provision of academic, economic, and social opportunities; social intervention; gang suppression; and organization change and development.

The community mobilization component includes citizens, youth, community groups and agencies. This strategy is deeply rooted in social disorganization theory, stressing that disorganized communities are a barrier for youth to get involved in productive programs and therefore they revert to gang life to find a sense of community and belonging. Strictly community mobilization began as a result of the rapid population and institutional changes that were believed to contribute to the formation of gangs (Howell, 2000). This approach deals with getting the community involved in forming programs that youth can be involved in to take their attention away from gang activity. One of the problems with this method is that often times the community denies a gang problem or is too fearful to get involved.

The next component, provision of academic, economic, and social opportunities, focuses on special school training and job programs. This is one of the few approaches that attempts to address individuals already involved with gangs. It aims at reaching out to the gang members who are not in school, but are maturing and may be ready to leave the gang (Howell, 2000). These programs are created to help them reenter society as productive members and give them the confidence to succeed without the help of a gang.

Social intervention also attempts to reach youth already wrapped up in gang life by using street outreach workers to engage gang-involved youth. Specific outreach efforts would include youth serving agencies such as schools, faith-based organizations, etc. to reach out to gang youth and provide a link between the youth and the conventional world (Howell, 2000). An example of a program like this that has proven successful is the Aggression Replacement Training (ART) program, which was started in schools. This program includes training in aggression-related social skills, anger control, and moral reasoning. In research regarding this program it showed that only 13 percent of ART participants were rearrested during an eight-month tracking period, compared to 52 percent of the control subjects (Carylon and Jones, 1999). Another example would be using police in conjunction with the schools, as studied through the Gang Resistance Education and Training (GREAT) program. This program consists of police officers teaching a nine-week course including lessons on "crime/victim and your rights; cultural sensitivity/prejudice; conflict resolution; meeting basic needs; drugs/neighborhoods; responsibility; and goal setting" (Esbensen & Osgood, 1999:199). The results of this study from 11 sites found that students that participated in the GREAT program reported significantly more prosocial behaviors and attitudes than those not in the program in addition to lower rates of delinquency (Esbensen & Osgood, 1999). A longitudinal follow-up study by Esbensen et al. (2001) confirms a beneficial effect of the program, but comments that the magnitude of the positive impact is small. Additionally, the 2001 longitudinal research shows some opposition to the 1999 results which showed a more significant impact on high-risk youth, by stating that students at high risk were not more or less likely to benefit from the program, bolstering the conclusion that there is an overall "modest beneficial effect" regardless of the individual (Esbensen et al., 2001).

Gang suppression is one of the most well known approaches. This strategy includes formal and informal social control procedures of the juvenile and criminal justice systems and community agencies and groups. It can be viewed as a collaboration of official and unofficial agencies to increase surveillance and exchange information that will lead to the apprehension and suppression of gang members. The Dallas Anti-Gang Initiative is a successful example of gang suppression tactics that compared targeted areas to matched control areas during an anti-gang initiative designed to reduce gang violence. The targeted areas received saturation patrol, aggressive curfew, and truancy enforcement. The results of this study found that both aggressive curfew and truancy enforcement were successful in leading to a significant reduction in gang violence (57%), although saturation patrol did not (Fritsch et al. 1999). Another study assessing the effectiveness of gang suppression and apprehension strategies looked at the communities fears before and after Operation Roundup in California. This was a project in Santa Ana, CA that consisted of increased surveillance of a known gang area and an arrest sweep to eliminate a specific gang. The results of this study showed that community members' attitudes about their neighborhood improved significantly from somewhat dissatisfied prior to the arrest sweep to somewhat satisfied three weeks after the sweep. In addition their feelings on their safety in the community also increased at a significant level (Vogel & Torres, 1998).

The final component is a culmination of the previous four, the organizational change and development strategy. It can be described as "the appropriate organization and integration of the above strategies and potential reallocation of resources among involved agencies." (Howell, 2000:34). One of the goals of this strategy is to lead to an awareness of a gang problem in order to mobilize efforts to reduce it. Although the preliminary research in this area shows positive results, rigorous evaluation of these programs have not yet been completed because they are a new phenomena.

The prevalence of these different strategies varies and is mostly concentrated in suppression (44%) and social intervention (31%). This breakdown is not surprising because as research became more methodologically sound and popular, these were the developing strategies (Howell, 2000). Therefore, looking at the prevalence of the strategies prior to social intervention have been phased out due to a lack of effectiveness and the most recent comprehensive approach is still very new and has not expanded yet. I would propose that the percentage for the comprehensive approach found in the organizational change and development section would continue to increase. Despite the fact that it is the most recent, its prevalence and use has already surpassed the earliest interventions.

After thinking about the comprehensive approach I tried to think of a way to put it into simpler terms by logically looking at how youth spend their day and trying to maximize their everyday encounters. Youth spend a majority of their time in school or school programs. A typical school day has the attention of juveniles for at least six hours a day. Knowing this, simple life skills programs need to be implemented into the typical school day in order to combat the peer pressures of school and to boost youth self images and relations in school. Parental and community involvement are also necessary in prevention programs. Parents need to be informed as to how programs in school are being run and they should also be educated as to how to talk to their kids about gang violence and how to naturally combat some of the risk factors. There needs to be distribution of materials regarding school programs and direct parent training. The direct

Box 9.6
Prevalence of Gang Intervention Tactics

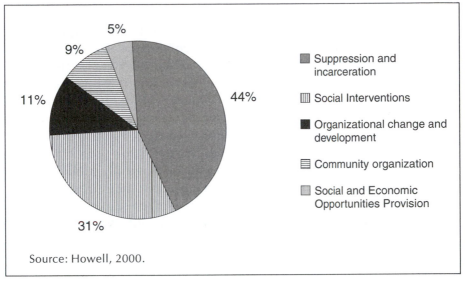

Source: Howell, 2000.

parent training can emphasize parenting skills, stress management, inter-personal skills in order to shift the focus from the troubled youth to the risk factors within the parents, and curbing those effects (Carylon & Jones, 1999). Programs within the community to build community relations are also necessary so that children realize that their neighborhood is a safe haven for them and that it is okay to coexist with others and have no vio-lence. This could be something as simple as the block parties to facilitate better community rapport. By having programs in each of these areas juve-niles' individual level risk factors will naturally be reduced.

Box 9.7
Maryland Methods Scoring Scale

Score	Definition
1	The study found a correlation between treatment program and a meas-ure of crime or crime risk factors.
2	The study found a temporal sequence between the program and the measure of crime or crime risk factors.
3	The study used a comparison between two or more groups, one with and one without the program.
4	The study used a comparison between a program group and one or more control groups, controlling for other factors; or a nonequivalent com-parison group that is only slightly different from the program group.
5	The study used random assignment and analysis of comparable program and comparison groups, including controls for attrition.

Source: MacKenzie, 1997.

What the Current Research Is Lacking

One of the major problems with gang research is that there is not enough of it and that some of it is not very good. The comprehensive approach appears promising because it incorporates all of the previous strategies of gang intervention. However, is the current research good? I reviewed a large number of studies of gang interventions, but could only identify a few that found positive significant findings (MacKenzie, 1997). Of those formally evaluated using the Maryland Methods Scoring System (explained in Chapter 1, see also Box 9.7), there was only one score of a 4, two scores of 3, and one score of 2 (Box 9.8). This shows that the current research is not always methodologically sound. They all lack random assignment, some lack pre and post measures, and some lack comparison groups. In addition, these research studies only encompass two of the comprehensive strategies, social intervention and gang suppression. That is because rigorous research on the other strategies does not exist.

Box 9.8
Maryland Methods Ratings Of Gang Research

Evaluation Study Review	Methods Score	Evaluation Study Findings
Carylon and Jones (1999)	3	13% of ART participants were rearrested during an eight-month tracking period, compared to 52% of the control subjects
Esbensen and Osgood (1999)	3	11 sites found that students that participated in the GREAT program reported significantly more prosocial behaviors and attitudes than those not in the program in addition to lower rates of delinquency
Fritsch et al. (1999)	4	aggressive curfew and truancy enforcement were successful in leading to a significant reduction in gang violence (57%), although saturation patrol did not
Vogel and Torres (1998)	2	community members' attitudes about their neighborhood improved significantly from somewhat dissatisfied prior to the arrest sweep to somewhat satisfied three weeks after the sweep; feelings on their safety in the community also increased at a significant level

Howell (2000) included a chart in his overview of youth gang strategies of gang research from 1936-1999. This chart (Box 9.9) highlights most of the problems with gang research. First, by looking in the study column you can see that there are few studies of the same program. This makes it difficult to evaluate the effectiveness of a specific program using the Maryland Methods Scoring system to examine similar programs. The Maryland system uses scores from multiple studies on each program to determine effectiveness. Therefore, the only way to use the Maryland Methods Scoring is to look at all of the research collectively. As noted previously, only four studies found a significant and positive impact of a program. In addition, Howell's chart shows very mixed results in the results column, which is slightly disheartening. However, we do not know whether the mixed results are due to poor research, poor implementation, or poor programming.

The type of intervention column in Howell's (2000) chart is also important to examine. Almost all interventions focus on prevention. There are few interventions designed to help youth already involved in gang life, which this analysis has shown to be an increasing number.

The nature of research is that studies create more questions to be addressed, and the area of youth gangs is no different. The Thornberry and Krohn study (1993) shows there is hope for helping gang members. According to their research, gang members have a lower rate of delinquency when they get out of the gang, which lends hope for rehabilitation programs. There are plenty of studies examining what should be done to prevent gang involvement, but research is lacking on how to help juveniles already involved. There are some success stories of gang members who have gotten out of a gang and turned their life around, so we need to focus some attention on helping the youth who have gotten caught up in the lifestyle. Possibly the hardest part of this will be getting juveniles to believe that leaving a gang is the right decision and that they will be safe. It is no secret that getting out of a gang is not an easy process. Many times there are repercussions and negative feedback from current gang members. However, if there are success stories of adolescents that have done it, then there must be a feasible way to go about it. How do we get juveniles to give up gang life and minimize the negative consequences in the process? This is an important area for future research.

Between the lack of multiple analyses of the same programs, the low Maryland Methods scoring on the existing research, the mixed findings, and the fact that we are neglecting the intervention tactic and only focusing on prevention, it seems logical to conclude that much more is needed in the area of gang research. I propose that this research should focus on the comprehensive approach. According to Howell's chart, the comprehensive approach found in the Little Village project has shown the best results. This program included prevention and intervention and found very favorable results (Howell, 2000), however, a rigorous statistical analysis of this program is lacking. Therefore, we need to look at what is promising and perform substantial research studies with sound methods in order to truly assess the effectiveness of programs and start implementing them.

Box 9.9
Appendix D: Chart of Current Gang Research (Howell, 2000)

Program	Study	Design	Type of Intervention	Results
New York City Boys Club*	Thrasher, 1936	Descriptive and case study	Prevention—general delinquency	Negligible impact
Chicago Area Project (CAP)	Kobrin, 1959; Schlossman and Sedlak, 1983	Descriptive and case study	Prevention—community organization	Indeterminable
Midcity Project (Boston)	Miller, 1962	Field observation and quasi-experimental	Prevention—community organization, family service, and detached worker	Negligible impact
Chicago Youth Project* Development	Caplan et al., 1967; Gold and Mattick, 1974; Mattick and Caplan, 1962	Quasi-experimental community comparison	Prevention—detached worker and community organization	No differential impact
Chicago YMCA Program for Detached Workers*	Short, 1963; Short and Strodtbeck, 1965	Field observation and quasi-experimental observation	Prevention—detached worker	Early results encouraging; no final results: evaluation suspended
Group Guidance Project (Los Angeles)	Klein, 1969, 1971	Quasi-experimental	Prevention—detached worker	Significant increase in gang delinquency
Ladino Hills Project (Los Angeles)	Klein, 1968	Quasi-experimental	Prevention—detached worker	Significant reduction in gang delinquency
Chicago Community Action Program (Woodlawn Organization)*	Spergel, 1972; Spergel et al., 1969	Descriptive statistical trends	Social intervention	Ineffective
Wincroft Youth Project (U.K.)* 1972	Smith, Farrant, and Marchant, 1972	Quasi-experimental	Prevention—detached worker	No differential impact
Gang Violence Reduction Program (California)	Torres, 1981, 1985	Quasi-experimental	Suppression and crisis intervention	Declines in gang homicides and intergang violence
House of Umoja (Philadelphia)	Woodson, 1981, 1986	Descriptive, case study, statistical trends	Prevention, crisis intervention, and social intervention	Effected truce among warring gangs; effective sanctuary
Operation Hardcore (Los Angeles)	Dahmann, 1981	Quasi-experimental	Suppression (vertical prosecution)	Successful gang prosecution process

Box 9.9, *continued*

Program	Study	Design	Type of Intervention	Results
San Diego Street Youth Program*	Pennell, 1983	Quasi-experimental community comparison	Prevention—detached worker	Indeterminable
Crisis Intervention Services Project (Chicago)	Spergel, 1986	Quasi-experimental community comparison	Crisis intervention and suppression	Some reduction in serious and violent crimes
Broader Urban Involvement and Leadership Development (Chicago)	Thompson and Jason, 1988	Quasi-experimental school comparison	Prevention—discouraging adolescents from joining gangs	Marginal reduction
Youth Gang Drug Prevention Program (Administration on Children, Youth, and Families)*	Cohen et al., 1994	Quasi-experimental treatment and control comparison (multiple sites)	Prevention—discouraging adolescents from joining gangs; community mobilization	Little or no effect on gang involvement; some delinquency reduction
Aggression Replacement Training (Brooklyn)	Goldstein and Glick, 1994; Goldstein, Glick, and Gibbs, 1998	Quasi-experimental treatment and control comparison	Skills training, anger control, and moral education	Preliminary results positive with members of 10 gangs
Tri-Agency Resource Gang Enforcement Team (TARGET) (Orangese County, CA)	Kent and Smith, 1995; Kent et al., 2000	Quasi-experimental	Suppression—targeting gang members for prosecution, supervision, and incarceration	Successfully targeted hardcore gang members and showed serious crime reduction
The Neutral Zone (State of Washington)	Thurman et al., 1996	Direct observation, focus group, and crime statistics	Prevention and alternatives to gang involvement	Some positive results (but see Fritsch, Caeti, and Taylor, 1999:26)
Montreal Preventive Treatment Program	Tremblay et al., 1996	Longitudinal study from kindergarten; random assignment	Prevention via skills development (in pro-social skills and self-development)	Reduced delinquency, drug use, and gang involvement
Little Village Gang Violence Reduction Program (Chicago)	Spergel and Grossman, 1997; Spergel, Grossman, and Wa, 1998	Quasi-experimental community comparison	Social intervention and suppression	Positive results; best results with combined approach
Youth Gang Drug Intervention and Prevention Program for Female Adolescents* (Pueblo, CO; Boston, MA; and Seattle, WA)	Curry, Williams, and Koenemann, 1997	Quasi-experimental	Prevention and social intervention	Pueblo program showed positive results with culture-based programs for Mexican American females
Gang Resistance Education and Training Program (G.R.E.A.T.)	Winfree, Esbensen, and Osgood, 1996; Esbensen and Osgood, 1997, 1999	Quasi-experimental treatment and control comparison (multiple sites)	Prevention—discouraging adolescents from joining gangs	Modest reductions in gang affiliation and delinquency

Box 9.9, *continued*

Program	Study	Design	Type of Intervention	Results
Gang Resistance Education and Training Program (G.R.E.A.T.)	Palumbo and Ferguson, 1995	Quasi-experimental and use of a focus group (multiple sites, different from G.R.E.A.T. sites above)	Prevention—discouraging adolescents from joining gangs	Small effects on attitudes and gang resistance
Operation Cul-De-Sac (Los Angeles)	Lasley, 1998	Quasi-experimental before, during, and after comparisons with control area	Suppression—using traffic barriers to block gang mobility	Gang homicides and assaults appeared to be reduced
Antigang Initiative (Dallas)	Fritsch, Caeti, and Taylor, 1999	Quasi-experimental; compared target and control areas	Suppression—using saturation patrol, curfew, and truancy enforcement	Aggressive curfew and truancy enforcement appeared to be effective
*These programs are not described in the main body of the Summary.				

Conclusion

Juvenile gangs are a widely misunderstood issue surrounded by conflicting research. My personal opinion is that research must continue in this field in order to ensure a safe environment and a thriving future for the youth of today. The hardest part of looking at juvenile gangs is that there is so much research that covers a wide range of issues. Through doing this research I came upon two realizations that I believe need to be focused on. The first being that all prevention strategies need to start early in one's life. Current research demonstrates that gang life is now starting earlier in the life of children, therefore prevention efforts also need to start earlier. I am also a firm believer that we cannot give up on kids if they choose to become involved in gangs. We need more research on how to successfully divert gang members away from gang life and on a more pro-social path. In my readings of this issue there is one quote I repeatedly found myself returning to, which epitomizes my feelings on gang violence and why we need to care about it.

> Indeed, it is a primary responsibility of society's officialdom to protect its citizens; gang violence in its diverse and often intense form must be controlled. But much more must be done. Gang youths are our youths. They are among us now and, even if periodically incarcerated, most will be among us in the future. We deserve protection from their predations, but they deserve the opportunity to lead contributory and satisfying lives without resorting to individual or group violence. Punishment may be needed, but punishment fails to teach new, alternative ways to reach desired goals (Carylon & Jones, 1999).

The truth of the matter is that these juveniles are our future and we have a responsibility to educate them and prepare them for the world.

References

Akers, R.L. (1998). *Social Learning and Social Structure: A General Theory of Crime and Deviance*. Boston: Northeastern University Press.

Beccaria, C. (1764). *On Crimes and Punishments.* Upper Saddle River, NJ: Prentice Hall.

Carylon, E. and D. Jones (1999). "Youth Gangs, Cognitive-Behavioral Interventions in Schools, and System Change." In C. Branch (ed.) *Adolescent Gangs: Old Issues, New Approaches*, pp. 175-194. Philadelphia: Brunner/Mazel.

Craig, W.M., F. Vitaro, C. Gagnon, and R.E. Tremblay (2002). "The Road to Gang Membership: Characteristics of Male Gang and Nongang Members from Ages 10-14." *Social Development,* 11:53-68.

Curry, G.D. (1998). "Female Gang Involvement." *Journal of Research in Crime and Delinquency,* 35(1):100-118.

Egley, Jr., A.E., J.C. Howell, and A.K. Major (2004). "Recent Patterns of Gang Problems in the United States: Results From the 1996-2002 National Youth Gang Survey." In F.A. Esbesnen, S.G. Tibbetts & L. Gaines (eds.) *American Youth Gangs at the Millennium*, pp. 90-108. Long Grove, IL: Waveland Press, Inc.

Esbensen, F.A. and D.W. Osgood (1999). "Gang Resistance Education and Training (Great): Results From the National Evaluation." *Journal of Research in Crime and Delinquency*, 36:194-225.

Esbensen, F.A., L.T. Winfree, Jr., N. He, and T.J. Taylor (2001). "Youth Gangs and Definitional Issues: When Is a Gang a Gang, and Why Does It Matter?" *Crime & Delinquency,* 47:105-130.

Fritsch, E.J., T.J. Caeti, and R.W. Taylor (1999). "Gang Suppression Through Saturation Patrol, Aggressive Curfew, and Truancy Enforcement." *Crime & Delinquency,* 45:122-139.

Gottfredson, M.R. and T. Hirschi (1990). *A General Theory of Crime*. Stanford, CA: Stanford University Press.

Hill, K.G., J.C. Howell, J.D. Hawkins, and S.R. Battin-Pearson (1999). "Childhood Risk Factors for Adolescent Gang Membership: Results From the Seattle Social Development Project." *Journal of Research in Crime & Delinquency*, 36:300-323.

Hirschi, T. (1969). *Causes of Delinquency*. Berkeley, CA: University of California Press.

Horowitz, R. (1990). "Sociological Perspectives on Gangs: Conflicting Definitions and Concepts." In C.R. Huff (ed.) *Gangs in America,* pp. 37-45. Newbury Park: Sage Publications.

Howell, J.C. (2003). *Preventing and Reducing Juvenile Delinquency: A Comprehensive Framework*. Thousand Oaks, CA: Sage Publications.

Howell, J.C. (2000). "Youth Gang Programs and Strategies." Washington DC: Office of Juvenile Justice and Delinquency Prevention.

Howell, J.C., (1998). "Youth Gangs: An Overview." *Juvenile Justice Bulletin, August 1998*. Washington, DC: U.S. Department of Justice, Office of Juvenile Justice and Delinquency Prevention.

Mackenzie, D.L. (1997). "Criminal Justice and Crime Prevention." In Sherman et al. (1997) *What Works, What Doesn't, and What's Promising? A Report to Congress by the University of Maryland.* www.preventingcrime.org or www.evaluating corrections.org (chapter 9).

Miller, J. and S.H. Decker (2001). "Young Women and Gang Violence: Gender, Street Offending, and Violent Victimization in Gangs." *Justice Quarterly*, 18(1):115-140.

Miller, W.B. (2001). "The Growth of Youth Gang Problems in the United States: 1970-1998." Washington, DC: Office of Juvenile Justice and Delinquency Prevention.

Miller, W.B. (1992). "Crime by Youth Gangs and Groups in the United States." Washington, DC: Office of Juvenile Justice and Delinquency Prevention.

Moore, J.W. and J.M. Hagedorn (2001). "Female Gangs." *Juvenile Justice Bulletin Youth Gang Series.* Washington, DC: U.S. Department of Justice, Office of Juvenile Justice and Delinquency Prevention.

Sheley, J.F., J. Zhang, C.J. Brody, and J.D. Wright (1995). "Gang Organization, Gang Criminal Activity, and Individual Gang Members' Criminal Behavior." *Social Science Quarterly,* 76:53-68.

Spergel, I.A. (1992). "Youth Gangs: An Essay Review." *Social Service Review*, 121-140.

Sutherland, E.H. *Principles of Criminology*, Fourth Edition. Chicago, IL: Lippincott Co.

Swetnam, J. and J. Pope (2001). "Gangs and Gang Activity in a Non-Metropolitan Community: The Perceptions of Students, Teachers, and Police Officers." *Social Behavior and Personality,* 29:197-208.

Thornberry, T.P. (1987). "Toward an Interactional Theory of Delinquency." *Criminology*, 25(4):863-891.

Thornberry, T.P. and M.D. Krohn (1993). "The Role of Juvenile Gangs in Facilitating Delinquent Behavior." *Journal of Research in Crime & Delinquency* 30:55-83.

Thornberry, T.P., M.D. Krohn, A.J. Lizotte, C.A. Smith, and K. Tobin (2003). *Gangs and Delinquency in Developmental Perspective.* New York: Cambridge University Press.

Vogel, R.E. and S.Torres (1998). "An Evaluation of Operation Roundup." *Policing: An International Journal of Police Strategies & Management*, 21:38-53.

Wang, J.Z. (2000). "Female Gang Affiliation: Knowledge and Perceptions of At-Risk Girls." *International Journal of Offender Therapy and Comparative Criminology,* 44(5):618-632.

SECTION IV

Complex Motivations

Chapter 10

Serial Murder

Raven Korte and Susan Fahey

Introduction

Jack the Ripper is faceless and nameless; his identity still unknown after more than 100 years. He is the world's most infamous serial killer and is just as capable of invoking fear and fascination today as he was in Victorian London. Although the public has been disturbed and fascinated by the deeds of Jack the Ripper and other serial killers ever since that time, serial murder did not gain serious attention from law enforcement as a distinct form of criminal behavior until 1980. The 1980s witnessed the establishment of psychological profiling and the development of the FBI's Behavioral Sciences Unit. In the 1990s, serial murder achieved widespread public attention through the introduction of the fictional Hannibal 'The Cannibal' Lecter. In 2005 the American public's attention shifted to Dennis Rader, the infamous real-life BTK killer, who was tried and convicted of killing 10 people over a period of nearly 30 years. In fiction and in fact, serial murderers present a disturbing and difficult criminal element to identify and understand.

Definitions

Box 10.1
Multicide

The Killing of at Least Three People by a Single Offender	
Mass Murder	The killing of three or more people at one time and in one place.
Spree Murder	The killing of at least three people within a 30-day period that is accompanied by the commission of another felony.
Serial Murder	The killing of three or more people over a period of more than 30 days, with a significant cooling-off period between killings.

Holmes and Holmes (1998) define multicide as the killing of at least three people by a single offender. They outline three categories of multicide: mass murder, spree murder and serial murder. Mass murder is the killing of three or more people at one time and in one place (Holmes & Holmes, 1998). A classic example of a mass murderer is Charles Whitman, the man who climbed the bell tower on the University of Texas campus in 1966 with a high-powered rifle and proceeded to kill 16 people before turning the gun on himself (Hickey, 2005). Spree murder involves the killing of at least three people within a 30-day period that is accompanied by the commission of an additional felony (Holmes & Holmes, 1998). John Muhammad and Lee Malvo, the sniper killers who killed 10 and injured three others during their 2002 rampage in the Washington D.C. area, can be classified as spree murderers. Finally, serial murder, as defined by Holmes and Holmes (1998), is the killing of three or more people over a period of more than 30 days, with a significant cooling off period between killings. This definition is significant because it denotes a minimum number of murders (three) within a large window of time (more than 30 days) with a break between the murders (a cooling-off period). Jack the Ripper, Ted Bundy, John Wayne Gacy, Albert DeSalvo, Jeffrey Dahmer, and Dennis Rader all typify this definition. In this chapter we focus on serial murder.

Offender Characteristics

Core Elements of Serial Murder

Box 10.2
Core Elements of Serial Murder

Core Elements Distinguishing Serial Murder from Other Types of Homicide	
Repetitive Nature	Serial killers generally do not stop killing until they are apprehended or killed.
Lack of Pre-Existing Relationship	Killer and victim are often strangers prior to the murder. It is very rare for a serial murderer to harm someone with whom they are well acquainted.
Motivated by Compulsion	Serial murders feel a need to kill their victims. Their motives rarely involve jealousy or greed.
Lack of Motives	Investigators often have a difficult time finding a reason for these homicides.

Due to its violent, unpredictable nature, serial murder is the most fascinating, frightening, and disturbing form of multicide. In their research, Holmes and DeBurger (1988) have identified four core elements that distinguish serial murder from other types of homicide. These elements are repetition, lack of a pre-existing relationship, compulsion to kill and lack of an apparent motive. The first core element is the repetitive nature of the homicides. It is very important to note that serial murderers typically will not stop killing until they are either apprehended or die. Ted Bundy, for example, is believed to have begun killing when he was 15 years old and did not stop until he was arrested and charged with murder at the age of 32 (Holmes & DeBurger, 1988). The second and most unnerving core element is that there is typically no preexisting relationship between the killer and the victim (see Box 10.3). Seldom do serial killers harm those with whom they are well acquainted.

Box 10.3
Characteristics of Victim-Offender Relationships

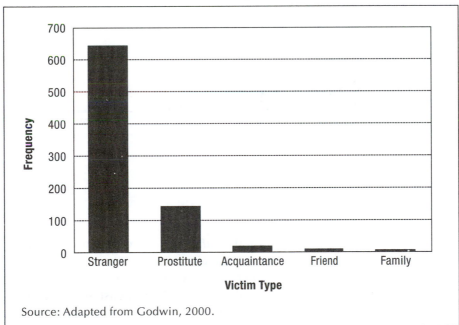

Source: Adapted from Godwin, 2000.

The third core element defined by Holmes and DeBurger (1988) is that serial killers are impelled to kill not by traditional motives such as jealousy or greed, but by a compulsion or need to do so (Holmes & DeBurger, 1988). Correspondingly, the fourth core element of serial murder is the lack of an apparent motive for the crime. Very often when dealing with cases of serial murder, investigators are unable to discover a clear motive behind the acts (Holmes & DeBurger, 1988).

Characteristics of Serial Murderers

Holmes and DeBurger (1988) report that the majority of serial murderers are Caucasian males between the ages of 25 and 35. It is extremely rare for a serial murder to be interracial (see Box 10.4), and the victims of serial homicide are usually Caucasian females.

Box 10.4
Characteristics of Victims' Ethnicity

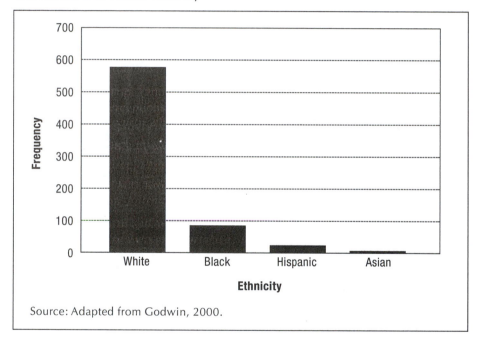

Source: Adapted from Godwin, 2000.

Despite the public perception that *all* serial murderers are Caucasian males, recent research shows that the racial composition of known serial murderers is actually similar to the racial demography of the United States (Rossmo, personal communication, 2004). While Caucasian male offenders are responsible for the vast majority of serial murders, Leyton (2000) indicates that female offenders could possibly account for as much as 17 percent of all serial homicides. According to Jenkins (1993), one of the reasons females have been under-represented as serial murderers is that their primary means of murder, asphyxiation or poisoning, are less apparent than methods used by male killers.

Box 10.5
Case Analysis of Ted Bundy

To shed further light on what defines a serial murderer, we offer a brief case analysis on the murders of Ted Bundy. Although Bundy is known to have started killing in the mid 1970s, it is suspected that he may have begun much earlier, at the age of fifteen. Bundy was a charming, physically attractive law student who participated in charity work and campaigned for the Republican Party. Throughout the 1970s, Bundy utilized his considerable charm to lure young, unsuspecting women, usually in their teens or early twenties, into his vehicle. Bundy abducted the young women, drove them to secluded areas, and then proceeded to rape and murder them either by strangulation or bludgeoning. Following the victims' death Bundy would usually discard the body in an isolated, preferably wooded area (Holmes & DeBurger, 1988). However, he is also known to have had sexual intercourse with the corpses of his victims (Hickey, 1997). Along with necrophilia, Bundy also practiced elements of sexual sadism. He inflicted physical, emotional and sexual pain on his victims through sodomy, foreign object penetration and sexual mutilations (Holmes & Holmes, 1998; Hickey, 1997). Although Bundy's first confirmed victim was killed in Washington State, he is known to have traveled extensively and also admitted to committing murders in Oregon, Utah, Colorado, Idaho, and Florida. Bundy was ultimately apprehended in Florida after savagely murdering two sorority coeds and a twelve-year-old girl. Bundy was tried, convicted and sentenced to death, and was electrocuted in 1989 (Holmes & Holmes, 1998).

Although Ted Bundy has been dead for nearly 20 years, this murderer continues to exist in the American consciousness as the ultimate serial killer. His murders explicitly validate the scholarly profile of a serial killer. Possessing an outward charm and pleasing physicality, he did not fit the 'dirty old man' or 'depraved killer' stereotypes. Through the image of normality he projected, Ted Bundy was able to conceal the depravity, anger, frustration, and sadism of the sexual torturer and murderer of as many as 40 young women and girls.

Prevalence and Risk of Victimization

Another widely debated topic concerns the actual threat posed by serial killers in the United States. While it is known that more cases of serial murder are reported in the U.S. than in any other country, and that the number of known serial murders has increased dramatically over the past 50 years, it is unclear why. Estimates of the number of serial murderers actively "working" in the United States in any given year commonly range from between 35 and 100, with some researchers asserting that the true number is closer to 200 (Holmes & Holmes, 1998; Hickey, 2005). States with the highest incidence of victimization such as California, New York, Texas, Florida and Illinois tend to have very large populations. In fact, between 1850 and 1995, California reported more than 50 serial murderers; nearly double the number of any other state (Hickey, 2005). The rate of serial homicide is very difficult to quantify due to the crime's rarity and clandestine nature (Holmes & Holmes, 1998). Although the victimization rate for serial homicide is very low, certain types of people tend to be at higher risk. These include young females (especially university students), both male and female children, prostitutes and travelers (especially hitchhikers). Occasionally the family of the offender will also be targeted (Hickey, 2005).

Behavioral Classifications

Classification System One: FBI

To further understand the acts of serial murderers, we now turn to the FBI's typology system as explained by Eric Hickey (2005). Using psychological profiling, the FBI's Behavioral Sciences Unit categorized serial killers into two types: organized and disorganized. The crime scenes left by an organized offender show a great deal of planning and tend to yield very few clues. Because research conducted by the FBI indicates that sexual gratification is an integral part of the organized offender's attack, these serial killers are sometimes referred to as serial sex murderers or lust killers (Hickey, 2005). Organized offenders are considered to be intelligent, socially skilled, sexually competent, employed, mobile and in emotional control throughout the commission of their crimes (Hickey, 2005). According to the FBI, the organized offender often demonstrates an interest in media coverage of the crimes.

Unlike organized offenders, disorganized serial murderers have impulse control issues and produce crime scenes that tend to be chaotic and messy. Disorganized offenders tend to be below average in intelligence, socially immature, nocturnal, underemployed, high school dropouts, who demonstrate high anxiety during the commission of their crimes (Hickey, 1997).

Classification System Two: Eric Hickey (2005)

Providing an interesting alternative to the classification system devised by the FBI, Hickey (2005) offers two typologies that consider three key aspects of serial murder: victims, methods and locations. Hickey's first typology divides offenders into four types based on the specificity or variety of their selected victims and methods.

Although many attempts have been made to classify serial killers into distinct behavioral groups, Hickey's second classification is unique in that it separates offenders based on whether they travel during the course of their criminal career (Hickey, 2005). First, a 'traveling offender'

Box 10.6
Hickey's Serial Murder Typology

Type A	**Type B**
Kills Specific Victims	Kills a Variety of Victims
Using Specific Methods	Using Specific Methods
Type C	**Type D**
Kills Specific Victims	Kills a Variety of Victims
Using a Variety of Methods	Using a Variety of Methods

Source: Adapted from Hickey, 1997.

is one who is willing to hunt and kill over thousands of miles, often crossing the borders of several states in the process. An example of this type of serial murderer is Ted Bundy, who admitted to killing women in at least six states (Holmes & Holmes, Eds., 1998). Second, a 'locally oriented' offender is one who remains within the borders of a single state throughout their criminal career (Hickey, 1997). David Berkowitz, the Son of Sam killer is an example of a local serial murderer because throughout the course of his murders he never left the confines of New York City (Holmes & Holmes, 1998). The final type of serial murderer is one who kills within his home or place of employment. Donald Harvey, the Angel of Death killer, murdered between 54 and 58 people in his own home and in nursing homes where he worked (Hickey, 2005).

Classification System Three: Holmes & Holmes (1998)

The third and most comprehensive attempt to classify serial murderers into distinct types comes from Holmes and Holmes (1998), who have developed a behavioral typology to describe four distinct offender types. Each of the four types has different victim preferences, methods of murder and motives. According to Holmes and Holmes (1998), motives are the most important and most meaningful way to classify serial murderers. They explain,

A serial killer becomes a human predator because of a unique combination of forces that lie within the psychogenic, sociogenic, and biogenic realms of 'inheritance.' It is not only what one has inherited from

> parents and the society/culture, it is the sequence of exposure to activities, experiences, and traits that shape and form the personality of the serial murderer . . . Motives then are either *intrinsic* or *extrinsic* in nature. Intrinsic motivations are within the personality of the offender. For example, there may be something deep inside the individual that is a part of his personality that makes or compels him to kill (1998:36-37).

An example of a common intrinsic motive that is offered to explain serial murder is sociopathy, or what is now referred to in psychology as psychopathy or antisocial personality disorder. Characterized by insincerity, pathological lying, poor judgment, impulsivity, lack of remorse and an inability to experience empathy for others, psychopaths often exhibit persistent lawlessness and rule breaking behavior from childhood into adulthood (Andrews & Bonta, 2003). Interestingly, psychopaths also frequently demonstrate a charming, smooth-talking personality. Psychopathy is often used as an explanation for the brutal crimes of those who seem outwardly friendly and attractive such as Ted Bundy. Holmes and DeBurger (1988) explain that although psychopathy may be a perfectly valid facilitating factor, it is neither the motive nor the only facilitator. In other words, while being a psychopath may have made it easy for Bundy to sadistically brutalize and murder as many as 40 women, it is not the reason he did so. To understand why Ted Bundy turned to murder, one must acknowledge that he received some sort of psychological gain from his activities. According to Holmes and DeBurger (1988),

> . . . the central motive is . . . the basic impellent toward commission of lethal violence, but the motive can be implemented because there exists, in the serial killer's mind-set, a sociopathic tendency and a sufficient capacity for interpersonal violence (1988:71-72).

Holmes and Holmes (1998) structure their classification system around the motives and psychological gain received by the perpetrator through the commission of murder. Whether the type of anticipated gain is psychological or material, and whether the motive is sexual gratification, power, or control determines the category into which a murderer is placed.

In order to promote a full understanding of the Holmes and Holmes (1998) typology, some terms must first be defined. The *act-focused* murder is one in which the act of murder is viewed as a job that must be accomplished. For the murderer there is no reason to extend the process or torture the victim. The murder will last only long enough to accomplish the kill, often only a few minutes. On the other hand, the *process kill* is drawn out to enhance the killer's enjoyment of the act. Those who employ the process kill enjoy the act of murder so much, that they may extend the process for hours, or even days, in order to fully enjoy each stage of the crime.

Another important facet of the Holmes & Holmes (1998) typology involves victim selection. Serial murderers either select victims randomly or they seek out those who correspond with their *ideal victim type*. Selection of victims on the basis of an ideal victim type often reflects a pathological drive toward a certain build, hair color, age or gender on the part of the murderer (Holmes & Holmes, 1998).

The last item to be defined is the organized/disorganized category, which is similar to the FBI classification system discussed above. One interesting distinction is that while the crime scenes created by disorganized killers are characterized by large amounts of physical evidence (blood, fingerprints, etc.), the crime scenes generated by organized killers reveal comparatively few clues. Another interesting distinction is that while disorganized serial murderers tend to utilize weapons found at the murder scene, organized murderers tend to come prepared with a weapon of their own choosing (Holmes & Holmes, 1998).

Box 10.7
Holmes and Holmes Typologies

Visionary Killer	Commits murder due to auditory or visual hallucinations.
Mission-Oriented Killer	Believes it is their duty to commit murder; murder creates feeling of accomplishment; plan attacks; victims are unknown.
Hedonistic Killer	Seeks pleasure from their crimes; includes three sub-categorizations: comfort killer, lust killer, and thrill killer.
Comfort Killer	Often mercenaries and assassins; motivated by material gain; no underlying pathology.
Lust Killer	Sexually motivated murder; often mutilate and pose victims; frequently stalk victims prior to the murder.
Thrill Killer	Motivated by the excitement associated with the process of killing, rather than the killing itself; thrill killers anticipate psychological gains, often sexual, from their crimes; will often torture victim prior to killing them; very organized in committing crime.
Power/Control Oriented Killer	Seek power and total control over their victim; gain is psychological and at times sexually gratifying.

The Visionary Killer

The visionary killer is the only type of serial murderer that can actually be classified as psychotic. Visionary killers suffer from psychotic episodes, a detachment from reality and are usually impelled to murder by auditory or visual hallucinations (Holmes & Holmes, 1998). Due to the presence of these hallucinations, visionary serial killers feel that their actions are unavoidable. In other words, visionary killers claim that they kill in order to be free of their psychoses, not because they actually *want* to commit murder (Holmes & Holmes, 1998). Harvey Carignan, a serial murderer who killed six women, believed that God had commanded the executions. Joseph Kallinger, driven by a considerably less divine source, claimed that a floating head named Charlie was responsible for his actions. While visionary killers claim that their hallucinations compel their criminal behavior, it is essential to understand that the gods and demons are a creation of their own disorganized psyche (Holmes & Holmes, 1998). The method of murder for the visionary killer is spontaneous and act-focused, and they have no ideal victim type (Holmes & Holmes, 1998). In fact, victims of visionary killers often have no physical traits in common and may appear to be selected at random.

The Mission-Oriented Killer

Rather than being motivated by auditory hallucinations or visions, mission-oriented murderers kill because they have decided it is their duty to do so (Holmes & Holmes, 1998). These murderers are generally motivated by a desire to eliminate a portion of the population that is, in their opinion, not worthy of living. As such, the murders themselves impart a feeling of accomplishment to mission-oriented killers. Mission-oriented murderers are predatory in nature and although they devote substantial time to planning their attacks, the murders themselves are act-focused. Whether the victims are prostitutes or drug addicts, they are always strangers to the mission-oriented killer and not reflective of an ideal victim type (Holmes & Holmes, 1998). While it may seem that these behaviors are reflective of an insane individual, mission-oriented killers are not out of touch with reality, and therefore not insane according to Holmes and Holmes (1998).

The Hedonistic Killer

Unlike visionary and mission-oriented killers, the third classification of serial murderers seeks pleasure from their crimes. They are therefore labeled hedonistic. Holmes and Holmes (1998) have created three sub-types within this classification: the comfort killer, the lust killer and the thrill killer.

The Comfort Killer

The first sub-type of the hedonistic serial murderer is the most difficult to classify. Comfort killers are frequently mercenaries or assassins (Holmes & Holmes, 1998). Motivated by material gain, usually money, comfort killers have no underlying pathology. They consider the taking of human life a means to an end. Victims chosen by comfort killers are often friends, business partners or acquaintances. The murders are usually well organized and carefully planned act-focused crimes.

The Lust Killer

The hedonistic lust killer is a sexually motivated offender. The ultimate goal of a lust killer is to obtain sexual gratification from the murder. These killers may experience orgasm during their crimes and may engage in necrophilia (sexual intercourse with lifeless humans). Lust killers are heavily involved in sexually sadistic fantasies that allow them to rehearse and relive their acts. These murderers often mutilate their victims and pose them in sexually provocative ways (Holmes & Holmes, 1998). One notorious lust murderer, Jerry Brudos, engaged in sexual intercourse with the dead body of one of his victims before removing her breasts. Lust killers seek out victims who embody their ideal victim type, typically a person with characteristics the killer finds sexually appealing. Although lust killers usually target strangers, they often stalk their victims prior to the crime. Lust killers are organized and enjoy the process kill (Holmes & Holmes, 1998).

The Thrill Killer

The thrill killer's motive is the excitement of killing, where "much of the pleasure is derived from the process of the kill rather than the kill itself" (Holmes & Holmes, 1998:106). Thrill killers murder not because they are impelled to do so out of obligation to their community or even in response to voices in their heads. They simply enjoy the act of killing. Victims of choice for thrill killers tend to be strangers; however, as with victims of lust killers, they may be people the killer has stalked for some time prior to the murder. Thrill killers are attracted to the unique physical characteristics of their ideal victim type. They are organized killers who will torture, rape, strangle, sodomize and penetrate their victims with objects prior to the victim's death. Interestingly, the thrill killer will seldom engage in necrophilia (Holmes & Holmes, 1998). John Muhammad, the D.C. area sniper, is an example of a thrill killer.

The Power/Control-Oriented Killer

The fourth and final type of serial murderer defined by Holmes and Holmes (1998) is the power/control-oriented killer. These murderers are motivated by the possibility of attaining total control over their victims prior to killing them. Power/control-oriented murderers have very developed fantasy lives with common themes of dominant male figures obtaining complete control over women, and then forcing the women to perform various illicit acts (Holmes & DeBurger, 1988). The ideal victims for power/control serial killers are similar to those described for lust and thrill killers, usually strangers who resemble each other in some physical way. A notorious power/control killer, Ted Bundy, was known for selecting attractive brunette women who parted their hair in the center. Bundy employed the process kill in order to enjoy the victim both before and after death. In addition, like most power/control killers, Bundy killed women in many states across the country, attempting to confuse law enforcement and evade capture.

Criticisms of Holmes and Holmes (1998)

The main criticism leveled against the Holmes and Holmes typology is the degree of possible overlap between the categories (Hickey, 2005). It is relatively easy to confuse the sexual sadism of the lust killer with the need for total power and domination of the power/control killer. The distinction is an important one, because the primary motivation for the lust killer is sexual gratification through sexual control of the victim while the power/control killer is primarily motivated by a need for control expressed through sexual and other forms of torture (Hickey, 2005). Although there are drawbacks to this typology, it is a meaningful way in which to classify a serial murderer.

The Role of Fantasy

Three of the categories proposed in the Holmes and Holmes (1998) typology, the lust killer, the thrill killer and the power/control-oriented killer, have been acknowledged to possess underlying sexual elements. In order to explore these types of serial murder in more detail one must first examine the roles played by fantasy and control in the lives of these unique serial killers. Fantasy allows the killers to relive past misdeeds, to reinforce the pleasure obtained from sadistic acts and to rehearse future crimes. Hazelwood and Douglas (1980) and Giannangelo (1996) explain that the potential serial murderer, devoid of any sense of self esteem or loving relationships with others retreats from his negative world into a fantasy world in which he is the all-powerful decision maker. It is this retreat from the real world that may lead a potential offender into the world of violent, sadistic pornography in which the reader or viewer has all the power, a scenario that would very much appeal to a powerless, potential serial murderer. Abel and Blanchard (1974) explain that a process of conditioning occurs that allows the offender to be sexually gratified by sadistic and murderous fantasies. This process is defined as masturbatory conditioning (Giannangelo, 1996). Masturbatory conditioning could associate the violent, sadistic pornography with the complete control of the fantasy world in the potential offender's mind, thereby making the connection between sex, control, and sadism. It is a natural progression for the potential offender to then associate death with sex, control and sadism (Giannangelo, 1996). During his recent trial, Dennis Rader, the self-proclaimed BTK or "bind torture kill" murderer, who terrorized Wichita, Kansas from the 1970s to the 1990s, described in detail how he killed ten people to satisfy his sexual fantasies. Rader admitted that he enjoyed masturbating while watching his victims die (*The Washington Post*, 8/19/05:A3).

Box 10.8
The Conviction and Sentencing of Dennis Rader

> In August of 2005, Dennis Rader, the serial murderer who called himself BTK, for "bind, torture, kill," was convicted and sentenced to 10 consecutive life terms in Wichita, Kansas. Rader, who had evaded justice for more than 31 years, pleaded guilty to ten murders committed between 1974 and 1991. Rader was not eligible to receive the death penalty because his murderous rampage ended three years before Kansas reintroduced capital punishment. During the trial, the court learned that Rader approached his crimes in an extremely organized manner, even using a squeeze ball to strengthen his hands to prevent them from going numb during strangulations.
>
> Also during Rader's trial, the court heard, in excruciating detail, the story of the Otero family who lost four members to Rader in 1974. Eleven-year-old Josephine, Rader's intended target, was kept alive until Rader had killed her parents and nine-year-old brother. Following the murder of her family, Rader removed Josephine's clothing and hanged her, having fashioned a noose in the basement of her home. As Rader watched Josephine hang he masturbated near her body. Through fantasy, Rader was able to relive his actions over and over with an extensive collection of photographs, drawings and newspaper clippings detailing the murders (*The Washington Post*, 8/19/05:A3).

Prentky, Burgess, Rokous, Lee, Harman, Ressler & Douglas (1989) found that offenders frequently attempt to bring their sexually sadistic fantasies to life. Each successive act generates new fantasies, and each

new fantasy incites the desire to kill anew. This frightening cycle reinforces the killer's taste for violence and over time, greater acts of violence
and sadism are required to satisfy the offender (Prentky et al., 1989).

The Role of Control

Another element that emerges from the Holmes and Holmes (1998)
typology is the importance of control in the acts and motivations of the
three types of serial murderers discussed previously. With the lust
killer, the anticipated psychological gain is sexual gratification through
the sexual control of the victim. Hickey (2005) uses the example of the
rapes and murders of elderly women as an example of the inseparable
nature of sexual assault and power, "the reality of these killings suggests
that raping women has much more to do with power, control, and
desecration than it does sexual desire" (2005:172). Further, on sadism,
Fromm (1973) wrote,

> The core of sadism, common to all its manifestations, is the passion to
> have absolute and unrestricted control over a living being, whether an
> animal, a child, a man or a woman. To force someone to endure pain or
> humiliation without being able to defend himself is one of the mani-
> festations of absolute control, but is by no means the only one . . . The
> person who has complete control over another living being makes this
> being into his thing, his property, while he becomes the other being's
> god (1973:322-323).

The above elements demonstrate how an obsessive need for control man-
ifests itself in the extreme actions of these offenders.

In order to show his complete and utter control over his victims,
Douglas Clark, a serial murderer who killed Los Angeles area prostitutes
in the early 1980s, engaged in a very unusual form of necrophilia. After
decapitating his victims, Clark masturbated on and engaged in sexual
activity with the heads (Holmes & Holmes, 1998). Needless to say,
Holmes and Holmes classify Clark as a power/control-oriented serial
murderer.

Theoretical Perspectives

As the fascination with serial killers has grown, researchers and
laypeople alike have begun to theorize about the causes of this terrifying
and bizarre behavior. Perhaps the most prevalent belief held by the modern public is that all serial killers are insane. Though clinicians and
researchers initially sought to validate this assessment, current research

has not supported this conclusion. In an early theory, Lunde (1976) hypothesized that many serial killers suffer from paranoid schizophrenia that is characterized by delusions of grandeur or persecution and bizarre religious ideas. At the time of his research, there had been no attempt to categorize serial murderers into distinct groups based on behavioral characteristics. Therefore Lunde (1976) considered all serial murderers to have similar thought patterns. More recently, Holmes and Holmes (1998) have asserted that the only serial murderers who can be considered psychotic are those who have been known to experience visions and hallucinations (visionary killers).

Three social/psychological theories have been proposed to explain the development of serial murders: Trauma Control, Frustration-Aggression, and Diathesis.

Box 10.9
Social/Psychological Explanations for Serial Murder

Trauma Control Model	Links serial murder to severe childhood trauma; offenders never found a healthy way to overcome early trauma.
Frustration-Aggression Hypothesis	Based on Freud's notion of basic human drives; assumes that aggression is always a consequence of frustration; when a person experiences humiliation rather than approval, frustration and aggression result; motivation is caused by some previous and unresolved humiliation.
Diathesis-Stress Model	Risk factors for serial murders include psychological anomalies, a history of severe emotional trauma, antisocial behavior and/or early, less serious forms of crime as well as problematic sexual deviance and episodes of dissociation into fantasy.

The Trauma Control Model

The trauma-control model directly links severe childhood trauma to the violent behavior of serial murderers. Hickey (2005) defines trauma as physical punishment, sexual abuse, an unstable home environment and parental death. The traumatized child internalizes a sense of anxiety and mistrust of others from an early age. Although most children who are abused never turn to violence, those who grow up to be serial killers are the ones who have never found a healthy, acceptable way to overcome their early trauma. Instead, they begin harming people "as a way of regaining the internal equilibrium that has been taken from them by those in authority" (Hickey, 2005:65-68).

Echoing this sentiment, Sears (1991) hypothesizes that the childhood abuse inflicted upon serial murderers by women, specifically their mothers, causes an inclination toward violence later in life. The idea that a serial murderer's hatred for a person, such as his mother, can be manifested in violent crimes toward another person is what psychologists call "displaced aggression" (Holmes & Holmes, 1998:54). Instead of harming their wives or mothers, serial killers seek out and kill women who share some characteristic with the women who hurt them. While the hatred is still directed at the mother or the wife, the violent behavior is directed toward strangers. In 1984, Edmund Kemper was convicted of killing eight women. He admitted in a televised interview that it was his mother he was trying to kill from the beginning. As a child, Kemper's mother had allegedly punished him by locking him in her basement for hours at a time.

The Frustration-Aggression Hypothesis

Another similar theory, based on Sigmund Freud's notion of basic human drives, is Dollard and Miller's (1950) frustration-aggression hypothesis. The frustration-aggression hypothesis explains that aggression is a normal consequence of frustration. According to Robert Hale (1993) the frustration-aggression hypothesis paired with social learning theory helps explain not only the behavior but also the internal motivation of a serial killer. Hale believes that the murders of a serial killer are a means to overcome some past humiliation. The killer has previously experienced a situation that has left him feeling humiliated, and he feels that the situation will be set right only through his act of murder (Hale, 1993). Ted Bundy, for example, was thought to have chosen victims who resembled his former fiancé because he felt humiliated and frustrated by her decision to break off their engagement. According to Hale, humiliations only lead to violent criminal acts if the killer internalizes the humiliation and recognizes it as a motive for his murders. According to Dollard and Miller's (1950) theory of learning, each child learns to seek approval from others. When individuals fail to receive approval and are instead met with humiliation, they become frustrated and aggressive. Serial killers avoid taking out their aggressions on the original instigator of the frustration because, in their minds, the person who humiliated them still maintains a level control over them (Hale, 1993).

The Diathesis-Stress Model of Serial Murder

Giannangelo (1996) has attempted to create a predictor-based theory of serial murder. He has done so by examining both biological and social stressors to understand their interaction in the creation of a serial murderer. Giannangelo (1996) attempts to discover why some people become serial murderers and others do not. He does so by using a case study analysis of four well-known serial murderers. Giannangelo (1996) gleaned the information used in his study from books, magazines, television, personal communications, police reports and interviews. To construct his model, he looked for evidence of physiological anomalies in the subject's history, severe emotional trauma, clinically antisocial behavior from early age, lesser crimes prior to first murder, prior sexual deviance, dissociative episodes and that the predatory murders were serial in nature (Giannangelo, 1996). These characteristics form the backbone of Giannangelo's (1996) theory of serial violence. He believes the risk factors for serial murderous behavior are physiological anomalies, a history of severe emotional trauma, antisocial behavior and/or early less serious forms of crime, problematic sexual deviance, and episodes of dissociation into fantasy. Because Giannangelo (1996) used case studies of known serial offenders, his first model is not predictive in nature; it is simply a recitation of what he believes are the necessary conditions to create a serial murderer.

However, despite these limitations it is worth examining Giannangelo's (1996) explanation of the transformation process of troubled youth into potential offender, potential offender into first time murderer and first time murderer into serial murderer as seen below.

Box 10.10
Stage 1
Foundation of Pathology

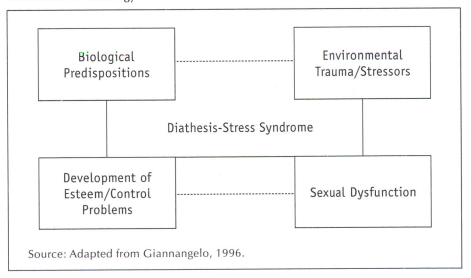

Source: Adapted from Giannangelo, 1996.

Stage one of the process involves the interplay between a biological predisposition towards crime and environmental trauma or stressors in creating a Diathesis-Stress Syndrome (literally, biological and social stress syndrome). Diathesis-Stress Syndrome can lead to the development of self-worth or impulse control problems as well as sexual dysfunction. The development of these problems completes stage one, turning a troubled youth into a potential offender.

Box 10.11
Stage 2
Path of Stressors Leading to First Murder

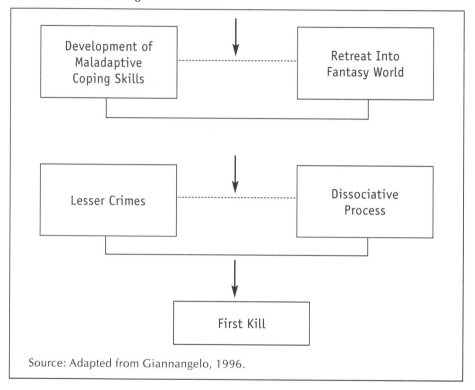

Source: Adapted from Giannangelo, 1996.

Stage two examines how stage one leads to the development of maladaptive coping skills such as an inability to deal with family or friend trouble, a retreat into a fantasy world that leads to lesser crimes like robbery and sexual assault, and a further descent into fantasies that can lead to the first kill. Herein lays the mechanism by which a potential offender can be transformed into a first time murderer.

The final stage involves a feedback loop of a renewed urge to kill, a kill, a cooling off period and a continuation of the cycle. Thus, all three stages are complete and a serial murderer has been created. However, the main assumption in this model is that if something can lead to another thing, it necessarily will lead to that thing. We still do not know what explains the opting out of so many offenders. For example, many offenders could progress from lesser crimes and an active fantasy world into a first kill but do not. Giannangelo's (1996) model cannot answer the question of why not.

Box 10.12
Stage 3
Obsessive-Compulsive Ritualistic Cycle

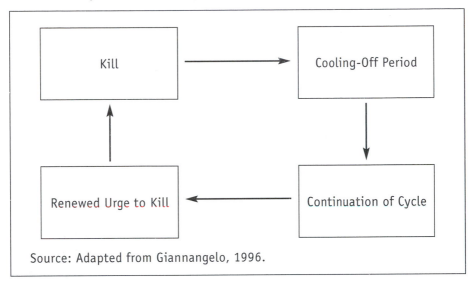

Source: Adapted from Giannangelo, 1996.

Biological Influences

While social theories may be most prevalent in the study of serial murderers, researchers have also recognized the possible biological influences that lead to this unusual and violent behavior. Heredity and genetics have long been considered contributing factors to criminal behavior, and the hunt for the so-called 'crime gene' has been ongoing. When it was discovered that serial murderer Richard Speck, who killed eight nurses in 1966, might have had an extra Y chromosome, research ensued in an attempt to link violent criminal behavior to chromosomal abnormalities in men. Research findings showed that men with the extra Y chromosome did have more criminal convictions than men without the aberration. However, most of the offenses these men were convicted of were of a non-violent nature. Furthermore, the particular chromosomal abnormality was found to be extremely rare, and would not explain the number of serial murderers that have been identified (Andrews & Bonta, 2003).

Research has also examined the possible correlation between head injuries and murderous behavior. Norris and Birnes (1988) developed a theory of serial murder based on certain physical injuries including head trauma. Their findings have been challenged because they fail to provide any way to verify or replicate their results. More promising research has indicated a link between violent behavior and certain neurotransmitters in the brain. Low levels of serotonin have been consistently linked to aggressive and violent behaviors. Pihl and Peterson

(1993) concluded that "reduced brain serotonin function is associated with heightened vulnerability to depression, increased risk of violent suicide, propensity to exhibit aggressive or impulsive behavior, and susceptibility to alcohol abuse . . . among the general public." Other research conducted by Kruesi & Jacobsen (1997) suggests that low levels of serotonin in the brain can lead to impulsive forms of violent behavior. Regrettably, no single theory has conclusively identified a precise cause for the violent behavior of serial killers. It is likely a combination of these persons' psychological adjustment, their early socialization and their biological makeup that explains their transformation into serial murderers.

Treatment/Prevention

Researchers have recently begun to consider preventative measures that could address the issue of serial homicide. Johnson and Becker (1997) emphasize the importance of early intervention by stating, "Although many would believe that a serial killer may not be treatable once he or she has begun to kill, one wonders whether, if they had been identified early enough, treatment might have succeeded in preventing them from actually starting their stream of killing" (1997:336). If adolescents at risk of homicidal violence could be identified, they could be treated using cognitive behavioral therapy (Johnson & Becker, 1997). Methods of identification including questionnaires given in school could assess students' violent thoughts and fantasies. Adolescents who admit to homicidal or sadistic sexual fantasies could receive early intervention in order to extinguish these deviant ideations (Johnson & Becker, 1997).

Another possible intervention could address lack of empathy as a predictive factor in the development of a serial killer. As lack of empathy characterizes psychopathy, acknowledged by Holmes and DeBurger (1988) to be a facilitating factor in the commission of serial murders, questionnaires could also assess students' empathetic capacity. Students who receive particularly low scores on measures of empathy could then be identified as being at risk for violent behavior. Since cognitive behavioral therapy has been reported to increase empathy through the understanding of others' feelings and perspectives, high-risk students could potentially benefit from these therapies (Simons, Wurtele & Heil, 2002).

Apprehension Techniques

Psychological/Behavioral Profiling

In addition to the contribution of researchers and clinicians, law enforcement officials have also addressed the unique crime problem posed by serial murderers. In the 1980s, in an attempt to identify violent serial criminals, the FBI began training agents to create psychological or crime scene profiles (Homant & Kennedy, 1998). Crime scene profiling operates on the following two assumptions: the crime scene will reflect the offender's personality and the unique manner of killing, or signature, will remain the same over time. Although federal profilers initially claimed responsibility for solving difficult cases, the validity of profiling has since been called into question.

Wilson, Lincoln, and Kocsis (1997) caution that profiling is reductive rather than productive. This means that while a profile can focus an investigation on a smaller pool of suspects, it cannot identify a single suspect as the guilty offender. Indeed, Egger (1999) points out that a survey of 192 cases involving the use of profiles revealed that 46 percent were beneficial to the investigation but only 17 percent actually identified a single suspect. However, the study also showed that 77 percent of investigators found that profiles focused their investigations, increasing their chances of apprehending a suspect (Pinizzotto & Finkel, 1990).

Research into the validity of profiles is scarce because very little can feasibly be studied. According to Homant & Kennedy (1998), less than one-half of the cases in which profiles have been employed have resulted in an arrest. This means that the number of solved cases where results can be verified is fairly small. The process of comparing how well an individual in custody fits a profile is also extremely subjective, because profiles tend to be somewhat vague. One of the few comprehensive studies relevant to the use of crime scene profiling involves interviews of 36 sexual murderers, some of whom killed serially (Ressler, Burgess, Douglas, Hartman & D'Augustino, 1986). Ressler et al. (1986) classified offenders as organized or disorganized according to the FBI classification system. They also compiled and divided crime scene and victim information into four categories: background of the offender, nature of the offense, nature of the victim, and nature of the crime scene. When organized and disorganized offenders were compared on these variables, the researchers found significant differences between the two, and felt these differences could be used to generate accurate profiles (Ressler et al., 1986). This study indicates that crime scenes reveal enough information about the behavior of the offender to provide insights into the type of person responsible for the crime.

Finally, a study by Pinizzotto and Finkel (1990) revealed that when compared with students and investigators untrained in profiling, FBI trained profilers were superior at generating profiles in cases involving sexual offenders. In cases involving other types of offenders, profilers were not significantly more adept at identifying the guilty party. This finding supports the assertion that crimes suitable for profiling involve unusual crime elements that are indicative of psychopathology such as sadistic torture, postmortem mutilation, lust murder and evisceration (Egger, 1999). According to the typologies of Holmes and Holmes (1998), profiling would be especially advantageous to investigations involving lust and thrill killers as well as power/control-oriented killers. Profiles alone cannot solve crimes, but evidence supports the conclusion that that they can be accurate enough to greatly reduce the number of suspects and help focus police investigations.

Geographic Profiling

Another innovation that may assist in the identification and capture of serial murderers is geographic profiling. Kim Rossmo, a former Detective Inspector with the Vancouver Police Department, developed this technique in the early 1990s. Geographic profiling uses a computer-mapping program that incorporates crime locations to identify the probable residence of an unknown offender. Geographic profiles have been found to narrow the area of interest to a mere five percent of the entire area in question. This reduction can be even greater if more crime sites are available to the investigator (Rossmo, 2000). Geographic profiling is sometimes used in conjunction with a psychological/behavioral profile in order to narrow the search even further (Homant & Kennedy, 1998).

Conclusion

Serial killers inspire a disturbing combination of curiosity and abhorrence. Despite their repulsive actions and mysterious motivations serial killers never fail to command attention. The recent upsurge of scholarly research and popular fiction about those who kill serially illustrates the demand for more knowledge on the topic. However, as a noted forensic psychiatrist once said, "there are far more people interested in studying serial killers than there are serial killers" (Reisner, McGee & Noffsinger, 2003). Indeed, the number of known serial murderers is so small as to inhibit reliable empirical research. For now, refinement of existing classification systems as well as collection of anecdotal data from incarcerated serial murderers must serve to augment our understanding of the causes and motivations of these offenders. Until more research can be conducted to this end, scholars must look to prevention strategies and law enforcement officers must look to apprehension techniques because one thing is certain, serial murderers cannot stop themselves.

References

Andrews, D.A. and J. Bonta (2003). *The Psychology of Criminal Conduct,* Sixth Edition. Cincinnati, OH: Anderson Publishing Co.

Coates, S. (Aug. 19, 2005). "Rader Gets 175 Years for BTK Slayings." *The Washington Post,* (August 3):A3.

Dollard, J. and N. Miller (1950). *Personality and Psychotherapy.* New York, NY: McGraw Hill Book Co.

Egger, S.A. (1999). "Psychological Profiling: Past Present and Future." *Journal of Contemporary Criminal Justice,* 15(3):242-261.

Fromm, E. (1973). *The Anatomy of Human Destructiveness.* New York, NY: Fawcett Crest.

Giannangelo, S. (1996). *The Psychopathology of Serial Murder: A Theory of Violence.* Westport, CT: Praeger.

Godwin, G. (2000). *Hunting Serial Predators: A Multivariate Classification Approach to Profiling Violent Offenders.* Boca Raton, FL: CRC Press.

Hale, R. (1993). "The Application of Learning Theory to Serial Murder, or 'You Too Can Learn to be a Serial Killer.'" In R. Holmes & S. Holmes (eds.) *Contemporary Perspectives on Serial Murder,* pp. 75-84. Thousand Oaks, CA: Sage.

Hazelwood, R. and J. Douglas (1980). "The Lust Murderer." *FBI Law Enforcement Bulletin.*

Hickey, E. (2005). *Serial Murderers and Their Victims,* Fourth Edition. Belmont, CA: Wadsworth Publishing Company.

Hickey, E. (1997). *Serial Murderers and Their Victims,* Second Edition. Belmont, CA: Wadsworth Publishing Company.

Holmes, R. and J. DeBurger (1988). *Serial Murder.* Newbury Park, CA: Sage.

Holmes, R. and S. Holmes (1998). *Serial Murder.* Thousand Oaks, CA: Sage.

Holmes, R. and S. Holmes (eds.) (1998). *Contemporary Perspectives on Serial Murder.* Thousand Oaks, CA: Sage.

Homant, R.J. and D.B. Kennedy (1998). "Psychological Aspects of Crime Scene Profiling: Validity Research." *Criminal Justice and Behavior,* 25(3):319-343.

Jenkins, P. (1993). "African-Americans and Serial Homicide." In R. Holmes and S. Holmes (eds.) *Contemporary Perspectives on Serial Murder,* pp. 17-32. Thousand Oaks, CA: Sage.

Johnson, B.R. and J.V. Becker (1997). "Natural Born Killers? The Development of the Sexually Sadistic Serial Killer." *Journal of the American Academy of Psychiatry and Law,* 25:335-348.

Kruesi, M.J.P. and T. Jacobsen (1997). "Serotonin and Human Violence: Do Environmental Mediators Exist?" In A. Raine, P.A. Brennan, D.P. Farrington, and S.A. Mednick (eds.) *Biological Bases of Violence.* New York, NY: Plenum.

Leyton, E. (2000). *Serial Murder.* Burlington, VT: Ashgate Publishing Company.

Lunde, D. (1976). *Murder and Madness.* New York, NY: Norton.

Norris, J. and W. Birnes (1988). *Serial Killers: The Growing Menace.* New York, NY: Dolphin.

Pihl, R.O. and J.B. Peterson (1993). "Alcohol, Serotonin, and Aggression." *Alcohol, Health & Research World,* 17:113-116.

Pinizzotto, A.J. and N.J. Finkel (1990). "Criminal Personality Profiling: An Outcome and Process Study." *Law and Human Behavior,* 14:215-233.

Prentky, R.A., A.W. Burgess, F. Rokous, A. Lee, C. Harman, R. Ressler, and J. Douglas (1989). "The Presumptive Role of Fantasy in Serial Sexual Homicide." *American Journal of Psychiatry,* 146(7):887-891.

Reisner, A.D., M. McGee, and S.G. Noffsinger (2003). "The Inpatient Evaluation and Treatment of a Self-Professed Budding Serial Killer." *International Journal of Offender Therapy and Comparative Criminology,* 47(1):58-70.

Ressler, R.K., A.W. Burgess, J.E. Douglas, C.R. Hartman, and R.B. D'Augustino (1986). "Sexual Killers and Their Victims: Identifying Patterns Through Crime Scene Analysis." *Journal of Interpersonal Violence,* 1:288-308.

Rossmo, D.K. (2004). Personal Communication with the Authors.

Rossmo, D.K. (2000). *Geographic Profiling.* Boca Raton, FL: CRC Press.

Sears, D. (1991). *To Kill Again.* Wilmington, DE: Scholarly Resources.

Simons, D., S.K. Wurtele, and P. Heil (2002). "Childhood Victimization and Lack of Empathy as Predictors of Sexual Offending Against Women and Children." *Journal of Interpersonal Violence,* 17(12):1291-1307.

Wilson, P., R. Lincoln, and R. Kocsis (1997). "Validity, Utility and Ethics of Profiling for Serial Violent and Sexual Predators." *Psychiatry, Psychology and Law,* 4:1-11.

Chapter 11

Arson

Sara Betsinger

Introduction

Very few crimes cause as much widespread destruction as that caused by arson. Arson is defined by the FBI's Uniform Crime Report as "any willful or malicious burning or attempt to burn, with or without intent to defraud, a dwelling, house, public building, motor vehicle or aircraft, personal property of another, etc." (Snyder, 1997). According to Doherty (2002), 25 percent of the fires that occur in the United States are the result of arson. Arson is estimated to claim between seven hundred and eight hundred lives each year (Bartol, 2002). On top of this cost in human lives, the 1992 Uniform Crime Report reported that arson caused over \$1 billion in property damages in 1991 alone (Sapp, Huff, Gary & Icove, 1999), and this figure has since expanded to more than \$2 billion annually (Bartol, 2002). Additionally, while violent crime and most property crime arrest rates for juveniles began to decline in the late 1990s, juvenile arrest rates for arson increased by 1 percent in 1999, despite showing decreases during the previous four years (Bartol, 2002). Yet, as Holmes and Holmes (1996) point out, "the arrest rate per 100,000 population for arson is lower than for any other Part I or Part II offense" (1996:94). In fact, the nationwide clearance rate for arson in 1999 was an astonishingly low 17 percent (Bartol, 2002), and the average annual clearance rate hovers around 15 percent (Bartol, 2002). The conviction rate is even lower, with only about two percent of arrested arson suspects being found guilty (Doherty, 2002). These low clearance and conviction percentages are, of course, due largely to the fact that much of the evidence of the crime is destroyed in the fire.

Even though the media and the general public have paid some attention to the extensive human and property costs associated with arson, surprisingly little empirically sound research has focused on the crime and the individuals who engage in it. In a 1980 piece, Rider discussed five major obstacles to researching and acquiring information

about arsonists; these problems include: "(a) the problem of apprehending arsonists; (b) the legal disposition of arson crimes with the few
who are incarcerated; (c) the sources of arson statistics was not centralized until 1978; (d) the legal constraints on information exchange;
and (e) the focus and conclusion of past research" (Davis & Lauber,
1999:276). Existing research tends to be in the form of clinical studies
with small sample sizes (Sapp et al., 1999).

Box 11. 1
Obstacles Confronting Arson Research

1. Properly identifying fires as arson and arresting arsonists is problematic.

2. Arson statistics were not centralized until the late 1970s.

3. Legal constraints prevent the free flowing exchange of information
   about offenders.

4. Existing research has traditionally utilized small sample sizes.

5. Subjects of arson research are usually confined in prisons, mental
   hospitals, or other institutions; these institutionalized offenders
   may not be representative of the general population of arsonists.

6. Existing research has been focused almost exclusively on developing offender typologies.

Additionally, as Barnett and colleagues (1999) point out, "With the
exception of a study of 83 arsonists in England and Wales, all previous studies were based upon samples drawn either from psychiatric hospitals, from
prisons, or from pre-trial psychiatric expert assessments" (1999:50).
Studies such as these obviously may cause a skewed interpretation of arsonists and their behavior since most arsonists are not arrested or institutionalized. Further, the research that has been conducted has focused
almost exclusively on developing different typologies of arsonist motivation. As Kocsis and Cooksey (2002) point out, "The majority of current
social science research on arson is dominated by psychiatric or psychological studies that examine issues of mental status and/or offender etiology, or criminological studies that propose either varying motive-based
classification taxonomies or anecdotal case studies" (2002:631). This is
exemplified by Geller's 1992 literature review, which identified more than
20 different typologies of arsonists (Sapp et al., 1999); Geller even added
his own typology to this already extensive collection.

Although several typologies that have been developed will be
briefly reviewed, this chapter is not intended to duplicate Geller's
efforts. Instead, the intention here is to understand arsonists' behavior
by providing a general description of who arsonists are and what kind

of lives they lead. Additionally, although the research that has been developed about arsonists has not always been explicit about the theoretical basis for understanding their behavior, theoretical approaches will be examined here, as will proposed methods for prevention and for treating individuals who begin problematic fire-setting behaviors in childhood.

Offender Characteristics

Major Typologies

As was already mentioned, there have been an abundance of typologies offered by researchers studying arsonists. Many of these typologies overlap, and a few emerge as widely accepted. However, a few caveats should be noted before these categorizations are presented. First, it is not likely that all arsonists have the same motivations (see Holmes & Holmes, 1996), and this is true even for supposedly similar arsonists. For example, not all "revenge-motivated" arsonists are motivated by the same type of revenge, and these arsonists may not be motivated by revenge alone. It is possible that many arsonists have mixed motivations that do not fit in one exclusive category (see Sapp et al., 1999). Unfortunately, most major typologies do not include "multiple motivation" or "mixed motivation" categories. Second, as Durkheim suggested, "human intention is too intimate a thing to be more than approximately interpreted by another person" (Barker, 1994:17). Thus, trying to fit all possible human motivations into a simple classification scheme is impossible and may be even dangerous. Third, and perhaps most importantly, there have not been extensive empirical tests of the existing typologies. As Wooden and Berkey (1984) state, ". . . it is lamented that . . . little is known about the etiology or cause of fire setting, as so much of the accounts has been impressionistic and conjectural, based primarily on the authors' experiences with a limited number of fire setters and with limited statistical backing" (1984:21). This is unfortunately true even in the case of serial arsonists, where a solid empirical foundation could prove helpful for individuals investigating repeat arson offenses (see Kocsis & Cooksey, 2002).

Box 11. 2
Challenges to Creating Typologies of Arsonists

1. It is unlikely that all arsonists have the same motivations. Arsons may have mixed motivations and not fit into one category.

2. Human motivations are impossible to fully identify.

3. Most existing typologies have not been empirically substantiated.

As such, current typologies may serve little practical use. However, despite the difficulties in developing typologies, it remains important to develop or revise classification schemes for future empirical testing so that arson can be better understood and so that prevention and individualized treatment options can be explored.

Box 11. 3
The Evolution of Arson Typologies

	Lewis and Yarnell (1951)	Macy (1979)	Rider (1980)	Crime Classification Manual
Description	This classic categorization system is the foundation for many modern arson typologies.	Although perhaps useful at one time, this categorization system is outdated.	More specific than the Macy version regarding motivations, this classification is similar to more recent typologies.	This widely cited typology was based on literature and case reviews and interviews with arsonists.
Categories of Arson	Accidental or unintentional Delusional Erotic Revenge Arson committed by children	Organized Crime Insurance/ Housing Fraud Commercial Residential Psychological	Jealousy-Motivated Adult Male Would-Be Hero Excitement Fire-Setter Pyromaniac	Vandalizing Arsonists Excitement Arsonists Revenge Arsonists Crime Concealment Arsonists Profit-Motivated Arsonists Extremists

In a 1979 study, Macy identified five different types of arson: organized crime, insurance/housing fraud, commercial, residential, and psychological (Holmes & Holmes, 1996). Although this classification system may have been useful in its time, the influence of organized crime is no longer very significant, making this category unnecessary. Additionally, newer typologies would probably combine the insurance/housing fraud and commercial categories since the motivation for both is ostensibly monetary gain. Finally, newer typologies are also more specific in recognizing actual motivations for arson, while this typology simply lists broad categories. For instance, the psychological category, as Macy identifies it, includes children and juveniles, pyromaniacs, and those motivated to set fires for political reasons. Newer typologies break up psychological motivations into multiple categories, given that the broad category of "psychological" cannot adequately describe the specific motivations that drive different offenders.

Only a year after Macy's suggestions were made, Rider (1980) adapted the 1951 work of Lewis and Yarnell into another typology (Holmes & Holmes, 1996).[1] Unlike Macy's piece, Rider's work is more specific about the precise motivations of arsonists in his categorization. His categories are as follows: the jealousy-motivated adult male; the would-be hero; the excitement fire-setter (excluding those motivated by sexual factors); and the pyromaniac (Holmes & Holmes, 1996). The inclusion of the pyromaniac may be controversial, as will be discussed later in the chapter. Otherwise, this categorization is very similar to more recent typologies, which include several of the same offender types but modify the categories slightly.

Perhaps the most widely cited typology comes from the *Crime Classification Manual* by Douglas and colleagues (1992), which summarizes the efforts of the Arson and Bombing Investigative Services (ABIS) subunit of the National Center for the Analysis for Violent Crime (NCAVC). This classification system identifies six different groups of arsonists, including: vandalizing arsonists, excitement arsonists, revenge arsonists, those committing arson to conceal other crimes, profit-motivated arsonists, and extremists. This typology was developed after an extensive review of existing arson cases and research literature as well as interviews with incarcerated arsonists across the United States (Sapp et al., 1999). The six categories outlined by this research have been the most prevalent and effective identifications of arsonist motivations (Sapp et al., 1999); therefore, the remainder of this chapter will utilize the Douglas et al. classification system in identifying arsonist characteristics and patterns. Still, the strengths and weaknesses of this classification system will become obvious, as some categories are better defined and better researched than others. Because the typology was developed by reviewing known arson cases and by interviewing incarcerated arsonists, it is possible that the categories included do not represent the motivations of arsonists who manage to elude arrest and incarceration. Similarly, this typology does not cover all possible motivations for arson in general; for example, Davis and Lauber (1999) list a plethora of reasons for arsonists' behavior: "revenge, excitement (including sexual), vandalism, vagrancy, cry for help, attempted suicide, rehousing, psychosis, carelessness, insurance fraud, cover-up, heroism, arson by proxy, vanity, political arson, pathological jealousy, antidepressant, fire buff, hero syndrome, other manipulations, and unknown or no obvious motive arson" (1999:277-278). Several of the motivations included on this list are not included in the six categories put forth by Douglas and colleagues. Finally, the Douglas et al. typology still requires further empirical evaluation. Thus, while the Douglas et al. classification scheme provides a useful overview for understanding arsonists' behavior, it should be utilized only with the understanding that it is not perfect and that there is still room for improvement.

Description of Arsonists' Motivations, Lives, and Behavior

Although emphasis will be placed on the behaviors and motivations of arsonists in general, serial arsonists will also be described.[2] Serial arsonists are defined as individuals who set three or more separate fires with some "cooling off" period between fires (Bartol, 2002; Sapp et al., 1999). Most of the information concerning serial arsonists included in this chapter comes from a two-phase study conducted by the ABIS involving the voluntary participation of 83 convicted serial arsonists (see Sapp et al., 1999). Even though serial arsonists may have the same motivations for setting fires as their less frequently acting counterparts, the backgrounds of serial offenders tend to differ significantly from general arsonists. Such differences may be critical to identify and target if effective treatment is to be offered.

Box 11. 4
A Serial Arsonist Captured

> In April of 2005, police arrested Thomas Sweatt, who was suspected of setting 46 fires to apartments and homes in Maryland, Virginia, and the District of Columbia in a two-year time span. One of the fires took the life of an elderly woman. Prior to the arson arrest, Sweatt had only a minor criminal history, which included arrests in 1985 for receiving stolen property and unauthorized use of a vehicle. Sweatt, a 50-year-old fast-food restaurant manager, was described by neighbors as "nice" and was often seen collecting trash and maintaining the lawns in his neighborhood. While some questioned whether the kind man they knew could be the cause behind the series of malicious fires, Sweatt admitted to setting the fires but gave no motive. However, one law enforcement official did say that the offender mentioned voices and demons. Sweatt was linked to the arsons through DNA evidence found at several of the crime scenes (Ruane & Duggan, 2005; Wilber, 2005).

Vandalism-Motivated Arsonists

A study by Icove and Estepp (1987), which involved more than 1,000 juveniles and adults who had been arrested for fire-related crimes in Prince George's County, Maryland, found that vandalism was the most frequent motive (49% of the sample) for fire-setting. Individuals who set fires for vandalizing purposes typically do so to challenge authority or to relieve boredom (Bartol, 2002). Additionally, they may set fires simply to cause destruction (Sapp et al., 1999). When arson is committed by juveniles, this is typically the form their acts take; in the Icove and Estepp (1987) study, 96 percent of the vandalism fires in their sample were set by juveniles. Not surprisingly, targets of these arsonists tend to be schools and other educational facilities (Sapp et al., 1999), but residential areas or places with thick vegetation may also be selected (Holmes & Holmes, 1996). Vandalism-motivated arsonists usually live less than a mile away from their targets, and they commit their crimes on weekends or on weekday afternoons without the influence of drugs and alcohol (Holmes & Holmes, 1996). Arsonists in this category may act alone but usually act in groups or pairs, and they are not motivated by sexual excitement in setting fires or in selecting their targets (Holmes & Holmes, 1996). There is some disagreement in the research literature about what vandalism-motivated offenders do after they set their fires; Holmes and Holmes (1996) suggest that most of these arsonists flee the scene, but the research conducted by Icove and Estepp (1987) found that approximately one-half of the offenders who committed vandalism-motivated arson remained at the scene after their fires were set.

Offenders who are motivated to set fires for vandalizing purposes tend to be males. Most vandalizing arsonists come from lower-class families and live at home with their parents (Holmes & Holmes, 1996); however, Sapp et al. (1999) note that most vandalism-motivated serial arsonists in the ABIS study came from stable middle-class backgrounds with one or both parents present during childhood. It should be noted that there were only six individuals in this category of serial arsonists in the ABIS study. It is difficult to make generalizations based on such a small sample. However, it can be noted that serial arsonists in this category in the study tended to have extensive histories of misdemeanor and felony arrests, time spent in juvenile detention centers, jails, and prisons, and stays in mental health institutions (Sapp et al., 1999). These individuals usually began setting fires at an average age of 8 years and set fires based on opportunity, using no special accessories or accelerants. Additionally, unlike their less frequently acting vandalism-motivated counterparts, serial arsonists in the ABIS study in this category typically acted alone when they committed their crimes.

Box 11. 5
Description of Arson Motivations

Motivation	Description
Vandalizing Arsonists	Empirically found to be most frequent motive; purpose is to challenge authority, relieve boredom, and cause destruction; often juveniles and young adults.
Excitement Arsonists	Second most frequent motivation; can be subdivided into thrill-seekers, attention seekers, recognition seekers, and sexual deviants; predominantly juveniles and young adults; often seen as socially inadequate.
Revenge Arsonists	Separated lovers, neighbors in dispute, disgruntled employees, and people who generally want to get back at someone; often adults, typically from lower-class socioeconomic backgrounds, but better educated than vandalism- and excitement-motivated arsonists. Women may be found in this category.
Crime Concealment Arsonists	Arson is secondary to the crime that is being concealed; often males who live alone and come from lower-class socioeconomic backgrounds.
Profit-Motivated Arsonists	Often the least passionate of the arsonist types; typically hired by struggling business owners or individuals wishing to collect insurance money; often use a more sophisticated method of arson such as explosives; live farthest from their crime scenes.
Extremists	Commit crimes for purposes of frightening or deterring; this is the least common and least researched of the six arson motivations.

Excitement-Motivated Arsonists

In the above mentioned study by Icove and Estepp (1987), excitement was the second most frequently mentioned motive for fire-setting, accounting for 25 percent of their sample. Excitement-motivated arsonists can be subdivided into thrill seekers, attention seekers, recognition seekers, and "sexual perverts" (Holmes & Holmes, 1996; Sapp et al., 1999). Pyromaniacs are sometimes grouped along with these offenders but are examined separately here. Arsonists who commit their crimes for excitement do so because they desire stimulation, and the stimulation they seek may be achieved by both setting the fire and by witnessing the excitement and confusion that is caused by the fire they set. Excitement-motivated arsonists consist predominantly of juveniles and young adults, and these offenders are usually unemployed and still living with their parents (Bartol, 2002). Additionally, Holmes and Holmes (1996) note that these offenders usually come from middle-class backgrounds and usually have arrest records. Unlike vandalism-motivated fire-setters, excitement-motivated arsonists tend to carefully select their targets based on the vantage point that they will have for viewing the fire after it is set (Bartol, 2002). Their targets may include trash bins, construction sites, residential areas, or areas thick with vegetation (Holmes & Holmes, 1996) Additionally, these offenders are known to mingle with the crowds that gather to witness the fires they set so that they can better experience the excitement their fire has caused (Bartol, 2002). Sapp and colleagues (1999) note that excitement-motivated arsonists may include firefighters or security guards; these individuals may engage in arson so that they can later gain recognition by taking part in the efforts to extinguish the fires they set.

Box 11. 6
A Firefighter and an Arsonist

> In February of 2004, a 20-year-old Colorado volunteer firefighter, Austin Gene Mayo, pleaded guilty to first degree arson. Mayo had been a volunteer firefighter for a year and a half and had previously been recognized as the Livermore Fire Protection District firefighter of the year. He set fire to the Virginia Dale Community Church, and he was one of the first emergency personnel at the scene of the blaze. Mayo also admitted to three other fires in the same area. Charges for the other three fires were dropped in exchange for a guilty plea in the Church arson. Mayo's defense attorney suggested that her client was depressed and suicidal, and she said that Mayo had stopped taking his medications when he committed the acts of arson (Lingle, 2004).

Excitement-motivated arsonists vary in their selection of fire-starting materials; some use simple materials, such as cigarettes or matches, while others may use more sophisticated methods and devices (Holmes & Holmes, 1996). It is noted, however, that the use of these more advanced incendiary devices is often associated with older offenders who have had experience with setting more fires. Excitement-motivated fire-setters are often seen as socially inadequate individuals (Bartol, 2002). Thus, it is perhaps not surprising that these offenders are likely to commit their crimes alone, although they may occasionally set their fires in the company of another person (Holmes & Holmes, 1996).

A great deal of attention has been given to the idea of sexual gratification as motivation for arsonists' behavior. Most modern day researchers have all but discounted the idea of sexual excitement as the sole motivation for fire-setting. For instance, researchers have noted that "all of the evidence for the sexual motivation of fire setting consists of case studies, anecdotes, literary analyses, and uncontrolled group studies" (Davis & Lauber, 1999:279). At the same time, many researchers do acknowledge that there may be some sexual component involved for some fire-setters; Barker (1994), for example, states that "fire fetishists almost certainly do exist" (1994:32; see also Davis & Lauber, 1999). Still, a study by Wolford (1972) failed to find evidence of sexual abnormality in a sample of 68 imprisoned arsonists in the southern United States. In a 1989 study, Quinsey and colleagues conducted an experiment in which they played various audio taped scenarios and measured the associated penile arousal of the participants. While both arsonists and volunteer controls showed similar arousal patterns to the audiotapes, the one individual who had been caught masturbating at the scene of a fire showed no response to the scenarios involving fire (Barker, 1994). Thus, the exact role that sexual gratification plays in motivating arsonists has yet to be sufficiently explained. Even so, Bartol (2002) points out that the sexual arousal from fire may be possible due to the fact that classical conditioning can allow virtually anything to become associated with sexual satisfaction. Accordingly, Holmes and Holmes (1996) note that fire investigators should be aware of the possible presence of pornography and semen at arson crime scenes.

Box 11. 7
Pyromaniacs

Pyromaniacs have sometimes been grouped along with the excitement-motivated arsonists. The DSM-IV definition of pyromania is "the presence of multiple episodes of deliberate and purposeful firesetting" (Bartol, 2002:362). Individuals who are considered pyromaniacs are also characterized by the high levels of tension they experience before a fire and the release of tension they experience after setting fires or witnessing the aftermath of the fires they set (Bartol, 2002). Pyromaniacs are additionally described as having an irresistible impulse to set fires. Like the excitement-motivated fire-setters, pyromaniacs are known to mingle with the crowds at the fires they set, and they are also known to be in the crowds at other fires in their neighborhoods and communities (Bartol, 2002). Additionally, these individuals may also set off false alarms (Bartol, 2002; Holmes & Holmes, 1996) and collect firefighter gear. Pyromaniacs are typically white males whose ages range from 16 to 28. The range of their intelligence varies widely, as do the socioeconomic backgrounds from which they emerge. Psychopathy and psychotic disorders are frequently associated with pyromaniacs (Holmes & Holmes, 1996), and most pyromaniacs come from broken and unhappy homes with neglectful parents.

It is believed that pyromaniacs may set hundreds of fires before they are finally caught. However, it should be noted that pyromania is a very controversial phenomenon among researchers because many studies have failed to find any pyromaniacs among samples of arsonists. As such, estimates of pyromania vary widely, with percentages ranging from 40 percent of all arsonists (Davis & Lauber, 1999) to zero, with some researchers not convinced that pyromania even exists (Sapp et al., 1999).

Several different motivations have been identified for the actions of pyromaniacs. First, it has been suggested that pyromaniacs set fires so that they will have the opportunity to act as heroes and be the centers of attention; this is evident in situations where pyromaniacs set fires and then arrive at the scene in order

Box 11. 7, *continued*

to help victims, assist firefighters, and play detective (Holmes & Holmes, 1996). Second, pyromaniacs may try to prove their intelligence or cleverness by setting fires that appear to baffle the experts or cause them a great deal of problems (Holmes & Holmes, 1996). Third, pyromaniacs may simply delight at watching the destruction they cause. Fourth, pyromaniacs may be acting under the force of an irresistible impulse and may not be able to offer any other explanation for their behavior (Holmes & Holmes, 1996). Fifth, pyromaniacs may unconsciously seek revenge by setting fires. Finally, a small percentage of pyromaniacs are believed to set fires for the purpose of sexual satisfaction (Holmes & Holmes, 1996).

With respect to serial arsonists, research on 25 excitement-motivated serial arsonists conducted by the ABIS depicts these individuals as single white males with an average of 11 years of education (Sapp et al., 1999). Again, this relatively small sample size makes generalizations about these arsonists difficult. However, a description of the excitement-motivated serial arsonists in the ABIS study will be offered here to provide a comparison with general excitement-motivated arsonists. Excitement-motivated serial arsonists in the ABIS study were likely to have felony arrests as well as stays in foster homes, juvenile detention centers, jails, and prisons in their backgrounds, but they were less likely to have experienced misdemeanor arrests (Sapp et al., 1999). Like vandalism-motivated serial arsonists, serial arsonists in the ABIS sample who were motivated by excitement tended to come from middle-class socioeconomic backgrounds with one or both parents present (Sapp et al., 1999). However, these serial arsonists started their fire-setting behavior at a later age than their vandalism-motivated counterparts, with the average starting age being 12 years. Additionally, excitement-motivated serial arsonists set an average of 40 fires, although the range in number of fires set by these offenders varied widely depending on subgroup classification (Sapp et al., 1999). For example, excitement-attention-motivated serial arsonists in the ABIS sample committed an average of 4 fires, while the excitement-thrills-motivated serial arsonists set an average of 56 fires (Sapp et al., 1999).

Revenge-Motivated Arsonists

In the study conducted in Prince George's County, Maryland, by Icove and Estepp (1987), revenge was found to be the third most frequently present motivation for arson, with 14 percent of the individuals in their sample engaging in fire-setting for this reason. Unlike vandalism-motivated and excitement-motivated arsonists, revenge-motivated arsonists consist mainly of adults. As pointed out in a 1977 study by Boudreau and colleagues, arsonists motivated by revenge may include separated lovers, neighbors in dispute, disgruntled employees, and individuals who generally want to get back at someone who they believe wronged them. The injury for which these arsonists are attempting to gain revenge may be real or imagined (Holmes & Holmes, 1996; Sapp et al., 1999). Additionally, these arsonists tend to commit no further acts of arson after the one-time act of seeking revenge (Holmes & Holmes, 1996). Targets of revenge-motivated arsonists may include individuals, businesses, government facilities, or groups of individuals, such as rival gangs (Holmes & Holmes, 1996).

Revenge-motivated arsonists usually have lower-class socioeconomic backgrounds, but they tend to be better educated than vandalism-motivated and excitement motivated arsonists (Holmes & Holmes, 1996:106). Additionally, while the other categories outlined by Douglas et al. typically do not include women, women are present in the revenge-motivated arson category. Individuals who act out their revenge by setting fires often have prior records and tend to use alcohol or drugs either before or during their offenses (Bartol, 2002), and they avoid staying at or returning to their crime scenes in an effort to distance themselves both physically and psychologically from their crimes (Holmes & Holmes, 1996). Finally, as with most other arsonists, these arsonists are not sexually motivated.

Box 11. 8
Women and Arson

Bourget and Bradford (1989) suggest that between 10 and 18 percent of fire-setters are women. Even so, as with many areas of social science research, most of the research on arsonists has focused exclusively on male offenders. Much of the information that is put forward about female arsonists is either anecdotal or predominantly theoretical. Existing research that is focused on female offenders shares many of the problems of general arson research, including small samples which consist primarily of institutionalized offenders.

Descriptions of female arsonists have tended to be condescending or psychological in nature. One 1837 account of a female arsonist traced her behavior back to the sexual arousal and overheating she experienced as a result of a dance (Wooden & Berkey, 1984). Over 100 years later, in the 1950s, Lewis and Yarnell put forth the notion that female adolescents who engaged in arson suffered from a high incidence of retardation (Kaufman, 1990; Bourget & Bradford, 1989). Studies in the 1970s suggested that female arsonists suffered from immaturity (Bourget & Bradford, 1989).

During the 1980s, Harmon, Rosner, and Wiederlight studied the characteristics of twenty-seven convicted female arsonists in New York. These individuals tended to be in their mid-thirties, African American, uneducated, unmarried, earning low

Box 11. 8, *continued*

incomes, and suffering from alcohol and drug problems (Bartol, 2002). Additionally, these women were usually motivated by revenge, acted in a hasty manner, and set fire to the places in which they lived (Bartol, 2002). Both Bourget and Bradford (1989) and Holmes and Holmes (1996) seem to support this assessment of female arsonists' motivations; both note that women who commit acts of arson are typically motivated by revenge. However, women typically target personal possessions or items that belong to persons with whom they are intimately involved, while men tend to target residential and business properties (Holmes & Holmes, 1996). Kaufman (1990) notes that women may also direct their aggression onto themselves by setting their clothes or their bodies on fire.

Female adolescents who engage in deliberate fire-setting may additionally be motivated to do so to protest their parents or to simply attract attention (Bourget & Bradford, 1989). Bourget and Bradford (1989) note that factors such as parental separation, poor parental identification, lack of family cohesiveness, poor impulse control, promiscuity, and early onset of sexual activity have been cited in various research studies as factors that are associated with arson by females. Their own study, which included a sample of 15 female and 77 male arsonists examined at the Royal Ottawa Hospital before trial, found that, compared to the sample of males, females in their sample were slightly older on average, had slightly lower IQs (but were not mentally retarded), were more likely to be single, and were more likely to have histories of "suicidal gestures or self-mutilation" as well as histories of drug and alcohol abuse (Bourget & Bradford, 1989). They also stated: "All these women exhibited psychopathic features, although some did not meet the full criteria of antisocial personality disorder" (Bourget & Bradford, 1989:298). However, it should be noted that some of these differences were not statistically significant, and the sample of females is too small to be generalizable. The study may be further biased due to the fact that all of the subjects were institutionalized. As with arson research in general, further empirical studies are necessary before generalizations and useful suggestions for treatment for female arsonists can be made.

When serial arsonists are found in the revenge-motivated category, they are more likely to target institutions and society than individuals or groups (Sapp et al., 1999). In fact, the study by the ABIS on 34 revenge-motivated serial arsonists found that 59 percent of these individuals targeted their acts of fire-setting at society in general and 20.6 percent targeted societal institutions, while only 14.7 percent set fires for personal revenge and only 5.9 percent set fires to achieve revenge against a group (Sapp et al., 1999). Typical revenge-motivated serial arsonists are single, white males with lower- or middle-class backgrounds and an average of 10 years of education (Sapp et al., 1999). Additionally, these offenders, like other serial arsonists, tend to have extensive criminal histories and have experienced a mental health institutionalization at some point in their lives. These offenders set an average of 35 fires during their criminal fire-setting careers, and they typically begin setting fires at around age 15 (Sapp et al., 1999).

Crime-Concealment Motivated Arsonists

Icove and Estepp (1987) found arson for the purpose of crime concealment to be the motivation for two percent of the 1,016 individuals in their sample. As noted by Holmes and Holmes (1996), the arson is obviously secondary to the crime that is being concealed. Arsonists in this category typically use an excessive amount of liquid accelerant with the belief that it will destroy all of the evidence of their primary crime; however, this is not usually the case because these arsonists tend to leave disorganized crime scenes (Holmes & Holmes, 1996).

Icove and Estepp (1987) found that 72 percent of the crime-concealment motivated arsonists in their study were adults, and almost all of these types of offenders had prior arrest records. These arsonists also tend to be males who live alone and come from lower-class socioeconomic backgrounds (Holmes & Holmes, 1996). Additionally, crime-concealment motivated arsonists usually have to travel farther from their homes to set their fires than do arsonists who are motivated by vandalism, excitement, or revenge (Holmes & Holmes, 1996). Further, these arsonists may commit their crimes with other individuals (except when covering up murders), may use drugs or alcohol to lower their inhibitions, and are not motivated by sexual gratification (Holmes & Holmes, 1996).

Except in cases where crime-concealment offenders are acting to cover up murders, these arsonists may be serial offenders. In the study by the ABIS on serial arsonists, only four crime-concealment serial arsonists were in the sample. Because this sample size is so small, it may be difficult or dangerous to make generalizations about other crime-concealment serial arsonists. However, it should be noted that all four of these offenders were covering up crimes of burglary, and they were a much more racially diverse group than the other serial arsonists studied by the ABIS.

Profit-Motivated Arsonists

Icove and Estepp (1987) found one percent of their sample of 1,016 individuals to be motivated by profit. Despite this small representation in their sample, this motivation is usually the first to be considered by individuals investigating arson (Battle & Weston, 1960). Redsicker and O'Connor (1997) state that arson for profit accounts for about one-half of all property damage caused by fire in the United States. Even so, according to Holmes and Holmes (1996), individuals who set fires for profit are the least passionate about their crimes. They are often hired by struggling business owners or by individuals wishing to collect insurance money. Battle and Weston (1960) note that individuals may also profit from arson indirectly; for example, an individual who works in the construction industry may deliberately set a fire to a structure so that he will be hired to rebuild it. Individuals may also engage in arson as a form of welfare fraud, either for the purpose of moving to a new location or as a way to receive cash (Redsicker & O'Connor, 1997). Like most other arsonists, individuals who set fires for profit are not motivated by sexual gratification. These arsonists usually set their fires in the evening or early morning hours (Holmes & Holmes, 1996), and they may utilize more sophisticated incendiary methods and devices, including explosives. As such, the crime scene left by this type of arsonist is usually seen as "organized" (Holmes & Holmes, 1996:109). The experience and skills displayed by profit-motivated arsonists may prevent them from being caught, which may explain why they are underrepresented in the Icove and Estepp study.

Profit-motivated arsonists tend to be single males ranging in age from 25 to 40 years (Holmes & Holmes, 1996), and they live the farthest away from their crime scenes of all the arsonists profiled so far. These arsonists may work alone or with one other person, and they have at least average intelligence. Additionally, these arsonists tend to have very extensive criminal histories involving a wide range of crimes. Finally, these arsonists are likely to be serial arsonists, especially if they are hired by others to set fires, and they usually have extensive fire-setting experience.

As was the case with many other categories of serial arsonists, the sample size of serial arsonists motivated by profit included in the ABIS study was too small (N=4) to be generalizeable. However, it can be noted that all of these offenders were white males with an extremely wide variation in both their educational histories and their first experiences with setting fires. Additional research needs to focus on offenders in this motivational category before generalizations can be made.

Extremist-Motivated Arsonists

Arsonists who commit their crimes for purposes of "intimidation, extortion, terrorism, [or] sabotage" (Bartol, 2002:361) may be included in the extremist-motivated category. As Barker (1994) notes: "Until the development of modern weapons of mass destruction, fire has been the one means by which a single individual could create more havoc and devastation than by using any other tool" (1994:82). Individuals who engage in extremist-motivated arson commit their crimes in order to frighten or deter (Bartol, 2002). This is the least common category of arsonists, and this type of arson is considerably rare. In fact, the research literature provides little information on these arsonists, and there were no extremist-motivated serial arsonists in the ABIS study.

Sapp and colleagues (1999) note that arsonists in the extremist-motivated category commit their crimes to "further social, political, or religious causes" (1999:402). The individual or individuals responsible for extremist-motivated acts of arson commit their crimes with the intent of making their social, political, or religious cause or group appear larger or more important than it really is (Krzeszowski, 1993). Examples of these crimes include fires set at abortion clinics and animal laboratories. French (1979) states that fires were often set during the 1960s and 1970s to make political points. However, it is likely that as technological advances such as the internet have made information on bomb-making more readily available, individuals whose intent is to frighten or deter have turned, or will turn, to these alternative and more destructive strategies to make their points. This may be seen through numerous abortion clinic bombings, the bombing in Oklahoma City, the events of September 11, 2001, and numerous other terrorist events.

Theoretical Perspectives

As was previously mentioned, the research literature on arsonists has not typically included extensive information about theoretical approaches to explain their behavior. However, it is possible to interpret arson through the biological/psychological and social learning approaches.

Although many serial arsonists have histories of mental institutionalizations, "arsonists appear on the whole very unlikely to be mentally ill" (Barker, 1994:46). Davis and Lauber (1999) suggest that only about 10 percent of those arrested for arson suffer from a mental illness. Still, psychological disorders such as psychopathy and obsessive-compulsive disorder have been used to explain arson offending behavior, especially in the case of pyromaniacs. In a 1963 study, Kaufman and colleagues attempted to tie arson and other violent crimes to schizophrenia (Kaufman, 1990). Additionally, psychological tests such as the WAIS-R, WISC-R, Rorschach, and versions of the MMPI have been used in attempts to assess arsonists (Davis & Lauber, 1999).

In addition to psychological disorders, for many decades researchers have attempted to explain fire-setting via offender "sexual disturbance and urinary malfunction" (Bartol, 2002:362). This explanation can be linked to the psychoanalytical framework of Sigmund Freud (Davis & Lauber, 1999). Freud believed that the pyromaniac regressed or was fixated in the phallic-urethral stage of psychosexual development (Davis & Lauber, 1999). In later years, the 1945 work of Fenichel and the 1967 work of Halleck also suggested that offenders connect fire-setting with pleasurable urination. Thus, it has been believed that a high proportion of arsonists have experienced problems with bedwetting (Bartol, 2002). Kaufman and his colleagues, on the other hand, took exception to the explanation of phallic stage fixation and instead asserted that arson was related to a fixation in the oral stage of psychosexual development (Kaufman, 1990).

Other researchers have attempted to explain arson through other biological functions or processes; for instance, in a 1953 book, Michaels tried to explain that arson and other delinquent behaviors resulted from difficulty in gaining control of the sphincter (Kaufman, 1990). Note also the earlier discussion in this chapter of sexual excitement as a motivation for excitement-motivated arsonists. However, biological links such as those listed here have not been conclusively shown, and more recent research efforts have moved away from these explanations and toward other psychological and biological theories and factors. For instance, Davis and Lauber (1999) cite five studies that have found correlations between neuro-transmitted or metabolic abnormalities and repeat fire-setting. These and other biological and psychological connections may be promising to understanding and treating fire-setting behavior. Accordingly, future research should continue to utilize psychological and biological theories and factors until they are thoroughly researched and can be eliminated as possible explanations for fire-setting behavior.

With respect to social learning theory, some researchers have suggested that the behavior of arsonists should be viewed in terms of their antecedent environmental conditions, organismic factors, actual fire-setting behavior, and the consequences of fire-setting (Barker, 1994). This approach considers both individual and environmental characteristics that may influence arsonists' behavior. Experiences that individuals had at one time or another may be consciously or unconsciously remembered and modeled later in life. Research cited by Barker (1994) suggests that individuals who engage in arson may have been abused as children through cigarette burns, had friends or loved ones who worked with or died in fire, been heavily exposed to hellfire in religious teachings, or may have been raised with the understanding that it is socially acceptable to destroy things with fire.

Box 11. 9

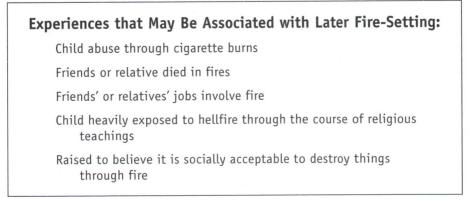

Experiences that May Be Associated with Later Fire-Setting:

Child abuse through cigarette burns

Friends or relative died in fires

Friends' or relatives' jobs involve fire

Child heavily exposed to hellfire through the course of religious teachings

Raised to believe it is socially acceptable to destroy things through fire

This is substantiated by a study by Ritvo, Shanok, and Lewis (1983), which found that a large number of adult arsonists were burned or otherwise injured with fire when they were children. This type of punishment may result in the adolescent receiving "the message that the use of fire [is] an acceptable mode of retaliation" (Bartol, 2002:365).

Social learning theory also emphasizes the reinforcement aspect of learning behavior. Positive reinforcements for setting fires may include "the warmth and visual stimulation of the fire, the confusion which the fire creates, praise from peers for an act of defiance, praise from authority for helping to put out the fire, and economic gains" (Barker, 1994:18). Additionally, lack of parental response to fire-setting behavior or general lax parenting may also be interpreted by young offenders as indifference and may have a reinforcing effect. Alternatively, fire-setting may be reinforced through masturbatory experiences involving fire fantasies (Barker, 1994).

As with psychological and biological theories, the components of social learning theory have not been thoroughly tested for fire-setting behavior. Testing of these theories would greatly improve the theoretical interpretations of arson. Additionally, theory testing and theory development in general may provide insight into both fire-setting behavior and the methods that may be used to treat offenders who set fires.

Treatment/Prevention

It is perhaps not surprising, given the lack of concentration in the literature on the theoretical approaches to understanding arsonists, that there is a dearth of information in the research literature regarding the approaches which should be taken to treat arsonists. Research studies that do discuss treatment for arsonists usually focus exclusively on juveniles. The treatments and prevention efforts examined in the research literature, in addition to the individuals and the risk factors targeted, will be highlighted here.

The Federal Emergency Management Agency (FEMA) utilizes a screening instrument to assess children who engage in fire-setting activities (Kolko, 1999; Garry, 1997). This instrument includes guides for interviewing children in three different age groups: those under age 7, those who range between ages 7 and 12, and those who are 13 years old or older. As noted by Kolko (1999), the purpose of these interviews is to rank the risk for recidivism presented by each child as either little, definite, or extreme risk. Children with little risk for recidivism are those who are found to have "no major individual problems or disorders, positive peer and family circumstances, and an intact family with no salient precipitants for fire activity" (Kolko, 1999:96). Those who are at definite risk for repeat fire-setting activity are children who experience some psychological problems, some personal problems such as problems in school, some parental problems such as insufficient discipline, and family difficulties such as a single-parent household (Kolko, 1999). Additionally, these individuals typically engage in setting fires for the purpose of gaining attention (Kolko, 1999). Finally, children who are identified as presenting an extreme risk for repeat fire-setting are believed to have started several fires for which they were not held responsible. They exhibit "severe behavioral and emotional problems (e.g., disorders, impulsivity, aggression or violence), parental pathology, minimal family support, peer rejection, school failure, and family stressors" (Kolko, 1999:97).

Kolko notes the importance of obtaining additional information concerning children's fire-setting. He states that the intention, social context, reactions, impact, and the child's involvement in the fire, in addition to the factors examined by the FEMA instrument, are important to understanding the incident. Such information has been previously documented in studies using the Fire Incident Analysis-parent version (FIA-P) and the Fire Incident Analysis for Children (FIA-C). Kolko (1999) notes that a study utilizing the FIA-P found that "heightened (vs. low) curiosity was associated with greater fire involvement out of the house and less costly fire damages, whereas heightened (vs. low) anger was associated with greater aggression and defiance just prior to the fire and peer rejection following the fire" (1999:99). A 1994 study by Kolko and Kazdin which utilized the FIA-C found that the factors associated with the severity of future fire-setting were: occurrence of the fire out of the home, the child's acknowledgment that he was likely to set another fire, a neutral or positive reaction to the fire, and no response by the child's parent(s) to the fire (Kolko, 1999). Studies such as these provide insight into factors that may be important to address in order to prevent further arson involvement by juveniles. Individual risk factors that should be targeted will now be reviewed.

As has already been mentioned in the Theoretical Perspectives section, efforts to link fire-setting behavior to biological factors such bed-wetting and sexual dysfunction have not been fruitful. However, other risk factors, which have been linked to both fire-setters and other offenders, seem more logical and may be promising targets for intervention and prevention. Räsänen and colleagues (1995), in their study comparing juvenile arsonists (N=34) to other violent juvenile offenders (N=33), found that 44 percent of the arsonists had been treated in a psychiatric hospital prior to committing the act of arson compared to only 24 percent of the violent offender group. The group of arsonists was also more likely to use psychiatric outpatient care and public health services, to be alcoholics, and to have suicidal thoughts or to have attempted suicide prior to committing their offense. Räsänen et al. (1995) thus state at the end of their article that "the recognition of the mental health problems of these juveniles and their psychiatric treatment in all sectors of the public health service is very important in the prevention of arsons" (1995:46).

Bailey, Smith, and Dolan (2001) cite additional studies which found psychopathology among young arsonists and which found that the act of arson occurred only after a string of other antisocial symptoms. Their own study also found that juvenile arsonists were more likely than a violent offender control group to be victims of physical abuse and to have mothers who exhibited signs of dysfunctional parenting (Bailey, Smith & Dolan, 2001). It should be noted, however, that both the Räsänen et al. (1995) study and the Bailey et al. (2001) study utilized small sample sizes, making it dangerous to generalize their findings. Additionally, both studies drew their samples from offenders who were being treated by psychiatric professionals, making it difficult to get a clear picture of how the general population of juvenile arsonists looks. Even so, studies such as these are useful in presenting risk factors (i.e., abuse or neglect, substance abuse, psychiatric problems, and suicidal tendencies) which may be worth examining in future research and which may be essential to identify in order to prevent future acts of arson.

Other individual risk factors are identified by Kolko (1999). He states that a study which used the Children's Fire setting Inventory (CFI) found that, compared to children who were non-fire setters, children who engaged in fire-setting displayed "more attraction to fire, past fire play, family interest in fire, exposure to friends or family who smoke, and, somewhat surprisingly, knowledge of things that burn, but tended to show less fire competence (skill) on role-plays than nonfiresetters" (Kolko, 1999:100). Kolko (1999) also cites studies that have found associations between juvenile fire-setting and heightened aggression, psychiatric distress and/or marital discord among the child's parents, failure of the parent(s) to monitor the child's behavior, and other forms of family dysfunction. These factors, in addition to those discussed by Räsänen et al. (1995) and Bailey et al. (2001), should be further tested in future studies involving juvenile arsonists to determine their value in addressing fire-setting behavior.

Prevention and early intervention approaches are emphasized in government literature as the primary treatment options for juvenile arsonists (see Garry, 1997). Accordingly, community prevention programs have commonly focused on fire safety techniques, such as stop-drop-roll, even though these techniques have not been extensively researched (Kolko, 1999). Kolko (1999) notes that the Learn Not to Burn program, which teaches fire drills, safe use of matches, and safe smoking practices, is possibly the only prevention program with a proven impact on knowledge of fire safety. Other fire safety programs, including Group Fire Safety/Prevention Skills Training (FSST) and "Smokey the Bear" programs, have received some research support for reducing the fire-setting of children in hospital or residential treatment settings (Kolko, 1999). However, most of the prevention programs that are already widely used still need to be empirically evaluated to determine how effective they have actually been.

Box 11. 10
Individual Risk Factors for Arson (Kolko, 1999)

1. Deep attraction to fire
2. Previous fire play
3. Interest among family members in fire
4. Exposure to smoking by friends and family members
5. Understanding of things that burn
6. Heightened aggression
7. Psychiatric distress
8. Marital discord among child's parents
9. Failure of parents to monitor the child's behavior
10. Other forms of family dysfunction

Different approaches have been suggested to treat juvenile arson offenders. Treatment options typically include either therapy, social or psychological skills training, or some combination of these approaches along with safety skills education. Kaufman (1990), for example, recommends therapy for juvenile arsonists, and he suggests that this therapy should involve both the offender and his or her family members. However, he notes that offenders often deny responsibility for their offenses and that they need a "sufficiently lengthy period of restitution, of caring, constancy, and limit setting to fill in the gaps in [their] development" (Kaufman, 1990:156). Kolko (1999) notes that other efforts, such as pro-social skills training, have been utilized in order to teach young fire-setters alternative techniques to deal with anger or emotional arousal and to solve problems in a non-destructive way. However, these efforts, which have shown reductions in fire-setting behavior, still require further empirical evaluation. Thus, while the treatment options available for juvenile arsonists may hold some promise, they still require further evaluation to determine which options work best.

The studies mentioned here have all focused on juveniles; information about treating adult offenders is seemingly nonexistent. There are two probable reasons for this spotlight on youth offenders. First, juveniles make up a large proportion of the arsonist population. As noted by Kolko (1999), "arson has a higher percentage of juvenile involvement than any other serious offense" (1999:96). Bartol (2002) notes that roughly one-half of all arsonists are under the age of 18. Twenty-six percent of reported juvenile arson cases are committed by youth between the ages of 10 and 14 (Holmes & Holmes, 1996). On the other hand, only 17 percent of known adult arsonists are between the ages of 25 and 34, and adults gradually desist from arson offending after the age of 35 (Holmes & Holmes, 1996).

Second, most adult arsonists began offending as juveniles. Although interest and experimentation with fire by children are fairly common (Bartol, 2002; Barker, 1994), continuation of fire-setting behavior past a certain age is a warning sign of a serious problem. What is described as "'normal' human interest" in fire begins between ages 2 and 3 and continues to increase up through age 5 (Barker, 1994). Most children cease experimentation with fire around the ages of seven or eight, and those who continue to set fires after this age tend to be male, experience abuse, have poor relationships with their parents, act out more than their peers, and may be labeled as "conduct problems" (Bartol, 2002:364-365). However, it should be noted that serial arsonists who set fires beginning in childhood lead lives that are quite different from their aggressive, impulsive, and hyperactive pasts (Bartol, 2002); as adults, these individuals "tend to be unassertive, have limited interpersonal skills, be underemployed or unemployed, and be prone toward depression and feelings of helplessness" (Bartol, 2002:364). Regardless of these differences, the point is that fire-setting among youth is a warning sign for future problem behavior.

Although the focus on youth fire-setting is important so that intervention and prevention of future acts of arson can occur, it should be emphasized that there is still a lack of scientifically rigorous studies that focus on juvenile arsonists. As Kolko (1999) states: "Absence of prospective, empirical studies make it difficult to determine which children have clinically significant problems with fire and are likely to set additional ones, and what interventions they should receive" (1999:102). Additionally, it is unfortunate that existing studies have not examined possible treatment methods and applications for adult arsonists. Although it is commonly assumed by the general public that adult arsonists cannot be reformed, there is simply not enough research to substantially validate this claim. Thus, there exists the need for more research on treatment for arsonists at both the juvenile and adult levels.

Conclusion

The six different types of arsonists described within this chapter vary a great deal with respect to their motivations and backgrounds. However, different types of arsonists have in common fire-setting experiences beginning in childhood or adolescence, and this link may provide some insight into possible treatment of arsonists. However, it should be stressed that much of the information that is known regarding arsonists' behavior and the methods used to treat them comes from clinical studies involving small samples of offenders who are known to the police. Additionally, theoretical approaches to understanding arsonists' behaviors have not been discussed in much detail in the existing research literature. Future research efforts should focus on improving these deficits so that a more realistic portrayal of the population of both juvenile and adult arsonists—not just those who have been caught—may be advanced and so that prevention and intervention methods may be refined.

Notes

[1]   As noted by Barker, most modern typologies have been based on the work of Lewis and Yarnell. Their typology was based on "mental reasons" and so did not include arson for profit but could be broken down as: (1) accidental or unintentional; (2) delusional; (3) erotic; (4) revenge; and (5) arson committed by children (Barker, 1994).

[2]   Readers who are interested in serial arsonists should read the 2002 study by Kocsis and Cooksey, as it provides a more detailed and empirical look at serial arsonists and their behaviors without being confined to the six categories outlined here.

References

Bailey, S., C. Smith, and M. Dolan (2001). "The Social Background and Nature of 'Children' Who Perpetrate Violent Crimes: A UK Perspective." *Journal of Community Psychology,* 29:305-317.

Barker, A.F. (1994). *Arson: A Review of the Psychiatric Literature*. Oxford: Oxford University Press.

Barnett, W., P. Richter, and B. Renneberg (1999). "Repeated Arson: Data from Criminal Records." *Forensic Science International,* 101:49-54.

Bartol, C.R. (2002). *Criminal Behavior: A Psychological Approach*, Sixth Edition. Upper Saddle River, NJ: Prentice Hall.

Battle, B.P. and P.B. Weston (1960). *Arson: A Handbook of Detection and Investigation*. New York: Arco.

Boudreau, J., Q. Kwan, W. Faragher, and G. Denault (1977). *Arson and Investigation*. Washington, DC: USGPO.

Bourget, D. and J.M.W. Bradford (1989). "Female Arsonists: A Clinical Study." *Bulletin of The American Academy of Psychiatry and the Law,* 17:293-300.

Davis, J.A. and K.M. Lauber (1999). "Criminal Behavioral Assessment of Arsonists, Pyromaniacs, and Multiple Fire Setters: The Burning Question." *Journal of Contemporary Criminal Justice,* 15:273-290.

Doherty, J. (2002). "Parent and Community Fire Education: Integrating Awareness in Public Education Programs." In D.J. Kolko (ed.) *Handbook on Fire Setting in Children and Youth,* pp. 283-303. New York: Academic Press.

Douglas, J.R., A.W. Burgess, A.C. Burgess, and R.K. Ressler (1992). *Crime Classification Manual.* Lexington, MA: Lexington Books.

Fenichel, O. (1945). *The Psychoanalytical Theory of Neurosis.* New York: WW Norton.

French, H.M. (1979). *The Anatomy of Arson.* New York: Arco.

Garry, E.M. (1997). *Juvenile Fire Setting and Arson: Fact Sheet #51.* U.S. Department of Justice. Retrieved October 16, 2003 from the World Wide Web: http://www.ncjrs.org/txtfiles/fs9751.txt.

Geller, J.L. (1992). "Arson in Review: From Profit to Pathology." *The Psychiatric Clinics of North America,* 15:623-645.

Halleck, S. (1967). *Psychiatry and the Dilemmas of Crime: A Study of Causes, Punishments, and Treatment.* New York: Harper and Row.

Holmes, R.M. and S.T. Holmes (1996). *Profiling Violent Crimes: An Investigative Tool.* Thousand Oaks: Sage Publications.

Icove, D.J. and M.H. Estepp (1987). "Motive-Based Offender Profiles of Arson and Fire-Related Crime." *FBI Law Enforcement Bulletin,* 56:17-23.

Kaufman, I. (1990). "Arson: From Creation to Destruction." In E.C. Viano (ed.) *The Victimology Handbook,* pp. 147-157. New York: Garland.

Kocsis, R.N. and R.W. Cooksey (2002). "Criminal Profiling of Serial Arson Crimes." *International Journal of Offender Therapy and Comparative Criminology,* 46:631-656.

Kolko, D.J. (1999). "Firesetting in Children and Youth." In V.B. Van Hasselt and M. Hersen (eds.) *Handbook of Psychological Approaches with Violent Offenders: Contemporary Strategies and Issues,* pp. 95-115. New York: Kluwer Academic.

Kolko, D.J. and A.E. Kazdin (1994). "Children's Descriptions of their Firesetting Incidents: Characteristics and Relationship to Recidivism." *Journal of the American Academy of Child and Adolescent Psychiatry,* 33:114-122.

Krzeszowski, F.E. (1993). "What Sets Off an Arsonist." *Security Management,* 37:42-47.

Lewis, N.D.C. and H. Yarnell (1951). *Pathological Firesetting (Pyromania).* Nervous and Mental Disease Monographs, No. 82. New York: Coolidge Foundation.

Lingle, C. (2004). "Virginia Dale Arsonist: Guilty: Volunteer Firefighter Pleads Guilty to First-Degree Arson." *Fort Collins Coloradoan* (February 21). Retrieved June 22, 2004 from the World Wide Web: http://www.coloradoan.com/news/stories/20040221/news/453080.html.

Quinsey, V.L., T.C. Chaplin, and D. Upfold (1989). "Arsonists and Sexual Arousal to Fire Setting: Correlation Unsupported." *Journal of Behavior Therapy and Experimental Psychiatry*, 20:203-209.

Räsänen, P., R. Hirvenoja, H. Hakko, and E. Väisänen (1995). "A Portrait of the Juvenile Arsonist." *Forensic Science International*, 73:41-47.

Redsicker, D.R. and J.J. O'Connor (1997). *Practical Fire and Arson Investigation*, Second Edition. Boca Raton: CRC Press.

Rider, A.O. (1980). "The Firesetter: A Psychological Profile (Part 1)." *FBI Law Enforcement Bulletin*, 49:6-13.

Ritvo, E., S.S. Shanok, and D.O. Lewis (1983). "Firesetting and Nonfiresetting Delinquents." *Child Psychiatry and Human Development*, 13:259-267.

Ruane, M.E. and P. Duggan (2005). "Arson Suspect's Low-Key Life: Neighbors Characterize Southeast Man as 'Average, Everyday Guy'." *The Washington Post* (April 28). Retrieved October 5, 2005 from the World Wide Web: http://www.washingtonpost.com/wp-dyn/content/article/2005/04/27/AR2005042702006.html.

Sapp, A.D., T.G. Huff, G.P. Gary, and D.J. Icove (1999). "Serial Arson and Fire-Related Crime Factors." In V.B. Van Hasselt and M. Hersen (eds.) *Handbook of Psychological Approaches with Violent Offenders: Contemporary Strategies and Issue*, pp. 397-416. New York: Kluwer Academic.

Snyder, H.N. (1997). *Juvenile Arson: Fact Sheet #91*. U.S. Department of Justice. Retrieved October 16, 2003 from the World Wide Web: http://www.ncjrs.org/txtfiles1/fs9991.txt.

Wilber, D.Q. (2005, April 28). "Man Arrested in D.C. Area's Arson Wave." *The Washington Post* (April 28). Retrieved October 5, 2005 from the World Wide Web: http://www.washingtonpost.com/wp-dyn/content/article/2005/04/27/AR2005042700599.html

Wolford, M.R. (1972). "Some Attitudinal, Psychological and Sociological Characteristics of Incarcerated Arsonists." *Fire and Arson Investigator*, 16:8-13.

Wooden, W.S. and M.L. Berkey (1984). *Children and Arson: America's Middle Class Nightmare*. New York: Plenum Press.

SECTION V

Special Offender Population

Chapter 12

Violent Offenders
with Schizophrenia

Michael Krezmien and Nancy Minniti

Introduction

Over the past five decades, persons with serious mental illness (PSMI) have become a growing part of the corrections system nationwide. Of particular concern are the violent offenders who are diagnosed with a serious mental illness. Current research has indicated that PSMIs are more likely than the general population to commit a violent crime, and to be arrested and incarcerated for violent offenses (Rice & Harris, 1995). It is unclear whether or not PSMIs are more likely to commit violent crimes than other offenders, but it appears that PSMIs who have committed violent offenses exhibit similar scores on static risk assessment scales such as the Violence Risk Appraisal Guide (VRAG) as non-mentally disordered violent offenders (Rice & Harris, 1997). Persons with schizophrenia have a higher risk of criminal behavior than other PSMIs. Furthermore, schizophrenics who also have substance abuse problems are more prone to violent recidivism (Blanchard, Brown, Horan & Sherwood, 2000). While these data could be interpreted to suggest that PSMIs who have committed violent offenses should not be treated differently than other violent offenders, current research in the fields of psychology and psychiatry has shown that effective treatments for PSMIs can result in more successful outcomes than routine care typically provided by mental health providers in prison settings (Tarrier, Kinney, McCarthy, Witkowski, Yusupoff & Gledhill, 2001).

This paper focuses on the assessment and treatment of one type of PSMI offender—the violent offender with schizophrenia. Cognitive behavioral therapy (CBT) and associated treatments combined with effective pharmacological treatments can positively affect outcomes for persons with schizophrenia, particularly those with dual diagnoses of schizophrenia and substance abuse disorder. Experts are unclear whether a cure for schizophrenia exists, but like substance abuse disorders, schizophrenia is treatable. Most would agree that for the majority of schizophrenics (including those with dual diagnosis) this is a lifelong treatment and requires commitment on the part of mental health care providers and compliance on the part of patients. The theoretical model we propose relies on two essential components: Comprehensive and effective assessment procedures and effective and scientifically supported treatments.

Box 12. 1
Proposed Theoretical Model

Theoretical Model—Essential Components

1. Comprehensive and Effective Assessment Procedures

2. Effective and Scientifically Supported Treatments

These treatments, if appropriately applied in prison and community settings with schizophrenics who have committed a violent offense, can result in decreases in recidivism for violent offenses by this population.

Offender Characteristics

Persons with Mental Illness

In order to appropriately address the issues of effective treatment for schizophrenics who have committed some type of violent criminal offense, we discuss the characteristics of PSMIs and some of the identification processes and procedures. We discuss the characteristics of schizophrenia and then address issues related to persons with dual diagnoses of schizophrenia and substance use disorder. It is important to identify and define these specific disorders because the overall classification of PSMI is too large and poorly defined to adequately direct treatment, particularly for violent offenders who may be at high-risk for violent recidivism.

Mentally disordered offenders. Mentally disordered offenders (MDO) are a heterogeneous and operationally poorly-defined group. Mentally disordered offenders is a term typically used in the field of criminal justice to define criminals with mental disorders. Mentally disordered offender is a legal term that includes disordered sex offenders, sexual predators, persons found guilty and mentally ill, persons found not

Box 12. 2
Mentally Disordered Offenders (MDOs)

> Overall this is a poorly defined group. The criminal justice system often uses this term to describe disordered sex offenders, sexual predators, persons found guilty and mentally ill, persons not found guilty by reason of insanity, and prisoners who have been transferred to mental health facilities. Estimations of the prevalence of MDOs in prison populations vary. MDOs should be distinguished from offenders with "serious" mental illness (or persons with "serious mental illness, PSMI). The latter group includes persons with schizophrenia, bipolar disorder, and major depressive disorder. These are the most severe of mental disorders PSMIs are the focus of the present paper.

guilty by reason of insanity, prisoners who have been transferred to mental health facilities, and others (Lurigio & Swartz, 2000; Rice & Harris, 1997). Estimations of the prevalence of this group in correctional settings vary greatly. Some studies suggest that 7 percent of the prison population consist of MDOs, while others suggest this rate is as high as 54 percent (Rice & Harris, 1997). These numbers are problematic, however, because they tend to include persons who have been identified with antisocial personality disorder. The MDO label itself is problematic because of issues with accurate diagnosis and a tendency to over-identify offenders with antisocial personality disorder (Andrews & Bonta, 2003). In fact, Andrews and Bonta (2003) suggest that all violent offenders could be diagnosed with antisocial personality disorder, and that current assessments utilized by corrections facilities are insensitive to differentiating between violent offenders and PSMIs.

According to Lurigio and Swartz (2000) there is a difference between mentally ill offenders and the class of offenders classified as having "serious" mental illness. The term PSMI includes persons with schizophrenia, bipolar disorder and major depressive disorder. While other types of psychiatric disorders (e.g., antisocial personality disorder, posttraumatic stress disorder) can have severe and negative effects on an individual, schizophrenia, bipolar disorder and major depressive disorder have the most severe and chronic effects upon the sufferer, and are among the most debilitating of psychiatric disorders (Lurigio & Swartz, 2000). The term PSMI, however, is still extremely broad because it includes three distinct mental disorders. These disorders differ on characteristics of identification, symptomatology, and even on the types of appropriate treatment. In this paper we discuss PSMIs as they relate to the criminal justice system, but we are primarily focused on violent offenders with schizophrenia. We identify effective treatments for schizophrenia: treatments that can assist individuals in managing their disorders as well as treatments that can reduce recidivism for violent offenses. Most studies, however, tend to measure mental illnesses as an aggregate of either MDOs or PSMIs. We continue to utilize these terms when necessary, but focus on schizophrenia as the disorder of primary concern for the purposes of this paper.

Schizophrenia. Schizophrenia is part of a spectrum of psychotic disorders characterized by disturbances of thought, delusions, inappropriate affect or inappropriate and disturbed interpersonal relations. Schizophrenia is characterized by an array of positive and negative symptoms. Positive symptoms are those symptoms generally associated with abnormal or deviant behavior. Positive symptoms include disorganized thinking (or thought disorder), delusions, and hallucinations. Disorganized thinking reflects a diminished ability to think clearly and logically. Often disorganized thinking is manifested in disconnected, tangential and/or nonsensical language, and interferes with the ability of persons with schizophrenia to maintain appropriate social interactions. Delusions include paranoid delusions (feelings that the person is being conspired against by others), broadcast delusions (feelings that one's thoughts can be heard by others) and others. Like disorganized thinking, delusions impede the development and maintenance of interpersonal relationships and render social interactions extremely troubling and difficult for persons with schizophrenia. Hallucinations take several forms, but are usually auditory hallucinations, typically taking the form of voices heard only by the affected person. These voices may vary in number and frequency. Voices may describe the afflicted individual's actions, may warn the person of danger, may tell the individual what to do, or may take on the form of conversations.

Without treatment, positive symptoms are extremely difficult for persons with schizophrenia to manage. As described, they often interfere with an individual's ability to socialize, and often alienate them from society. Additionally, positive symptoms are the symptoms commonly perceived by the general public as generally associated with violent behaviors. Blanchard et al. (2000) suggest that the presence of positive symptoms is directly related to violent or aggressive acts.

Negative symptoms are less obvious than positive symptoms, but they are equally, if not more devastating to persons with schizophrenia. Negative symptoms include blunted affect, lack of emotional expression, anhedonia, apathy, and social withdrawal (Cooper, 2003). One unfortunate consequence of negative symptoms is the tendency toward depression. While negative symptoms have not been associated with acts of violence or crime, some suggest that the presence of negative symptoms render a person with schizophrenia less able to control their actions in the presence of positive symptoms (Sreenivasan, Kirkish, Eth, Mintz, Hwang, VanGorp & VanVort, 1997). Additionally, Blanchard et al. (2000) posit that negative symptoms are closely associated with alcoholism and substance abuse in schizophrenics.

Box 12. 3
Schizophrenia

Schizophrenia: Experiences and Symptoms	
Experiences	Disturbances of thought
	Delusions
	Inappropriate affect
	Inappropriate and disturbed interpersonal relations
Positive Symptoms	Disorganized thinking/thought disorder
	Delusions
	Hallucinations
Negative Symptoms	Blunted affect
	Lack of emotional expression
	Anhedonia
	Apathy
	Social withdrawal

Schizophrenia has both biological and environmental factors. It is characterized by onset in late adolescence and in early adulthood. There is a strong genetic component to schizophrenia, and there is evidence of the hereditary nature of the disease. Onset is most common between the ages of 16 and 25, and occurs earlier in men than in women. Onset of schizophrenia is extremely rare after the age of 40. Treatments for persons with schizophrenia vary, although most treatments include strong psychotropic medications. Oftentimes sufferers do not regularly medicate, causing extreme variability in the frequency and severity of psychotic episodes. Additionally, many persons with schizophrenia also have substance abuse problems which impede their ability to manage their behaviors, and are linked with increased rates of crimes (Blanchard et al., 2000). Schizophrenics who have committed crime often have had difficulty in receiving appropriate treatment in correctional settings, and may be at risk for recidivism upon release.

Box 12. 4
Dual Diagnosis

- Most often used to refer to mental illness diagnosis with a substance abuse diagnosis

- Approximately 50 percent of those diagnosed with schizophrenia also have substance abuse problems

- Alcohol abuse is the primary substance abuse among persons with schizophrenia

- The combination of substance abuse and schizophrenia makes treatment more difficult

- Little is know about why the two diseases are related

Dual diagnosis. One of the emerging issues for treatment of persons with schizophrenia is the high rate of dual diagnoses in this population. Dual diagnosis is most often used to refer to a mental illness diagnosis with a substance abuse diagnosis. Of particular concern for correction officials and mental health providers are schizophrenics with dual diagnosis (with comorbid substance use disorder). Current research finds that approximately 40 to 50 percent of individuals with schizophrenia have a substance use disorder, and that as many as 92 percent of incarcerated schizophrenics have a comorbid substance use disorder (Blanchard et al., 2000). For the purposes of this paper, when we refer to dual diagnosis, we are referring specifically to persons with schizophrenia and comorbid substance use disorder.

In a review of related literature, Blanchhard et al. (2000) found that comorbid substance use disorders are present in more than 70 percent of schizophrenics evaluated in prison settings. Dual diagnosis is linked to increased rates of homelessness, violence, and incarcerations. Evidence supports that substance abuse can precipitate positive symptom relapses (those most closely associated with violent behaviors), and are among the most important predictors of rehospitalization for persons with schizophrenia (Blanchard et al., 2000). Although little is understood about the causes of the prevalence of dual diagnosis, the issue is of grave importance to persons with schizophrenia. Dual diagnosis exacerbates problems of treatment for mental health providers. Substance abuse interferes with effects of psychotropic medications and inhibits compliance with treatment. Dual diagnosis is of particular concern for corrections officials because substance abuse in schizophrenia is associated with increased criminal offenses.

Despite the current understanding of the prevalence of dual diagnosis, little is understood about the underlying etiological structures responsible for high rates of comorbidity of schizophrenia and substance abuse disorders. Blanchard et al. (2000) discuss three current explanations: (1) the self-medication model which implies that schizophrenia causes substance use disorders, (2) substance use disorders cause schizophrenia, and (3) schizophrenia and substance use disorders share a common genetic origin. The self-medication model proposes that individuals with schizophrenia find temporary relief from the negative symptoms (anhedonia, apathy, depression) of the disease, and engage in a self-regulated medication process. A problem with this model is the lack of a clear and replicable correlation between substance abuse and occurrence of negative symptoms. The second model (substance abuse causes schizophrenia) proposes that repeated exposure to drugs with strong psychotropic properties (LSD, cocaine, cannabis) is a causal factor in the development of schizophrenia. This model is also subject to criticism because there has been a lack of research that has found a preponderance of substance abuse preceding schizophrenia. Furthermore, this model does not incorporate alcohol as a causal factor in the development of schizophrenia. The failure to include alcohol is problematic because alcohol abuse is the primary substance abused among persons with schizophrenia.

Box 12. 5

Explanations of the Relationship between Schizophrenia and Substance Abuse

Model	Rationale	Problems with Model
Self-Medication	Individuals gain relief from schizophrenia symptoms through self-medication with substances. Substances provide temporary relief from negative symptoms of schizophrenia	No clear, replicable correlation between substance abuse and the negative symptoms of schizophrenia
Substance Abuse Causes Schizophrenia	Repeated exposure to drugs with psychotropic properties (LSD, cocaine, cannabis) causes schizophrenia	Little evidence of substance abuse preceding schizophrenia Alcohol is not proposed to be a causal factor but alcohol abuse is the primary substance abuse among schizophrenics
Common Genetic Origins	Schizophrenia and substance abuse have common genetic origins	Lack of research evidence showing genetic relationship between schizophrenia and substance use disorder
Separate Genetic Risks	Comorbidity reflects two separate genetic risks in a single individual	Lack of research evidence showing genetic relationship between schizophrenia and substance use disorders

The third proposed model stems from evidence that schizophrenia and substance use disorders share a common genetic component. This model, however, is spurious because of a lack of definitive evidence supporting a genetic relationship between schizophrenia and substance use disorders (Blanchard et al., 2000). A rival hypothesis is that the comorbidity reflects two separate genetic risks in a single individual. Although these three models have failed to definitively isolate etiological underpinnings of the dual diagnosis, in combination they suggest that treatments for the individuals with dual diagnosis should address both of these disorders in unison.

None of these models provide definitive explanations for causes or prevalence of dual diagnosis. They fail to pinpoint what physiological phenomena predispose schizophrenics to substance abuse. Nonetheless, it is important for mental health care workers and corrections officials to recognize that there are behavioral and emotional explanations for substance abuse among dually diagnosed individuals that consider environmental factors as well as genetic factors. Most mental health professionals agree that an effective treatment for dual diagnosis must address both biological and psychological concerns. Biological components are addressed through psychotropic medications, while psychological aspects are treated through various psychotherapeutic interventions.

Dual diagnosis presents a number of complications for assessment, placement, and treatment, particularly for violent offenders. Without accurate assessments, dually diagnosed offenders may be inappropriately placed, and treatments may be ineffective. Mental health care providers are often unable to manage the behaviors of violent offenders, while prisons are unable to manage the mental health needs of this population. Understanding the relationship between the two diagnoses is essential to providing appropriate care to violent offenders and for reducing recurrences of violent offenses. Blanchard et al. (2000) propose that an understanding of the complexity of schizophrenia, and additionally the existence of dual diagnosis requires an approach that examines individual differences in temperament, personality, and substance abuse.

Currently, corrections officials have had difficulty accurately differentiating clinical groups. One reason may be the insensitivity of risk assessments to differentiate PSMIs from other violent offenders. Andrews and Bonta (2003) suggest that current psychological assessments are also ineffective for differentiating disorders. They state clinicians found the 10 scales of the Minnesota Multiphasic Personality Inventory (MMPI) used to differentiate disorders were highly correlated. As a result, they suggest accurate differentiation of schizophrenia from other major affective disorders (major depressive, bipolar disorder) is difficult. The failure of these assessments, however, may be a result of their ineffectiveness in isolation. Psychological disorders and mental illness are complex issues that require assessments by trained mental health professionals. Individual assessment tools are not intended to be used alone or in isolation without convergent data from other sources.

The lack of proper assessment tools is extremely problematic when formulating placement and treatment decisions for violent offenders because most intake facilities require only limited assessments, likely the result of the time-consuming and costly nature of thorough psychological evaluations. Andrews & Bonta (2003) suggest that assessments that evaluate individual differences on criminogenic risk factors may yield more reliable information regarding offending PSMIs than traditional psychometric scales. However, they present a perspective that is primarily concerned with criminogenic risk factors. From this perspective, the issues of concern are the behaviors associated with criminality, not the underlying causes of the behavior. We believe the underlying causes of schizophrenia (and dual diagnosis) are of fundamental concern because schizophrenia and associated substance abuse can be treated, thereby reducing risk for recidivism.

Blanchard et al. (2000) propose measurements that evaluate individual differences in temperament, personality, and substance abuse that are important for evaluating antisocial behaviors and impulsivity in schizophrenics both with and without substance use disorders. Differences in negative affectivity/neuroticism subscales and disinhibition/ impulsivity subscales have been useful in differentiating schizophrenics with and without substance use disorders. The finding is important because it suggests that violent behaviors among schizophrenics are highly correlated with comorbid substance abuse. Before discussing effective treatment for persons with schizophrenia, we describe the history of the criminalization of mental illness and the development of the relationship between mental illness and the criminal justice system. We believe that this examination reveals inadequacies of current approaches to offenders with schizophrenia, and supports our proposal for effective treatment-based measures.

Criminalization of Mental Illness

Prior to 1960, persons with mental illness were "warehoused" in large state institutions in deplorable situations and without adequate mental health care. In the 1970s, government recognized a constitutional right to treatment for persons with mental illness. In *Wyatt vs. Stickney* (1972) the court found that many of the individuals detained in institutions did not require long-term care, and further recognized that custodial care was not sufficient for providing PSMIs with an opportunity to be cured, or to improve their mental condition. The resulting goal of government was to reintegrate PSMIs into the community so they could live dignified and productive lives (Perez, Leifman & Estrada, 2003). Advocates for persons with mental illness pressured legislatures to amend mental health policies and to place a greater emphasis on treatment of mental illness. Additionally, new psychotropic drugs were introduced, capable of limiting and reducing positive symptoms (e.g., aural hallucinations and paranoia) of schizophrenia—the most salient features that are likely to be perceived as dangerous by the general public. Changes in public policy, increased advocacy, and advances in pharmacology led to deinstitutionalization of state mental institutions.

One unanticipated consequence of deinstitutionalization was the failure to appropriately implement the intent of the court. Many states used deinstitutionalization as a means for saving money. Many large state mental institutions were closed, but the resources for these centers were not transferred to other types of community mental health services (Perez et al., 2003). A large number of persons with mental illness were left without adequate treatment or mental health resources. As a result, over the past four decades communities have experienced an increase in homelessness and frequent incarcerations of persons with mental illness (Perez et al., 2003; Lurigio & Swartz, 1997). According to Perez et al., the number of persons served in psychiatric hospitals decreased from 560,000 in 1955 to 60,000 in 2000. This decrease is accompanied by a marked increase in the number of PSMIs incarcerated in jails and prisons. Today there are at least 300,000 people with serious mental illness in correctional facilities.

One speculation for the high rates of persons with mental illness in prison populations is the belief that the justice system has become a surrogate mental health provider for those with mental illness (Perez, Leifman & Estrada, 2003). The public mental health system has failed to provide adequate services to PSMIs following deinstitutionalization when large numbers of PSMIs were released from state psychiatric hospitals and mental institutions (Godley, Finch, Dougan, McDonnell, McDermeit & Carey, 1999). Prior to deinstitutionalization, as Lurigio and Swartz (2000) suggest, persons with serious mental illness were no more dangerous, and no more likely to commit violent crimes than the general population. More recent research suggests that PSMIs are more likely to be incarcerated, and are more likely to commit violent crimes than the general public. One suggestion for the different findings stems from the belief that PSMIs were not considered dangerous prior to deinstitutionalization because the most dangerous patients were detained in state institutions for long periods of time. Regardless, it appears deinstitutionalization has led to an increase of PSMIs placed into the community with inadequate or no support care. These changes in policy have resulted in increased involvement with PSMIs on the part of criminal justice systems (Lurigio & Swartz, 2000).

Box 12. 6
Problems with Detainment Policies for PSMIs

- Lack of communication and shared vision between corrections officials and mental health providers, resulting in a lack of consistent services to PSMIs.

- Public mental health does not provide adequate follow-up services for PSMIs released from correctional settings.

Revolving door policies. Mentally ill individuals are often detained with either no criminal charges or on trivial charges (Godley et al., 1999). The lack of appropriate services for PSMIs has led to a revolving door phenomenon in corrections settings. For instance, each day 1,000 inmates (10% of the total population) receive some type of mental health services from the Cook County Department of Corrections (CCDOC), making it the largest provider of psychiatric treatment in Illinois (Lurigio, Fallon & Dincin, 2000). Inmates with serious mental illness receive inadequate follow-up services, and often find themselves having multiple encounters with mental health providers, criminal justice personnel, or combinations of both. There are two primary problems with policies for PSMIs. First, there is a lack of communication and shared vision between corrections officials and mental health providers, resulting in a lack of consistent services provided to PSMIs. Second, public mental health does not provide adequate follow-up services for PSMIs released from correctional settings. Follow-up services, when provided appropriately, are likely to provide needed supports to PSMIs, positive outcomes, and decreased interactions with the justice system. While this is important for most offenders with schizophrenia, it is especially important for violent offenders who have schizophrenia. These offenders contribute to high social costs of the criminal justice system.

Violence and Mental Illness

One purpose of this paper is to examine the prevalence of violent criminal offenses by persons with schizophrenia, and to suggest directions for treatment. Psychopathy has consistently been associated with violence, but similar links between high rates of violence for PSMIs has been a matter of conjecture. Emerging evidence, however, shows that persons with dual diagnosis have greater risk for committing a violent offense than both persons in the general population and persons with either disorder alone (Rice & Harris, 1995). In an analysis of 618 individuals incarcerated for violent offenses, Rice & Harris (1995) found schizophrenics were less likely to recidivate violently, but only when compared to the population of violent offenders (non-violent offenders and the general population were not examined). This finding should be considered with caution because it failed to examine the interaction between schizophrenia and substance abuse, a known contributor to increased violence and corresponding violent recidivism.

Rice & Harris (1995) postulate that schizophrenic offenders were more likely to be under follow-up care than non-schizophrenic offenders. They further indicate that offenders with schizophrenia, by virtue of their mental disorder, were subject to involuntary committal to a psychiatric hospital by a doctor who believed they were likely to commit a violent crime, even if the behavior responsible for committal was dependent upon substance abuse or antisocial behavior as opposed to their psychotic symptoms. This suggests that part of the reason for decreased recidivism was a decreased opportunity for persons with schizophrenia to recidivate violently. An interesting finding was that men diagnosed with schizophrenia were less likely than other men to be psychopaths. They suggest that this may be due to serotonin hyperactivity that exists in schizophrenics, as opposed to serotonin deficits underlying psychopathy. This finding indicates that there are measurable differences between violent offenders with schizophrenia and other violent offenders, even those with ASPD.

Box 12. 7
The Influence of Rice and Harris (1995)

> Rice and Harris (1995) investigated a schizophrenic offender population. Their findings were important because they found that there are fundamental differences between schizophrenics who commit violent crimes and non-schizophrenic psychopaths who commit crimes. The two groups differ on risk-assessment tests. Furthermore, the researchers support the present authors' belief that effective assessment procedures require psychological measures as well as risk assessment.

The findings of the Rice & Harris (1995) study are important for two reasons. First, they suggest that there are fundamental differences between schizophrenics who commit violent crimes, and non-schizophrenic psychopaths who commit crimes. They, unlike Andrews and Bonta (2003), believe it is possible to differentiate schizophrenic violent offenders from violent psychopathic offenders on risk assessment measures. They point to specific indicators on the Psychopathy Checklist (PCL-R; Hare, 1991) that detect these differences. Specifically, they found that the "Juvenile delinquency," "Early behavior problems," "Glibness/superficial charm," and "Conning/manipulative" items were least likely to be endorsed for schizophrenic offenders. There were significant differences between schizophrenic and non-schizophrenic offenders on these scores. No items on this checklist, however, positively correlated with a diagnosis of schizophrenia (Rice & Harris, 1995). In other words, the PCL-R is able to differentiate psychopaths from schizophrenic violent offenders, but unable to identify schizophrenia. These findings are important for the development of guidelines for assessment, placement, and treatments for schizophrenic violent offenders. They provide further support for our belief that effective assessment procedures require psychological measures as well as risk assessments.

Rice and Harris (1995) reported a high rate of comorbid substance abuse among violent offenders with schizophrenia. While they could not report that this dual diagnosis was likely to increase the recidivism for violent crimes among the sample of schizophrenics, they did find 16 percent of the studied schizophrenics had violent recidivisms in the following year, and that alcohol was a significant contributor to violent recidivism overall (Rice & Harris, 1995). This suggests that schizophrenics may be likely to have violent recidivism (although not as likely as non-schizophrenic offenders), and that schizophrenia and alcohol abuse may increase the risk of recidivism. Furthermore, the assertion that follow-up care directly affected recidivism rates for schizophrenic violent offenders suggests a response to treatment (Rice & Harris, 1995) by violent offenders with schizophrenia. An important step for corrections officials and mental health providers is identifying effective treatments for improving outcomes for decreasing violent recidivism by persons with schizophrenia.

Theoretical Perspectives

Theoretical Treatment Model

We will now define a theoretical framework for treating violent offenders with schizophrenia. We use psychological and psychiatric research data to support a model of treatment that may be effective for reducing violent recidivism by offenders with schizophrenia. We identify the known precipitators to violent behavior among schizophrenics, reiterate the role of substance abuse in acts of violence, and discuss a treatment model that incorporates regulatory drug therapy and cognitive behavioral therapy (CBT). Both drug therapy and CBT have been effective treatments for persons with schizophrenia (Kingdon & Turkington, 2005; Turkington, Kingdon & Turner, 2002), and may be extremely effective for improving outcomes for violent offenders with schizophrenia. This model is also appropriate because it has been shown to be effective for treating substance use disorders, the comorbid disorder of concern among violent offenders with schizophrenia.

Assessment

Assessment procedures used in correctional settings should determine the type and severity of mental illness. The procedures should follow those used in psychology, psychiatry, and associated mental health fields. Assessment procedures should be comprehensive and should be conducted by trained mental health professionals. The assessment should include structured or semi-structured clinical interviews, one or more self-report instruments, such as the Minnesota Multiphasic Personality Inventory (MMPI-2; Butcher, Graham, Tellegen & Kaemmer,

1989), the Personality Assessment Inventory (PAI; Morey, 1991), or the Symptom Checklist Revised (SCL-R; Derogatis, 1994)), a clinician-based rating scale such as the Brief Psychiatric Rating Scale (BPRS-A; Kolakowska, 1976), risk assessments, and other drug and alcohol assessment measures as needed. For persons diagnosed with schizophrenia, the Positive and Negative Syndrome Scale (PANSS; Kay, Opler & Fishbein, 1987) is useful for providing a more detailed picture of the spectrum of positive and negative symptoms. The PANSS includes an assessment of aggression risk.

Precipitators. There has been a dearth of information regarding the precipitators of violent behavior for persons with mental illness, and an accompanying lack of clinical profiles of schizophrenics that can assist clinicians and mental health providers in decisions regarding the appropriate placement and treatment of violent psychiatric patients (Sreenivasan, Kirkish, Eth, Mintz, Hwang, VanGorp & VanVort, 1997). Recent studies have sought to identify precipitants to violent behavior. These studies have indicated that violent behavior among mental health patients is directly linked to psychotic symptomatology. Findings assert that certain psychotic symptoms override internal controls and lead to uncontrollable and violent behaviors. These symptoms may be caused by paranoid fears that the individual is in danger of harm from others, or from AXIS I symptoms such as hallucinations and severe depression (Sreenivasan et al., 1997). Alcohol and other substance abuse have been found to increase the impact symptoms have on behavior. Furthermore, negative symptoms have a direct relationship to substance abuse, increasing the likelihood of violent offenses for a person with schizophrenia (Blanchard et al., 2000).

Box 12. 8
Treatments for PSMIs

Cognitive Behavior Therapy (CBT)	Empirically-based treatment is based on the belief that psychopathology is caused by faulty and irrational thinking. CBT attempts to change dysfunctional thinking.
Drug Therapy	Medication has been shown to improve schizophrenic symptoms. Such drugs include haloperidol, chlorpromazine, droperidol, clozapine, and respiradol.
Combined Approach	Includes the use of both CBT and Drug therapy. Both therapies have been shown to improve positive symptoms.

Treatment/Prevention

Cognitive Behavioral Therapy

Cognitive-behavioral therapy (CBT) is an empirically based therapeutic technique used to treat a variety of psychological disorders. Fundamental to CBT is the belief that psychopathology originates from faulty, irrational, distorted or dysfunctional self-statements a person makes to him or herself. CBT interventions center on altering these negative or distorted thought patterns into more positive, rational, and appropriate ones. CBT adheres to the principle that if changes in thinking occur, then changes in behavior and affect will follow. CBT is highly collaborative; patients take an active role in setting goals and designing treatment plans tailored to their individual needs. Cognitive-behavioral therapists use psychoeducation to keep patients highly informed about their condition, and homework assignments are given to encourage people to actively participate in their recovery. Treatment goals are expressed in measurable terms, and progress is continually evaluated and discussed (Beck, 1976).

The use of CBT in schizophrenia was initially described by Beck in 1952. Recently, CBT has been found to be an effective treatment for persons with schizophrenia. Research indicates that CBT has been shown to improve overall symptomatology, ameliorating positive symptoms in chronic patients, and decreasing chance of relapse among schizophrenics (Gumley et al., 2003; Turkington, Kingdon & Turner, 2002). One study examined the effects of CBT (delivered by community psychiatric nurses) on outcomes of 257 patients with schizophrenia receiving secondary psychiatric treatment (Turkington et al., 2002). Patients who received CBT improved significantly in overall symptomatology and readmissions to hospital as compared to the control group. Another study evaluating the effects of CBT and supportive counseling was conducted with 72 patients with schizophrenia receiving psychiatric care (Tarrier, Kinney, McCarthy, Wittkowski, Yusupoff & Gledhill, 2001). The study reported that delusions, hallucinations, and thought disorder improved significantly for persons receiving CBT. Hallucinations and thought disorder improved significantly compared to the supportive therapy group and the routine care group. Additionally, there were significant differences in negative symptoms with an advantage to the CBT group compared to the routine care group.

The findings indicate a significant improvement in positive symptoms for schizophrenics who receive CBT, those most closely associated with criminal and violent offenses. Additionally, two studies found improvements in negative symptoms, those symptoms shown to be associated with substance abuse among schizophrenics. Turkington et al.

(2002) revealed another interesting implication for CBT. Treatment was provided by trained psychiatric nurses in secondary care settings, indicating treatment can be provided by trained individuals other than clinical psychologists or psychiatrists, and that treatment can be provided in low risk settings in the community.

One study compared the long-term effects of 21 persons with schizophrenia receiving CBT to those receiving supportive counseling through hospital in-patient care (Haddock, Tarrier, Morrison, Hopkins, Drake & Lewis). At a two-year follow-up, the CBT group had lower numbers of relapses and readmissions to hospitals. Another study examined differences of frequency of relapses and readmissions to hospitals between a group of persons with schizophrenia receiving CBT and a control group receiving treatment as usual (Gumley et al., 2003). The CBT group was readmitted less often than the treatment-as-usual group, and there was a significant difference in relapse, with the CBT group having significantly fewer relapses. Like the previous studies, the CBT group showed significantly greater improvement in positive symptoms, negative symptoms, global psychopathology, and performance on independent functions and pro-social activities.

It is clear that CBT, when implemented appropriately, can be an effective treatment for persons with schizophrenia. It has been shown to have significant effects on both frequency of relapse and readmission to hospitals. This suggests an overall increase in functioning by persons with schizophrenia who receive CBT. A decrease in readmissions should be seen as extremely important to both mental health care providers and corrections officials. These findings indicate that it is possible to repair the revolving-door policy that has entrapped numerous persons with mental illness. Furthermore, these studies found that CBT causes significant improvement in both positive and negative symptoms of schizophrenia. Positive symptoms are a known precipitator to violence among schizophrenics, and these findings suggest that improvements in positive symptoms due to CBT may result in a decrease in instances of violent behavior. Additionally, negative symptoms are directly associated with alcoholism and substance abuse, and improvements in negative symptoms of schizophrenia may affect the rate of substance abuse (another known precipitator of violence) among schizophrenics.

Drug Therapy

Use of psychotropic medications has been shown to improve overall symptomatology in schizophrenia. Emerging evidence also suggests that drug therapy decreases aggression and violent behavior (Chengappa, 2002; Citrome, 2000; Suda, 1999). Drug therapy for patients with schizophrenia generally involves daily medications of haloperidol, chlor-promazine, droperidol, clozapine, respiradol and others. These medications have been known to decrease positive symptoms that have been associated with violent behaviors. One study examined the effects of clozapine with 137 patients in a psychiatric hospital (Chengappa, 2002). Patients who received clozapine had significant decreases in the numbers of restraints and seclusions due to violent behavior, and experienced an overall improvement in aggressive behavior. Two problems are commonly associated with drug therapy; the acquired immunity to the effects of the medications and neurological impairments (e.g., tardive dyskenzsia) associated with long-term medications.

Box 12. 9
Problems with Drug Therapy

1. Eventual immunity to the medications' effects.

2. Neurological impairments are associated with long-term use of some of the medications.

Combined Approach

We believe that the most effective treatment for schizophrenia is a combination of CBT and drug-therapy. Both of these therapies have been shown to improve positive symptoms associated with schizophrenia. Improvements in positive symptoms could result in decreases of violent behavior, while improvements in negative symptoms have shown corresponding decreases in depression and substance abuse. Furthermore, CBT has demonstrated reductions in relapses and readmissions, and drug therapy has been shown to reduce violent behavior and aggression in persons with schizophrenia. Additionally, CBT is an effective approach for helping persons with substance use disorder to manage their substance abuse problems. The multiple problems associated with violent offenders with schizophrenia may be most effectively treated through the integration of CBT and drug therapy.

Effective treatment programs should be based upon four basic principles: (1) treatments should directly address criminogenic factors, (2) treatments should have therapeutic integrity, (3) treatments should target offenders who are at risk for recidivism, and (4) treatment should be delivered in a mode that addresses individual learning styles (MacKenzie, 2000). The CBT/drug therapy model that we propose does include these four basic principles. The treatment addresses those factors directly associated with violent recidivism; the precipitators of violence, access to treatment, and comorbid substance abuse. Additionally, this treatment should be based upon individual risk assessments as proposed by Blanchard et al. (2000) and Rice & Harris (1995). Second, this treatment model requires highly regulated therapy by trained professionals in the field. Third, this model targets violent offenders with schizophrenia, including those with dual diagnoses, or who are at risk for violent recidivism on risk assessment scales. Finally, CBT is one of the most individualized approaches to therapeutic treatment. It requires active participation by the therapist and the patient, and facilitates the individual learning styles of persons with serious mental illness.

Box 12. 10
Principles of an Effective Treatment (Mackenzie, 2000; Andrews & Bonta, 2003)

---

1. Treatments should directly address criminogenic factors.

2. Treatments should have therapeutic integrity.

3. Treatments should target offenders who are at risk for recidivism.

4. Treatment should be delivered in a mode that addresses individual learning style.

Current Research on Schizophrenia and Violent Recidivism

In order to determine the type and effectiveness of treatments currently employed for the treatment of violent offending among schizophrenics, we conducted a review of the literature. We ran an electronic search using the Psychinfo database using the descriptors "schizophrenia," "violence," and "recidivism," and using the descriptors "schizophrenia," "violence," and "treatment." We also conducted an ancestral search of the journals related to the field of criminal justice. Our search yielded only three studies that measured the effects of treatments on the rates of violent reoffending among persons with schizophrenia. We reviewed these studies, and evaluated them based upon their methodological rigor.

Baxter, Hesketh, and Parrot (1999) evaluated the effects of treatment in a medium security detention facility on the rates of recidivism and violent reoffending of 63 offenders with schizophrenia. Data were collected ex post facto. Official records were examined to determine the amount of psychiatric care received, rates of violent offending, and rates of comorbid substance abuse prior to commitment in the facility and after release from the facility. Subjects were included if they received psychotropic medications, were discharged directly to the community, and were discharged at least one year prior to data collection. Five behaviors were included as violent offenses: (a) violence against the person, (b) violence toward property, (c) threats to kill, (d) arson, and (e) sexual offenses.

Public disorder and possession of a weapon were not included as violent offenses. Reconviction and violent reoffending data were obtained from official criminal records. Length of follow-up ranged from one year to ten years.

On average, the sample was 33.6 years old. Most were single (81%), black (63%), and male (75%). A high percentage of the subjects had received psychiatric treatment prior to incarceration. Illicit drugs had been abused by 71 percent, and 29 percent were excessive alcoholics.

At referral, 68 percent of the subjects had previous convictions for violent offenses. The majority of these were violence against person offenses. Additionally, 68 percent of the subjects had been convicted for non-violent or minor offenses. Previous psychiatric treatment had been received by 86 percent of the subjects. At outcome, 67 percent of the subjects were convicted for violent offenses. Ninety-two percent of the sample had retained links with psychiatric services or had new encounters with psychiatric care facilities. The contacts with mental health facilities ranged from hospitalization to consistent contact with a social worker from local psychiatric service providers. Additionally, logistic regression analysis revealed that substance abuse and alcoholism were significant predictors of violent recidivism.

This study revealed that typical correctional treatments for violent offenders with schizophrenia are not effective for reducing violent reoffending among schizophrenics. The treatment evaluated was incarceration with provision of psychotropic medications. The pre and post results revealed no differences for violent reoffending or for new encounters with the justice system. Furthermore, the authors found a significant relationship between violent offending among schizophrenia and coexisting substance abuse. One major problem with the data, however, was the failure to disaggregate substance abuse at the pre and post measures. As a result, it was impossible to tell if schizophrenics with substance abuse problems exhibited higher or lower rates of violent reoffending than those without substance abuse problems.

This study had some methodological shortcomings. The authors did not clearly describe the treatment during incarceration. They also failed to adequately identify the types of services subjects received after release. Additionally, the length of time out of treatment was highly variable, and could not have been controlled. As a result, this study has severe limitations with regard to the findings. However, it does provide important descriptive data regarding the types of outcomes that schizophrenic offenders might experience. Furthermore, this study highlights the failure of corrections officials to investigate and provide treatments that reduce positive and negative symptoms which have been shown to contribute to reduced violent behavior among schizophrenics.

Box 12. 11
Review of Treatment Evaluations

Treatment Evaluations	
Baxter, Hesketh, and Parrot (1999)	Looked at the effects of treatment in a medium security detention facility on the rates of recidivism and violent reoffending of 63 schizophrenic offenders; results showed that typical correctional treatments for violent offenders with schizophrenia are not effective for reducing violent reoffending among schizophrenics. Treatments evaluated included incarceration with provisions of psychotropic medications.
Hodgins, Lapalme, and Toupin (1999)	Examined a sample of schizophrenics with criminal histories; reported rates of reoffending for schizophrenics were high after release from hospitalizations. Found alcohol abuse and substance abuse were significant predictors of violent offending.
Godley, Finch, Dougan, McDonnell, McDermeit, and Carey (2000)	Examined the effectiveness of a case management model for dually diagnosed individuals involved in the court system on the rate of encounters with the law and arrest rates for 54 persons with schizophrenia and a dually diagnosed substance use disorder; found that case managers made home visits and worked with families to involve significant others in treatment, all measures related to involvement with the police and the legal system showed significant decreases at follow-up, the number of subjects jailed in the previous six months decreased; attrition was high.

Hodgins, Lapalme, and Toupin (1999) reported different results in their analysis of 74 persons with schizophrenia who had a history of offending. The authors collected follow-up data for the subjects for two years after their release from a forensic hospital and two general psychiatric hospitals. Subjects were aged between 18 and 55, and had full scale IQs above 70. The authors collected data on instances of drug abuse, assessments of psychological functioning, and convictions for criminal offenses. At discharge, 47 percent of the subjects had a lifetime history of drug abuse, 49 percent had been convicted of violent crimes, but only 31 percent had been sentenced to prison for any offense. The percent of violent offenders who were sentenced to prison was not reported. The authors reported the length of previous hospitalizations, but did not report the percent of subjects who had been hospitalized previously. Additional demographic data was not reported.

Follow-up data were collected through a series of interviews. The percentages of subjects reassessed were as follows: 89 percent at 6 months, 78 percent at 12 months, 62 percent at 18 months, and 46 percent at 24 months. During the interview visit, research staff collected urine samples and breathalyzer tests. At the conclusion of the 24-month follow-up period, official records were examined to determine frequencies and types of offenses committed by subjects. Proportions of substance abuse were moderately high according to self-report data (33%) as well as by urine analysis (32%). Rates of alcohol abuse were high when reported by the subjects (70%) as well as when evaluated by the breathalyzer (82%). Unfortunately, the authors did not state which follow-up session these data were from. Only 15 percent of the subjects were convicted for a criminal offense, and only 10 percent were convicted for a violent crime after the 24-month follow-up.

The authors reported that rates for reoffending for schizophrenics were high after release from hospitalizations. Additionally, they found that alcohol and substance abuse were significant predictors of violent reoffending. There are, however, a number of methodological concerns with this study. First, the type of treatment received after discharge was not reported. Additionally, there was a high rate of attrition which severely limits the generalizability of these findings. Considering that subjects were voluntary participants, it is conceivable that subjects with better outcomes continued their participation, while persons with poorer outcomes dropped out. Furthermore, not all of the subjects had been convicted of violent offenses prior to discharge, so there is no rationale for hypothesizing that these subjects would offend violently. Finally, the data were not presented so that comorbidity of schizophrenia and substance abuse were correlated with violent offending prior to discharge and after the follow-up. Instead, these data were aggregated for these two conditions. Therefore, it is impossible to determine if persons with schizophrenia who have lifelong histories of substance abuse are more or less likely to violently reoffend than those without substance abuse problems.

The final study (Godley, Finch, Dougan, McDonnell, McDermeit & Carey, 2000) examined a case management model for dually diagnosed individuals involved in the court system. Specifically, this study examined the effectiveness of this program on the rates of encounters with the law and arrest rates for 54 persons with schizophrenia and a dually diagnosed substance use disorder. The subjects participated in an intensive case management program upon release to probation. Case managers were assigned to each client, and provided services in community-based sites. The ratio of managers to clients was 1:10. The study reported that case managers made home visits and worked with families (when possible) to involve significant others in treatment. No other descriptions of the treatment were presented; however, the authors indicated that each subject received different types of services. Length of stay in the case management service varied dependent on length of probation. An average contact with case managers was .82 times per week. Follow-up data were collected for each subject. The authors evaluated the effects of the treatment on recurrence of substance abuse, encounters with the law, and arrests.

Most subjects were between the ages of 25 and 35 (46%), male (72%) and white (63%). The most common substance abuse diagnosis was alcohol (76%), followed by cannabis (37%), and cocaine (26%). Sixty-three percent had more than one substance abuse diagnosis. One major methodological problem with this study is the high rate of attrition. Only 23 of the subjects completed all of the follow-up measures.

Outcome measures were sporadic, and results must be considered in view of the high attrition rates. Each of the outcome measures were reported based upon the number of subjects who completed that particular outcome measure. Of the 44 subjects who completed treatment, 57 percent successfully completed their probation, 16 percent experienced new arrests on minor charges or violent activity, and 27 percent had no records. The authors reported that all measures related to involvement with police and the legal system showed significant decreases from intake to follow-up. The number of subjects with legal problems in the previous six months decreased from 95 percent at intake to 70 percent at follow-up (N = 44). The number of subjects jailed in the previous six months decreased from 74 percent at intake to 26 percent at follow-up (N = 44). Of the 23 subjects who completed follow-up, there was no significant decrease in substance abuse, although 72 percent moved to an advanced stage of treatment, indicating these subjects were active participants in the substance treatment program.

Results from this study should be considered with caution. The treatment provided to subjects was highly variable, and never clearly described. Length of stay in the program was also highly variable. Similar to the previous study, there was a high rate of attrition. Many of the outcome measures were conducted on less than one-half of the original subjects, a major threat to the validity of the findings. The authors did not report the actual number of violent reoffenses committed by the subjects, nor did they report correlations between substance abuse and violent reoffending. As a result, it is difficult to assess the effectiveness of the treatment on the outcome measures. While this study has shortcomings, it does provide some evidence that community treatment programs may be effective for reducing criminal behavior and substance abuse among schizophrenics dually diagnosed with substance use disorders. We found the reported success of the drug treatment program of particular note, considering the apparent adherence to the treatment by the subjects.

Implications for Future Research

These three studies had methodological problems but do contribute to an initial understanding of effective treatments for offenders with schizophrenia who are dually diagnosed with substance abuse problems. The authors of these studies experienced difficulty maintaining controls on the treatment, limiting the impact of the findings. The treatments in these studies do not adhere to the four basic principles proposed by MacKenzie (2000), and lack sufficient descriptions be adequately evaluated. An issue across each of these studies is to examine the symptomology of the subjects at the time of investigation—a known predictor of violent behavior among schizophrenics. Another was the failure to systematically measure the role of comorbid substance abuse as a factor of violent offending.

In order to evaluate effective treatments for violent offenders with schizophrenia, more research needs to be conducted by the criminal justice system. Researchers need to examine those factors most closely associated with violent behavior: symptomatology and comorbid substance abuse. The field of psychology has shown clear evidence of the role of these factors as predictors of violent behavior, and has found some promising treatments for reducing these behaviors. They have learned that certain psychotic symptoms override internal controls and lead to uncontrollable and violent behaviors and that alcohol and other substance abuses have been found to increase the impact symptoms have on behavior. The criminal justice system needs to examine research conducted by the field of psychology, and incorporate those practices that are known to be effective for treating schizophrenics who exhibit violent behavior. Future treatments should include CBT and drug therapy, be developed in accordance with the four basic principles of effective treatment, and be rigorously examined by the research community to determine the most effective practices for delivery of treatment.

Conclusion

In this paper we addressed the issues surrounding violent offenses by persons with schizophrenia (particularly those with dual diagnosis), and the problems associated with identification and treatment of this population. We discussed the salient features of schizophrenic symptomatology, and their effect on patterns of violent behavior. We also addressed the prevalence of comorbid substance use disorder among the population of violent offenders with schizophrenia. We identified some of the issues surrounding this population's overrepresentation in the criminal justice system, and proposed some approaches to better identify and assess persons with schizophrenia and their risks for violent recidivism. We then examined current research of violent offenders with schizophrenia, and found a need for more seminal research that examines effective treatments that reflect the knowledge learned by the field of psychology. Finally, we proposed a treatment model of CBT/drug therapy that we believe will be effective for improving symptoms of schizophrenia, decreasing relapses and readmissions, and reducing rates of violent recidivism for offenders with schizophrenia. This model relies on a comprehensive assessment process and an effective and scientifically-based treatment. If employed appropriately by corrections officials, we believe this model will be successful in improving outcomes and reducing violent recidivism for persons with schizophrenia.

References

Andrews, D.A. and J. Bonta (2003). *The Psychology of Criminal Conduct*, Third Edition. Cincinnati, OH: Anderson Publishing Co.

Baxter, R., S. Rabe-Hesketh, and J. Parrot (1999). "Characteristics, Needs and Reoffending in a Group of Patients with Schizophrenia Formerly Treated in Medium Security." *The Journal of Forensic Psychiatry,* 10:69-83.

Beck, A. (1976). *Cognitive Therapy and the Emotional Disorders.* New York, NY: Penguin Books, USA Inc.

Blanchard, J., S. Brown, W. Horan, and A. Sherwood (2000). "Substance Use Disorders in Schizophrenia: Review, Integration, and a Proposed Model." *Clinical Psychology Review*, 20:207-234.

Butcher, J. N., W. Dahlstrom, J. R. Graham, A. Tellegen, and B. Kaemmer (1989). "Minnesota Multiphasic Personality Inventory (MMPI-2)." *Manual for Administration and Scoring.* Minneapolis: University of Minnesota Press.

Chengappa, K. (2002). "Clozapine: Its Impact on Aggressive Behavior Among Patients in a State Psychiatric Hospital." *Schizophrenia Research*, 53:1-6.

Citrome, L. (2000). "Management of Violence in Schizophrenia." *Psychiatric Annals*, 30:41-52.

Cooper, B. (2003). "Evidence-Based Mental Health Policy: A Critical Appraisal." *British Journal of Psychiatry*, 183:105-113.

Derogatis, L.R. (1994). *Symptom Checklist-R: Administration, Scoring, and Procedures Manual.* Minneapolis, MN: NCS Pearson.

Godley, S., M. Finch, L. Dougan, M. McDonnell, M. McDermeit, and A. Carey (2000). "Case Management for Dually Diagnosed Individuals Involved in the Criminal Justice System." *Journal of Substance Abuse Treatment*, 18:137-148.

Gumley, A., M. O'Grady, L. McNay, J. Reilly, K. Power, and J. Norrie (2003). "Early Intervention for Relapse in Schizophrenia: Results of a 12-Month Randomized Controlled Trial of Cognitive Behavioral Therapy." *Psychological Medicine*, 33:419-431.

Haddock, G., N. Tarrier, A. Morrison, R. Hopkins, R. Drake, and S. Lewis (1999). "A Pilot Study Evaluating the Effectiveness of Individual Inpatient Cognitive Behavioral Therapy in Early Psychosis." *Social Psychiatry and Epidemiology*, 34:254-258.

Hodges, S., M. Lapalme, and J. Toupin (1999). "Criminal Activities and Substance Use of Patients with Major Affective Disorders and Schizophrenia: A 2-year Follow-Up." *Journal of Affective Disorders,* 55:187-202.

Kay S.R., L.A. Opler, and A. Fishbein (1987). *Positive and Negative Syndrome Scale (PANSS) Rating Manual.* San Rafael, CA: Social and Behavioral Sciences Documents.

Kolakowska T. (1976) *The Brief Psychiatric Rating Scale.* Oxford University, Oxford.

Kingdon, D.G. and D. Turkington (2005). *Cognitive Therapy of Schizophrenia.* New York, NY: Guiford Press.

Lurigio, A. and J. Swartz (2000). "Changing the Contours of the Criminal Justice System to Meet the Needs of Persons with Serious Mental Illness." *Policies, Processes, and Decisions of the Criminal Justice System*, 3:45-108.

MacKenzie, D. (2000). "Sentencing and Corrections in the 21st Century: Setting the Stage for the Future." Manuscript and Overheads. www.evaluatingcorrections.org

Morey, L.C. (1991). *The Personality Assessment Inventory Professional Manual.* Odessa, FL: Psychological Assessment Resources.

Perez, A., S. Leifman, and A. Estrada (2003). "Reversing the Criminalization of Mental Illness." *Crime & Delinquency*, 49:62-78.

Rice M. and G. Harris (1997). "The Treatment of Mentally Disordered Offenders." *Psychology, Public Policy, and Law*, 3:126-183.

Rice M. and G. Harris (1995). "Psychopathy, Schizophrenia, Alcohol Abuse, and Violent Recidivism." *International Journal of Law and Psychiatry*, 18:333-342.

Sreenivasan, S., P. Kirkish, S. Eth, J. Mintz, S. Hwang, W. VanGorp, and W. VanVort (1997). "Predictors of Recidivistic Violence in Criminally Insane and Civilly Committed Psychiatric Inpatients." *International Journal of Law and Psychiatry*, 20:279-291.

Suda, K. (1999). "Effectiveness of Clomipramine for Obsessive-Compulsive Symptoms and Violence in Schizophrenia." *Clinical Psychiatry*, 41:751-753.

Tarrier, N. and R. Calam (2002). "New Developments in Cognitive-Behavioral Case Formulation. Epidemiological, Systematic and Social Context: An Integrative Approach." *Behavioral and Cognitive Psychotherapy*, 30:311-328.

Tarrier, N., C. Kinney, E. McCarthy, A. Wittkowski, L. Yusupoff, and A. Gledhill (2001). "Are Some Types of Psychotic Symptoms More Responsive to Cognitive-Behavior Therapy?" *Behavioral and Cognitive Psychotherapy*, 29:45-55.

Turkington, D., D. Kingdon, and T. Turner (2002). "Effectiveness of a Brief Cognitive-Behavioral Therapy Intervention in the Treatment of Schizophrenia." *British Journal of Psychiatry*, 172:523-527.

Wyatt v. Stickney, 324 F. Supp. 781 M.D. Ala. (1972).

Chapter 13

White-Collar Crime

Natalie Schell

Introduction

The four news items shown in Box 13.1 have one thing in common: they describe alleged cases of white-collar crime. White-collar crime is a relatively new addition to criminology. The concept was introduced by Edwin Sutherland (1940) to differentiate a group of offenders that were not ordinarily considered criminals. In his groundbreaking work, *White Collar Crime*, Sutherland's definition of white-collar crime revolved around the social position of the offender; this new category of crime was described as "any crime committed by a person of respectability and high social status in the course of his occupation" (Shapiro, 1990:347). Sutherland (1940) introduced this crime committed exclusively by the upper and middle classes in order to debunk criminological theories that claimed crime was due to poverty or psychopathic and sociopathic conditions associated with poverty.

A large debate, however, centers on this offender-based definition of white-collar crime. According to Sutherland's original definition, only the first two examples in Box 13.1 would be clear-cut cases of white-collar crime because they were committed by people of high social status in the course of their occupations. The third example would not qualify as white-collar crime because someone on welfare is not a person of high social status and the crime did not occur within an occupational setting. The last example above would be a questionable case because it is unlikely that this crime was committed in conjunction with employment and that the couple is of high social standing. While Sutherland's definition of white-collar crime would not encompass these last two offenses, they have both been considered white-collar crimes because they are cases of fraud.

Box 13.1
Opening Quotes

Prosecutors say Kozlowski, 57, and Swartz, 43, stole $170 million to finance their lavish lifestyles by taking unauthorized bonuses and abusing company loan programs. They say the two netted an additional $430 million by pumping up Tyco stock prices and selling their shares from 1995 through 2002.

—Maull, S. (2004)

The whistle-blower lawsuit challenges the pricing methods of the entire carbon fiber industry, including seven goliaths named in the suit: Toray Composites, Mitsubishi Rayon, Boeing, Hexcel, BP Amoco Polymers, Cytec-Fiberite and Toho Tenax . . . Beck said industry executives talked "matter of factly" about fixing prices and charging the U.S. government high prices for carbon fiber used in defense programs.

—Taylor & Bigelow (2002)

Inspector General Albert H. Masland today announced that Lois J. Worrell (also known as Lois J. Ballenger), 54, of Gettysburg, Adams County, faces felony welfare-fraud charges for allegedly collecting more than $10,650 in cash assistance for which she was not eligible from November 1997 to December 2001.

—PR Newswire (2002)

A Narragansett couple has been indicted on federal charges of mail fraud, wire fraud, conspiracy and other charges for allegedly bilking elderly victims out of thousands of dollars through a telephone solicitation scam.

—Davis, M. (2002)

The alternative way to define white-collar crime is to focus on the criminal acts rather than on offender characteristics. Scholars on this side of the debate argue that until white-collar crime as a concept is disentangled from the characteristics of the perpetrators, the phenomenon of white-collar crime will be misinterpreted and misunderstood (Shapiro, 1990, Griffin, 2002, Braithwaite, 1985). An example of an offense-based definition of white-collar crime is provided by Wheeler, Weisburd and Bode (1982), who defined it as "economic offenses committed through the use of some combination of fraud, deception, or collusion" (1982:642). This definition of white-collar crime is a broader definition that encompasses all four examples of white-collar offenses provided in Box 13.1.

Within the debate over the definition of white-collar crime, there is also dissension over the number of subsets of white-collar crime. There are three categories that seem to cover most white-collar crime: occupational crime, corporate crime, and job-less white-collar crime.

Box 13.2
Three Categories of White-Collar Crime

Occupational Crime	Offenses are largely related to occupation such as offenses against employer or offenses that use technical expertise.
Corporate Crime	Any act committed by corporations that is punished by the state, regardless of whether it is punished under administrative, civil, or criminal law (Clinard & Yeager, 1980:16).
Jobless White-Collar Crime	Does not require the use of an occupation; can include welfare fraud, identity theft, and postal fraud.

Occupational crime is largely perpetrated by individuals in connection with their occupation such that the crime is against an employer or makes use of technical expertise (Clinard & Yeager, 1980; Daly, 1989). It includes crimes such as tax evasion, fraudulent repair of cars and appliances, embezzlement, misappropriation of public funds, and employee theft of supplies. Corporate crime is "any act committed by corporations that is punished by the state, regardless of whether it is punished under administrative, civil, or criminal law" (Clinard & Yeager, 1980:16). Corporate crime encompasses tax and securities violations, intentional pollution of the environment, knowingly failing to provide a safe work environment, and a wide range of anticompetitive behaviors like price-fixing. The third subset of white-collar crime does not require the use of an occupation and is the most controversial subset of white-collar crime. This job-less white-collar crime can include welfare fraud, identity theft, and postal fraud (Daly, 1989).

In this paper, I use the offense-based definition of white-collar crime provided by Wheeler, Weisburd and Bode (1982) since it is more inclusive, and I attempt to include all three subsets of white-collar crime in my discussion. First, I will discuss the prevalence of white-collar crime and its effects on society. Then I will describe the known characteristics of white-collar criminals and the justifications commonly used in committing white-collar crime. The next section will cover some of the popular theoretical perspectives of white-collar crime. After this, I will discuss the historical and current enforcement response to white-collar crime, and I will conclude with the treatment/prevention options available to combat white-collar crime.

Prevalence

The prevalence of most types of white-collar crime is not known for certain. The number of victims and the amount of monetary losses are matters of speculation because data has not been systematically collected on the incidence or cost of white-collar crime (Shover & Wright, 2001; Jesilow, Klempner & Chiao, 2001; Cohen, 2000). The only well-known fact about the prevalence of most white-collar crimes is that they are not often brought to the attention of the authorities. One reason for this is that white-collar crime is more hidden than street crime, and so the victims commonly do not know they have been victimized (Shover & Wright, 2001; Jesilow, Klempner & Chiao, 2001; Clinard & Yeager, 1980). Another reason is that the public does not know where to report white-collar crime, and if they do know, they tend to think little can be done to recover their losses (Jesilow, Klempner & Chiao, 2001). Finally, even when studies of the prevalence and cost of white-collar crime do exist, the crime types and definitions can vary so dramatically and be so convoluted that comparability across crime types is difficult (Cohen, 2000). For these reasons, reports on the prevalence of white-collar crime usually underestimate the actual incidence of this crime.

The Uniform Crime Reports (UCR), which is arrest data collected by the FBI from state and local police departments, contains measures of forgery, fraud, and embezzlement. Recent UCR data from 2002 showed that arrests for forgery and counterfeiting made up .8 percent of all arrests in the United States. Fraud arrests accounted for 2.5 percent of all arrests in the U.S., and arrests for embezzlement made up .1 percent of all arrests in the U.S. Overall, these fraudulent offenses accounted for 3 percent of all arrests in the U.S. in 2002 (FBI, 2002). This data describes a very low prevalence of these three white-collar crimes. However, it has been argued that UCR data does not provide an accurate picture of white-collar crime. Studies show that most occupational and corporate crime does not come to the attention of police agencies, and even if it does come to the attention of authorities, it may not result in an arrest (Steffensmeier, 1989; Titus, 2001). These numbers, therefore, underestimate the true prevalence of white-collar crime.

The Bureau of Justice Statistics provides yearly reports on the arrests for federal white-collar crime offenses. In 2000, arrests for fraudulent offenses, like embezzlement, fraud, and forgery, made up 11.6 percent of all federal arrests with fraud accounting for 9.1 percent of arrests. Regulatory offenses, like antitrust and food and drug violations, only made up 0.5 percent of all arrests, and tax law violations constituted 1 percent of all federal arrests. Taken together, white-collar crime accounted for about 13 percent of all federal arrests made in 1999 (BJS 2002).[1] Once again, the available arrest data do not demonstrate a high prevalence of white-collar crime, but it should be noted that federal arrest data face the same limitations as the UCR data with regard to white-collar crime offenses.

Self-report studies of victims and employees provide more accurate estimates of the prevalence of white-collar crime. Household surveys with questions concerning fraud victimization discovered that one in three Americans reported having been cheated out of money through various deceptive means (Titus, 2001). Titus et al. (1995) conducted a national telephone survey and found that 58 percent of the 1,246 respondents had been the victims of successful fraudulent acts in their lifetime. Fifteen percent of the sample had been successfully victimized within the past year, and 8 percent of the sample reported being repeat victims of personal fraud.

Self-report studies conducted on employees to discover the prevalence of employee-theft, an occupational crime, have found that it is a common phenomenon. Several studies of employees in retail, hospital, and manufacturing jobs found that about one-third of employees admitted to some sort of workplace theft (Mustaine & Tewksbury, 2002). Dabney (1995) interviewed 25 nurses in a hospital; 23 admitted to personally stealing supplies and all of them claimed to have seen other nurses stealing supplies. These self-report surveys suggest much higher rates of white-collar crime.

Effects on Society

Box 13.3
Effects of White-Collar Crime on Society

Monetary costs (e.g., loss of house, unable to pay health care)

Stress

Depression

Anger

Health Problems

Lost time from work

Generalized Anxiety Disorder

Injury and Death (e.g., from medical crimes or violations of Occupational Safety and Health Act)

As mentioned above, the monetary costs of white-collar crime to society are also matters of speculation. Estimates vary by crime type and source; however, most sources seem to show that the monetary losses associated with white-collar crime far exceed the monetary losses associated with street crime (Cohen, 2000; Shover & Wright, 2001). Cohen

(2000) reported that employee theft and fraud cost society $435 billion a year, which was about four times the monetary losses from street crime reported in the same study. Cohen (2000) also reported that false claims on insurance cost $120 billion a year, telemarketing scams cost up to $40 billion a year, and theft of services in the telecommunications industry cost society between $3.7 and $5 billion a year. Liederbach (2001) reported that the estimates of the cost of health-care fraud range from $50 to $80 billion annually. Calavita and Pontell (2001) reported that the costs of the savings and loans scandals in the late 1980s, in which operators of the companies stole millions and brought their institutions to financial ruin, will range from $300 billion to $473 billion by the year 2021. Clinard and Yeager (1980) reported that corporate crime, including faulty goods, monopolistic practices, and other violations cost consumers between $174 and $231 billion a year. They also reported that the Internal Revenue Service estimated that about $1.2 billion goes unreported each year in tax returns.

These numbers demonstrate the staggering monetary costs of white-collar crime. They do not, however, depict the emotional harm caused to white-collar crime victims. Elderly victims of white-collar crime sometimes lose their houses or are unable to pay for Medicare, which can increase the intangible costs, like stress and depression, of white-collar crime (Cohen, 2000). In one study, interviews with victims who have lost investments in businesses due to criminal activities of employees revealed bitter and angry feelings up to 10 years after victimization, and a small group of victims reported depression and intense anger due to their victimization (Titus, 2001). In another study, 10-20 percent of victims of white-collar crime suffered health problems and lost time from work following their victimization. Ganzini, McFarland, and Bloom (2001) found that victims of a fraud scam were as likely to experience generalized anxiety disorder and major depressive episodes as victims of violent crime.

White-collar crime can also cause injury and death. Medical crimes, such as unnecessary medical procedures and prescription violations can exact an enormous physical toll. Liederbach (2001) reported that up to two million patients are needlessly subjected to physical risks through unnecessary (fraudulent) operations each year. Sickness and death can result from air and water pollution caused by corporate violations, and the sale of unsafe foods and drugs and defective cars and appliances can cause serious injuries and death (Clinard & Yeager, 1980). Companies that violate workplace safety regulations also place people at risk; it is estimated that poor working conditions kill at least 100,000 workers annually and disable another 390,000 annually (Donnelly, 1982).[2] Clinard and Yeager (1980) assert that more people die as a result of corporate crime than as a result of criminal homicides.

While these monetary, emotional, and physical costs to society are enormous, Sutherland argued that the greatest cost of white-collar crime was the damage to social relations. White-collar crime is a violation of trust and can, therefore, breed distrust. This distrust can, in turn, lower social morale and create social disorganization on a large scale (Sutherland, 1940). Moore and Mills (1990) elaborated on this cost to society by explaining that white-collar crime diminishes faith in business leaders, business institutions, and even the capitalist system as a whole. If the American public does not trust businesses, they will stop investing in them, and if criminal actions persist, they may begin to distrust capitalism entirely.

White-collar crime could also lead to a loss of confidence in political institutions, processes, and leaders (Moore & Mills, 1990). If the American public witnesses violations of the law by public officials, they naturally will question the integrity of the individuals and the government they serve. Furthermore, if the criminal justice system treats white-collar criminals more leniently than street criminals, the public may begin to distrust the criminal justice system and its officials. The last consequence of white-collar crime described by Moore and Mills (1990) is a general erosion of public morality. They explain that citizens who witness crimes committed by their business leaders, politicians, and other public officials will more easily rationalize their own criminal actions. When these issues of distrust are added to the enormous financial losses and the emotional and physical costs mentioned above, the effects of white-collar crime on society appear considerable.

Offender Characteristics

It is difficult to generalize characteristics of white-collar criminals since they commit such a wide variety of economic offenses. The stereotypical white-collar offender invoked by Sutherland's definition is an upper-class white male. He is well-educated and older than the average street criminal. He has a family and a house in the suburbs. In other words, he is the antithesis of the average street criminal, who tends to be young, black, single, undereducated, and poor.

Weisburd et al. (1990) used a sample of 1,090 offenders who participated in various white-collar crimes, including both occupational and corporate offenses, to investigate the traits of white-collar criminals.[3] They found that only 8 percent of the sample was unemployed at the time they committed their crimes, which differs greatly from offenders of street crime who are usually unemployed. The sample of offenders also included a larger number of white offenders than is usually found in a sample of street criminals, and the offenders were much older than typical street criminals. For example, the average criminal convicted for property offenses like burglary and larceny in 1992 was 28 years old (Langan & Cohen, 1996). In Wesiburd et al.'s (1990) study, bank embezzlers were 31 years old on average, securities offenders were 44 years old, and tax offenders were 47 years old.

Interestingly, in Daly's (1989) analysis of the same data set, she discovered that the females in the sample (N=194) tended to possess more of the traits associated with offenders of street crime. Compared to the men in the sample, a higher percentage of women convicted of postal fraud, credit fraud, and false claims were unemployed. Of those females who were employed, most were clerical workers rather than managers or administrators. Daly (1989) also found that the female white-collar criminals in the sample were less educated and younger than the men. For instance, on average female embezzlers were 26 years old and those committing postal fraud were 30, whereas males were 31 and 41, respectively. There were also higher proportions of nonwhite women than men for all offenses but false claims. The characteristics of the female white-collar offenders more closely resembled those of street criminals than the characteristics of the male offenders.

Similarly, studies of employee theft produce evidence that white-collar offenders, at least those that commit employee theft, tend to be comparable to street criminals. These studies show that, as with street crime, young males tend to be the perpetrators. Mustaine and Tewksbury (2002) report that men account for 60-65 percent of arrests for workplace theft and that they are typically in their twenties.

Weisburd et al. (2001), in an updated analysis of their data, focused more on the different characteristics possessed by different groups in their white-collar crime sample. For instance, they reported that demographics of offenders tended to vary by crime type. Antitrust and securities fraud offenders were generally middle-aged, wealthier, white males with college degrees and steady employment in a white-collar job. Credit fraud and mail fraud offenders, on the other hand, were younger, less educated, less financially stable, female, and nonwhite (Weisburd et al., 2001). These findings emphasize the point that white-collar crimes include a variety of crimes and that a variety of people commit them. While many white-collar criminals fit Sutherland's description, others more closely resemble the typical street criminal.

Propensity for Crime

Another debate in the white-collar crime literature regarding offender characteristics surrounds not these demographic characteristics but characteristics of criminality, such as the propensity of crime. Hirschi and Gottfredson (1987) have argued that white-collar criminals are likely to share the same propensity as offenders of street crime. This assertion is consistent with their general theory of crime, which they claim accounts for all forms of criminal behavior. In this theory, they define criminality as the "tendency of individuals to pursue short-term gratification in the most direct way with little consideration for the long-term consequences of their acts" (Hirschi & Gottfredson, 1987:960). They claim that people with low levels of self-control will be unwilling or unable to delay gratification and will be impulsive, active, and risk-taking. According to Hirschi and Gottfredson (1987), all criminals possess low self-control and its associated characteristics. They also claim that all criminals, because of these shared traits, should offend at similar rates and should participate in several types of crime and deviance rather than specialize in any one specific crime type, like white-collar offenses.

In support of Hirschi and Gotffredson's theory, Mustaine and Tewksbury (2002) reported that college students who had participated in past criminal or deviant acts were more likely to steal from work. For instance, those most likely to steal from work tended to use or abuse alcohol. They also had stolen from strangers, broken into a vehicle in the past six months or had been to prison. In other words, they exhibited low self-control and the deviant acts associated with it. Similarly, Wright and Cullen (2000) found that high school students with high levels of occupational delinquency also had higher levels of delinquency outside of their workplace. Additionally, the students with high rates of occupational delinquency also had lower grades, materialistic values, delinquent co-workers, and low levels of self-control. These studies both support Hirschi and Gottfredon's (1987) position that occupational criminals possess the same traits as street criminals.

While there is some evidence for Hirschi and Gottfredson's (1987) propositions, other prominent studies found that most white-collar criminals do not share the criminal propensity characteristics of street criminals. Benson and Moore (1992) compared the characteristics of 2,462 white-collar criminals convicted of bank embezzlement, bribery, income tax violations, false claims, or mail fraud, to 1,986 offenders convicted of narcotics offenses, postal forgery, or bank robbery. They found that as a group, white-collar criminals were much less likely to have prior arrests than street criminals. They also found that white-collar offenders appeared to specialize in white-collar offending in contrast to street offenders who tended to commit a variety of offenses (Benson & Moore, 1992). Furthermore, white-collar offenders' lives tended to be more stable; they exhibited fewer characteristics associated with low self-control. For instance, white-collar criminals were less likely to have a drinking problem, although neither group showed a high prevalence for drinking. The white-collar criminals also were less likely to receive poor grades in school or be below average in social adjustment. The largest difference between the two groups was in drug use; nearly one-half of the street crime offenders used drugs compared to 6 percent of the white-collar criminals (Benson & Moore, 1992).

Weisburd et al. (2001) also found that, contrary to Gottfredson and Hirschi's theory, white-collar criminals, on average, offended at a much lower frequency than that of other types of offenders. The white-collar criminals also had a much older average age of onset of offending (35 years) than street criminals who are usually arrested for the first time as teenagers. Interestingly, the authors did find a subset of the white-collar offenders that offended at high rates similar to those of street offenders. These chronic offenders were much more likely to commit other deviant acts and have less stable lives than the low-frequency white-collar offenders.[4] Chronic offenders were less likely than low-frequency offenders to own their own homes, be steadily employed and be married and were more likely to be substance abusers (Weisburd et al., 2001). Aside from this subset, though, most white-collar criminals in the sample possessed fewer characteristics associated with low self-control than street criminals.

The applicability of Gottfredson and Hirschi's idea of low self-control to white-collar crime has been tested more directly by Simpson and Leeper-Piquero (2002). Using data collected from a sample of managers and managers-in-training, they tested the ability of both organizational theory and Gottfredson and Hirschi's theory to explain the managers' intention to violate the law. They found that both organizational and individual-level processes were related to the offending intentions of their sample, but they found little support for Gottfredson and Hirschi's theory. The authors reported that they failed to find a direct relationship between corporate offending intentions and behavioral indicators of low self-control (Simpson & Leeper-Piquero, 2002).

In Their Own Words: Why They Do It

One of the more difficult aspects of white-collar crime is understanding the motivation of offenders for such crimes. As Wheeler (1992) states, "many white-collar offenders have led lives not only unmarked by prior trouble with the law, but characterized by positive contributions to family and community life" (1992:109). Because of their unique positions as employed, upstanding citizens most people assume that white-collar criminals have more to lose than average criminals (Weisburd et al., 1995; Willott et al., 2001). So why do they risk it? What motivates white-collar criminals to commit their economic crimes?

Two answers seem to re-occur in white-collar criminals' accounts. The first answer to this question is that these crimes, like common property offenses, are need-based. Interviews with white-collar offenders reveal that, in some cases, the offense was committed out of sense of personal financial need. Cressey (1953) interviewed 133 prison inmates who had been convicted of embezzlement. He determined that violating financial trust through white-collar crimes like embezzlement required a psychological process that begins with the emergence of a financial problem that the offender thinks cannot be shared with others. Offenders then recognize that one way to solve their personal financial problem is by violating the financial trust of their place of employment. The final step in this psychological process, according to Cressey (1953), was to rationalize the act so that the offender's view of himself as a law-abiding citizen was not altered.

Box 13.4
Why Do Offenders Commit White-Collar Crime?

1. These crimes, like common property crimes, are need based. This need does not come solely from professional motives but also family need as well.

2. White-collar criminals' transgressions are common practices in their field.

3. Maintaining status.

4. Coercion or being ordered to by bosses.

5. Sense of entitlement.

Personal need is not the only motive cited by white-collar offenders. Many offenders also cited family need as the motive for their crime. In the Wheeler et al. sample, 25-40 percent of men's motives were need based, either for themselves or their families. Thirty to 35 percent of the women cited their families' financial needs as the reason for their criminal act (Daly, 1989). In Willott et al.'s (2001) interviews with white-collar criminals, several of them also expressed the need to support their families as the reason for their white-collar crime.

Among the sub-category of corporate crime, need is often stretched to include the employees and the business itself. Willot et al. (2001) reported that several white-collar criminals felt a huge responsibility to maintain failing companies by "digging into funds" (2001:451) for the benefit of the employees who would lose their jobs and for the company as a whole. Similarly, Benson (1985) found that offenders convicted of tax violations claimed to have supplied employees with cash payments in order to save the employees money in taxes. Benson (1985) also reported that antitrust violators claimed their actions were necessary in order for the company to remain competitive and make a profit in the business world. Likewise, Sutherland's (1983) case studies revealed that many companies claimed to have committed crimes over long periods of time in order to remain competitive in their industry.

The second motive frequently cited by white-collar criminals is that their transgression is common practice in their field. Benson's (1985) interviewees argued that they were just following established business practices. Many felt they were blameless for their actions since it was a "harmless business practice that happened to be a technical violation" (1985:592). Other white-collar criminals convicted of price-fixing have explained that illegal activity was an established practice when they began their jobs with their respective companies (Clinard & Yeager, 1980). Some employees who commit workplace theft also explain that it is common practice and so acceptable under certain circumstances. Registered nurses in Dabney's (1995) interviews said that, despite knowing it was against the law and hospital policy, they frequently took supplies, scrubs, and non-prescription medicine because it was a common practice among nurses.

Other motives cited by white-collar criminals include maintaining status, being coerced or ordered, and because of a sense of entitlement. Some white-collar offenders reported that they committed their crime in order to live up to certain expectations associated with the high social standing. They felt compelled to commit their crimes in order to maintain a high level of achievement and their status in society (Willott et al., 2001). Other white-collar offenders argued that they were coerced or ordered to commit their crimes. Daly (1989) reported that women convicted of postal fraud and false claims often said they were coerced, following orders, or doing a favor for someone else. Similarly, in a survey conducted by Brenner and Molander, employees ranked superiors as the primary influence in unethical decisionmaking, citing pressure from these superiors to sign false documents, overlook wrong-doing, and do business with superiors' friends (Clinard & Yeager, 1980). Simpson and Leeper-Piquero (2002) also reported that a manager's likelihood of offending increased substantially if they were ordered by a supervisor to violate the law. Another reason cited for committing white-collar crimes is out of a sense of entitlement. For instance, the nurses in Dabney's (1995) study said that theft of supplies was used as a way of supplementing otherwise inadequate incomes.

Theoretical Perspectives

Box 13.5
Theories Proposed to Explain White-Collar Crime

Differential Association	Explains that criminal behavior is learned through interaction with intimate others; in terms of white-collar crime, employees might learn criminal techniques, like how to embezzle funds, and positive views about such acts, from a group of co-workers.
Rational Choice Theory	According to this theory, humans possess free will or the ability to make decisions. They make these decisions by rationally calculating the costs and benefits of their actions. If the benefits outweigh the costs, they commit the illegal act. This applies to white-collar criminals because such crimes are rarely crimes of passion.
Revised Rational Choice Theory	Integrates opportunity and focuses on the costs and benefits (both formal and informal) of actions. Informal costs include negative publicity and disapproval.
Routine Activities Theory	In order for crime to occur, offenders must be motivated, there must be suitable targets, and there must be an absence of a capable guardian. Because white-collar criminals are often in positions of power and responsibility, this allows them to gain targets and control the presence of guardians.
Organizational Theory	Theory created specifically for corporate and organizational crime based on the structural organization of a company and the culture and beliefs that form within the organization.

Theories of White-Collar Crime

Due to the wide variety of white-collar crimes, it is not possible to cover all the theories that apply; however, there are several prominent theories commonly associated with white-collar crime. Sutherland, the originator of the concept of white-collar crime, applied his theory of Differential Association to white-collar criminals as well as common criminals. In his theory, Sutherland claims that criminal behavior is learned in interaction with intimate personal groups. The techniques for committing the crime and the motives, rationalizations and attitudes are learned in the process (Sutherland & Cressey, 1960). The motives learned depend on the favorable or unfavorable definitions of laws held by the group. The greater the frequency, duration, and intensity of contacts with groups who condone or participate in criminal activity, the more likely a person will become delinquent (Sutherland & Cressey, 1960). Accordingly, an employee might learn criminal techniques, like how to embezzle funds, and positive views about such acts, from his group of co-workers. This theory receives some support as an explanation for white-collar crime; however, others have argued that it does not fully explain white-collar crime. For instance, Wheeler (1992) claims that Sutherland's theory is unable to explain the fact that most white-collar criminals lead upstanding lives until their conscious decision to engage in illegal activity.

Since white-collar crime is generally seen as a highly rational form of criminality, in which potential offenders thoroughly weigh the risks and rewards of the criminal action, rational choice theory is commonly applied to white-collar crime. According to this theory, humans possess free will or the ability to make decisions. They make these decisions by rationally calculating the costs and benefits of their actions. If the benefits of crime are perceived as outweighing the costs, then the person will decide to commit the crime (Vold, Bernard & Snipes, 2002). In order to increase the costs and deter potential offenders from criminal behavior, the theory contends that society must increase the swiftness, certainty, and severity of punishment (Vold, Bernard & Snipes, 2002). This theory seems to apply well to white-collar crimes because they are rarely crimes of passion. Most white-collar crimes are complex and require forethought and planning and so rational choice theory makes sense. One problem with this simple form of rational choice theory is that it does not incorporate the opportunity for crime, which is increased with occupational and corporate crime because it occurs in the workplace where the offender is present on a daily basis.

Paternoster and Simpson (1993) address opportunity in their revised version of rational choice theory. They propose a rational choice theory that focuses on perceived costs and benefits and includes informal as well as formal costs and benefits of actions. The informal costs include negative publicity for the corporation and disapproval from friends and family (Paternoster & Simpson, 1993). The authors also include the perceived certainty and severity of loss of self-respect and the perceived costs of rule compliance and perceived benefits of rule violation. Finally, Paternoster and Simpson (1993) also include factors that affect the opportunity to commit crime in their revised version of rational choice; such factors include the internal organization of the firm and political, economic, and cultural forces. The empirical tests of this theory show that it might more accurately capture the decisionmaking of corporate offenders (Simpson, 2002). Managers tended to adjust their intentions of criminal behavior based on informal threats, like threats to significant relationships, feelings of guilt, and the negative impact on the reputation of the firm (Simpson, 2002).

Another theory associated with white-collar crime that accounts for opportunity is Routine Activity theory. This theory is based on the offender's lifestyle and daily routines. Cohen and Felson (1979) argue that in order for crime to occur, three elements must be in place: motivated offenders, suitable targets, and the absence of a capable guardian. The likelihood of all three of these elements occurring at the same time and providing the opportunity for crime depends on one's daily routines. In the case of white-collar crimes committed at work, the motivated offender's routine of showing up for work increases the opportunity for criminal activity. Furthermore, many white-collar criminals are in positions of responsibility that increase their access to suitable targets, like cash registers or accounting books, and lessen the presence of guardians. Managers and CEOs of businesses are the guardians, and so have few people guarding them. Cashiers and bank tellers might have guardians, but they are still frequently entrusted with the control of large sums of money. Routine activity theory addresses the important aspect of opportunity in white-collar crime.

The final theory I would like to mention is Organizational theory, which applies solely to corporate and organizational crime, subsets of white-collar crime. Organizational theory is based on the structural organization of a company and the culture and beliefs that form within the organization. Vaughan (1998) explains that decision making is influenced by the politics, culture and beliefs that form in a company. Within companies, capitalist goals of profit and success may become the dominant culture in such a way that corporate crime becomes a normalized way of operating when faced with certain decisions in the company (Vaughan, 1998). Further, decision making can be constrained by the actual structure of the organization. As companies grow larger, subsidiaries and sub-units with their own decision-making processes are formed. Due to the distance between these units and the corporate headquarters, decisions by sub-units may rarely be assessed. Additionally, the hierarchy of power in a company can obscure the criminal actions from employers or prevent objections to the criminal actions from being heard by employers. In other words, the structural organization of the company allows for criminal actions to become part of the accepted work culture so that committing crimes becomes "business as usual."

Enforcement Responses

Despite the large costs of white-collar crime discussed above, white-collar crime has not received a great deal of attention from authorities and prosecutors. It is widely accepted that white-collar criminals, especially corporate criminals, are less likely to be punished by the criminal justice system for their crimes than other criminals (Benson et al., 1992). One reason for this is, as stated earlier, most white-collar crimes are difficult to detect and frequently unreported by victims so certainty of punishment is low. When they are discovered and reported, they often require a more proactive approach from authorities and prosecutors (Albonetti, 1998) and more resources (Gurney, 1985). Further, civil or regulatory actions might be taken rather than criminal ones (Weisburd et al., 1995).

Box 13.6
Benefits and Drawbacks of Civilly Prosecuting White-Collar Offenders

Benefits

1. Evidence is often difficult to collect for white-collar crimes thus civil suits are more successfully prosecuted.

2. Treble and punitive damages are available from civil courts, which can increase the amount of money awarded to the victim.

Drawbacks

1. Only individuals, not the state, can bring civil charges

2. Treble sanctions are limited by the offender's ability to pay them, which means that the high monetary awards may not be guaranteed.

Some white-collar crime victims choose to prosecute in civil rather than criminal courts. There are several benefits of choosing to use civil suits to prosecute white-collar crimes. First, since evidence is often difficult to collect in white-collar crime cases due to the complexity of the crimes, civil suits tend to be better because the standard of proof is more lenient. In civil courts, the prosecution must simply prove their case according to a preponderance of the evidence rather than beyond a reasonable doubt. This can mean that cases move through the system faster and that victims have a greater chance of winning the case than in criminal court. Second, treble and punitive damages are available from civil courts, which can increase the amount of money awarded to the victim.[5] However, civil suits also have their drawbacks. One drawback is that individuals, not the state, bring civil suits. This requires that the victim has knowledge of the victimization, which, as stated previously, tends to be rare in cases of white-collar crime. Another drawback is that treble sanctions are limited by the offender's ability to pay them, which means that the high monetary awards are not guaranteed. Still, civil courts are an option for the prosecution of white-collar offenders.

Corporate crimes most frequently are handled by regulatory agencies, such as the Securities and Exchange Commission (SEC), the Environmental Protection Agency (EPA), and the Occupational Safety and Health Administration (OSHA). Within these federal agencies, the goal is not to punish corporations but to keep them in compliance; therefore, they tend to focus on persuasion rather than punishment (Simpson, 2002). When these agencies do resort to punishment, the fines and sanctions are not usually high (Bartel & Thomas, 1985; Weil, 1996). Another problem with regulatory enforcement has been agency capture. Agency capture occurs when there is a high-degree of personal exchange between the regulating agency and the regulated organizations, which results in lenient enforcement, few regulations, and minimal penalties (Sabatier, 1975). However, a benefit of regulatory enforcement is that these agencies tend to be more proactive and focus on preventing violations rather than simply reacting to them. Further, these agencies have the resources and ability to follow-up on cases and ensure that compliance is achieved.

The criminal justice system tends to focus more of their effort on street crime, and so has faced scrutiny for the way white-collar criminals are handled. Some studies have shown that white-collar criminals receive more lenient forms of punishment (Mann et al., 1980).

Both legally relevant and legally irrelevant variables typically are offered to account for these more lenient punishments (Mann et al., 1980; Wheeler et al., 1982).

Box 13.7
Enron

HOUSTON, April 21—Two former Merrill Lynch & Co. executives convicted in Enron's bogus sale of power barges to the brokerage were sentenced Thursday to prison terms far shorter than the punishment sought by the government.

James A. Brown, former head of the brokerage's asset lease group, was sentenced to three years and 10 months in prison and a year's probation. Daniel H. Bayly, former head of investment banking for Merrill Lynch, was sentenced to 2¹/₂ years' incarceration and six months' probation. Each was ordered to pay $840,000 in fines and restitution.

Federal probation officers had recommended up to 15 years for Bayly and up to 33 for Brown. Their case illustrated Wall Street participation in Enron crimes through the brokerage's choice to take part in a sham deal to make a client happy.

(From: Former Merrill Execs Sentenced; Pair Convicted of Fraud in Enron Brokerage Barge Deal By Kristen Hays; Associated Press, Friday, April 22, 2005; Page E05)

First, as previously mentioned, white-collar offenders tend to have impeccable prior records. Judges have reported difficulty in deciding sentences for white-collar criminals because the crimes might include large sums of money and violations of trust, but the offender has no prior criminal record and has contributed positively to society (Mann et al., 1980; Wheeler et al., 1982). There are two legally irrelevant assumptions that account for the lower rates of punishment for known white-collar offenders. First, is the assumption by judges that, due to their status as upstanding citizens, the shame and humiliation of adjudication is enough punishment for white-collar criminals (Benson, 1985; Mann et al., 1980). Second, it has been assumed that prison will exact a much harsher punishment than necessary on white-collar offenders. It would be harsher than it is on street criminals because of white-collar offenders' unfamiliarity with such deprivations (Willott et al., 2001; Mann et al., 1980), and it would be harsher than necessary because white-collar criminals are considered to be "one-shot" offenders, unlikely to be processed in the system more than once (Weisburd et al., 1995).

Box 13.8
Why White-Collar Crime Punishments Tend to be More Lenient

1. White-collar criminals tend to have clean records.

2. Judges assume that shame will be enough punishment for these upstanding citizens.

3. Many believe that prison is too harsh a punishment for such criminals.

Despite these reported assumptions, other studies have shown that white-collar offenders actually receive harsher sentences. These studies found that offenders of higher status were perceived as more blameworthy and so deserving of harsh punishments (Wheeler et al., 1982; Weisburd et al., 1980). Whether it is true or not that white-collar criminals receive more lenient punishments, the perception that they were able to avoid the most serious penalties in the justice system led to increased severity in sanctions for federal white-collar offenders. It also led to a larger number of criminals being sentenced to imprisonment (Weisburd et al., 1995). Still, even with these changes, the system should focus more attention on white-collar criminals given the enormous costs that white-collar crimes have on society.

Treatment/Prevention

There is very little mention of treatment in the white-collar crime literature; the closest the literature comes to this topic is to discuss prevention through ethics classes. Most debates on the sentencing side of the literature focus on punishment and prevention of white-collar crime. In debates on punishment, scholars have tried to determine the appropriate level of punishment for white-collar criminals. As mentioned in the section above, it has been assumed that prison sentences are too harsh for the white-collar criminal because of their backgrounds and lack of experience in the criminal justice system. In Willott et al.'s

Box 13.9
Martha Stewart

NEW YORK (CNN/Money)—A jury found Martha Stewart guilty Friday on all four counts of obstructing justice and lying to investigators about a well-timed stock sale, and the former stockbroker turned style-setter could face years in jail.

Her ex-broker, Peter Bacanovic, was found guilty on four of the five charges against him. Each of them faces up to five years in prison and $250,000 in fines for each count. Sentencing is set for June 17.

Stewart avoided a loss of about $51,000 by selling nearly 4,000 shares of ImClone stock on Dec. 27, 2001, rather than the next trading day, when the stock tumbled after regulators rejected the company's application for a key cancer drug.

"The word is—beware—and don't engage in this type of conduct because it will not be tolerated," David Kelley, U.S. attorney for the Southern District of New York, said outside the courthouse.

One of the jurors said, "This is a victory for the little guys. No one is above the law."

(From: Stewart convicted on all charges; Jury finds style maven, ex-broker guilty of obstructing justice and lying to investigators; March 5, 2004; www.money.cnn.com)

(2001) interviews with white-collar offenders, the offenders tended to support this assumption. The offenders compared prison to the "bowels of the earth," and described the criminal world of prison as an unsophisticated, hellish place (Willott et al., 2001:457). They also said they thought that prison does not disrupt the life of the working class criminal and could even be educational; whereas for themselves, prison destroyed the structure of their lives (Willott et al., 2001).

However, when Benson and Cullen (1988) interviewed white-collar offenders who had been incarcerated, they found that, like ordinary offenders, there was a period of stress and shock, but they adapted to prison life. Most reported their treatment was better than expected and that fellow inmates were less crazy and threatening than expected. Benson and Cullen (1988) reported that research has suggested that personal social resources, like an education, family ties and non-criminal identities, increase the offender's ability to manage the prison experience. Since white-collar offenders are more likely to possess these resources than street criminals, they actually could be better suited for adjusting to prison. Benson and Cullen (1988) and Willott et al. (2001) reported that offenders expressed a sense of superiority over fellow inmates and resisted the criminal label by seeing themselves as exceptions and different from street criminals. Benson and Cullen (1988) concluded that white-collar criminals are not more sensitive to prison and can adapt just as well, if not better, than street criminals. The authors do note, however, that their sample was incarcerated in federal prisons so these findings cannot be generalized to state prisons or jails. Still, this study provides some evidence that the assumption of the sensitive white-collar criminal may be false.

Weisburd et al. (1995) found in their study that, regardless of whether white-collar criminals are too sensitive for prison, it might not be the best option because it provides no deterrent effect. Because white-collar crimes are considered to be more rational crimes, it is assumed that white-collar criminals will be susceptible to deterrence through punishment. However, Weisburd et al. (1995) examined the impact of sanctions on the criminal careers of 742 convicted white-collar criminals and found no significant deterrent effects of prison. In fact, they actually found that those in the prison sample were slightly more likely to recidivate than those in the no-prison sample, though this was not statistically significant. While this finding is not isolated to white-collar criminals, it shows that prison might not be the preferred method to prevent future white-collar crime.[6]

Suggestions for preventing white-collar crime are understandably wide-ranging due to the numerous varieties of white-collar crime itself. Most prevention ideas for white-collar crime take a routine activity theory approach to prevention and focus on target-hardening rather than focusing on the offender's behavior. In order to prevent employee theft, many companies have contracted security personnel and have instituted programs of pre-employment screening and projects that encourage "whistle blowing," or reporting co-worker misbehavior. Such projects include hotlines for employees to report misconduct and incentives for their "whistle blowing" (Traub, 1996).

There are also many ideas that focus on reducing opportunity in order to prevent corporate crime. According to Clinard and Yeager (1980), one is to increase the enforcement budget of federal regulatory agencies so that they can hire additional and more experienced investigators. A second option is to re-organize the structure of corporations by allowing stockholders to exercise more control over the corporation in order to discourage violations. A third option is to decrease the secrecy in and complexity of corporations by forcing large corporations to disband. This would reduce the opportunity for cultural beliefs that normalize offending to form (Clinard & Yeager, 1980). Other prevention plans for corporate crime focus on increasing the consequences of crime. These ideas function on the concept of deterrence through reducing profits. For example, the penalties for corporate crime could be larger and publicity surrounding misdeeds could be increased. This bad publicity would discourage consumers from doing business with the corporation in particular, thereby hurting the profits (Clinard & Yeager, 1980).

The one prevention idea that does focus on the offender is to develop stronger business ethics in employees. Employees and managers should be taught that it is unethical to embezzle funds and to participate in price-fixing. They should be taught the importance of product safety and regulations on pollution. Disseminating effective ethical standards through codes, manuals, or seminars should help to create stronger business ethics in employees (Clinard & Yeager, 1980). There is evidence that these ethical programs both do and do not work. Simpson (2002) found that managers were less likely to offend when an ethical program was present. Interestingly, it was the operation of the ethical program that prevented criminal behavior; the components of the program did not matter. However, McKendall et al. (2002) discussed several studies that found ethical codes did not prevent crime, and they found in their study that ethical compliance programs did not work to prevent Occupational Safety and Health Act violations. Still, others have argued that if managers set an example of ethical behavior, it can correct employee misconduct (Clinard & Yeager, 1980).

Box 13.10
Bank of America

> Bank of America Corp. touched off a chain of events that ultimately led to the resignation of First Marblehead Corp. chief executive Daniel M. Meyers when the bank fired a high-ranking student loan executive several weeks ago, then alerted First Marblehead's general counsel that Meyers had given expensive personal gifts to her. The gifts violate the codes of ethics at both companies, which place limits on such exchanges to avoid appearances that the firms' business could be swayed.
>
> In the initial disclosure of Meyers's resignation as CEO and chairman, First Marblehead, a Boston firm that specializes in student loans, said its chief executive had given gifts worth $32,000, but it did not name the client that had received the gifts, disclose what they were or how the board had discovered them. In fact, several weeks ago, Bank of America executives received a tip from a whistleblower alleging that Cannon had accepted gifts from First Marblehead.
>
> Bank of America's ethics policies prohibit employees from giving or receiving gifts valued at more than $100. First Marblehead's board decided that Meyers had violated that company's ethics policy.
>
> (From: Tip on improper gifts led to CEO's exit; Client informed First Marblehead of Meyers' moves; By Sasha Talcott and Chris Reidy; *Boston Globe*; September 29, 2005)

Finally, another idea for preventing white-collar crime is to focus on educating the consumer or general public. Griffin (2002) suggested that consumer education is the key to preventing white-collar crime, especially securities fraud. He explained that an informed and educated investor has fewer chances of becoming the victim of fraud. Similarly, Titus (2001) recommended public information campaigns to teach people how to recognize scams and how to terminate attempted scams quickly and effectively. He also reported that the likelihood of a fraud attempt being successful decreased if the potential victim had heard of this type of fraud before or had attempted to investigate the scam.

Conclusion

White-collar crime varies extensively and covers many types of economic crimes. There are on-going debates regarding the definition of this range of illegal actions, but it tends to include occupational crime, corporate crime, and even some crimes that do not require employment. Offenders tend to possess characteristics different from those of the average street criminals but this depends upon the sample and type of white-collar crime. Historically, white-collar criminals have been treated leniently by the justice system, although there are definite signs of change within the system. While white-collar criminals are not as threatening as street criminals tend to be, their crimes take a large toll on society. More research needs to be done to further investigate white-collar criminals' motivations and techniques in order to prevent such costly crimes.

Notes

[1]   The federal arrest rates consist of more white-collar crime arrests than do the arrest rates of local and state police departments. This could be due to the limitations of the UCR data, the nature of the offenses, or the prosecution and arrests habits of federal prosecutors and U.S. Marshals. Hagan, Nagel & Albonetti (1980) reported that in some federal jurisdictions, prosecutors actively seek out white-collar crime cases, which might account for the higher arrest rates in federal jurisdictions.

[2]   Not all of these injuries and illnesses are due to companies that intentionally violate regulations. These numbers reflect all workplace injuries and illnesses, including those caused by employers (either willfully or due to neglect) and employees through accidents on the job.

[3]   The sample was drawn from the Wheeler et al. (1982) study and included antitrust offenses, securities and exchange fraud, postal and wire fraud, false claims and statements, credit and lending institution fraud, bank embezzlement, IRS fraud, and bribery.

[4]   Low frequency offenders were defined as those with one or two arrests in their official criminal histories while chronic offenders were defined as having three or more arrests in their official criminal histories (Weisburd et al., 2001).

5   Treble damages are the tripling of the damages awarded in a lawsuit; punitive damages are damages awarded in a lawsuit as a punishment and example to others for malicious, evil or particularly fraudulent acts.

6   Weisburd et al., (1995) provide several references for studies of street crimes where this finding is replicated. Spohn & Holleran (2002) also find a similar effect of prison on felony drug offenders.

References

Albonetti, C.A. (1998). "Direct and Indirect Effects of Case Complexity, Guilty Pleas, and Offender Characteristics on Sentencing for Offenders Convicted of a White Collar Offense Prior to Sentencing Guidelines." *Journal of Quantitative Criminology*, 14(4):353-377.

Bartel, A.P. and L.G. Thomas (1985). "Direct and Indirect Effects of Regulation: A New Look at OSHA's Impact." *Journal of Law & Economics*, 28:1-25.

Benson, M.L. (1985). "Denying the Guilty Mind: Accounting for Involvement in a White Collar Crime." *Criminology*, 23(4):583-607.

Benson, M.L. and F.T. Cullen (1988). "The Special Sensitivity of White-Collar Offenders to Prison: A Critique and Research Agenda." *Journal of Criminal Justice*, 16:207-215.

Benson, M.L., F.T. Cullen, and W.J. Maakestad (1992). "Community Context and the Prosecution of Corporate Crime." In K. Schlegel and D. Weisburd (eds.) *White Collar Crime Reconsidered*, pp. 269-288. Boston: Northeastern University Press.

Benson, M.L. and E. Moore (1992). "Are White-Collar and Common Offenders the Same? An Empirical and Theoretical Critique of a Recently Proposed General Theory of Crime." *Journal of Research in Crime and Delinquency*, 29(3):251-272.

Braithwaite, J. (1985). "White Collar Crime." *Annual Review of Sociology*, 11:1-25.

Bureau of Justice Statistics (2002). *Compendium of Federal Justice Statistics, 2000*. Online. Available: www.ojp.usdoj.gov/bjs

Calavita, K. and H.N. Pontell (2001). " 'Heads I Win, Tails You Lose': Deregulation, Crime, and Crisis in the Savings and Loan Industry." In N. Shover and J.P. Wright (eds.) *Crimes of Privilege: Readings in White-Collar Crime*, pp. 99-126. New York: Oxford University Press.

Clinard, M.B. and P.C. Yeager (1980). *Corporate Crime.* New York: The Free Press.

Cohen, M.A. (2000). "Measuring the Costs and Benefits of Crime and Justice." *Criminal Justice*, 4:263-315.

Cohen, L.E. and M. Felson (1979). "Social Change and Crime Rate Trends: A Routine Activity Approach." *American Sociological Review*, 44:588-608.

Cressey, D. (1953). *Other People's Money: A Study in the Psychology of Embezzlement.* New York: Free Press.

Dabney, D. (1995). "Neutralization and Deviance in the Workplace: Theft of Supplies and Medicines by Hospital Nurses." *Deviant Behavior: An Interdisciplinary Journal,* 16:313-331.

Daly, K. (1989). "Gender and Varieties of White-Collar Crime." *Criminology,* 27(4):769-793.

Davis, M. (2002). "Couple Accused of Phone Scam of Elderly." *Providence Journal-Bulletin* (July 5): News Section.

Donnelly, P.G. (1982). "The Origins of the Occupational Safety and Health Act of 1970." *Social Problems,* 30(1):13-25.

Federal Bureau of Investigation (2002). *Uniform Crime Reports: Crime in the U.S. Online.* Available: www.fbi.gov/ucr.

Ganzini, L., B. McFarland, and J. Bloom (2001). "Victims of Fraud: Comparing Victims of White-Collar and Violent Crime." In N. Shover and J.P. Wright (eds.) *Crimes of Privilege: Readings in White-Collar Crime*, pp. 87-95. New York: Oxford University Press.

Griffin, S.P. (2002). "Actors or Activities? On the Social Construction of 'White-Collar Crime' in the United States." *Crime, Law & Social Change,* 37:245-276.

Gurney, J.N. (1985). "Factors Influencing the Decision to Prosecute Economic Crime." *Criminology,* 23(4):609-628.

Hagan, J., I. H. Nagel, and C. Albonetti (1980). "The Differential Sentencing of White-Collar Offenders in Ten Federal District Courts." *American Sociological Review,* 45:802-820.

Hirschi, T. and M. Gottfredson (1987). "Causes of White-Collar Crime." *Criminology,* 25(4):949-974.

Jesilow, P., E. Klempner, and V. Chiao (2001). "Reporting Consumer and Major Fraud: A Survey of Complainants." In K. Schlegel and D. Weisburd (eds.) *White-Collar Crime Reconsidered,* pp. 149-168. Boston: Northeastern University Press.

Langan and Cohen (1996). "State Court Sentencing of Convicted Felons, 1992." *Bureau of Justice Statistics.* Online. Available: www.ojp.usdoj.gov/bjs

Liederbach, J. (2001). "Opportunity and Crime in the Medical Professions." In N. Shover and J.P. Wright (eds.) *Crimes of Privilege: Readings in White-Collar Crime,* pp.144-155. New York: Oxford University Press.

Mann, K., S. Wheeler, and A. Sarat (1980). "Sentencing the White-Collar Offender." *American Criminal Law Review,* 17:479-500.

Maull, S. (2004). "Jurors Begin Day 3 in Tyco Deliberations." *Associated Press* (March 22): Domestic News Section.

McKendall, M., B. DeMarr, and C. Jones-Rikkers (2002). "Ethical Compliance Programs and Corporate Illegality: Testing the Assumptions of the Corporate Sentencing Guidelines." *Journal of Business Ethics,* 37(4):367-383.

Moore, E. and M. Mills (1990). "The Neglected Victims and Unexamined Costs of White Collar Crime." *Crime & Delinquency,* 36(3):408-418.

Mustaine, E.E. and R. Tewksbury (2002). "Workplace Theft: An Analysis of Student Employee Offenders and Job Attributes." *American Journal of Criminal Justice,* 27(1):111-127.

Paternoster, R. and S. Simpson (1993). "A Rational Choice Theory of Corporate Crime." In F.T. Cullen and M. Felson (eds.) *Routine Activity and Rational Choice: Advances in Criminological Theory*, pp. 37-58.

PR Newswire (2002). "Office of Inspector General: Felony Welfare Fraud Charges Filed Against Adams County Resident." *PR Newswire* (November 27): State and Regional News Section.

Sabatier, P. (1975). "Social Movements and Regulatory Agencies: Towards a More Adequate, and Less Pessimistic, Theory of Clientele Capture." *Policy Sciences,* 301-344.

Shapiro, S.P. (1990). "Collaring the Crime, Not the Criminal: Reconsidering the Concept of White-Collar Crime." *American Sociological Review,* 55:346-365.

Shover, N. and J.P. Wright (eds.) (2001). *Crimes of Privilege: Readings in White-Collar Crime.* New York: Oxford University Press.

Simpson, S.S. (2002*). Corporate Crime, Law, and Social Control.* New York: Cambridge University Press.

Simpson, S.S. and N. Leeper-Piquero (2002). "Low Self-Control, Organizational Theory, and Corporate Crime." *Law & Society Review,* 36(3):509-548.

Spohn, C. and D. Holleran (2002). "The Effect of Imprisonment on Recidivism Rates of Felony Offenders: A Focus on Drug Offenders." *Criminology,* 40(2):329-357.

Sutherland, E.H. (1983). *White-Collar Crime: The Uncut Version.* New Haven: Yale University Press.

Sutherland, E.H. (1940). "White-Collar Criminality." *American Sociological Review,* 5(1):1-12.

Sutherland, E.H. and D.R. Cressey (1960). "A Theory of Differential Association." In F.T. Cullen and R. Agnew (eds.) *Criminological Theory: Past to Present*, pp. 131-133. Los Angeles: Roxbury Publishing Company.

Steffensmeier, D. (1989). "On the Causes of White-Collar Crime: An Assessment of Hirschi and Gottfredson's Claims." *Criminology,* 27(2):345-357.

Taylor, M. and B.V. Bigelow (2002). "Small S.D. Company's Lawsuit Alleges Global Price-Fixing; Executives Went Undercover for 2 Years Gathering Information About Makers of Carbon Fiber, Which Is Used in Military Aircraft." *The San Diego Union-Tribune* (August 25): Business Section.

Titus, R.M. (2001). "Personal Fraud and Its Victims." In N. Shover and J.P. Wright (eds.) *Crimes of Privilege: Readings in White-Collar Crime*, pp. 57-66. New York: Oxford University Press.

Titus, R.M., F. Heinzelmann, and J. Boyle (1995). "Victimization of Person by Fraud." *Crime & Delinquency,* 41:54-72.

Traub, S.H. (1996). "Battling Employee Crime: A Review of Corporate Strategies and Programs." *Crime & Delinquency,* 42(2):244-256.

Vaughan, D. (1998). "Rational Choice, Situated Action, and the Social Control of Organizations." *Law & Society Review,* 32(1):23-61.

Vold, G.B., T.J. Bernard, and J.B. Snipes (2002). *Theoretical Criminology.* New York: Oxford University Press.

Weil, D. (1996). "If OSHA Is So Bad, Why Is Compliance So Good?" *RAND Journal of Economics,* 27(3):618-640.

Weisburd, D., E.F. Chayet, and E.J. Waring (1990). "White-Collar Crime and Criminal Careers: Some Preliminary Findings." *Crime & Delinquency,* 36(3):342-355.

Weisburd, D., E Waring, and E. Chayet (2001). *White-Collar Crime and Criminal Careers.* New York: Cambridge University Press.

Weisburd, D., E. Waring, and E. Chayet (1995). "Specific Deterrence in a Sample of Offenders Convicted of White-Collar Crimes." *Criminology,* 33(4):587-606.

Wheeler, S. (1992). "The Problem of White-Collar Crime." In K. Schlegel and D. Weisburd (eds.) *White-Collar Crime Reconsidered,* pp. 108-123. Boston: Northeastern University Press.

Wheeler, S., D. Weisburd, and N. Bode (1982). "Sentencing the White Collar Offender: Rhetoric and Reality." *American Sociological Review,* 47:641-659.

Willott, S., C. Griffin, and M. Torrance (2001). "Snakes and Ladders: Upper-Middle Class Male Offenders Talk About Economic Crime." *Criminology,* 39(2):441-466.

Wright, J.P. and F.T. Cullen (2000). "Juvenile Involvement in Occupational Delinquency." *Criminology,* 38(3):863-896.

SECTION VI

Conclusion

Chapter 14

Final Thoughts: What Have We Learned and Where Are We Going?

Summer Acevedo and Lauren O'Neill

The primary goal of this book was to provide an in-depth examination of several different types of crime and the offenders that commit those crimes. Additionally, theoretical perspectives for each crime type, along with treatment and prevention strategies were explored. It was the objective of the authors to provide the reader with the most up-to-date information about research and treatment methods, while also keeping the work grounded with practical examples of real-life scenarios. With this integration of theory, practice, and true-to-life illustration, the reader is able to gain a better sense of the stories behind certain crimes, and can formulate a more informed opinion about the motivations of offenders and the many potential causes or correlates of their crimes.

The crimes that were selected for this work are not an exhaustive list; rather they were chosen as unique examples to provide the reader with broad information about several extremely different types of criminal behavior. Additionally, this work was not intended to explore every facet of each type of crime featured. To do so would require separate books on each subject, with multiple contributions from opposing specialists in the field. Instead, the intention here was to provide an overview of several crimes of interest by evaluating the existing research and the merit of the methods used to draw conclusions about these offender types. Our goal was to simplify the statistical and highly technical research (which is necessary from a methodological standpoint) into general and easy to understand conclusions about what is known about these crimes and ways of addressing them. What results is the groundwork and background research an interested scholar could begin with upon deciding to investigate a certain type of crime.

There has been an ongoing discussion in the field of criminology over the specialization of offenders and whether individualized treatment programs are necessary based on crime type (Gibbons, 1975, 1988; Blumstein et al., 1988). While some may believe that this book is illustrative of specialization due to the classification of offenders, it is important to mention that we do not take a stringent stance on offender specialization. While the chapters are organized by crime type, this was done so for clarity and we are not suggesting that these types are mutually exclusive. In fact, there are several characteristics that offenders share across each chapter, which allows for versatility of offending that has been supported in criminological research (Simon, 1997). With the exception of infanticide, offenders tend to be male, and with the exception of corporate crime, offenders tend to be lower or lower middle class.

In addition, there are a broad range of theories that are used to offer explanations of these crimes. Many focus on crime as a learned behavior or part of a mental or personality disturbance, although it is noteworthy that there does not appear to be a single theory that adequately accounts for all of these criminal actions. Another area of significant overlap deals with prevention strategies. A theme present in multiple chapters is educational programming which can operate in two ways. First, some programs are aimed at informing individuals of consequences and myths surrounding certain behaviors (i.e., gang, rape, and arson prevention). Second, other programs work towards successful re-entry of offenders or altering one's propensity toward committing certain offenses, such as parenting and anger management classes for infanticide and domestic violence offenders.

While treatments mentioned include multiple types of therapy, there is some overlap between the chapters. For example, the use of Cognitive Behavioral Therapy (CBT) is present in the majority of the chapters, specialized courts (i.e., drug courts and domestic violence courts), and biological treatments through the use of medications such as antidepressants in domestic violence offenders, lithium to treat personality disorders in stalking offenders, chemical castration for rapists, and drug therapy for schizophrenics.

It should be noted that no chapter lists the only treatment method as incapacitation. Although there is wide variability in seriousness of offense, ranging from crimes against property (arson), to business (corporate crime), to persons (domestic battery, serial murder), each crime and the perpetrators involved are examined under the pretense that all is not lost. There is an overall understanding that the underlying mechanisms involved in criminal offending need to be addressed and that there may be some prevention strategies that thwart criminal acts from occurring or a treatment that helps facilitate reintegration back into the community. Of course, this may be easier for some of the less serious offenses, but even research on serial murder shows some promise, although still needs adequate investigation.

Some of the crimes profiled in this work are relatively new. A few decades ago, one would be hard-pressed to find an offender population to study that was convicted for stalking, domestic battery, or even any corporate crime. Of course, the acts that comprise these crimes are nothing new, but their formal recognition has only happened in relatively recent history. As a result, what was commonly known as assault now has several forms; it could be domestic battery among partners, stalking among former acquaintances, or a hate crime among strangers. This is in part due to an influx of coverage of these crimes by the organized media. Many of the crimes covered here are said to be sensationalistic or 'sexy crimes.' They draw people in with their uniqueness, which media reports sometimes exploit. However, while the media illustrations of these crimes may be intriguing, they are not always accurate or thorough depictions of the offenders or criminal events. Therefore, it was our goal to educate the public from a perspective other than the media by making information more readily available about the underlying processes involved in these criminal incidents.

The increase in media reports, coupled with more extensive classifications of crimes as well as increased data availability within these areas, speaks for the prior and likely future innovative advancements in the field. There are numerous advantages to categorizing crimes with increasing specificity, the most important being the ability to better understand, and thus attempt to treat the underlying causes of various deviant behaviors, which are highlighted by this book.

Future research in this area should focus on the effects of particular treatments by capitalizing on the similarities as well as accounting for the differences among specific offenses. This is not to say that every offender should receive an individualized treatment, but the reality of finding one successful global treatment is also unlikely. Therefore, research of this nature has many policy implications. For example, once certain treatments have been identified as having positive effects, they can be applied to groups of similar offenders. The crimes featured in this book can be thought of on a macro level to aid in determining what types of treatment could work for multiple populations. For example, if future research discovers that a CBT model works in reducing recidivism in offenders convicted of violent crimes such as domestic battery or rape, a treatment program for those offenders could be built into their sentence. This may result in a more effective method of rehabilitating and reintegrating convicted offenders into the community.

It should also be mentioned that the treatments discussed in this work are taken from the most up to date research at this point in time. It is more than likely that this information will change in the upcoming years, perhaps drastically so. Such changes are welcomed, as they are demonstrations of the dynamic nature of the fields of criminology and psychology and their determined pursuit of better treatment and rehabilitation methods. However, before we can advance, we should be fully educated about the state of our problems and the efficacy of current programs to be sure that we are not abandoning valuable means.

As demonstrated in each chapter, there are still lingering questions about the motivations and decisions to offend for each type of criminal. This contributes in part to the allure for researchers to study these types of crime. The examples given that were 'ripped from the headlines' are further evidence of a fascination and desire to understand these criminals that exists on a national level; not just among the fields of sociology, criminology or psychology. It was the goal of this work to facilitate such understanding and arm the reader with enough knowledge to know which questions to ask next, and where to go from this point. Criminology may be established as its own discipline, but it certainly leaves the door open for contributions from psychology and theories of individual behavior to help tell the story of some types of offending.

References

Blumstein, A., J. Cohen, S. Das, and S.D. Moitra (1988). "Specialization and Seriousness During Adult Criminal Careers." *Journal of Quantitative Criminology*, 4:303-345.

Gibbon, D.C. (1988). "Some Critical Observations on Criminal Types and Criminal Careers." *Criminal Justice and Behavior*, 15:8-23.

Gibbons, D.C. (1975). "Offender Typologies: Two Decades Later." *British Journal of Criminology*, 15:140-156.

Simon, L.M.J. (1997). "Do Criminal Offenders Specialize in Crime Types?" *Applied & Preventive Psychology*, 6:35-53.

Contributors

Summer Acevedo is a Graduate Research Assistant currently enrolled in the Ph.D. program in the Department of Criminology and Criminal Justice at the University of Maryland, College Park. She is originally from Grant, FL and received her B.A. in Criminology and Psychology from Florida State University. Her research interests include psychology of criminal behavior, stalking, and victimology.

Sara Betsinger received her master's degree from the University of Maryland, College Park in 2005 and is currently seeking her Ph.D. While her thesis focused on the impact of gambling venues on crime rates, her other research interests include juries, sentencing, and probation and parole.

Susan Fahey attained her Master of Arts degree in Criminology and Criminal Justice from the University of Maryland–College Park in 2005. She also received her Bachelor of Arts degree in Justice from American University in 2002. She is currently studying terrorism at the National Center for the Study of Terrorism and Responses to Terrorism and is pursuing a doctoral degree from the Department of Criminology and Criminal Justice at the University of Maryland–College Park.

Jennifer Gibbs is a visiting part-time assistant professor of Criminology at the College of Notre Dame of Maryland. She is the managing editor for the North American editor of *Criminal Justice: An International Journal of Policy and Practice*, as well as a member of several criminal justice organizations. Her other publications include work on trends in police research with the student-run Police Research Group at the University of Maryland (supervised by Professors David Weisburd and Jean McGloin), and she also is working on a corporate criminal sentencing project and other projects involving violence against women, including the fathers' rights movement and police investigation of rape (with Martin D. Schwartz). Jennifer received a Master's degree in Criminal Justice from Niagara University (New York) and is presently finishing a doctoral degree in Criminology from the University of Maryland, College Park.

Danielle Harris is a criminologist researching the nature of specialization and versatility of sexual aggression. She has worked as a clinical residential worker in the United Kingdom and as a research officer for the Commission of Inquiry into Child Abuse in Government Institutions in Queensland (the Forde Inquiry). She completed her undergraduate degree in Justice Studies at the Queensland University of Technology, Australia, and the University of Westminster, London; her Masters in Criminology at the University of Maryland; and is currently pursuing a Ph.D. in Criminology at Griffith University, Australia, in collaboration with researchers at Brandeis University, Massachusetts.

Raven Korte has a Bachelor's degree in psychology from UCLA and a Master's degree in Criminology and Criminal Justice from the University of Maryland at College Park. She is originally from Santa Monica, California and currently lives in Arlington, Virginia. Raven will begin training as a Special Agent with the Naval Criminal Investigative Service.

Michael P. Krezmien conducts research with the National Center on Education, Disability, and Juvenile Justice at the University of Maryland. He is interested in issues of mental health and educational services for delinquent youth. He spent several years teaching in a residential treatment center for students with severe emotional disturbance. He is currently working with several juvenile corrections facilities to develop effective mental health and education screening intake procedures. He is also currently researching suspension and expulsion practices in public school systems. Mike enjoys shuffleboard, biking, and has dedicated himself to breaking par.

Doris Layton MacKenzie, Ph.D., is Professor in the Department of Criminology and Criminal Justice at the University of Maryland. She earned her doctorate in Psychology from The Pennsylvania State University, was on the faculty of the Louisiana State University where she was honored as a "Researcher of Distinction," and was awarded a Visiting Scientist position at the National Institute of Justice, U.S. Department of Justice. She has an extensive publication record on such topics as examining what works to reduce crime in the community, rehabilitation, inmate adjustment to prison, the impact of intermediate sanctions on recidivism, long-term offenders, methods of predicting prison populations, self-report criminal activities of probationers and boot camp prisons. Dr. MacKenzie has recently completed a book, "What Works in Corrections," to be published by Cambridge Press and an edited book on "Correctional Boot Camps." At the University of Maryland, she teaches courses on: Psychology of Criminal Behavior; Professional Development; Evaluation; and Corrections. She was just elected Vice-President in the American Society of Criminology (ASC) and in the past has served as Executive Secretary of ASC and Chair of the Division on Corrections and Sentencing as well as serving on numerous committees.

Nancy Minniti is currently a doctoral candidate at Widener University in Chester, PA. Her clinical specialization is in neuropsychology. She has a diverse range of interests, including the biological bases of behavior and psychopathology, traumatic brain injury, health psychology, chronic mental illness, psychodynamic theory, and psychopathy. She has worked with individuals with chronic mental illness and those with brain injuries in residential, inpatient, and outpatient settings. Nancy's other interests include fine arts and literature, and more recently, tennis.

Lauren O'Neill is currently pursuing her Ph.D. at the University of Maryland Department of Criminology and Criminal Justice. She completed her undergraduate degree in Law and Justice at The College of New Jersey and her Master's degree at The University of Maryland. Her research interests include peer influences on behavior, discretion, court processes, and rehabilitative programming. Her most recent research involves situational crime prevention within schools, prosecutorial discretion in offering charge reductions, and educational programming within correctional institutions.

Ashlee Dale Parker graduated Magna Cum Laude in May of 2003 from the University of Wyoming with a Bachelor of Arts degree in Sociology and Communications, and a minor in Women's Studies. Her interest in criminal justice brought her to the Criminology program at the University of Maryland, College Park, where she completed her Master of Arts degree in May of 2005. Her interests are primarily centered on sexual assault and violence against women.

Wendy Povitsky received her Bachelor's degree from St. Mary's College of Maryland. She recently completed her Master's degree in Criminology from the University of Maryland. Her Master's Thesis was entitled "Teen Court: Does it Reduce Recidivism?" She is currently in her first year of the Doctoral Program in Criminology and Criminal Justice, also at the University of Maryland. Her research interests include juvenile delinquency and prevention/diversion programming.

Natalie Schell is a Ph.D. student in Criminology and Criminal Justice at the University of Maryland. Her research interests include white-collar crime, gender, and theory. Her Master's thesis, which she completed at the University of Maryland, was titled, "Exploring the Relationship between Profit-Squeeze and Occupational Safety and Health Violations."

Elizabeth Smith is a recent graduate from the University of Maryland where she obtained her Master's degree in Criminology and Criminal Justice. Her research interests include juvenile justice issues, using geographical analysis for crime prevention, and terrorism.

Jaclyn Smith received her undergraduate degree from the University of Texas at Arlington and her Master's degree from the University of Maryland, College Park. She works at the National Institute of Justice in the Office of Research and Evaluation. She also works at the Center of Excellence for Behavior and Social Research on Terrorism and Counter-Terrorism at the University of Maryland.

Index